MAP AND TOP
Communications
Standards and Applications

ELECTRONIC SYSTEMS ENGINEERING SERIES

Consulting editors   **E L Dagless**
University of Bristol

J O'Reilly
University College of Wales

OTHER TITLES IN THE SERIES

MAP AND TOP

Communications

Standards and Applications

A. VALENZANO • C. DEMARTINI
L. CIMINIERA

Polytechnic of Turin

**ADDISON-WESLEY
PUBLISHING
COMPANY**

Wokingham, England · Reading, Massachusetts · Menlo Park, California · New York
Don Mills, Ontario · Amsterdam · Bonn · Sydney · Singapore
Tokyo Madrid · San Juan · Milan · Paris · Mexico City · Seoul · Taipei

Cover designed by Chris Eley and
printed by The Riverside Printing Co. (Reading) Ltd.
Printed in Great Britain by T J Press (Padstow) Ltd, Cornwall.

First printed 1992.

British Library Cataloguing in Publication Data
Valenzano, Adriano
    MAP and TOP communications : standards and applications
    I. Demartini, Claudio II. Ciminiera, Luigi
    004.62

    ISBN 0201416654

Library of Congress Cataloging in Publication Data
Valenzano, Adriano.
    MAP and TOP communications : standards and applications /
A. Valenzano, C. Demartini, L. Ciminiera.
        p.   cm.
    Includes bibliographical references and index.
    ISBN 0-201-41665-4
    1. Computer integrated manufacturing systems.   2. Computer net-
work protocols — Standards.   3. Manufacturing automation protocol.
I. Demartini, C. (Claudio) II. Ciminiera, Luigi. III. Title.
TS155.6.V347 1991
004.6'2 — dc20   91-22441
                                                             CIP

Preface

Developments in computer and networking technology will have a profound influence on how manufacturing and office systems are designed, operated and controlled.

Computer Integrated Manufacturing (CIM) is today a goal for most industries, which can be achieved only with the support of well established factory computer networks. The same need is also emerging in the fields of banking, insurance and government activities, which are mostly based on office work. In general, the possibility of freely exchanging information in digital form is an ever increasing need in our society, and it is a prerequisite for a real integration of many of the working activities.

Accepted international standards for computer communications are an essential component of this process of enhanced integration. Since the end of the seventies, the International Organization for Standardization (ISO), with its Open Systems Interconnection project, has set the basis for providing such standards.

Computer network standards have now reached a maturity that allows commercial products based on them effectively to compete with proprietary network solutions. A proof of acceptance of international standards is given by the large number of products available which comply with the Manufacturing Automation Protocol (MAP) and Technical Office Protocol (TOP); these protocols represent the two most important standardization efforts, based on ISO-OSI standards, in the field of manufacturing and office automation.

Aim of this book

Technical descriptions of protocols are often important in order to understand what a network can or cannot do; however, when a new technology has the potential to introduce important changes in a specific field, examples and experiences showing how it can be used are also very important.

The objective is to describe MAP and TOP protocols showing both aspects: technical descriptions of each single component and illustrations of how different companies are beginning to use the whole system.

Most of the book will be devoted to technical descriptions, because the complexity of the protocols involved does not allow short descriptions, without the risk of incurring over-simplification. We have tried, however, to avoid all the details and the formal language used in the thousands of pages of the original standard documents, instead focusing our attention on describing the functionalities characterizing each component.

Intended Audience

This book is suited to computer engineering professionals who face the problem of choosing, installing, operating and maintaining a MAP/TOP communication system for the factory and/or office environment. Planning and implementing such a network require a good knowledge of the MAP/TOP architecture and of the related standards that is hard to find in a single book. Our intent is to provide the reader with all the basic elements needed to reach this goal, by dropping those details that can be considered inessential to understanding the MAP/TOP main characteristics.

Postgraduate students and engineers will find this material useful to keep up-to-date their technical background; moreover several topics covered in this book are often ignored or too briefly presented in the literature on computer networks and communications.

The reader should be familiar with the basic concepts of data communications such as those usually presented in a first-level course on computer networks. These aspects are discussed throughout the book only from the MAP and TOP points of view. In fact, our aim is to cover advanced topics that are particularly related to the factory and office application fields.

Organization

The subdivision into chapters of the book is roughly tailored in accordance with the layered structure of the protocols profile used in MAP and TOP. Particular emphasis is given to the application layer, since its services (and underlying protocols) are directly accessed by the applications designers and by the users. The presentation of the characteristics of the lowest protocol layers is focused on the choices that have been carried out in MAP and TOP, since these aspects can affect significantly the performance of the network and must be well known to the system designer.

- Chapter 1 summarizes the main reasons that led to the development of the MAP and TOP projects and outlines the basic characteristics of a MAP/TOP network concerning the system topology, the connected devices and the interconnection of different subnetworks.

- Chapter 2 introduces the two lowest communication layers of the MAP/TOP protocol profiles. Topics such as transmission techniques, transmission media, physical and data-link protocols and services are discussed. This chapter also contains some material on fiber optics and the FDDI standard for supporting data communications by using the emerging fiber optics technology.

- Chapter 3 is devoted to the so-called 'intermediate' protocol layers of the ISO–OSI reference model. Thus those aspects that are usually confined in the network, transport and session layers are introduced and discussed in the MAP/TOP framework.

- Chapter 4 describes the presentation layer, pointing out its main functions dealing with the manipulation of data structures, their description in terms of abstract types and their representation according to the requirements to be satisfied for achieving efficient data transfer operations.

- Chapter 5 introduces some of the application modules located in the application layer. In particular the association common service elements (ACSE) services are presented together with the network management and directory service functions, with emphasis on those aspects considered in the MAP and TOP specifications.

- Chapter 6 deals with the manufacturing message service (MMS) which provides a standard model for interactions among different application processes located on different nodes of the network.

- Chapter 7 is devoted to the description of the companion standards to MMS; these provide new objects and services which take into account the peculiar characteristics of the different devices that can access the MMS services.

- Chapter 8 introduces the file transfer and access management and describes the model for supporting file transfer in an open system.

- Chapter 9 is devoted to the description of the message interchange functions and the virtual terminal support which play a basic role for the efficient progress of activities in the office environment.

- Chapter 10 introduces the ISO standards for interchanging integrated text and graphics documents between dissimilar systems in an open system interconnection environment.

- Chapter 11 deals with the application interface to the user, which must be the same in all the MAP/TOP implementations because the user has to be allowed to choose between competing MAP/TOP products on the basis of performance and price.

- Chapter 12 deals with some issues related to the development of MAP/TOP applications, discussing the experimentations of MAP/TOP based solutions for factory communications; specific pilot projects are described and a case study related to the development of a time-critical prototype network is presented.

Adriano Valenzano
Claudio Demartini
Luigi Ciminiera
October 1991

Contents

Chapter 1

LANs for Factory and Office Automation

1.1　CIM and computer networks

Computer integrated manufacturing (CIM) is a term used to express the pervasive presence of computers in designing, planning, dispatching and controlling manufacturing operations. But this book is about computer networks in industrial environments, not about CIM, so why should we talk about CIM here? First, to say that an industrial computer network **is not CIM**. CIM implies the integration of, hopefully, all the manufacturing functions, by means of a distributed data processing system. System distribution is required for two main reasons: first, it is very difficult to implement all the functions in a single system; secondly, it is necessary, in some cases, to locate the 'intelligence' close to the area where it is needed. The efficiency and effectiveness of a distributed computer system depends on the characteristics of its communication system, and local area networks provide a good (though not the only) solution to this type of problem. Hence they are only a *tool* to support CIM; this is the reason why the two concepts are often related to each other, and in

1

many cases are also confused.

But not all computer networks are created equal. Several solutions are available and it is necessary to choose the one that best matches the communication requirements of the information system to be built.

The functions performed by the information system in an industrial environment may be classified according to a hierarchical model, such as that proposed by NIST [McLeMi83] and shown in Figure 1.1. Using Figure 1.1, it is possible to identify two needs for integration, and then communication: *vertical* and *horizontal*. Vertical integration designates the need to integrate the operations from product design down to programming of the basic manufacturing device; this implies a flow of information up and down the hierarchy which is not shown in the figure for the sake of simplicity. Horizontal integration designates the need to integrate all the operations required to process each single piece of raw material, in order to obtain the final product; this implies direct communication between peers in the hierarchy. An example of this type of horizontal communication is given by a flexible manufacturing cell, whose processing plan for working different small batches can be varied according to the state of the other cells that should receive the batches produced; in this case, the exchange of state information among the different cells can take place without the intervention of a general controller, except for handling some special exceptions.

Local area networks often allow one transmitter to address all the receivers (or a selected group of receivers) in the system by sending a single 'broadcast' message; thus they seem to be a suitable solution to the communication requirements implied by both vertical and horizontal integration. However, a single local area network is not necessarily sufficient, because it will be necessary to intermix on the same communication channel different types of traffic, with different requirements for delivery.

The need to separate local communications from global ones, in order to obtain short delivery times for some urgent messages, leads to the definition of a hierarchy of networks to be used as communication infrastructures to support CIM. This hierarchy may be composed of three types of networks:

Type 1

This kind of network interconnects mainframe, minicomputers and workstations implementing the functions of the two top levels of the model in Figure 1.1, with several type 2 subnetworks. The typical traffic flowing over this type of network comprises file transfers, database query/update operations and mail exchanges, hence there is no need for real-time operations, but the flexibility of the communication system can be important.

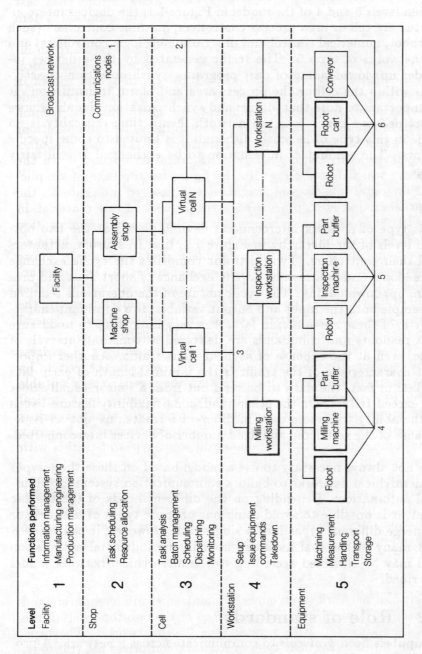

Level	Functions performed
Facility 1	Information management Manufacturing engineering Production management
Shop 2	Task scheduling Resource allocation
Cell 3	Task analysis Batch management Scheduling Dispatching Monitoring
Workstation 4	Setup Issue equipment commands Takedown
Equipment 5	Machining Measurement Handling Transport Storage

Figure 1.1   Hierarchical model for the automated manufacturing facility.

Type 2

This type of network provides the support for communications between levels 3 and 4 of the model in Figure 1.1; the devices interconnected are cell or area process controllers, machine controllers (such as robot, numerical control and programmable logic controllers) and subnetworks of type 3. The traffic generated by these devices includes up/downloading of part programs, synchronization of activities within the cell or the process area and alarm transmission. It is important to note that alarms and synchronization signals require short delivery times over the network, hence time criticality is an issue in this type of network, although it is limited to some specific events. The amount of information to be exchanged is still fairly large.

Type 3

This type of network interconnects devices placed at the two bottom levels of the hierarchy in Figure 1.1, that is, sensors, actuators and their controllers. Typical traffic comprises the cyclic exchange of readouts and commands, acyclic exchange of short data and program up/downloading. The cyclic nature of the operations required to sample both the input and output variables is a dominant characteristic of these networks; in fact, it is very important to make sure that readouts and commands are delivered at constant intervals of time, even at the expense of asynchronous traffic. Another important characteristic of the traffic is the minimal length of each data packet; in fact, the data to be read out from a sensor usually does not exceed 16 bits. On the other hand, some flexibility features, such as the ability to handle data in different formats, are not an issue, because of the restricted and fixed number of devices interconnected.

It is not always necessary to use a model based on these three types of hierarchical networks to build a communication system for industrial automation. Depending on the different needs of the specific plant, it is possible to avoid using one or more types of network, or to merge different types into a single one. However, it can be seen that many of the real networks used in the industrial automation field may be classified according to the hierarchical network model described.

1.2   Role of standards

Computers need *protocols* to communicate across a network. A protocol is a set of common communication rules that should be followed in order for them to understand each other, in a similar way to the rules used in natural languages for human communications. Establishing common rules sounds like defining a standard, and in fact the real issue in computer networks is not whether it is necessary to have a standard, but *who should define the standard*?

If we look at the real world of computer networks, there are only two possible answers to this question: computer manufacturers (each one with their own standard) and international standards bodies, with contributions from both manufacturers and users.

The majority of installations consist of *proprietary* networks, that is, networks based on protocols specified by a computer manufacturer. The reason for the wide diffusion of proprietary networks is twofold: first, their competitors (international standards) have been available in their final form for a shorter time, and secondly computer manufacturers give full support to their own solutions, both technically and commercially.

But general-purpose computers are not the only devices in a network for industrial applications. The small and medium manufacturers of automation devices, such as robots, programmable logic controllers (PLCs) and sensors/actuators, are faced with the problem of either interfacing their products to all the major proprietary networks or of choosing one of them and restricting their possible market to the end users adopting the selected network.

The end users have a similar problem, because the presence of different *de facto* standards fragments the market into incompatible 'worlds' of products, each one related to a specific proprietary solution. Hence, having once adopted a network, the user is forced to restrict the selection of computers and automation devices to only those offered by manufacturers adopting the same type of network. This situation may be fine, so long as the user wants to stay with the same group of manufacturers; but it is almost impossible to build a system using devices belonging to different 'worlds', and it is also difficult to exchange information between industrial plants or departments adopting different networks.

Moreover, the technical evolution of the protocols in a proprietary network, which can be needed to update the network characteristics, is totally out of the control of both users and medium/small automation device manufacturers, as the standard is set by a (usually big) computer manufacturer.

The proliferation of proprietary solutions to communication between different computers and automation devices does have a cost. At the end of the 1970s, General Motors realized that more than half of their automation budget was dedicated to implementing custom interfaces between intelligent automation components; furthermore, most of the programmable devices in use by that time were unable to communicate outside their plant area. A similar situation was found by Boeing when they tried to interconnect their several different data centers; the incompatibility presented by different computers from more than 85 vendors was total. These two experiences gave a clear picture of the communication world in a typical industrial and office environment, and pushed GM and Boeing to find a solution to overcome these problems that eventually resulted in the Manufacturing Automation Protocol (MAP) and Technical and Office Protocol (TOP) projects, whose description forms a large part of this book.

1.3   Brief history of MAP and TOP

1.3.1   Industrial environment

The first MAP version was only a procurement specification, and it was adopted in fall 1982; GM also stated it would only purchase equipment complying with that specification.

This first attempt was not really successful, because the products offered were custom implementations of the procurement specification rather than a widely supported standard, hence their costs were higher than proprietary solutions.

To overcome this problem, GM needed to expand the number of users interested in MAP-compatible networks, so that the potential market for such networks could be widened and the cost of each interface could be lessened. The foundation of a MAP User Group in March 1984, including also McDonnell Douglas, Ford, Chrysler, Deere and Kodak, marked a turning point in MAP's history, because it became a real standardization effort with wide industrial support, rather than solely an initiative of GM. A demonstration conducted at the National Computer Conference (NCC) in 1984 showed the feasibility of MAP networks in their first version (MAP 1.0) [MAP1.0].

Since the NCC demonstration, several successive versions of MAP have been defined. In February 1985, the MAP 2.0 specification was published; this new version introduced in the lower layers the standard protocols defined for the ISO–OSI reference model. This is the first version with a practical application of the strategic decision made by the MAP management to use, as far as possible, international standards developed for ISO–OSI, selecting those options in the standards that would be best suited for industrial applications; when a suitable standard was not available, the choice was to promote the definition of such a new standard.

The first version of MAP producing real commercial products was MAP 2.1 [MAP2.1], which added missing protocols to the previous version, and was demonstrated in 1985 at the AUTOFACT exhibition. The main drawback of the commercial implementations of MAP 2.1 was that, in most cases, the devices were interfaced to the network via a separate communication box, implementing the two bottom layers; this box was connected to the device by a parallel or serial port whose data transfer rates were far below the transmission rate of the network, hence creating a performance bottleneck. This drawback led to limited commercial success of such devices; however, there is still a market for them even today.

Up to version 2.1, the MAP specification included only a type 1 network, in accordance with the classification presented in Section 1.1. MAP 2.2 [MAP2.2] first introduced the Enhanced Performance Architecture (EPA) and MiniMAP nodes, which were intended to provide a means to implement type 2 networks. Moreover, the Mini-MAP segments are allowed to use carrierband transmission rather than broadband, in order to cut the cost of the network attachments.

Finally, the MAP 3.0 version [MAP3.0] specification, published and demonstrated in preliminary form in June 1988 at the ENE exhibition in Baltimore, is the first stable version; in fact there is a commitment not to publish any incompatible new version within six years from the publication of MAP 3.0. This new version is incompatible with MAP 2.2 because it introduces new protocols for the network and presentation layers, and adds new services to the application layer. As MAP 3.0 should last at least six years, it is the version that most of the commercial products implement, and it will be the subject of a large part of this book.

1.3.2 Office environment

Incommunicability was also the major problem faced by Boeing when they tried to interconnect their data center and office stations throughout the United States. They discovered that their computers, purchased from 85 different manufacturers, were almost unable to communicate with other manufacturers' devices, without complex *ad hoc* protocol translations. This characteristic caused the economic failure of a Boeing project aimed at interconnecting all their computers by adopting a subset of IBM SNA. In fact, the Boeing solution was based on *ad hoc* interfaces, like those for MAP 1.0, with a cost higher than that for proprietary solutions and a spectrum of available services too narrow for real office applications.

The success of the MAP User Group stimulated the formation, in late 1985, of a User Group for the Technical and Office Protocol (TOP), with the same goal as for MAP, but oriented to the office environment. Furthermore, the two groups worked together, in order to differentiate the two solutions only where it was necessary to meet the specific requirements of the two environments.

The first outcome of the work of the TOP User Group was TOP 1.0 [TOP1.0], demonstrated at AUTOFACT 1985 along with MAP 2.1, with which it was able to communicate, by means of suitable bridges.

The close relationship with MAP has also been kept in TOP 3.0 [TOP3.0] (TOP version numbers have skipped 2.x to be aligned with MAP versions, in order to stress this relationship). The presentation and demonstration of TOP 3.0 took place at ENE '88, together with MAP 3.0. This version introduces new services such as those provided by office document architecture/office document interchange format (ODA/ODIF) for document exchange, initial graphics exchange specification (IGES) for technical product information exchange, and by network management and directory services.

1.4   MAP and TOP profiles

The definition of the protocol profiles for both MAP 3.0 and TOP 3.0 has been based on some well defined criteria:

- adoption of the ISO–OSI reference model, along with a selection, for each layer, of protocols defined by an international standards body, as far as already existing standards match the industrial and office automation requirements;

- promotion of new protocols, to be submitted to international bodies for standardization, in the areas where no satisfactory standard protocol already existed.

The result is a set of profiles mostly composed of standard protocols, selected from the set of possible ones defined in the standards, but with some components whose definition has been influenced by MAP/TOP activities, such as MMS (ISO DIS 9506) and token bus access protocol (IEEE 802.4 or ISO 8802/4).

In this section, only the profiles for the end systems will be illustrated; such systems perform both data processing and communication tasks, as opposed to intermediate systems that perform only communication tasks and are merely used to implement the communication infrastructure, without any application program running on them. The intermediate systems will be illustrated in Section 1.7.

1.4.1   MAP 3.0

Three different types of end systems are included in the MAP 3.0 specification, according to the different roles played in the whole network.

The first type is the so-called FullMAP station, whose protocol profile is shown in Figure 1.2. It includes a full seven-layer OSI stack whose components will be the subject of the following chapters.

This type of profile is clearly intended to provide a lot of flexibility for the communicating stations, while this type of station is not suitable for real-time applications, as the number and complexity of the protocols used perhaps do not provide enough communication speed. In the hierarchical network model introduced in Section 1.1 this kind of station is intended to be connected to type 1 networks, and the types of applications to be run on them could be those related to corporate and/or plant management.

OSI layer:

File transfer access and management (ISO 8571) Manufacturing message specification (ISO 9506) MAP/TOP network management Directory service (ISO 9594) Association control service element (ISO 8649)	7
Presentation kernel (ISO 8822)	6
Session kernel (ISO 8326)	5
Transport class 4 service (ISO 8072)	4
Connectionless network service (ISO 8348)	3
Logical link control classes 1 and 3 (ISO 8802/2) Token–bus medium access control (ISO 8802/4)	2
Token–bus 10 Mbps broadband (ISO 8802/4) Token–bus 5 Mbps carrierband (ISO 8802/4)	1

Figure 1.2   Protocol profile for FullMAP stations.

In fact, the application layer includes protocols for file transfer (FTAM, Chapter 8) and for manufacturing messaging (MMS, Chapter 6), in addition to management and directory services.

The FullMAP profile does not satisfy all needs in the factory automation field, as the three bottom layers of the diagram in Figure 1.1 require time-critical communication. These requirements for a type 2 network are satisfied in MAP 3.0 by the so-called MiniMAP profile, shown in Figure 1.3.

MiniMAP protocol architecture represents a major departure from the standard OSI profiles, as layers 3 to 6 are absent or empty. However, this reduced protocol profile guarantees better response times for the messages sent over the network, which is paid for with a loss of communication functionalities leading to the following re-

Layer number:

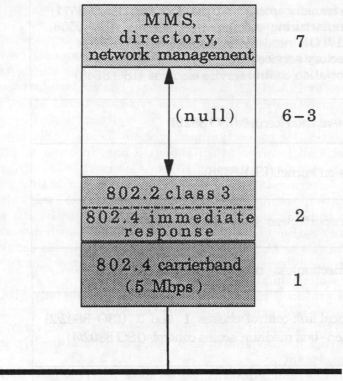

Figure 1.3 Protocol profile for MiniMAP stations.

strictions with respect to FullMAP stations:

- owing to the absence of a transport layer, no fragmentation is performed and the size of the application messages is constrained by the maximum frame size allowed on the channel;
- no real routing is possible, as there is no network layer, thus MiniMAP networks should be limited to a single segment;
- only full-duplex communication may be used, as no session layer functionalities exist;
- reliable packet delivery, mostly guaranteed by transport and network layers, is implemented by introducing acknowledging at the data-link layer, by using an LLC class 3 (see Section 2.3);
- message formats are fixed, as no presentation layer is used, unless ASN.1 (see Chapter 4) encoder/decoder routines are

included in the application layer.

However, the performance advantages were believed to be worth the limitations listed above.

It is important to note that the MiniMAP profile has prompted the work of international standards bodies on computer networks with time-critical communication requirements. The MiniMAP has been revised by ISA SP 72, in its definition of a standard for a process control architecture [ISASP72]; it was recognized that MMS, in its final version [ISO9506], relies heavily on services provided by ACSE (see Chapter 5) for connection management, hence a thin layer has been introduced between MMS and data-link, in order to provide a minimum set of such functionalities. Also in the field of discrete part manufacturing, ISO TC 184 started a work item on time-critical communication architecture, although it is not yet clear whether the profile to be defined is similar to MiniMAP. Finally, it is worth mentioning the IEC FIELDBUS standard project which uses almost the same profile as MiniMAP, even though the protocols defined for each layer are different, as FIELDBUS is aimed at defining type 3 networks, while MiniMAP falls in the type 2 class.

The protocols in the application layer include only MMS for manufacturing messaging, management and directory services; hence the MiniMAP station is essentially devoted to the control of some manufacturing device, and it does not participate directly in the plant management.

FullMAP and MiniMAP nodes have different protocols and even a different number of layers, thus they cannot communicate with each other. It turns out that a third type of station is needed to fill the gap between the other two types. The Enhanced Performance Architecture (EPA) nodes play this role; as can be seen from Figure 1.4, the protocol profile adopted is a merging of FullMAP and MiniMAP architectures. In particular, the bottom layers are the same as in MiniMAP; they support two types of protocol stacks: a full stack with all the intermediate layers (3 to 6), and a reduced stack with only layer 7. The two stacks merge on the top, since both use the application layer; however, some restrictions apply, as FTAM can only be used on the full stack, while MMS may be used with both. A multiplexing/demultiplexing mechanism is also required at the merge of the two stacks, in order to route correctly the packets from and to the selected stack.

The EPA nodes are best suited to implementing cell or area process controllers, implementing the functions of level 3 in the model of Figure 1.1. In fact, they are able to communicate, using the full stack and a router, with FullMAP nodes that implement high level functions in the model, where flexibility of the communication is a primary issue. They can also communicate with MiniMAP ones, using the reduced stack, as time-critical communication is more

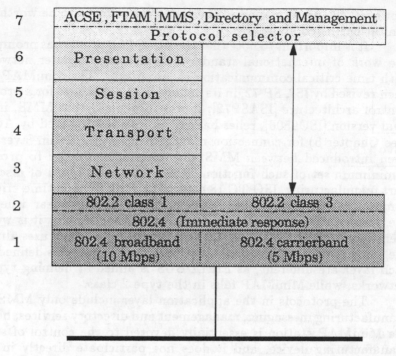

Communication medium

Figure 1.4   Protocol profile for enhanced performance architecture.

important in the lower functional levels of the model in Figure 1.1.

An example of a MAP 3.0 configuration is shown in Figure 1.5. It uses a two-level hierarchical network: a type 1 network, referred to as a backbone, interconnecting FullMAP stations performing different high-level tasks, and a cell subnetwork (type 2), connected through a bridge, with a cell controller implemented in a distributed fashion on two EPA stations, with manufacturing devices controlled by MiniMAP networks. Furthermore, it is possible to have a connection to X.25 wide area networks (WANs) for interplant communication, as well as possible gateways to proprietary networks and routers to TOP 3.0 networks.

1.4.2 TOP 3.0

Unlike MAP 3.0, only one architecture is defined for the station, which is shown in Figure 1.6. A unique architectural definition, however, does not mean that all the TOP stations should be equal; in fact, TOP 3.0 specifies a well-defined set of so-called 'building

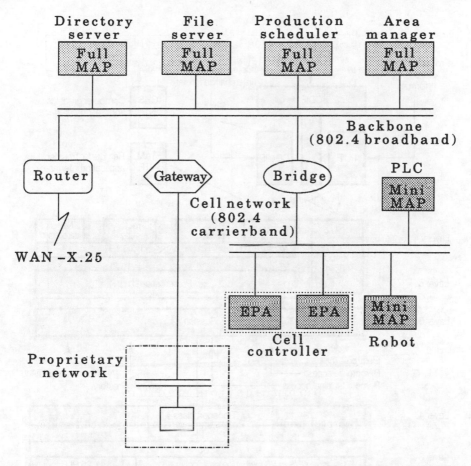

Figure 1.5   Example of MAP 3.0 network configuration.

blocks' (designated with shadowed and dashed boxes in the figure), indicating which type of TOP subset may be implemented in a product, in order to conform with TOP 3.0 specification. It is important to note that the TOP 3.0 architecture includes both communication components (layers 1 to 7) and some other standards for system components not related to computer network communication as well. This is in recognition that, in the office environment, it is necessary to have standard formats for documents (ODA/ODIF), product information (PDIF) and computer graphics (CGMIF) interchange, in addition to a standard computer network interface.

The communication building blocks are organized in two classes: the bottom one encompasses layers 1 to 4 and is oriented to data communication; the upper one encompasses layers 5 to 7 and is oriented to data processing support.

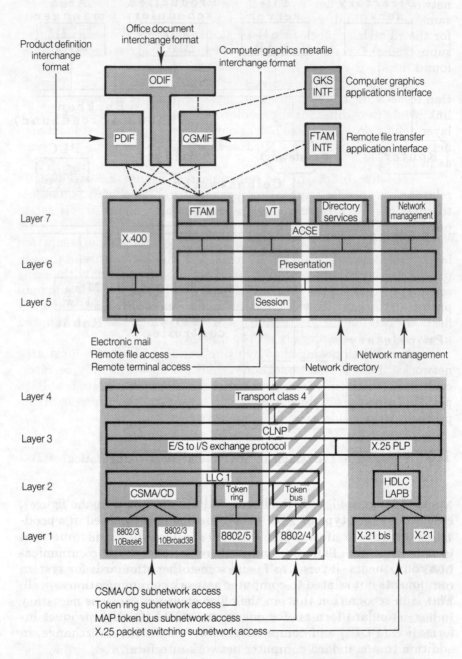

Figure 1.6   Architecture and building blocks defined in TOP 3.0.

Four blocks are defined in the bottom class, three for local area networks and one for wide area networks. All the blocks have the same network and transport layers as for FullMAP stations, except for the rightmost block that uses X.25 as bottom network sublayer, supported by layer 2 and layer 1 protocols in a standard configuration found in public packet switched networks.

The three blocks devoted to local area networks share, in addition to network and transport protocols, the upper sublayer of data-link; while they differ for the medium access mechanism and physical layer definition. The three blocks cover all the commonest local area networks, namely CSMA/CD, token ring and token bus (the same as in FullMAP).

The five blocks in the upper part of Figure 1.6 are directly related to a specific application layer protocol, so that it is possible to configure a TOP station with only a subset of the whole set of protocols shown.

Four out of the five blocks use the session and presentation layers (identical to FullMAP choices), and they differ only in the application protocol put on top. The leftmost block uses only the same session protocol supporting directly the CCITT X400 electronic mail protocol (Chapter 9); the different profile selected for this block reflects the original CCITT definition of X400, which has been adopted in several products already on the market.

It is worth noting that by using building blocks for local area networks, TOP 3.0 and backbone MAP 3.0 networks may be interconnected using (in the worst case) an intermediate system able to perform a protocol translation up to layer 2, as all the rest of the protocol stack is identical for both networks.

1.5 Why and when should I use MAP and TOP?

Modern production systems rely heavily on the ability of electronic information exchange to reach very high levels of efficiency. Large companies such as those involved in the MAP and TOP user groups were already facing this problem several years ago, when the MAP/TOP projects were at the very first stage. It is worth pointing out, however, that the integration of the production environments in both offices and factories is also a key point for medium and small industries who wish to win the competition for marketable products in their own areas of interest.

It is a fact that higher efficiency leads to improved productivity, an improved quality of product and, last but not least, improved profits. Often it is not so obvious, however, that these goals are strictly related to planning and organizing the flows of information inside the organization being considered, and even between different

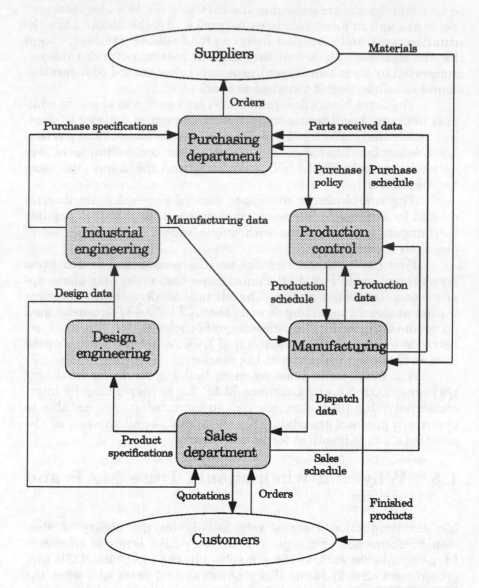

Figure 1.7   Typical information flows in a manufacturing environment.

organizations. Data exchange is a crucial issue for CIM: without efficient solutions for moving and handling information between different equipment several of the benefits expected from adopting CIM would be lost.

Figure 1.7 outlines some typical requirements for the information flows in a production environment. Boxes represent production processes, while arrows are used to show the paths for data that are to be exchanged among the processes.

As one can immediately realize, the number of paths in a real situation can also be significantly larger than those in Figure 1.7, and the complexity of the information management system must not be underestimated. In the recent past, *ad hoc* solutions were widely adopted and this led to two typical kinds of situations:

(1) Suitable hardware/software mechanisms and interfaces were specifically developed for the user's own account to allow the interconnection of groups of intelligent devices produced by different manufacturers. These systems, often known as *user-build* networks, allowed users to reach a certain degree of integration with the advantage that the user had exactly what he/she wanted. However, this approach also showed several drawbacks: for instance, when a new device and/or computer had to be introduced in the system, suitable interfaces had to be implemented. In this way investments were not preserved, since changing a machine or modifying the network of information paths could result in partially (or even totally) re-designing and re-implementing the hardware/software communication supports. In other words, this kind of interconnection was neither *flexible* nor *open* to enable devices from different manufacturers to exchange information without any additional specific mechanism.

(2) The user adopted and bought machines from a single (preferred) manufacturer, or from a very small number of manufacturers. In this case the vendor was usually able to offer a more or less large set of devices equipped with data exchange capabilities, building up a so-called *proprietary* solution. This approach had a number of advantages: for instance the user was able to introduce a new machine or replace an old one in a graceful way, without being concerned with the problem of interfacing it to the existing environment; the required hardware/software was supplied directly by the vendor, together with the devices sold to the user. Another advantage was often reached in terms of performance: an integrated system produced by a single manufacturer is usually able to offer better performance, since several hardware/software components can be optimized during their design phase.

Nevertheless, the proprietary solution had a major drawback: it forced the user to be locked into a particular supplier. This meant that the proposed solutions (hardware and software products) were not particularly tailored to the user's needs and, even worse, it was very difficult (or impossible) to introduce in the system equipment from other vendors when the user wished to do so. The conclusion in this case also is that the level of flexibility and openness that could be obtained was far from satisfactory.

With the advent of MAP and TOP the integration scenario has started to change radically. The keyword in this case is *standard* as the way to reach interoperability of equipment from different vendors without significant (additional) efforts. The aim of the MAP and TOP projects, in fact, is to select a set of standard rules for the exchange of information between intelligent devices that should be adopted by each vendor wishing to sell data communication products for the factory and office environments. In this way the user can satisfy his/her own requirements by including in his/her system heterogeneous machines with the only condition being that they conform to the selected standard specifications. This solution offers both the advantages of the user-build and proprietary approaches, that is, the system fits in well with the user's needs and it is *flexible* and *open*. The openness is granted by the set of standards adopted for MAP and TOP that were chosen in the OSI framework and are both becoming well established and continuously gaining international credit.

To be fair, the reader must be warned that usually the performance reachable with the MAP/TOP approach cannot be compared with an optimized proprietary solution, given the size and complexity of the communication protocols adopted in MAP/TOP. Nevertheless, the advantage of achieving the full integration and interoperability in a multivendor scenario cannot be measured; thus it does not seem meaningless to give up some performance to obtain a significant improvement in flexibility. Besides the larger number of products that can be obtained by different vendors, the MAP/TOP solution is also attractive from other points of view:

- The cost of the communication equipment is reduced, since standard interfaces and protocols are used. It is not necessary to replace significant parts of the existing hardware/software as the system grows.
- The software maintenance costs are reduced: this aspect is also due to the adoption of internationally accepted standards.
- The system is modular and easily expanded: this is granted by the layered ISO–OSI architecture which supports a complete set of communication services.
- The maintenance costs are reduced: a blend of proprietary networks is harder and more expensive to maintain than a homogeneous and well-structured system oriented to openness.
- The factory and office environments can be easily integrated because MAP and TOP use the same protocol profiles.

1.6 Necessary steps for implementing MAP and TOP

When considering the implementation of a MAP/TOP system from scratch one must be conscious that there is no well-defined and unique set of rules that must be obeyed; moreover, the same is true when a user wishes to migrate to MAP/TOP starting from an existing proprietary or 'personal' network. In the real world each user has his/her own specific requirements and he/she is often in some kind of particular situation which cannot be generalized easily. Thus the following considerations must not be interpreted as a list of precepts that the MAP/TOP user must observe, instead they have to be considered mainly as a summary of common and important issues that the wise customer should take into account when he/she plans to move towards a MAP/TOP network.

(1) The first step for achieving integration both in the industrial and office automation fields is to determine the required user services and functions. The task is not simple, especially when the user does not have any previous experience with other kinds of networks. This involves a deep and detailed analysis of the user requirements, taking into account the present needs but also the growth and changes that can reasonably be expected in the future. Since this point is crucial it is desirable that the user be supported by a team of people expert in planning communications networks for industrial and/or office automation. It is worth noting that the complexity of this step can be significantly high: aspects such as the analysis of the possible network strategies to satisfy the different communication requirements (data, voice, video, and so on) in the whole organization have to be carefully considered.

(2) The different options that can be adopted to meet the user requirements should be compared to select the most reasonable solution. This step involves evaluation of the capabilities of the hardware/software products offered by the different manufacturers and suppliers. As in step 1, the aid of experts in factory/office communications could be valuable because they can help in saving money by selecting the set of products that best suits the user's needs. MAP and TOP products are still beginning to appear, nevertheless the choice has always to be aimed at obtaining the best performance and functionality while preserving the hardware/software investments.

(3) Another step that is strictly related to the options comparison is the costs analysis: typically costs include cables, interfaces, interconnection devices such as bridges, routers and gateways and communication equipment such as head-ends, broadband/carrierband modems and amplifiers. However, the

costs of installing and maintaining the network also have to be considered together with the costs of acquiring and/or developing and maintaining the communication and application software.

(4) Once the previous three preliminary (but strategic) steps have been completed, the network implementation can be started. A reasonable approach is to plan and install either a broadband backbone or a baseband subnetwork, in order to satisfy at the very beginning only a selected number of user requirements. The choice depends on the user's situation: when broadband is not necessary or the user is introducing MAP/TOP in a pre-existent context made up of proprietary solutions the installation of a (small) carrierband subsystem is a good starting point. By contrast, if a new system has to be built and multiple information flows have to be supported, the backbone installation can precede the implementation of the subnetworks. There are two main reasons for doing this:

(a) First a MAP/TOP network is a complex system involving a large number of aspects that are unfamiliar, or even unknown, to the user; thus it is not wise to start by trying to implement the whole system in a single stage since the risk of losing control of the situation is very high. A graceful migration towards MAP and TOP allows the user to master this (new) technology and to obtain the expected benefits as he/she proceeds along the migration path.

(b) A step-by-step approach is suitable to develop pilot implementations that can be used to replace existing parts of the proprietary network(s) already owned by the user. Thus 'obsolete' cables and interfaces can be progressively replaced and the new solutions tested without causing rude changes in the user operating methodologies. In other words, a user is allowed to experience and explore the MAP/TOP potentialities while moving towards a MAP/TOP system.

(5) Once a certain degree of experience has been reached (and possibly any residual suspicion and reluctance have been overcome) the initial installation can be completed either by introducing the remaining cables and interfaces or by progressively replacing the existing communication equipment with MAP/TOP products. Obviously these further phases are needed only if the user requirements can only be satisfied by means of a large and complete system (i.e. not limited to a carrierband subnetwork as in the simplest cases). When the user migrates to MAP from a proprietary solution this involves a substantial upgrade/replacement of the existing ma-

chines. Upgrades are generally possible for host computers and for some kinds of high-end intelligent equipment since their manufacturers will provide suitable cards and packages to allow the interconnection in a MAP/TOP-based system. Simpler or less intelligent devices (such as several types of PLCs) have to be replaced to obtain the full benefits of the open environment. In this case the user has to consider carefully the adoption of remote-addressable devices that enable the downloading/uploading of part-programs and data tables through the network.

(6) A final point concerns the integration of MAP and TOP with other non-standard and/or proprietary networks: the solution to these problems is based on the availability of special interconnection devices in general and gateways in particular. The problem of finding such devices on the market is related to the development and widespread use of MAP and TOP systems. Lower layer (physical and data-link) interfacing is well supported as MAP and TOP use well-established international standards; the same is often true in proprietary networks. Thus it is not difficult to find bridges and routers to interconnect MAP/TOP to the most popular proprietary environments.

The upper layer protocols are the real problem. The lack of international standards and profiles for a very long time has led to an uncontrolled proliferation of 'special' solutions. In fact, many proprietary networks were designed as stand-alone, local area networks, hence some functions such as routing and end-to-end acknowledgment were not deemed worth implementing as they are not usually needed in a LAN. Therefore, the major challenge in integrating MAP, TOP and the (already existing) proprietary networks is the availability of software packages interfacing the upper layer protocols of these networks, since the hardware interfaces for the lower layer are already available.

1.7 Intermediate systems

A basic requirement for achieving full integration in both the manufacturing and office environments is the ability to interconnect heterogeneous networks/subnetworks (such as those depicted in the model of Figure 1.5) and to link different segments belonging to the same network.

In the OSI world interconnections can occur at the first, second, third and seventh layer of the reference model [ISO7498], while no type of link is possible at the transport and the session layers between distinct subnetworks. The reason for this comes from practical situations where the interworking of real networks is needed. In fact

the protocol profile adopted in a given network can either fit satisfactorily in the OSI architecture or be completely OSI incompatible
(such as all the proprietary networks). In the latter case it does not
make sense to bridge the differences between a pair of networks at a
level different from the application layer, since non-OSI systems are
not forced to use a layered communication architecture and, even
in this case, they can adopt a non-OSI subdivision of the communication functionalities among the different protocol layers. The only
acceptable solution, in these conditions, is to connect the heterogeneous subnetworks directly at the application layer, by leaving the
task of translating a set of communication protocols into another to
those hosts that are directly connected to two or more subnetworks.

Distinct networks adopting OSI protocol profiles can still exhibit significant differences. However, in this case, the deepest dis-
similarities can be found in the three lowest layers of the reference
model, while common protocols are used in the transport and in the
session layers. This is not surprising since a number of functions and
mechanisms of the lowest communication layers are strictly related
to the techniques adopted for physically transferring the information
through the network, and each method has its own peculiar characteristics that are often incompatible with the solutions adopted in
any other system. Also in this case the interconnection of different
subnetworks requires the presence of machines interfaced to more
subnetworks in order to smooth the differences in the lowest communication layers. Nevertheless the application processes access the
communication facilities by means of a uniform interface that is offered by the upper (common) layers.

Repeaters

Repeaters are interconnection devices used at the physical level as
shown in Figure 1.8. Their presence is completely hidden from the
upper layers that see the network as consisting of a single uniform
element (i.e. segment). Since a repeater only concerns the physical
layer the network elements linked must be physically identical. MAP
and TOP make use of repeaters; typically they are amplifiers used
to strengthen the signal in order to reach longer distances (usually
not allowed for a single network segment).

Bridges

Bridges interconnect two subnetworks at the data-link level as shown
in Figure 1.9. Since the connection occurs at the second OSI layer
the data-link protocol should be the same in both the subnetworks,
while the physical layers can also be (and usually are) different.

A common data-link protocol also implies the same addressing scheme used to identify the data-link users in the subnetwork,
thus a bridge should be a 'transparent' device whose presence in the

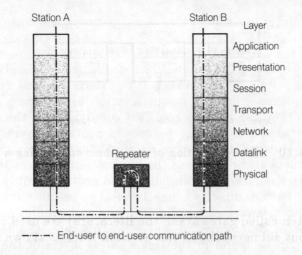

Figure 1.8   Interconnection of two subnetworks using a repeater.

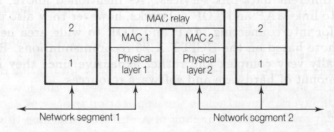

Figure 1.9   Interconnection of two subnetworks using a bridge.

network is not known to the clients who use the link service. Unfortunately the implementation of a bridge is not always a straightforward matter, even though the subnetworks to be connected adhere to the same set of international standards. This occurs, for instance, when different IEEE 802 (see Chapter 2) subnetworks must be linked (e.g. an 802.4 subnetwork which has to be connected to an 802.3 system) since the token-bus and the CSMA/CD channel access methods have different characteristics concerning the maximum message length allowed, the message priority and format. This is why the connection of an 802.4 MAP network with an 802.3 TOP system is carried out at the network layer. Bridges are used in MAP to interconnect different 802.4 segments or to link an 802.4 carrierband subnetwork to a baseband backbone. Different broadband channels can also be linked by a bridge. Bridges are more complex than repeaters and generally include intelligent equipment in order to enhance the overall network performance. For instance, an intelligent bridge can avoid repeating a message to another subnetwork when the address of the destination belongs to the same subnetwork as the sender.

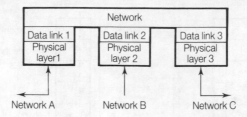

Figure 1.10   Interconnection of two subnetworks using a router

Routers

Routers (often called gateways in the literature) are used to connect heterogeneous subnetworks at the network level as shown in Figure 1.10.

Usually each subnetwork has its own data-link protocol and the router is able to support a common set of network layer functions by using different data-link services. As mentioned above, routers are used to link MAP and TOP networks, however they also provide a means for interconnecting MAP and TOP to wide area networks such as those based on the CCITT X.25 recommendations. Routers are generally very complex and rather expensive since they involve a large amount of hardware and software resources.

Gateways

Gateways, also called protocol converters, are the most complex (and often most expensive) way to interconnect two computer networks. A gateway is responsible for translating the functionalities of the whole protocol profile used in a given network into a suitable set of communication functions adopted in another subnetwork as shown in Figure 1.11.

Typically this operation also requires some enhancement/impairment of the service when passing from one network to the other that has to be obtained by means of a special mechanism designed *ad hoc*. This can involve considerable amounts of hardware and software and usually leads to some penalties in performance since the translation process can be unavoidably slow. Gateways are used to connect MAP and TOP to proprietary networks that are not based on the ISO–OSI model. It is worth noting that each interconnection of this kind requires a particular (non-standard) solution to be developed.

1.8   Conclusions

Local area networks are a really useful tool for implementing CIM and modern office automation, although they are not the panacea

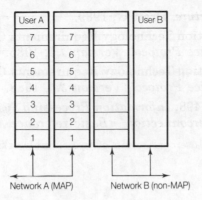

Figure 1.11   Interconnection of two subnetworks using a gateway.

for all the problems in this field.

In this chapter, the communication needs in a factory have been discussed in relation to the different functions to be performed. The communication requirements are different for different functional levels: more flexibility is required to support high-level management activities, while performance is the issue for time-critical communications required at the lower automation levels.

Requirements for three types of local area networks have been derived from this analysis, and the way in which MAP 3.0 and TOP 3.0 specifications try to meet these requirements has been shown by illustrating their general architecture. The following chapters will be devoted to a closer look at the components of these two local area networks, in order to understand better the functionalities offered.

References

[McLeMi83] McLean C., Mitchell M. and Barkmeyer E. A Computer Architecture for Small-Batch Manufacturing, *IEEE Spectrum*, n. 5, May 1983.

[MAP1.0] General Motors, *Manufacturing Protocol Specification, Version 1.0*, 1982.

[MAP2.1] General Motors, *Manufacturing Protocol Specification, Version 2.1*, 1985.

[MAP2.2] General Motors, *Manufacturing Protocol Specification, Version 2.2*, 1986.

[MAP3.0] General Motors, *Manufacturing Protocol Specification, Version 3.0*, 1988.

[ISO9506] ISO DIS 9506, *Manufacturing Message Specification, Part 1 & 2*, 22 December 1988.

[ISASP72] Instrument Society of America, *DS 72: Process Control*

Architecture, Draft G, 1989.

[TOP1.0]   Information Technology Requirements Council, *Technical and Office Protocol, Version 1.0*, 1985.

[TOP3.0]   Information Technology Requirements Council, *Technical and Office Protocol, Version 3.0*, 1988.

[ISO7498]   ISO IS 7498, *Information Processing Systems – Open System Interconnection – Basic reference Model*, 1984.

Chapter 2

Physical and Data-link Layers

2.1 Open systems interconnection model

The goal of this section is to introduce some common terms adopted in the OSI framework that will be used extensively throughout the remaining chapters of this book.

As is probably well known, the ISO–OSI model is an abstract way of describing the communications between processes residing on different stations in a network. The complexity of stations can range from very simple machines equipped with a single processor to large and powerful multiprocessor systems; the crucial issue here is that each station which adheres to the OSI model and supports the OSI standard protocols and services is an *open system* which is able to exchange information with other open systems without needing any other particular communication support.

Thus the OSI world can be thought of as consisting of systems (for our purposes we can assume that a system is equivalent to a station) structured into *subsystems* by means of a set of *layers* as depicted in Figure 2.1. Note that each layer is spread over the whole of the OSI scenario (i.e. the overall network), while each subsystem

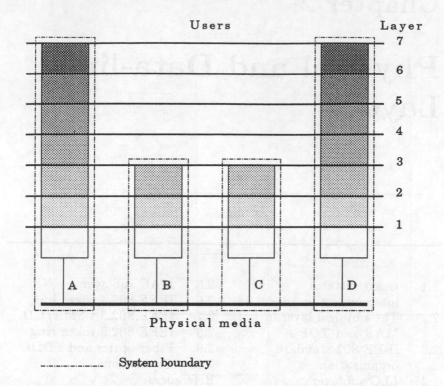

Figure 2.1   Systems, subsystems and layers in the OSI world.

is contained in just one station (A, B, C and D in the figure).

Inside a subsystem one or more *entities* exist representing hardware/software components devoted to performing some communication function that depends on the particular layer being considered. Entities belonging to the same layer but residing in different systems are called *peer entities*. Layers are numbered with progressively higher numbers in a bottom-up fashion: usually the attribute N is used to distinguish elements belonging to the Nth layer, so, for example, entities in this case are termed *N-entities*.

Seven layers are considered in the reference model; each layer offers a set of communication *services* to the next layer up by using and enhancing the services supported by the next layer down; in this way layer N offers a set of N-services to layer $N+1$ by using the $(N-1)$-services supported by layer $N-1$.

The users (or the application processes) are interfaced directly with the seventh (application) layer and are usually only allowed to invoke its communication services (i.e. the user does not have direct access to the lowest layers), while the first layer is attached to the physical communication media.

N-entities cooperate to support the N-services; this cooper-

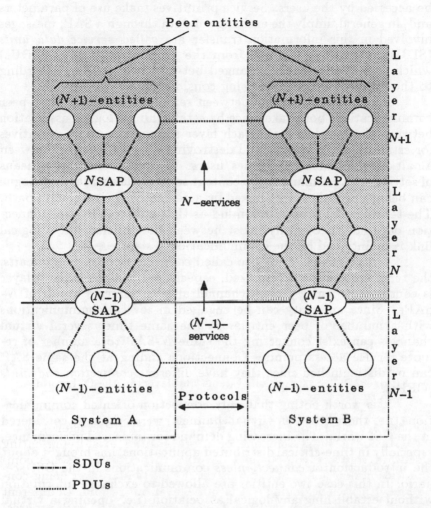

Figure 2.2   Entities, services, protocols and SAPs.

ation is obtained by exchanging data and control information according to a set of rules and using suitable message formats that build up an *N-protocol*. *N*-services are accessed by the users (that is, the $(N+1)$-entities) through *N-service access points* (N-SAPs) representing the logical interface between the entities of the two adjacent layers. Figure 2.2 shows the relationships between services, protocols and SAPs.

For the sake of simplicity a single SAP is shown for each layer/system; however, in general, several N-SAPs can interface with the N-entities and $(N+1)$-entities inside the same machine.

In the ISO documents, services are described in terms of *service primitives* representing an abstract model of the way services can be accessed by the users. Service primitives make use of parameters and, in general, imply the exchange of data through a SAP; messages involved in this information transfer are called *service data units* (SDUs) to distinguish them from the *protocol data units* (PDUs) which are the messages exchanged between peer entities according to the protocol of the layer being considered.

Information exchange between remote users and peer-to-peer communications both take place by establishing a logical association between the interlocutors. Each layer supports suitable primitives for establishing, managing and destroying a *virtual channel* between a pair of communicating entities/users. Virtual channels are a means of setting-up a communication context so that the entities in dialogue can behave as if they were linked by a dedicated (private) data path. The term virtual is used to remind us that a direct physical connection does not (necessarily) exist between the entities, but a logical link is maintained by the communication system.

Virtual channels are also called *connections* or *virtual circuits*; the term *association* is also used, especially when the seventh layer is considered. An N-virtual channel always connects a pair of N-SAPs. Since an entity can be engaged in several communications with a number of peer entities at the same time, several virtual channels can exist connecting the same N-SAP to a number of remote service access points. Connections ending at the same SAP can be distinguished since they have different *connection endpoints* (CEPs).

It is worth noting that only connection-oriented communications (i.e. those based on virtual channels) were originally considered in the OSI world. The increasing demand for improved performance, especially in time-critical distributed applications, has brought about the introduction of *connectionless* communications in the OSI scenario. In this case two entities are allowed to exchange information without establishing any logical association (i.e. opening a virtual channel) and PDUs are also called *datagrams*.

As mentioned above, each layer adds its own communication features to the services provided by the lower layers. The first and second layers, called *physical* and *data-link* layers, are responsible for transferring data packets between two adjacent stations in the network connected by some kind of physical link. In particular, the physical layer includes all those hardware/software mechanisms that are needed for accessing the physical medium and for sending/receiving bits over it, while the data-link layer provides services for assembling (disassembling) bits into packets (also called *frames*) and for detecting and (possibly) recovering transmission errors occurring inside the physical layer.

The third layer, or *network* layer, offers functions for relaying and routing the packets through the network, even though the network consists of several independent subnetworks that differ according to topology, physical media, access techniques and so on. Thus the network entities have to implement mechanisms for routing messages inside a given subnetwork as well as through a number of concatenated subnetworks.

The fourth layer, or *transport* layer, must provide transparent end-to-end data transfer services to its users, while adapting the quality of the service offered by the network layer to the users' needs. In practice this layer is responsible for hiding from the upper layers (which are application-oriented) all those mechanisms and details that are required to implement a reliable information transfer service and that are mostly confined to the lowest three (communication-oriented) layers.

The fifth layer or *session* layer has to offer services for controlling and managing the dialogue (exchange of information) between pairs of communicating users. These include the facility for half-duplex or full-duplex connections, the use of synchronization and resynchronization functions and suitable mechanisms for structuring the dialogue into a number of independent units and sub-units.

The sixth layer, or *presentation* layer, was conceived to provide users with the freedom to use their own data representations and to support security functions for protecting reserved data from unwanted interceptions by erroneous or malicious listeners/intruders.

Finally, the seventh layer, or *application* layer, is intended to contain services that can be accessed directly from the application processes; the nature of these services mainly depends on the particular type of applications being considered, although some common service elements, not related to any specific application field, can also be found within this layer.

2.2   The physical layer in MAP and TOP

As mentioned in the preceding section, the OSI physical layer is mainly concerned with setting up and maintaining a physical connection between two stations wishing to exchange data. In addition, the physical layer is also responsible for encoding/decoding and transmitting/receiving bits on the communication medium. At present a large variety of different techniques can be used to carry out such basic operations and a complete analysis of all the possible alternatives would fall beyond the goals of this chapter. For this reason the following sections present only those aspects of the physical layer that are relevant to MAP and TOP, together with the main characteristics of the transmission media that are commonly used in industrial and office communication systems.

2.2.1   Baseband and broadband systems

Each transmission medium is characterized by a *bandwidth* value representing the range of frequencies that can be transmitted over it; the larger the bandwidth the larger the difference between the lowest and highest frequency which can be used to send a signal from one station to another.

In practice, there are two basic approaches known respectively as *baseband* and *broadband* that use the bandwidth made available for transmission by the physical layer in two very different ways. On the one hand, baseband systems assign all of the available bandwidth to a single transmission; this approach implies that only one message at a time can be present on the communication channel and that multiple information flows (e.g. voice, images and data) and/or networks cannot use the transmission medium at the same time. On the other hand, broadband systems subdivide the whole frequency range into a number of intervals called *channels* and assign different channels to different traffics; in this way it is possible for multiple transmissions, each one having its own characteristics, to share the same physical medium simultaneously.

Broadband advantages are paid for with increased costs for both the equipment used to build the communication system and for network installation and maintenance, since broadband technology is more sophisticated, complex and hence expensive than baseband technology. Nevertheless, when high performance is a major issue, such as in the MAP backbone, the broadband solution is certainly very attractive. Baseband networks can only spread over relatively short distances (typically some hundreds of meters) and can only connect a small number of stations (i.e. some tens); baseband networks also make it difficult to reach very high data rates, particularly in critical environments such as most industrial plants (typical maximum values for baseband data rates are 1, 5 and 10 megabits per second). However, to be fair, the simplicity and cost-effectiveness of baseband systems make them suitable for cheaper applications such as cell control and office subnetworks.

Broadband networks have complementary characteristics: transmissions are less sensitive to electrical noise, links can be several kilometers long, hundreds of nodes can be connected to the same network and high data rates are allowed on multiple channels. Note that these are also the basic requirements for a network such as the MAP backbone which has to interconnect a number of less powerful subsystems.

Baseband networks use bi-directional propagation, while transmissions adopted in broadband systems are directional. The net result is that some trick must be used to implement multicast communications in a broadband network. Figure 2.3 shows the two possible solutions that are commonly adopted in this case.

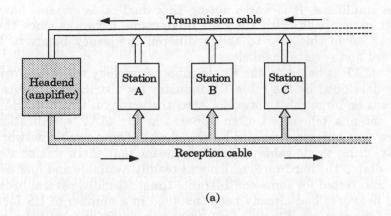

(a)

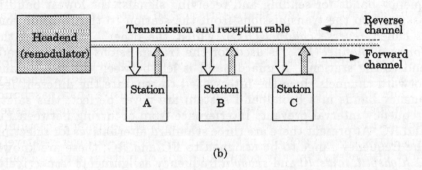

(b)

Figure 2.3 Possible architectures of a broadband system: (a) dual-cable; (b) single-cable.

In *dual-cable* systems each station is connected to a pair of physical links; the first link is used for transmissions, whilst the second is needed to receive the signals coming from the other stations. The *headend* device connecting the two links has to transfer the signals from the first to the second cable thus, since it needs to do nothing else, it can simply consist of an amplifier.

In *single-cable* systems two different broadband channels are used for signal transmission and reception, respectively. In this case the headend device must also perform a frequency shift to translate the incoming channels into the outgoing ones, so it is called a *headend remodulator*. The main drawback of any dual-cable network is that it requires a double cable length and the installation of two physical media; this is not needed for the single-cable solution. By contrast, single-cable devices, such as the headend remodulator and the stations' interfaces, are more complex and expensive than dual-cable amplifiers. It is worth noting that dual-cable systems have a larger useful bandwidth than do single-cable networks since there is no need in this case to assign different frequency bands to the forward and reverse channels.

MAP is based on the single-cable technology which was originally developed by the cable TV industry for distributing television stations on large cable networks, thus the acronym CATV (community antenna television) often appears in the MAP specifications. There were two main reasons for the choice of single-cable networks: firstly, using single-cable technology meant that there was no need to re-design the hardware, which was readily available and had been used and tested for some considerable time; secondly, several broadband networks had already been installed in a number of US factories to support other types of information transfer such as voice and television.

As mentioned above, each single-cable system needs two frequency bands for sending and receiving signals: the lowest band is assigned to the transmissions from the station to the headend and is called *reverse channel* (RC), whilst the other band, called the *forward channel* (FC), is used for the transmissions from the headend to the stations. A guard band is left between the reverse and forward channels since the filters used to separate the different frequency bands in a broadband system are never perfect; this safety frequency interval prevents interference from occurring between FC and RC. At present there are three standard alternatives for selecting the frequency range to be assigned to FC and RC; these are known as *highsplit*, *midsplit* and *subsplit* frequency assignments respectively.

Highsplit systems

Highsplit systems concern broadband media with an overall bandwidth equal to 400 MHz. In this case the range from 5 to 174 MHz is used for RCs while frequencies between 232 and 400 MHz are assigned to FCs. Modern coaxial cables can adopt such a subdivision since they have a larger bandwidth than their predecessors (which were typically limited to 300 MHz).

Midsplit systems

Midsplit systems are usually adopted for 300 MHz media and were developed to allow a balanced assignment of the frequency range to both RCs and FCs; in fact the former can fall inside the interval between 5 and 116 MHz, while the latter are found between 168 and 300 MHz.

Table 2.1   Highsplit and midsplit assignments for MAP broadband channels.

System type	Reverse channel (MHz)	Forward channel (MHz)
MAP	59.75 − 95.75	252 − 288
TOP	35.75 − 85.75	228 − 278

Subsplit systems

Subsplit systems are much older and do not permit a fair assignment to the reverse and forward channels, in fact the range from 54 to 300 MHz is reserved for FCs while only a 25 MHz wide band (comprising the frequencies between 5 MHz and 30 MHz) is assigned to RCs.

The MAP IEEE 802.4 backbone and the TOP IEEE 802.3 broadband networks are allowed to use either the midsplit or highsplit assignments mainly because several midsplit installations already existed before the development of the MAP/TOP specifications, even though there is a strong recommendation from the IEEE to use highsplit systems when a new IEEE 802.4 or 802.3 broadband network has to be installed.

Each basic broadband channel is 6 MHz wide since this bandwidth was sufficient to contain a US cable TV channel. MAP backbone networks operating at 10 Mbps require two pairs of adjacent 6 MHz channels to accommodate both RC and FC, while the broadband 802.3 used in TOP needs two larger frequency bands, each one consisting of three adjacent channels.

Table 2.1 summarizes the allowed frequency ranges currently assigned to MAP and TOP in both the midsplit and highsplit systems; it is easy to verify that the reverse and forward channels are separated by a frequency gap equal to 192.25 MHz. Since 6 adjacent channels are reserved for MAP three different MAP networks could coexist on the same cable, even though in most practical situations only one of the three possible choices is adopted. Similarly, one MAP and one TOP network could share the same medium in principle, but this event is also unlikely to occur very often.

2.2.2   Data signaling techniques

For our purposes, the numerous methods that can be used to send a stream of bits over a communication medium can be roughly grouped into two main classes known to the people interested in data communications as *digital* and *analog* transmission techniques.

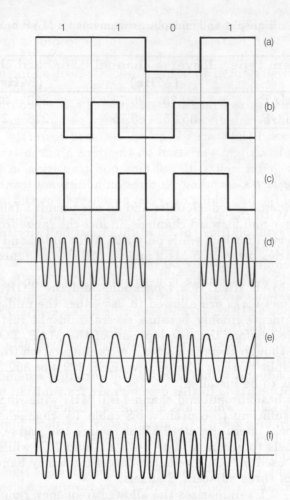

Figure 2.4   Different techniques for transmitting bit streams: (a) binary signal; (b) Manchester encoding; (c) differential Manchester encoding; (d) amplitude modulation (ASK); (e) frequency modulation (FSK); (f) phase modulation (PSK).

In practice, digital signaling does not make use of any modulated carrier: the data stream consisting of zeros and ones is sent directly on the communication channel at a suitable rate, for instance by using a square wave so that bit values are represented by two different voltage levels as shown in Figure 2.4(a). It is then conceptually simple for the receiver to extract the message bits by sampling the input signal at the same rate as that used by the transmitter. The main drawback of this method is in keeping the transmitter and receiver clocks synchronized, or, in other words, in detecting the start of each bit as it arrives at the receiver.

To circumvent this problem Manchester (Figure 2.4(b)) and differential Manchester (Figure 2.4(c)) encodings can be used. Manchester encoding has the following appealing characteristic: a 'one' bit is represented by a high-to-low transition in the middle of the bit period, whilst a 'zero' is encoded by a low-to-high transition. This scheme assures that each transmitted bit cell contains a signal transition in the middle so that the receiver's clock can be synchronized easily and the start of the bit detected correctly. Differential Manchester is a slight variation on the pure Manchester scheme: in this case each bit cell still contains one transition in the middle, however the zero's encoding requires an additional transition at the beginning of the bit, whilst ones can be detected by the lack of such a transition. With the Manchester schemes one bit of data is encoded into a 2-bit symbol, thus the baud rate must be twice the transmitted data bit rate; from this point of view Manchester encoding can be considered as being only 50% efficient.

Manchester encoding is used in the TOP IEEE 802.3 (baseband) subsystems working at 10Mbps, while differential Manchester is adopted by the IEEE 802.5 token ring access method also used in TOP. The main advantage of digital signaling is its high tolerance to electrical noise, since all information is conveyed as a sequence of discrete (binary) states.

In broadband systems the digital encoding schemes described above cannot be used. In this case bits are transmitted by modulating a carrier signal which has a frequency higher than the required data rate. Figures 2.4(d), (e) and (f) show the most popular modulation techniques adopted for this purpose.

Depending on the type of modulation, the amplitude, frequency or phase of the carrier is combined with the modulating digital signal and is allowed to take only two distinct values. Thus the modulating signal acts as a key shifting the value of the carrier parameter being considered and the term *shift keying* is used in this case. For instance, the digital amplitude modulation (amplitude-shift keying, ASK) encodes zeros and ones by using two different values of the carrier's sine wave height; when zeros are encoded by annihilating the carrier amplitude, bits are recognized on the receiver side by the presence or absence of the carrier.

Digital frequency modulation or frequency-shift keying (FSK) is another possible alternative: bits are encoded by changing the carrier's own frequency. Usually zeros are represented by a frequency equal to f_1, whilst ones are transmitted with a different frequency f_2 as shown in Figure 2.4(e). Note that with this type of modulation the receiver must be able to detect a change in the carrier's frequency in a very short time. Obviously FSK can also be adopted in a baseband system: for instance MiniMAP subnetworks are based on an FSK scheme which uses signals at 5 MHz and 10 MHz, thus allowing a data rate equal to 5 Mbps.

Phase modulation or phase-shift keying (PSK) encodes bits to be transmitted by changing the phase of the carrier at regular time intervals as exemplified in Figure 2.4(f). The PSK method can also be adopted to encode groups of bits rather than a single zero or one. For instance, a two-bits value can be associated to a phase shift of ±45 or ±135 degrees, so saving medium bandwidth and allowing higher data rates to be reached.

Basic modulation techniques can also be combined in more complex schemes to obtain more efficient systems, usually at the expense of both increased complexity and increased cost of the transmission equipment: for instance an amplitude modulation can be added to the basic PSK so that several amplitude values are associated with each phase shift. In this way it is possible to have more bits transmitted for each symbol; schemes working at 3 or 4 bits per symbol are currently used.

Bits sent over the MAP backbone are encoded by using a combined AM and PSK method known as *multilevel duobinary AM/PSK*. The term *duobinary* means that data to be sent are precoded in such a way that a reduced frequency range is needed for their transmission, while *multilevel* reminds us that more than two amplitude values are used for the amplitude modulation. The IEEE 802.4 broadband standard specifies a three-level duobinary AM/PSK scheme allowing the transmission of one bit per baud at the MAC level (see Section 2.3), and this recommendation has been adopted in the MAP specifications. However, it is worth noting that the 802.4 document also suggests three additional schemes to enhance the multilevel duobinary AM/PSK signaling at higher data rates (namely at two and four bits per baud).

2.2.3   MAP/TOP transmission media

In the world of standards, transmission media are strictly related to the techniques adopted for accessing the network. This is also the case with MAP and TOP: MAP is based on the token-bus approach which requires coaxial cables to conform to the IEEE 802.4 standard. The TOP situation is only slightly different because TOP can make use of different access techniques, each one having its preferred medium; thus it is possible to have TOP-compatible subnetworks working with twisted pairs, coaxial cables and even fiber optics.

At this point it is worth reminding ourselves of the main characteristics of the commonest transmission media:

Twisted pair

A twisted pair is made up of two insulated copper wires, twisted in a spiral as shown in Fig. 2.5(a). The main advantage of this solution

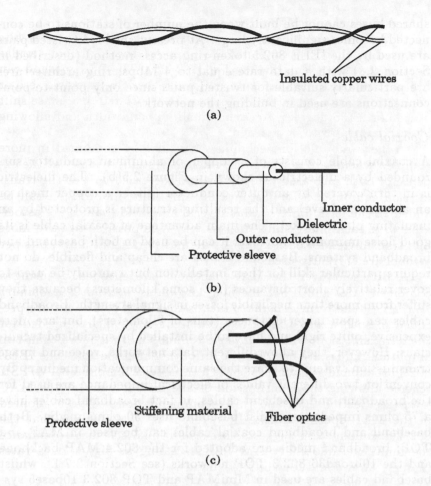

(a)

(b)

(c)

Figure 2.5   Transmission media for local area networks.

is reduced cost, since twisted pairs are significantly cheap when compared to coaxial cables and fiber optics. In addition these wires do not require skillful technicians for their installation and this aspect should not be underestimated when new systems have to be built. Unfortunately, twisted pairs also have a number of drawbacks: for example, they are affected by electrical noise and electromagnetic interference and this aspect makes them not very attractive for factory applications. The reason for twisting the wires is that it has a shielding effect; this can be enhanced by surrounding the wires with an additional shield (shielded twisted pair). However, this method can still be unsatisfactory in industrial environments. Another limitation is that twisted pairs operate with a relatively small bandwidth which prevents them being used in broadband systems. Furthermore, it is not easy to reach high data rates when using this type of medium and shared buses cannot be built when the number of stations to be connected becomes significantly large. At present shielded twisted pairs are used by the IEEE 802.5 token-ring access method (described in Section 2.8) with a data rate equal to 4 Mbps; ring architectures are particularly suitable for twisted pairs since only point-to-point connections are used in building the network.

Coaxial cable

A coaxial cable consists of a copper or aluminum conductor surrounded by a dielectric as shown in Figure 2.5(b). The dielectric is in turn covered by an outer conductor (either a copper mesh or an aluminum sleeve) and the resulting structure is protected by an insulating plastic jacket. The main advantage of coaxial cable is its good noise immunity, moreover it can be used in both baseband and broadband systems. Baseband cables are cheap and flexible, do not require particular skill for their installation but can only be used to cover relatively short distances (i.e. some kilometers) because they suffer from more than negligible losses in signal strength. Broadband cables can span larger distances (tens of kilometers), but are more expensive, quite rigid and have to be installed by specialized technicians. However, they allow different data networks, voice and image transmission systems to share the same communication medium. By convention two different values of electrical impedance are used for the broadband and baseband cables, in fact broadband cables have a 75 ohms impedance, whilst baseband uses 50 ohms media. Both baseband and broadband coaxial cables can be used in MAP and TOP: broadband media are adopted for the 802.4 MAP backbone and the 10broad36 802.3 TOP networks (see Section 2.7.1), whilst baseband cables are used in MiniMAP and TOP 802.3 10base5 systems.

Fiber optics

Fiber optics networks make use of light instead of electrical signals to transfer information from one station to another. Figure 2.6 shows the main building blocks of an optical transmission system connecting a general sender to the receiver: inside the transmitting station the (binary) data carried by some electrical signal are converted into light pulses that are in turn launched into the fiber. On the receiver side an optical detector is responsible for converting the light pulses back into electrical signals that are then handled by the electronic circuits in the receiving interface of the destination equipment.

   The fiber is a dielectric waveguide usually consisting of two coaxial cylinders of glass or plastic material. The inner layer (core) is more refractive than the outer (cladding) while, from a practical point of view, the core diameter is significantly larger than the wave-

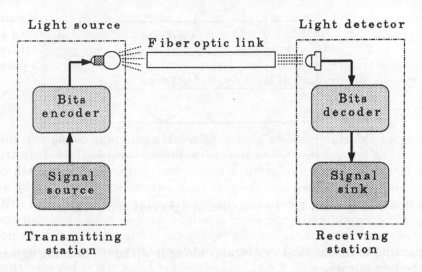

Light source   Fiber optic link   Light detector

Bits encoder

Signal source

Bits decoder

Signal sink

Transmitting station

Receiving station

Figure 2.6   Block structure of a fiber-based transmission system.

length of light used for the transmission (this is particularly true for *multimode* fibers).

Usually a fiber cable consists of several fibers surrounded by a protective sleeve as shown in Figure 2.5(c). The sleeve contains also some strengthening wires used to give mechanical robustness to the overall structure.

The light-guiding characteristics of fibers are mainly based on an optical parameter (n) which takes into account the optical properties of the material(s) building up the fiber. This parameter is known as the *refraction index* and can be computed as the ratio c/v where c is the speed of light in the free space and v is the speed of light in the specified medium (i.e. the material building up the core or the cladding of the fiber). The laws of geometric optics assert that a ray of light passing from one medium (core) with refraction index n_1 to another medium (cladding) with index $n_2 < n_1$ can experience total reflection at the interface between the two media if the incidence angle α of the ray exceeds a minimum (critical) value α_c. Otherwise the ray passes through the cladding and is refracted (i.e. deviated). This situation is sketched in Figure 2.7 where some rays emitted by an optical source are launched into a fiber. Ray A reaches the cladding-core boundary with an angle that is greater than the critical value, so it is totally reflected inside the core and continues to propagate along the fiber, bouncing against the core boundaries. By contrast the incidence angle α of ray B is too small and B is refracted through the cladding. The ray C in Figure 2.7 is particularly important for fiber technology since it enters the fiber

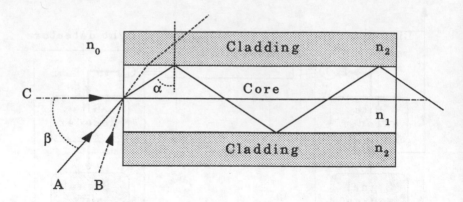

Figure 2.7   Propagation of light rays along a fiber.

parallel to its axis and propagates along it without bouncing against the boundaries.

It should be noted that since the light source is refracted when entering the fiber, not all the rays are able to propagate (i.e. are totally reflected) along the fiber; in fact a maximum value β_M of the *acceptance angle* in the figure exists so that each ray entering the fiber with an angle greater than β_M hits the cladding interface with an angle less then α_c and is refracted.

Each fiber has its own attenuation and bandwidth. Losses can be due both to the conversion of light energy into heat and to the radiation of the propagating rays. Typical values for the power losses of commercially available fibers fall between 1 and 4 $dBKm^{-1}$ depending on the wavelength of the light used (usually sources with wavelengths equal to 0.8 μm and 1.3 μm are adopted). In general the bandwidth of a (multimode) fiber depends on two factors known as *modal dispersion* and *material dispersion*. The first takes into account the fact that rays bouncing at different angles in the fiber follow different paths and consequently take different times to propagate along it, while the second considers the spreading of light pulses in fibers when incoherent light sources (such as light emitting diodes) are used. In practice, both these factors reduce the useful bandwidth of the medium.

Careful design of the fiber helps to increase the medium band-width; in fact the core diameter can be reduced to the order of a few light wavelengths, while the relative difference between the refraction indices of the core and the cladding (called the *step index*, δ_n) is kept small as shown in Figure 2.8(b). In this way a single type of ray (or *mode*) is able to propagate and the modal delay spread is eliminated. This kind of fiber is called *singlemode* and is more expensive and difficult to build than the 'conventional' *multimode* fibers.

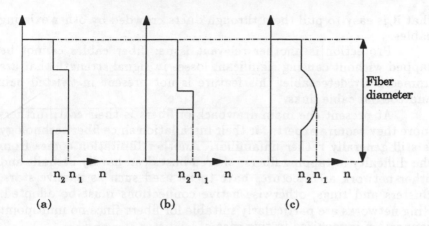

n_1 = maximum value of the core refraction index

n_2 = maximum value of the cladding refraction index

Figure 2.8   Refraction index profiles in fiber optics: (a) multimode step index fiber; (b) singlemode step index fiber; (c) multimode graded index fiber.

Another way to obtain optical links with larger bandwidth values is to use *graded index* multimode fibers. In this case the refraction index in the core is varied gracefully as shown in Figure 2.8(c). The final result is that the bandwidth is significantly larger (by as much as two orders of magnitude) than in a normal step index fiber (Figures 2.8(a) and (b)).

Light transmitters used with fibers can be either light emitting diodes (LEDs) or injection laser diodes (ILDs). The former generate weaker signals than the latter, however LEDs are significantly less expensive than laser diodes, which are typically used with singlemode fibers. Receivers are based on p-i-n and avalanche photodiodes that are able to convert a light pulse into an electric signal.

Digital transmissions are used with fibers, where zeros and ones are represented by means of light pulses. In addition, since light is used for transferring information, very high data rates can be achieved; for instance the emerging FDDI standard for fiber optics LANs specifies a data rate equal to one hundred megabits per second. The signal attenuation can also be satisfactorily low if high performance fibers are used; in this case efficient communications can be obtained over several kilometers without using repeaters.

Fiber optics has several other advantages that encourages its use in industrial communication systems: they are not affected by electrical noise and electromagnetic interference and can be installed in hostile chemical environments. They are lightweight and thin so that it is easy to pull them through ducts crowded by other existing cables.

Protection is another relevant issue: fiber cables cannot be tapped without causing significant losses in signal strength that are immediately detectable; this feature is not present in twisted pair and coaxial cable links.

At present the main drawback of fibers is their cost; furthermore they require experts for their installation since fiber technology is still generally rather unfamiliar. Another limitation comes from the difficulty in tapping fibers: shared buses can hardly be built and other network architectures have to be used such as passive stars, clusters and rings, otherwise active connections must be adopted. Ring networks are particularly suitable for fibers since no multipoint connection is required in this case.

2.3   IEEE 802 standard organization

Chapter 1 has shown that the protocol profiles used in MAP and TOP are based on the layered OSI reference model [ISO7498], [Zimmer83] and that services and protocols suited to industrial and office automation environments have been selected for each one of the seven communication layers.

Since both MAP and TOP concern local area networks, particular attention has been paid to those emerging standards that are both specifically oriented to LANs and are suitable to meet the MAP/TOP goals at the same time. The IEEE 802 project is perhaps the most important and widely accepted standard for LANs which deals in detail with the functionalities included in the two lowest layers of the OSI model, thus it is not surprising that the MAP/TOP physical and data-link layers have been based on the 802 specifications that have also been adopted as an ISO standard. For example, the logical link control sublayer (see Section 2.4) is described by the IEEE 802.2 and ISO 8802-2 documents, whilst the IEEE 802.3, 802.4 and 802.5 specifications correspond to the ISO standards numbers 8802-3 [ISO8802/3], 8802-4 [ISO8802/4] and 8802-5 [ISO8802/5], respectively.

Figure 2.9 shows the organization of the IEEE 802 standard: the two lowest layers of the OSI model are covered by a family of coordinate documents released by a number of working groups in the standardization committee, each one identified by a label of the form 802.x, where 'x' is a number used to denote a particular standard in the family. Thus the 802.1 documents concern the overall architecture of the 802 project but also contain guidelines for the network management procedure (see Chapter 5) and for internetworking multiple LANs.

The other standards appearing in Figure 2.9 define the services and protocols for the data-link and physical layers. In particular, the

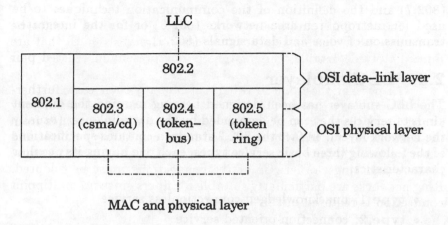

Figure 2.9 Organization of the IEEE 802 standard for local area networks.

data-link layer was split into two sublayers laid one upon the other in order to keep the interface to the network layer separate from the specifications of the mechanisms used to access the network that are dependent on the particular technique adopted to regulate the use of the communication channel.

The upper sublayer is called the *logical link control* (LLC) and is described in the 802.2 document. It contains a definition of the services offered to the network layer and of the protocols and message formats that are used to implement the data-link functions. The LLC specifications are totally independent of the method used to gain access to the network.

The second layer of the OSI model has several characteristics that are strictly related to the transmission of bits on the communication channel. These medium-dependent aspects have been confined in the 802 lower sublayer called *medium access control* (MAC). Because the MAC specifications share many details with the physical layer a single 802 document is used to cover the specifications of both. However, since different access protocols can be used to transmit messages on the network, each one having its advantages and drawbacks, different standards have been provided for the most significant access techniques. For instance, the IEEE 802.3 standard is concerned with the specification of the MAC and the physical layer for the CSMA/CD access method, while the 802.4 and 802.5 documents deal with the token-bus and token-ring systems, respectively. It is worth noting that the figure shows only those IEEE 802 elements that are relevant from the MAP and TOP points of view. However, other working groups, besides those shown in the diagram, exist in the 802 project which also has other primary goals such as, for instance, the standardization of a slotted ring access method (802.7) and the definition of the communication techniques to be used for metropolitan area networks (802.6) or for the integrated transmission of voice and data signals (802.9).

2.4   LLC sublayer

The LLC sublayer has been designed bearing in mind the different kinds of services that can be demanded by the data-link user (usually the network layer). In fact the 802.2 standard contains specifications of the following three basic service types, each one having its peculiar characteristics:

- **type 1**: unacknowledged connectionless service
- **type 2**: connection-oriented service
- **type 3**: acknowledged connectionless service.

Note that a system compatible with the IEEE 802.2 standard is not required to implement all three service types listed above. However, each implementation must support services that are included into a specific *service class* in order to conform to the standard. A service class consists of a suitable combination of the three basic service types and four classes are specified by the 802.2. Table 2.2 shows the correspondences between classes and types.

For example, hosts connected directly to the MAP backbone or to a TOP network make use of the type 1 service, whilst the type 3 service [8802dad] is needed by those machines connected to a MiniMAP subnetwork. Thus only classes 1 and 3 are considered in the MAP/TOP specifications, whilst other non-MAP/TOP systems can adopt the type 2 services and hence support the second and/or fourth class(es) shown in the table

Users access LLC services through data-link service access points (LSAPs). The service provider (LLC sublayer) is able to recognize different clients invoking data-link services since each user is connected to its own access point and each LSAP has a unique address in the network. Data exchanged across the user–LLC interface are usually called link service data units (LSDUs), whilst the messages exchanged between remote LLC entities are called link protocol data units (LPDUs). In the following we will also use the term *frame* to denote a generic message which is physically sent over the communication medium, whilst the terms *station* and *node* will be used interchangeably.

All the IEEE 802.2 services are described by means of *service primitives* that can be seen as an abstract way of specifying the meaning and the parameters concerning each LLC service without putting any constraint on its implementation. For instance, the same primitive can be implemented by a call to a procedure in one station

Table 2.2 IEEE 802.2 service classes.

Service class	Service type		
	Type 1	Type 2	Type 3
I	yes	no	no
II	yes	yes	no
III	yes	no	yes
IV	yes	yes	yes

or by means of message passing techniques in another machine. The only relevant aspect from the 802.2 point of view is that the same kind of capabilities with the same characteristics are offered to the users on both machines. In the following sections the three basic 802.2 services types will briefly be presented by using the related service primitives appearing in the 802.2 specifications.

2.4.1 Unacknowledged connectionless service

The type 1 service provides the user with simple functions for sending/receiving data to/from a remote entity and is based on a plain datagram scheme. In fact messages are sent without establishing any virtual connection between the source and destination stations and there is no acknowledgment message returned to the sender by the receiver to confirm that a message has correctly reached its destination. Furthermore, there is no flow control, message sequencing and error recovery mechanism. The MAC sublayer generates a confirmation for the LLC each time the transmission of a data LPDU has been completed, however this only means that the message has been transmitted correctly – no information is carried by the MAC confirmation concerning message reception.

The two following primitives are used to invoke the unacknowledged connectionless service:

(1) *L_DATA.request* allows the user to request the transmission of an LSDU by means of the datagram mechanism;

(2) *L_DATA.indication* is passed to the destination user by the LLC sublayer whenever a datagram is received addressing the user.

2.4.2 Acknowledged connectionless service

Type 3 is another connectionless service which adds some simple functionalities to the basic datagram scheme for granting reliable in-sequence data transfers.

Usually these goals are obtained by using either a connection-oriented service (such as type 2) or a protocols profile where the two lowest layers support a pure datagram service and the upper layers are responsible for implementing all the error recovery mechanisms and the sequencing procedures. The latter approach is followed in the full MAP and TOP stations, but it is not suitable for the Mini-MAP nodes where the complexity and the overhead introduced by the full stack of OSI protocols cannot be accepted. The solution in this case is based on the type 3 service which offers very simple, but also reliable, data transfer capabilities to the application layer. This is obtained by using a command/response protocol where each data transfer consists of two phases: first a command is sent from the initiating user to the remote destination and, secondly, a response is returned in the opposite direction which also carries the acknowledgment for the command frame. The service is completed with the reception of the response frame, so that any further transmission will be considered as non-related to the previous one.

Since no virtual circuit is established between any pair of communicating users, the sender/receiver is identified by its unique network address built up by concatenating the user source/destination LSAP address (SSAP/DSAP), which is unique for the node where the user resides, with the source/destination MAC address (SA/DA) which is unique for each station in the network.

Even though no virtual connection context is maintained and managed by the type 3 service provider, some mechanisms are needed to couple responses and commands in a correct way. Moreover, frames losses and/or duplications must be avoided because the service is assumed by the user to be reliable. For this purpose the communicating LLC entities use suitable sets of boolean variables called the *transmit sequence state* (TSS), *receive sequence state* (RSS) and *reception status* (RS) variables. TSS is used to check the incoming responses and to relate them to the outstanding commands that have still to be acknowledged, whilst RSS is needed to verify whether a command is being received for the first time or if it has been retransmitted by the remote LLC. Furthermore, RS is used to maintain the positive or negative result to be sent with the response to a given command when a retransmission of the response itself is needed.

A flow control mechanism for commands and responses is also included in the standard specifications, since the service provider must keep a TSS variable for each (DA, SSAP, priority) triple, whilst an RSS and RS pair has to be maintained for each combination of the (SA, SSAP, priority) values. This puts an upper bound on the maximum number of outstanding commands that can be sent by a user without waiting for any acknowledgment from the addressed interlocutors. In fact, each sender (SSAP) is enabled to transmit at most one command for each station in the network (DA) and service priority possibly supported by the MAC sublayer, then a response

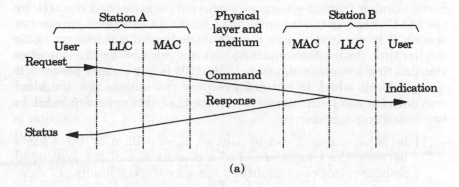

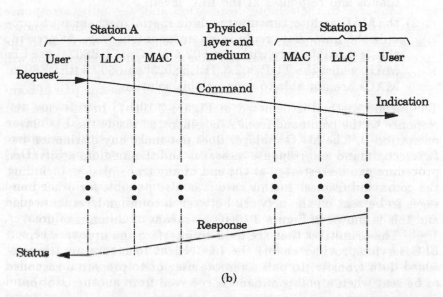

Figure 2.10   Sequences of primitives used to implement the type 3 services: (a) response generated at the MAC level; (b) response generated at the LLC level.

must be received before the user can send another command.

Basically there are two ways of implementing the acknowledged connectionless services: the diagrams in Figure 2.10 show the conceptual differences between the possible alternatives when an error-free data transfer is carried out by the data-link layer. As usual in this kind of diagram, the interfaces between adjacent layers are represented by vertical lines and the two dialoguing users are located on the left and right edges of the picture. The network, that is, the communication medium and the physical layer, is placed in the central zone.

In the first solution (Figure 2.10(a)) the response to a command coming from the user on station A is generated directly by the MAC sublayer in station B, that is, the LLC service provider of station B is not involved in the acknowledgment mechanism. This implies that the medium mastership is not released by MAC A after transmitting a command, instead, MAC B is left a short predefined time period in which to return its response as soon as the command transmission has been completed. Note that this approach exhibits two important aspects:

(1) no other message can be sent on the medium by these users between the transmissions of a command and the associated response; this can simplify to some extent the binding of commands and responses at the LLC level;

(2) the MAC architecture must include special mechanisms to provide the immediate reply in an autonomous way. At present, this is possible only with the 802.4 MAC [IEEE8024] used in MAP, whilst the TOP 802.3 [IEEE8023] and 802.5 [IEEE8025] MACs are not able to support this solution.

The second method is depicted in Figure 2.10(b). In this case the response to the command from A is generated inside the LLC layer on station B. The MAC sublayer does not make any distinction between command and response messages and the medium arbitration procedure can be restarted at the end of any transmission, including the command frames. In this case it is also possible for other messages to be sent on the network between a command/response pair and this is shown in Figure 2.10(b) by means of columns of dots.

The primitives that are used to interface the user to a type 3 LLC service provider enable the LLC client to invoke an acknowledged data transfer, to poll a remote user or to prepare a response to be sent when a poll command is received from another station.

Acknowledged datagram transmissions

Acknowledged datagram transmissions are invoked by means of the *DL_DATA_ACK.request* primitive and are based on the command/response scheme mentioned above. The destination user receives the message by means of a *DL_DATA_ACK.indication* primitive whilst a *DL_DATA_ACK_STATUS.indication* is returned to the initiator containing a positive or negative acknowledgment of the datagram reception. This service can be used to send either simple commands or data units to the destination LSAP.

Pollings of remote users

Pollings of remote users are performed by the *DL_REPLY.request* primitive and the polled users are notified by means of a *DL_REPLY.indication*. Data (if available) are returned to the initiator user by means of a *DL_REPLY_STATUS.indication*. Note that when a reply request reaches the destination LLC the data to be returned must be already available to the LLC entity since the reply is generated without the intervention of the polled user. In addition this service also allows bi-directional data exchanges between the communicating interlocutors since the request message can carry data to be delivered to the responding user.

Reply updates

Reply updates are obtained by invoking the *DL_REPLY_UPDATE.-request* primitive and are needed to pass new data to the LLC sublayer to be used in responding to a *DL_REPLY.request*. Thus this service has a pure local meaning and does not imply any exchange of messages on the network. The result of the update operation is returned to the user by means of a *DL_REPLY_UPDATE_STATUS.-indication* service primitive.

2.4.3 Connection-oriented service

Connection-oriented services are used neither in MAP nor in TOP, hence they are presented in this section only for the sake of completeness. In this case the messages are transferred over a virtual connection, which has previously been established between the two communicating users, by using an HDLC-like protocol [ISO7776] to grant an error-free, in-sequence data delivery service.

The 802.2 standard specifies suitable primitives for establishing and managing a virtual channel between a pair of LSAPs residing on different machines, for transferring data on the connection and for destroying the connection itself when it is no longer needed by the communicating users.

(1) **Connection establishment**. A user wishing to connect to a remote LSAP invokes an *L_CONNECT.request* primitive and this causes an *L_CONNECT.indication* primitive to be passed to the addressed user by the LLC service provider. As usual, the indication primitive is a signal to the remote entity notifying the attempt to open a new connection. Then a reply is returned to the initiating user by means of an *L_CONNECT.confirm* primitive containing the result (successful or unsuccessful) of the operation.

(2) **Data transfer**. Data-link service data units (LSDU) are transferred by means of the *L_DATA_CONNECT.request*, *L_DATA_CONNECT.indication* and *L_DATA_CONNECT.-confirm* primitives. The confirmation returns the sender information about the reception of the message. It can be seen as a positive or negative acknowledgment from the remote LLC entity, depending on the result of the LSDU transfer.

(3) **Disconnection.** Virtual connections can be destroyed by means of the disconnection service. In this case also, three primitives are provided, namely *L_DISCONNECT.request*, *L_DISCONNECT.indication* and *L_DISCONNECT.confirm*; they are used in the same way as the corresponding primitives for establishing a connection. However, it is worth noting that this disconnection is not graceful and the virtual circuit is destroyed as soon as the service request is passed to the LLC. Thus the user must be particularly careful in closing a virtual circuit since all the messages that were previously sent over the connection, but which are still undelivered when the disconnection is started, can be lost.

(4) **Connection reset.** When an error occurs at the level of the LLC user it can be necessary to reset a connection to the initial state. The 802.2 LLC supports this service by means of the *L_RESET* primitives provided in the usual request, indication and confirm versions. The reset service is also abrupt, and can cause the loss of undelivered data. However, unlike the disconnection service, the virtual circuit is not destroyed but it is cleared and reinitialized to an error-free state. Connection resets can also be started by the LLC layer itself when some internal error is discovered. In this case an indication primitive is passed to both the users at the connection endpoints since the reset request was not originated by either of them.

(5) **Connection flow-control.** Since the LLC user and the service provider can process data at significantly different speeds, a suitable mechanism is provided to control the flow of LSDUs that can cross the interface between the user and the LLC sublayer in both directions. The *L_FLOWCONTROL.request* primitive allows the user to specify the maximum amount of data that can be accepted from the LLC sublayer. Similarly the *L_FLOWCONTROL.indication* primitive is used by the LLC service provider to regulate the message flow coming from the user. Each flow-control primitive invocation concerns a single connection at a time, and each connection is independent from the others. A data flow can also be completely stopped by setting to zero the maximum amount of data that the user/LLC is ready to accept.

2.4.4   LLC message structure

Each LPDU exchanged between a pair of peer LLC entities that cooperate for implementing the link data services has the general format shown in Figure 2.11.

As can be deduced from the picture, there are two fields containing the message addressing information: the sender's address is

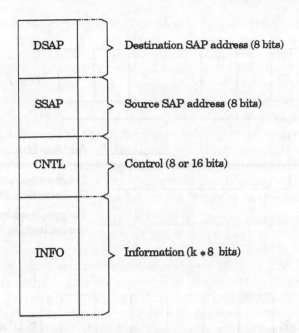

Figure 2.11   Format of the LLC protocol data units.

encoded in the eight bits of the SSAP field, whilst the destination is represented by the DSAP bits. The 802.2 document also specifies the way in which the address bits have to be used and this is shown schematically in Figure 2.12.

LLC destinations can be individual users (each user corresponds to an LSAP) or group of users. Thus the first bit of the DSAP field is used to distinguish individual from group (multicast) addresses. A special group address consisting of all '1's is handled by the LLC sublayer as 'global' and is used to broadcast messages to all the LSAPs active in the network. The standard also assigns special meanings to a number of other LSAP addresses: for instance the null address (consisting of all '0's) is used to address the LLC entity itself and does not correspond to any data-link user, whilst addresses having the first two bits equal to 01 or 11 are reserved for the 802 standard definitions.

Message senders are always single, thus only individual addresses are allowed in the SSAP field. Instead, the most significant bit in the SSAP field is used to distinguish commands from responses in both the type 2 and 3 procedures.

The control field in Figure 2.11 can be 8 or 16 bits long. It is used to encode the types of control messages needed to support the LLC service, but it can also carry other information such as the sequence numbers needed in the type 2 protocol or the values of the TSS and RSS variables used to grant the correct in-sequence data

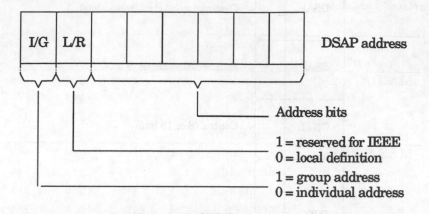

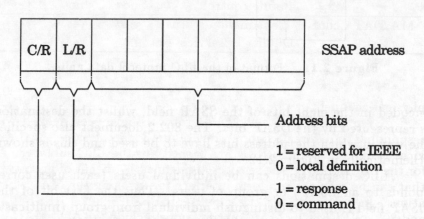

Figure 2.12   LSAP address structure.

delivery in the type 3 service.

Finally, the information field is normally used to carry data, and its maximum length depends on the particular MAC underlying the LLC sublayer. It is worth noting that this field is also used to transfer other useful information such as the positive or negative result of a type 3 command request and the reason for the possible failure.

2.5   MAC sublayer

The medium access control sublayer is responsible for carrying out all the operations concerned with the transmission and reception of frames according to the rules of the protocol for accessing the

Table 2.3   Service primitives exchanged at the LLC-MAC interface and related parameters.

Service primitive	Parameter	802.3	802.4	802.5
MA_DATA.req.	Destination address	yes	yes	yes
	LLC data	yes	yes	yes
	Quality of service	yes	yes	yes
	Frame control	no	no	yes
MA_DATA.ind.	Destination address	yes	yes	yes
	Source address	yes	yes	yes
	LLC data	yes	yes	yes
	Reception status	yes	no	yes
	Quality of service	no	yes	no
	Frame control	no	no	yes
MA_DATA.conf.	Transmission status	yes	yes	yes
	Quality of service	no	yes	yes

physical channel.

Even though different MAC protocols have been defined corresponding to different channel control methods, the same set of services is offered by each IEEE MAC entity to the LLC sublayer. As for the LLC sublayer, the services are defined by means of primitives that can be seen as a uniform interface for invoking the MAC operations. In particular the IEEE 802.3 [IEEE8023],802.4 [IEEE8024] and 802.5 [IEEE8025] MAC specifications include the LLC-MAC interface primitives listed in Table 2.3.

The *MA_DATA.request* primitive is used by the local LLC layer to send a message (that is a MAC service data unit) to a remote LLC entity. The LLC requesting this service must specify the MAC destination address, the data to be sent and the quality of service desired. The 'quality of service' parameter depends on the particular channel access method being used. For instance, when the 802.4 token-bus (see Section 2.6) is considered (the MAP medium access technique) the following two characteristics of data transmission can be selected with the quality of service parameter:

(1) the MAC priority to be assigned to the message (when the MAC sublayer supports multiple message priorities);

(2) the MAC delivery confirmation service.

By selecting a suitable value for the delivery confirmation parameter the user (LLC sublayer) can tell the MAC whether or not the message which is to be sent needs an immediate response (see Section 2.6.6); moreover, the same parameter is also used to distinguish the command messages from the responses to the incoming requests.

On the TOP side, the 802.3 MAC (see Section 2.7) does not allow the user to specify different values for the quality of service, whilst the 802.5 MAC (see Section 2.8) uses this parameter mainly to select the message priority.

The *MA_DATA.indication* primitive is passed to the LLC by the MAC sublayer each time a message is received from a remote station addressing the local LLC entity. The parameters used with this primitive are the destination and source addresses contained in the received frame and the data carried in the information field. Furthermore, the 802.4 MAC also returns the LLC the value of the delivered quality of service (with the same meaning as for the MA_DATA.request) whilst the 802.3 and 802.5 MACs pass a reception status parameter to the user containing the result (correct reception, frame received with errors etc.) of the frame reception operations. Note that the token-bus MAC simply discards any invalid messages that are received, whilst the 802.3 and 802.5 MACs report the reception errors to the LLC so that any possible recovery action can be undertaken at this level.

The *MA_DATA.confirmation* primitive is passed to the LLC entity by the MAC provider to report the successful or unsuccessful result of a previous MA_DATA.request invocation; this result is contained in the transmission status parameter. When the 802.3 and 802.5 MACs are considered, the meaning of this primitive is strictly local: it carries the confirmation that the corresponding data request frame has/has not been sent over the medium; this is also true for the 802.4 request_with_no_response service (see Section 2.6.6). However, when the 802.4 request_with_response service class is considered, the MA_DATA.confirmation is used to confirm to the local LLC that the message has really been received by the remote MAC entity. Hence, in this case, the confirmation becomes a sort of acknowledgment from the remote station.

Finally, it is worth remembering that the 802.4 and 802.5 confirmations specify the quality of service used in the transmission in the same way as that discussed for the request and indication primitives.

2.6   IEEE 802.4 token bus

2.6.1   Medium access method

The token-bus access method specified by the IEEE 802.4 MAC standard [IEEE8024] allows the stations sharing the transmission medium to gain access to the channel and send their messages without colliding while transmitting a frame. The 802.4 standard docu-

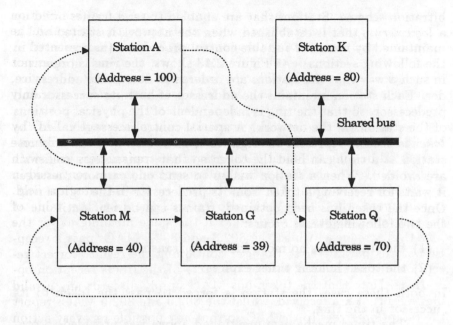

Figure 2.13   Structure of the token bus logical ring.

ment includes specifications for both baseband and broadband systems; in particular, baseband networks can have data transmission rates equal to 1 or 5 Mbps (the latter figure is used in MiniMAP subnetworks) whilst broadband networks work at 1, 5 or 10 Mbps (and the latter value has been adopted for the MAP backbone).

Receiving a message with the token-bus protocol is straightforward: all the stations are connected to a single cable as shown in Figure 2.13 and broadcast transmissions are used. In this way each receiver is able to listen to the channel and read all the frames sent over it. Each frame contains the addresses of both its sender and the intended destination and each station in the network has its own (unique) physical address. When the contents of the destination address field in the message match the station's physical address, the frame is copied by the receiving unit inside the buffer of the destination station and is then passed to the LLC sublayer by the 802.4 MAC entity.

It is worth noting that this mechanism can be used in some particular situations to implement special stations that are able to read and analyze all the messages sent over the network, for instance to carry out monitoring or to check system behavior in order to detect and recover faulty conditions and/or anomalous working modes.

Message transmissions are controlled by the token passing arbitration scheme. Stations that are enabled to send frames build up a *logical ring* that is established when the network is started and is maintained by means of suitable control procedures (as presented in the following sections). As Figure 2.13 shows, the ring is organized in such a way that the stations are ordered in decreasing address order. Each station maintains the addresses of both its successor and predecessor, so that the ring is independent of the physical positions of the stations in the network. A special control message called the *token* is used to represent the right to transmit frames, and only one station at a time can hold the token so that transmission collisions are avoided. When a station wishes to send one or more messages it waits for receiving a token from its predecessor in the logical ring. Once the token has been obtained, frames can be sent until one of the two following events occurs:

(1) the station has no more frames to transmit

(2) the token holding timer expires.

In both these cases the station is forced to pass the token to its successor in the ring.

The timer mechanism mentioned above was provided to prevent a station from being able to hog the network for an unacceptable period of time. This characteristic makes the timed token approach very attractive for industrial automation applications in general and MAP in particular, since the maximum waiting time experienced by a station in accessing the channel is upper bounded and can be computed and set when the maximum number of stations in the network is known. The value of the token holding timer is selected by each station when the network is started as described in Section 2.6.4.

Another advantage of the token-bus scheme is that the simplest devices do not need to be able to acquire medium mastership, that is they do not need to take part in the token arbitration, in order to be able to send frames to another station. In fact, it is sufficient for these simple stations not to be inserted in the logical ring, but to be polled by more sophisticated devices by using an extension mechanism of the 802.4 MAC (see Section 2.6.6) that allows a transmitter (i.e. a master station) to solicit and read data from a remote node (i.e. a slave station) without passing the token and releasing the channel control. In this way it is possible to connect cheap equipment to the network, since low-cost interfaces can be implemented that need only be able to reply to a poll command received as a normal frame.

Even though the token passing protocol can appear simple at a first glance, several problems must be tackled when the system is not working in a steady-state condition. In fact situations such as the insertion/deletion of stations in/from the logical ring, token losses, duplications and corruption must be handled explicitly by means of suitable mechanisms that complicate the basic access scheme introduced above.

These particular events are managed by the protocol with the aid of some special control frames whose formats and meanings are also included in the IEEE 802.4 standard. Each station is able to distinguish the special frames from the normal data messages by inspecting a control field present in each message sent over the network.

Timing mechanisms are another factor that plays a very important role in the token passing MAC. Several 802.4 timing specifications are described in the standard document as a function of the so-called *slot_time*. This term is used to denote '...the maximum time any station need wait for an immediate medium access level response from another station...' [IEEE8024], [ISO8802/4]. In other words the *slot_time* is the time a station must wait after having sent a frame before it is allowed to assume that the message did not reach its destination successfully since no response has been heard at the MAC level from the remote destination. Note that the actual value of the *slot_time* in a network is usually selected by the network administrator and must be the same at all stations. The duration of the *slot_time* τ_{st} is defined by the following formula:

$$\tau_{st} = 2(\tau_{pd} + \tau_{ed} + \tau_{sd}) + \tau_{sm} \qquad (2.1)$$

where τ_{pd} is the worst case delay due to the physical medium that a signal experiences in traveling from any station to another in the network; τ_{ed} is the overall delay caused by various pieces of equipment inserted in the communication path between the transmitter and the receiver such as amplifiers, repeaters, head-end remodulator, taps, splitters and so on; and τ_{sd} is the time taken by a station to receive a frame and generate an immediate response at the MAC level. Finally, τ_{sm} is a suitable safety margin used to ensure that τ_{st} is kept longer than the sum of the delays in Equation 2.1.

2.6.2   Joining and leaving the logical ring

Stations can join and leave the logical ring dynamically during the system's lifetime. When a station is booted (or rebooted) it is able to listen to the channel but is not allowed to send messages since it cannot receive the token. The insertion of a new station in the ring is based on a contention mechanism known as *response_window*. Every so often, the token holder looks for new stations wishing to join the ring by issuing a *solicit_successor* control frame. The *solicit_successor* frame contains the addresses of both the sender and a destination in the ring. After sending the frame the token holder pauses and listens to the channel for a predefined period of time, usually equal to one *slot_time*; that period of time is the response window. Three different situations can occur at this point:

(1) No transmission is heard before the response window expires: in this case no station, whose address falls between the addresses of the token holder and the destination, wishes to join the ring. The token holder passes the right to transmit to the next station as usual.

(2) The beginning of a valid transmission is heard before the end of the response window: the token holder waits for the end of the transmission even after the response window has expired. The answer of the responding station is a *set_successor* frame used to signal that a new station wishes to join the ring. Then the token holder changes its successor's address to the address of the responder and passes the token to its new successor (that is, the new station inserted in the ring).

(3) An invalid transmission is heard on the channel: this occurs when two or more stations try to reply to the same *solicit_successor* frame. In this condition the following arbitration algorithm is adopted in order to solve the contention and to allow only one station to join the ring.

   (a) first the token holder sends a *resolve_contention* frame;

   (b) each station that responded to the *solicit_successor* frame selects a two-bit delay value in order to defer its reply to the *resolve_contention* message for a time period equal to 0,1,2 or 3 *slot_times*;

   (c) whilst deferring its response the station listens to the channel: if something is heard the station abandons the arbitration and will try to join the ring when another *solicit_successor* frame is issued by the token holder, that is, when another response window is opened;

   (d) if only silence is heard during the deferring time period the station replies to the *resolve_contention* with a *set_successor* frame;

   (e) if another collision is detected by the token holder the arbitration is restarted by sending a new *resolve_contention* message; note that the number of colliding stations decreases at each iteration of the algorithm so that at last only one station will be able to reply to the token holder and will be inserted in the ring.

As a matter of fact the 802.4 standard mentions two different *solicit_successor* frames: *solicit_successor_1* and *solicit_successor_2*. The former is used by all the stations in the ring except for the one having the lowest physical address. In the latter case two response windows must be opened to solicit a new successor and this is accomplished with an additional *solicit_successor_2* frame: the first window is used to ask for stations with an address lower than the

sender's address, whilst the second window is intended for succes-
sors with addresses higher than the token holder's address. It is also
worth noting that, in order to keep the number of iterations of the
arbitration algorithm small, the 802.4 standard specifies a technique
for selecting the random delay value (called *demand delay*) directly
from the station's physical address using two bits at a time and starting with the most significant bits; this leads to sorting the colliding
stations in descending address order and to giving priority to those
stations with the highest addresses. In fact, if each address is k bits
long ($k = 16$ or $k = 48$), the arbitration takes at most $N = k/2 + 1$
iterations. At the ith iteration the demand delay τ_{dd} is chosen equal
to

$$\tau_{dd} = (3 - (2a_{k+1-i} + a_{k-i}))\tau_{st} \qquad 1 \le i < N \qquad (2.2)$$
$$\tau_{dd} = (rand(0,3))\tau_{st} \qquad\qquad i = N$$

where a_n is the nth bit of the station address, a_k is the most significant bit, and $rand(0,3)$ is an integer number randomly chosen
between 0,1,2 and 3. The Nth iteration was foreseen also to take
into account those (faulty) situations where two stations are present
in the network with the same physical address. In this case the random choice of the *demand_delay* values prevents the whole system
from being stuck indefinitely.

Since the insertion procedure for the new stations is time-
consuming, it can only be executed when the network load is not
too heavy and the upper bound on the access time to the channel
(which affects the maximum token rotation time) is not exceeded.

Leaving the ring is certainly simpler than adding a new station,
however there are two different ways of obtaining the same result.
On the one hand, a station wishing to abandon the network can
simply be detached from the transmission medium (i.e. it can be
switched off). When the token is passed to the absent station it will
be lost and consequently the recovery procedures (see Section 2.6.3)
will be started, thus leading the network to eliminate the missing
station from the logical ring. This approach should be avoided since
it is based on the time-consuming mechanisms included in the 802.4
protocol for recovering anomalous situations. A more convenient and
graceful solution is the following: the abandoning station waits to
receive the token and sends a *set_successor* frame to its predecessor
specifying its successor's address in the data field of the message.
Then it transmits the token to the next station, thus excluding itself
from the logical ring.

2.6.3   Token losses and corruptions

Passing the token from one station to its successor is another operation which needs particular attention. In fact, if the token is
corrupted by electrical noise or if it is lost, for example because the

intended destination has abandoned the ring, the protocol must recover the faulty situation automatically in order to keep the whole network working.

For this purpose, when the token holder passes the token to the next node in the ring, it also starts a timer equal to one *slot_time* and then begins listening to the channel. If a correct transmission is heard from the successor before the timer expires the station can safely assume that the token has been received and the current holder is now transmitting messages or passing the token in its turn. Otherwise, the station undertakes the following sequence of more and more drastic recovery actions for exiting the anomalous situation:

(1) If an invalid transmission or some noise is heard after passing the token, the station cannot rely on the source address field in the received frame in order to detect its sender. So the timer is restarted for up to four *slot_times* and the station continues listening to the transmission medium. If nothing is received during this period of time, the station assumes that its own token was corrupted and did not reach the successor, otherwise the successor is assumed to have obtained the token correctly. In the former case the station tries to pass the token a second time by repeating once more its monitoring actions after sending the token frame.

(2) If the second attempt to pass the token also fails, it is probable that the successor is not working, either because of a failure or an abrupt shutdown. In this case the token holder tries to locate a new successor by sending a *who_follows* frame containing its old successor's address. The other stations in the network check whether or not the address carried by the *who_follows* frame matches their predecessor's address. The result of this comparison is only true for one station, which then replies to the token holder by transmitting a *set_successor* frame containing its own address; this allows the logical ring to be reconfigured by excluding the non-responding (faulty) station.

(3) The most serious procedure is carried out when nobody replies to the *who_follows* frame. In this case a second attempt is performed to locate the token holder's successor. If another failure is reported, the station tries to build up a new logical ring by issuing a *solicit_successor_2* control frame containing its own address in both the source and destination address fields. This forces any other live station in the network to reply to join the ring. If some response is obtained the new ring is established with the *response_window* mechanism, otherwise a catastrophic event must have occurred (for example the transmission medium could be broken, all the other stations could have failed or left the ring, and so on). The soliciting station

then abandons its attempts to maintain the ring. It becomes silent and listens to the channel, looking for any transmission by a remote sender. However, if the station still has any data frame to transmit it sends all the remaining messages and then retries to pass the token before entering the idle state.

2.6.4 Ring initialization

When the system is started up nobody has the token and an original logical ring must be established. Each station can detect this initial state by means of another timer called the *bus_idle_timer* which is used to monitor the communication activity on the shared medium. The *bus_idle_timer* is restarted whenever a frame transmission is heard on the network. At initialization the *bus_idle_timer* expires, since no message is circulating over the network, and all the active stations start the initialization procedure trying to become the token holder. This procedure is based on a contention mechanism similar to the one used for inserting new nodes in the ring.

(1) To create a ring, a station sends a *claim_token* frame on the medium. The length of the information field in this frame can vary, but it is always a multiple of the *slot_time* and is chosen by the station using its physical address bits two at a time as for selecting the demand delay described in Section 2.6.2. In fact, during the ith iteration of the algorithm the duration τ_{ct} of the *claim_token* data part is given by:

$$\begin{aligned} \tau_{ct} &= 2(2a_{k+1-i} + a_{k-i})\tau_{st} & 1 \leq i < N \quad \textbf{(2.3)} \\ \tau_{ct} &= 2(rand(0,3))\tau_{st} & i = N \end{aligned}$$

where a_n and $rand(0,3)$ have the same meanings as in Section 2.6.2. In other words, τ_{ct} can be equal to 0,2,4 or 6 *slot_times*, according to the values of the bits selected from the station address.

(2) After sending the *claim_token* frame the station waits one more *slot_time* and then listens to the channel. If a transmission is heard the attempt to become the token holder is abandoned since another station with a higher address has been found which is still transmitting a longer *claim_token* frame.

(3) If instead, the medium is found to be silent after the *claim_token* transmission, the station performs another iteration of the algorithm by sending another *claim_token* frame whose length depends on the next two bits in its physical address.

(4) When the last iteration has been successfully ended the active station with the highest address has won the contention and

becomes the token holder. At this point the logical ring can be built using the *response_window* mechanism.

The protocol procedures for recovering from token losses/-corruptions and initializing/reinitializing the ring make the token bus access method quite slow in managing these particular events. This is because the station which tries to regenerate a token or restart the ring must be sure that the original token was either corrupted or lost and not delayed, for instance, inside some other station running at a slower clock speed. In other words, several delays in the protocol have been introduced to prevent the system from reaching a working condition where two tokens coexist on the same medium; it is easy to figure out that this would lead to catastrophic consequences for the network integrity.

Another critical situation could arise if a station having the same physical address as that used by another station could take part in the logical ring. To prevent this problem from occurring a duplicate address check is performed by each station by comparing its own address with the contents of the source address field in each frame received. If the checking station is not the token holder (this can be verified by testing a boolean variable inside the station) another transmitter exists in the network which has the same physical address, so an error message is reported to the management part of the checking station, which will then take appropriate recovery action (for instance disconnecting the station from the network).

2.6.5   Priority classes

One of the advantages of the token passing protocol is the facility to have different priority classes for the data frames transmitted by the MAC sublayer. This is particularly important in the process control and automation fields since some applications need prioritized communications in order to work correctly.

A major distinction which can be found in a token bus network is between synchronous and asynchronous messages. Some data traffic, such as the transmission of voice and/or image samples, are synchronous in their nature. This means that they are subject to strict delivery constraints and the data frames cannot wait for transmission indefinitely. Other types of messages can be equally time critical, even though they are not synchronous: for instance the alarm messages in a system supervising a manufacturing plant should not be delayed by communications such as file transfers, part-programs up/downloading or statistical data collection.

Often it is also useful to have different priority classes for transmitting the (less urgent) asynchronous messages. This allows the designer to give precedence to the communications of a given application, or to send some messages before other frames inside the same application.

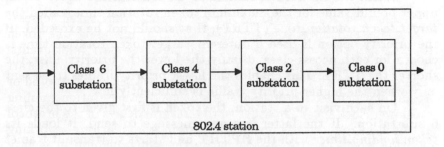

—→ Conceptual token passing sequence

Figure 2.14   Logical structure of an IEEE 802.4 station supporting the priority option.

The 802.4 standard specifies four priority classes (called *access_classes*) at the MAC level that are labeled, respectively, 0, 2, 4 and 6 (6 being the highest priority). However, the priority mechanism is an optional feature in the 802.4. Stations that do not use the priority option can coexist in the same network with stations transmitting prioritized messages; nevertheless, in the former case all the frames are transmitted by using the highest access class.

A station implementing the priority mechanism can be thought of as consisting of four cascaded substations as shown in Figure 2.14. Each substation is devoted to the transmission of a single class of frames; it has its own queue of messages waiting to be sent and, needless to say, a timer used to measure the token rotation time, that is the time elapsed between two subsequent visits of the token at the same substation. The substations are cascaded in priority order and the token, once obtained by substation 6, is passed to substation 4, 2 and 0 in sequence before leaving the station.

The priority mechanism has been designed bearing in mind that a suitable portion of the system bandwidth should be assigned to the most urgent (class 6) traffic. Thus a station, once it has obtained the token, can send class 6 frames up to a maximum time called the *high_priority_token_hold_time* (HPTHT), whilst frames of the lower classes can be sent only if the measured token rotation speed allows the delivery constraints for the class 6 messages to be satisfied. In fact, it is worth remembering that the higher the token rotation speed, the lower the network traffic, because when stations pass the token quickly, on average, they have few frames to transmit. In these situations lower priority frames can also be sent, since the unused part of the system bandwidth is sufficiently large. By contrast, slow token rotations show that the network load is high and no (or little) bandwidth is left for delivering low priority messages.

When the network is initialized all the stations agree on an upper bound value for the maximum token rotation time, called the *target_token_rotation_time* (TTRT), that should not be exceeded. If the priority option is used a different target token rotation time is chosen for each access class; usually the lower the priority class, the shorter the TTRT. This enables the lower priority frames to be sent only when the higher priority traffic is sufficiently low.

On each visit to a station, the token is first given to the class 6 substation. If the latter has any message to send, it loads its *token_holding_timer* with the HPTHT and starts to transmit frames until they are exhausted or the timer expires, then the token is passed to the following substation.

Substations 4, 2 and 0 all behave in the same way: they load their token rotation timer with the value of the target token rotation time for the corresponding access class on each token visit. However, before reloading the timer, a test is performed to check whether the timer has expired (i.e. the last token rotation has been longer than the TTRT) or not. In the former case the token is immediately passed to the next (sub)station, while in the latter situation the remaining time value is loaded in the *token_holding_timer* and the substation begins to send frames up to the holding timer expiration.

Setting the target token rotation times in a token-bus network is a critical issue, since it has been shown [CiVa88] that if too loose values are chosen all the classes are served in the same way, thus annihilating the effect of the priority mechanism. On the other hand, too tight values for the TTRTs prevent lower priority frames from being delivered, even though the overall system load would enable their transmission, and this also reduces the network throughput.

2.6.6   Immediate response mechanism

The 802.4 protocol allows for the implementation of the LLC DL_REPLY and DL_DATA_ACK services presented in Section 2.4.2 directly at the MAC level, that is without releasing the communication medium mastership (i.e. passing the token) while waiting for a reply from a remote user. In fact a suitable mechanism (acknowledged connectionless service) has been included in the 802.4 standard, which allows a station (initiator) to send a frame and then wait for a response message from the intended destination. The waiting state is exited when either a valid reply is received or a timer expires. In the latter case, a new attempt is performed by retransmitting the original request frame. The maximum number of unsuccessful attempts is a protocol parameter which is selected at initialization.

To keep the protocol as simple as possible, each station can manage a single *request_with_response* frame at a time; that is, no

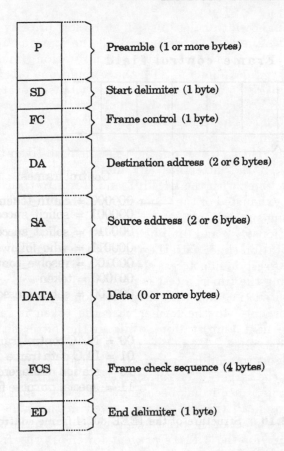

Figure 2.15 Organization of the IEEE 802.4 frame.

other service invocation is considered while transmitting the request and waiting for either a response or the maximum tries count to be reached. Moreover, the destination user (usually the LLC sublayer) is responsible for detecting and discarding possible duplicated requests sent by the initiator when its timer times out. By contrast, unacknowledged datagrams are transmitted by means of the *request_with_no_response* MAC frames.

2.6.7   802.4 MAC frame structure

The 802.4 frames are structured in a set of contiguous fields as shown in Figure 2.15. The meaning of each element in the frame is described in the following sections.

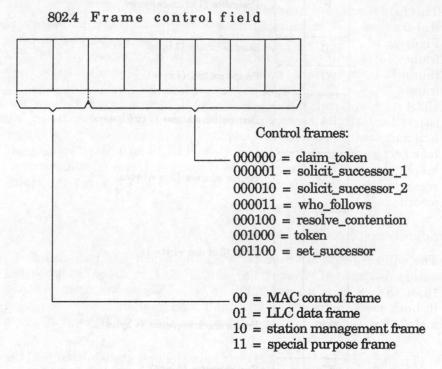

802.4 Frame control field

Control frames:

000000 = claim_token
000001 = solicit_successor_1
000010 = solicit_successor_2
000011 = who_follows
000100 = resolve_contention
001000 = token
001100 = set_successor

00 = MAC control frame
01 = LLC data frame
10 = station management frame
11 = special purpose frame

Figure 2.16   Structure of the IEEE 802.4 frame control field.

Preamble (P)

The main purpose of this field is to enable the receiver to synchronize its clock with the transmitter. In addition the preamble grants sufficient time spacing between two subsequent frames issued on the medium.

Start/end delimiters (SD, ED)

These fields have been provided to mark the beginning and the end of the frame, respectively. They are one octet long and are encoded by using special non-data symbols. In fact, one of the characteristics of the 802.4 physical layer is the encoding scheme, which includes non-data symbols as well as representations of the logical zero, one and idle medium status. This feature allows the frame boundaries to be completely defined by means of SD and ED as shown in Figure 2.15, so that a frame length field, such as the one included in the 802.3 frame (see Section 2.7.3), is not needed in this case.

Frame control (FC)

This field consists of 8 bits used to distinguish different data and control frames. The encoding scheme of the frame control is shown in Figure 2.16. Bits b_1 and b_2 allow for discrimination between control frames ($b_1b_2 = 00$), LLC originated data frames ($b_1b_2 = 01$), station management data frames ($b_1b_2 = 10$) and special-purpose data frames ($b_1b_2 = 11$) reserved for special functions not covered by the 802.4 standard. Bits $b_3 - b_8$ are then used to specify other characteristics: for instance control frames have their type (*claim_token, solicit_successor_1, solicit_successor_2, who_follows, resolve_contention, token, set_successor*) encoded in these bits, whilst data frames use $b_3b_4b_5$ to specify the required MAC action (*request_with_response, request_with_no_response, response*) and $b_6b_7b_8$ to detect the frame priority.

Source/destination addresses (SA,DA)

The address fields are used to locate the sender and intended destination of the MAC frame. Each 802.4 MAC address can be either 16 or 48 bits long, however only 48 bit addresses are used in MAP. In both cases, individual, global and broadcast addresses have been included in the standard specification as shown in Figure 2.17.

(1) *Individual addresses* always have the first transmitted bit (the leftmost bit in Figure 2.17) equal to zero. They are used to locate a single station in a LAN, so that each individual address must be unique in a network.

(2) *Group addresses* have the first transmitted bit equal to one. Groups have been provided for multicast transmissions, that is a single frame sent to a group is received by all the stations in the group at the same time. A station can join several different groups and receive any multicast frame addressing each one of them.

(3) *Broadcast address*: a special address consisting of all '1's has been reserved for broadcast transmissions. In this case all the stations in the network can be reached with a single message transmission.

It is worth noting that the IEEE 802 standard also specifies a method for administering 48 bit addresses. Addresses with the second transmitted bit equal to zero are managed by a global authority, otherwise the address administrator is local to the specific LAN. The purpose of a global authority (that is the IEEE in this case) is to ensure that there are distinct addresses even when different LANs are considered. In this way bridging two or more 802 LANs becomes a simple matter, since no duplicate station address can exist.

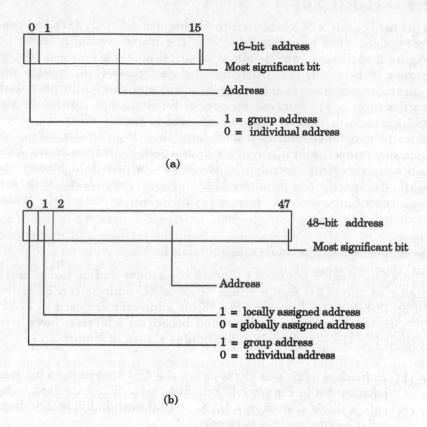

Figure 2.17   Format of the IEEE 802 MAC address.

Data

This field contains the information carried by the MAC frame. There is a limit on the data field length since the number of bytes between the SD and ED fields in Figure 2.15 can not exceed 8191.

Frame check sequence (FCS)

This field contains a 32 bit checking sequence used to detect transmission errors in the received frame. The FCS coverage includes the FC, DA and SA fields as well as the data information.

2.7 IEEE 802.3 CSMA/CD

2.7.1 Medium access method

The carrier sense multiple access with collision detection (CSMA/CD) access method is simpler and cheaper than protocols based on the token-passing techniques, such as the IEEE 802.4 and IEEE 802.5, and it exhibits characteristics that are complementary, to some extent, to those arbitration schemes.

In fact, token-passing protocols try to control simultaneous access to the physical medium by multiple stations in order to prevent possible collisions from occurring; by contrast, the CSMA/CD method allows two or more stations to begin a transmission at the same time and then starts to solve the contention.

The architecture of a typical IEEE 802.3 network is shown in Figure 2.18. As it can be deduced from the picture, all the stations are connected to the same transmission media having a 'common-bus' topology, even though multiple network segments can be present in the system connected by repeaters. Repeaters can be thought of as signal amplifiers and they are completely transparent to the data-link layer, thus from a logical point of view the network can be considered as consisting of a single segment. In fact, repeaters are needed only for networks spreading over relatively large areas (i.e. one or two kilometers) to bridge long distances between any pair of stations in the system.

The IEEE 802.3 standard document describes a whole family of CSMA/CD systems that are based on the same access protocol, even though they have different network parameters. In particular, each member of the family is given an identifier of the form RtD, where R is the data transmission rate in megabits per second, t is the type of transmission used (either *base* for baseband or *broad* for broadband) and D is the maximum length allowed for any network segment in hundreds of meters.

TOP systems can be designed based on either the 10base5 or 10broad36 specifications, that is, both 10 Mbps baseband networks with segments no longer than 500 meters and 10 Mbps broadband networks with segments no longer than 3.6 kilometers are allowed in TOP.

When the CSMA/CD method is used, messages are broadcast by the originating station to the other nodes in the network and each station is able to listen to all the frames traveling on the medium, as for the IEEE 802.4 protocol (see Section 2.6).

When a station has a frame to send it begins to listen to the channel; if some signal is heard, the message transmission is deferred because some other node in the network is currently using the physical medium. The deferring operations continue until the channel becomes silent; then the station waits for an additional short

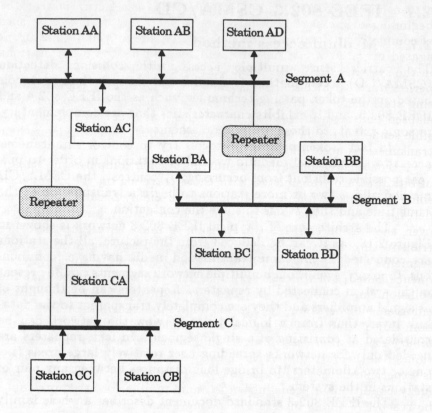

Figure 2.18   Structure of an IEEE 802.3 network.

time period, called the *interframe gap*, to elapse before it starts to send the message. If it's lucky, the transmission can be completed successfully because either no other station tries to send a message at the same time, or the other nodes find the medium busy and defer their transmissions. The *interframe gap* is needed to ensure that the destination physical layer is able to process the received frame before a new transmission is started. However, it is worth noting that this gap should be kept as short as possible, since it wastes system bandwidth and reduces the maximum (theoretical) reachable throughput for the network.

Frame reception is carried out in a similar way to the method adopted for the token-bus, that is, a message is copied inside the receiving station buffers when the destination address field contained in the frame is recognized by the receiver.

It is easy to see that the protocol introduced above is not sufficient to grant medium mastership to one station at a time. In fact some situations can arise where multiple stations start to send their messages when they find the channel silent and this results in a transmission *collision*. In particular, this can occur just at the beginning of message transmission. In fact, a station can be sure of completing its transmission successfully when its signal has propagated over the whole network and reached all the other stations in the system. The IEEE 802.3 standard [IEEE8023] calls the time period during which collisions can be experienced by the transmitting stations the *collision window*. After the *collision window* has elapsed and no transmission interference has occurred, all the possible senders but one will find the medium busy and will defer their transmissions accordingly.

For this reason each transmitting station compares the stream of bits that are transmitted with those traveling on the channel; if some difference is found a collision has probably occurred and been detected, and so the transmission is immediately aborted. Moreover, the station enforces the collision to make sure that the other transmitting nodes can recognize it and stop sending invalid frame segments on the network. This is done by sending a special bit sequence called *jam* which is set to be long enough to ensure that the collision can be noted by any other transmitter. After the collision enforcement operation, the station delays its transmission for a random time period selected by means of a method called the *truncated binary exponential backoff* algorithm, discussed in the following section. Another attempt is then carried out, and if a new collision is experienced the whole process is repeated. In particularly unlucky conditions a predefined maximum number of attempts could be reached without the station having been able to send the frame successfully; in this case the transmission failure is reported by the MAC to the LLC sublayer, since the LLC is responsible for deciding whether the transmission can be retried or an error message has to be reported to the user.

The width of the *collision window* is very important in each CSMA/CD system and depends on several factors such as the maximum distance between any pair of stations in the network, the characteristics of the physical medium and the data signaling rate. In the 802.3 document, the protocol timings are specified by using a parameter called *slot time* (τ_s) given by:

$$\tau_s = 2T_{ee} + T_j \tag{2.4}$$

where T_{ee} is the propagation delay experienced by a signal traveling from one end to the other in the network and T_j is the maximum time needed by the MAC sublayer to send the jam sequence. Hence τ_s can be considered as a worst-case bound in estimating the width of the collision window.

If the message to be sent is too short, a possible collision could not be detected before the end of the transmission. For this reason the MAC sublayer is responsible for appending a sequence of extra bits called *pad* to the shorter frames so that the minimum message length requirement is always satisfied.

As is easy to verify, the CSMA/CD method is simple and does not require complex procedures for arbitrating the right to transmit messages, moreover the access scheme is fully distributed since it does not depend on any special management station. These characteristics make this protocol very attractive for TOP applications because low-cost interfaces to the network can be implemented and satisfactory performance obtained. For example, the medium access time can be very short if the network load is not too high (this implies a low collision probability) and the overall system throughput is usually very good. By contrast, the CSMA/CD method was not considered suitable for MAP applications for the two following reasons:

(1) Since the access method is non-deterministic the protocol is not able to grant an upper bound to the maximum access time. This aspect is particularly important in a time-critical environment where the effect of repeated collisions experienced by a station could be catastrophic.

(2) The CSMA/CD scheme does not include any support for message priorities. This is a drawback in industrial environments where some communications must be prioritized. To these ends it is worth noting that some changes in the protocol, such as those proposed in [ChlFra80], [Tobagi] and [CiDeVa88], can be used to implement a sort of priority scheme, however these are particular solutions that are not taken into account in the standard specifications used in MAP and TOP.

In addition, the IEEE 802.3 access method does not allow for the implementation of the LLC services DL_DATA_ACK and DL_REPLY (see Section 2.4.2) at the MAC level, since medium mastership is released by the sending station whenever the current transmission is completed. This causes the contention mechanism to be restarted, so that other transmissions can occur before a response frame can be sent to the requesting station. This is another reason which prevents the CSMA/CD method from being used in time-critical environments where efficient immediate-response schemes are needed.

2.7.2   Backoff algorithm

A sending station which detects a collision has to delay its transmission. The length of the delay period is chosen so as to reduce the probability of experiencing another collision, but it is always a multiple of the network *slot time*. In general the station can decide to delay its transmission for k slot times where k is a randomly chosen integer value greater than or equal to zero and lower than N_m. The problem is to select a good value for N_m because if N_m is too small the colliding stations have a high probability of picking up the same k and a new collision will occur. By contrast, a large N_m can oblige a station to delay its transmission for several *slot times*, even when this is not necessary, as in the case of two stations colliding when the network load is very low.

The basic idea adopted for the backoff algorithm is to progressively increase the value of N_m as the number of collisions experienced for the same transmission becomes larger. In other words, the algorithm tries to reduce the collision probability after each unsuccessful attempt to send the same message. Thus, before trying the nth retransmission N_m is assigned the value 2^x where x is the lesser of n and ten. This means that N_m is no longer increased after the tenth attempt and the same value is used until the maximum number of tries is exhausted.

For example, when two stations collide the first time they can delay their transmissions for 0 or 1 *slot time* at random. This leads to a probability of having a second collision equal to 0.5. If the second collision occurs the stations can delay their transmissions for 0, 1, 2 or 3 *slot times* and this reduces the collision probability to 0.25. After the tenth attempt the collision probability is only 0.0009765.

2.7.3 802.3 MAC frame format

The basic format of the IEEE 802.3 frame is shown in Figure 2.19. As is easy to see each message consists of eight fields with the following meanings:

Preamble (P)

This field is a sequence of seven bytes used by the receiver to synchronize its clock for correctly decoding the incoming bits.

Start frame delimiter (SFD)

This one-byte field is needed by the receiving circuits for them to recognize the start of the frame.

Source and destination addresses (SA, DA)

These are the physical addresses of the sender and of the destination. The addressing scheme used by the 802.3 MAC is the same as that adopted by the token-bus access method which is described in Section 2.6.7.

Length (L)

This field is two bytes long and is used to detect the end of the frame. Since no end delimiter is included in the frame structure

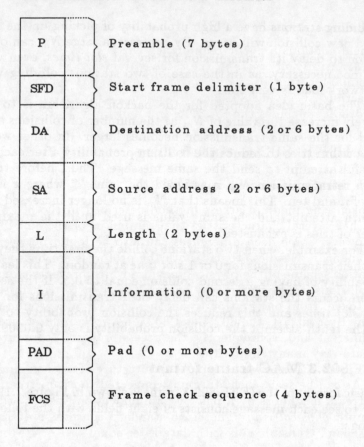

Figure 2.19   Structure of the IEEE 802.3 frame.

a length field must be present. It contains the number of bytes building up the information field; note that the standard documents specify a maximum length allowed for the information field so that a station is forced to restart the medium contention mechanism after a maximum period of time.

Information (I)

This field contains the data bytes sent by the LLC sublayer.

Pad (PAD)

This is a variable-length field used to keep the overall frame length longer than the predefined minimum value. If the information field contains a sufficient number of data bytes the *pad* is not inserted in the frame by the transmitting MAC.

Frame check sequence (FCS)

This field contains a cyclic redundancy check (CRC) value used to detect transmission errors in the received message. The generating polynomial for the CRC value is the same as that used by the 802.4 (see Section 2.6.7) and 802.5 (see Section 2.8.6) MACs, whilst the FCS coverage includes the SA, DA, L, I and P fields.

2.8 IEEE 802.5 token ring

2.8.1 Medium access method

The token ring medium access method described in the 802.5 document has several characteristics that remind us of the 802.4 token bus, however some deep differences can also be found between the two standards. Needless to say, both the protocols are based on an arbitration scheme of the physical medium which prevents transmission collisions from occurring by passing the right to transmit, that is the token, from one station to another in a circular, round-robin fashion. By contrast, the 802.4 and 802.5 network architectures are very different and, consequently, the access protocol procedures do not share very many similarities.

Figure 2.20 shows the typical architecture of a token ring network. As can be seen, each station is connected to its upstream and downstream neighbors by a pair of communication lines in order to build up a *physical ring*. The 802.5 standard concerns systems using baseband transmissions with data rates equal to 1 or 4 Mbps on shielded twisted pairs.

Unidirectional point-to-point transmissions are used: each station receives frames from the previous node in the ring and sends (or repeats) frames to the following downstream station.

This solution has a number of implications; for instance, network design and implementation can be kept quite simple and cost-effective, because no broadcast transmission is needed and the signal which is sent over the medium is regenerated inside each station. This eliminates the need to include amplifiers, headend remodulators and other similar devices in the system, even though the network can consist of a large number of stations. In addition the overall throughput is high when the network is heavily loaded as opposed to CSMA/CD where collisions can waste a significant fraction of the nominal bandwidth, whilst the maximum access time experienced by each station is upper bounded as for the token bus.

On the other hand, the ring structure lacks reliability. This weakness made the token ring unsuitable for MAP, since reliability is a primary goal for industrial automation and process control environments, one which must be obtained even at the expense of both the complexity and cost of the medium access method. In fact, if a

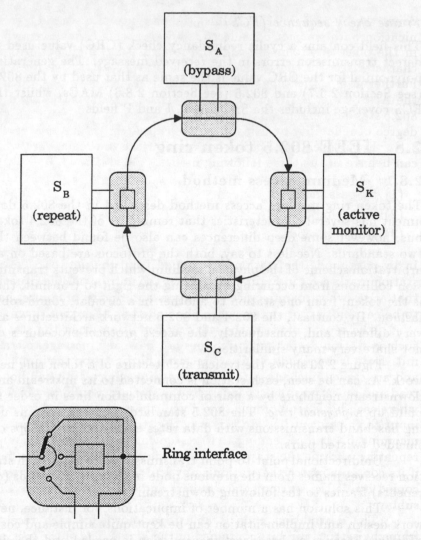

Figure 2.20   Architecture of a token ring network.

single station or a link connecting any pair of stations fails, the whole ring can be stuck. Usually the solution to this problem is based on two different types of mechanism:

(1) Each station is equipped with by-pass switches so that it can be excluded from the network when a failure occurs and the electrical continuity of the physical ring is maintained nevertheless.

(2) A redundant communication path is provided by duplicating the ring architecture.

It is worth noting that the original 802.5 specifications took into account the by-pass switches, whilst the presence of a second communication path was not considered. However, this is not a drawback in the office environment, and the low cost and high performance characteristics of the token ring make it very attractive for TOP. Furthermore, other non-standard and standard networks, such as the ANSI Fiber Distributed Data Interface (FDDI) [FDDI] and the 802.5 standard extension to the fiber optics media, can grant a higher degree of reliability by using a double-ring architecture.

Each token ring station has an interface to the network which can behave in the three following modes:

(1) by-pass mode

(2) repeat mode

(3) transmit mode.

In by-pass mode the station is excluded from the network like the station marked S_A in Figure 2.20; this is the normal off-line situation that arises when maintenance procedures and repairs of failures have to be carried out, or simply when the node has been shut down.

The repeat mode is the working condition when the station, such as station S_B in the figure, does not have any message to transmit. Data frames and tokens are received bit by bit on the input link and are copied unchanged to the output line. Since a bit can not be read and repeated simultaneously by the station, a buffer is provided where each bit is temporarily stored while being transferred from the input to the output line. In this way the station can also reverse an incoming bit before sending it to its downstream neighbor. While repeating a frame the station analyzes the destination address field: if its contents match the station's physical address the frame is also copied inside the station's data buffers and then passed to the LLC sublayer.

The destination node is able to acknowledge each received frame by setting two bits contained in the *status field* of the message (see Section 2.8.6). The *address recognized* (A) bit is used to notify the sender that the destination is present and working in the ring, whilst the *frame copied* (C) bit tells the source station that the frame has been copied into the receiver's buffer. These bits are returned to the sender since the receiving station also repeats the frame to its downstream neighbor.

Unfortunately, this form of implicit acknowledgment cannot be used to support the LLC DL_REPLY and DL_DATA_ACK services directly at the MAC level as discussed in Section 2.4.2 for the two following reasons:

(1) The frame status field is not covered by the frame check sequence (FCS) used to detect transmission errors in the message; thus the sender cannot rely on the values of the A and C

bits returned with the frame since this could result in incorrect acknowledged frames from possibly wrong destinations.

(2) No data can be appended to the frame by the destination, so the DL_DATA_ACK service cannot be implemented.

The transmit mode is entered when a station such as S_C starts to transmit a message. Since only the token holder can send frames, the station analyzes all the frames received on the input line looking for the token. When the token is detected it is captured and not repeated to the downstream station. This is possible because the token and the data frames have the same header (that is they begin with the same bit pattern) except for one bit called the *token bit* (TB) (see Section 2.8.6). A station can reverse the *token bit*, so changing the token into a data frame header; this is equivalent to capturing the token and starting the transmission of a message. Then the station appends data to the output stream, while incoming bits are no longer repeated but, on the contrary, are discarded.

The token holder can send frames up to a maximum time period controlled by a token holding timer. When there are no more messages to be transmitted or the timer expires the station releases the token to its downstream neighbor and then returns to work in the repeat mode.

A couple of important points must still be discussed: first, the transmitting station is also responsible for removing each frame that returns to the sender after a whole rotation on the ring. On the one hand this prevents frames from circulating indefinitely on the network, whilst, on the other hand, time-consuming recovery actions are avoided to eliminate messages from the network when they have reached their destinations. With regard to this aspect it is worth noting that frames are removed by the receiving station in the ring-based FDDI standard [FDDI] and this leads to a better use of the system bandwidth.

The second point is that the ring must always be sufficiently 'long' to contain a whole token frame, which consists of 24 bits. In fact, the network has its own latency time which depends on the data signaling rate, the lengths of the links connecting the stations and the number of stations (because of the interface buffers that introduce a delay between the input and output streams in each node). This latency time can be seen as the time period needed for a bit to complete a whole rotation on the ring.

When no frame is ready to be transmitted the token circulates on the ring and all the stations are in repeat mode, thus it is necessary for the ring latency to be greater or equal to the token length. However, the network latency time can change significantly, for instance because stations join or leave the ring dynamically. For this reason the 802.5 standard asserts that a latency buffer equal to the token length must be provided to ensure a sufficient value for the latency time. This buffer is supplied by a single station called the *active monitor* which also carries out other network management and supervising tasks. Even though each station must be prepared to act as a monitor there is always only one active monitor at a time in the system.

In practice the monitor latency buffer is larger than 24 bits. The active monitor is also responsible for compensating for those small differences that occur in the clocks of the different stations and which could result in the insertion or dropping of bits from the ring. The data rate and the values of the parameters used in the 802.5 specification lead to an estimate within ±3 bits of the maximum variation of the ring latency, thus an additional 6 bits-deep buffer is sufficient to keep the latency of the whole network constant. When the ring is started the monitor initializes its latency buffer to $24 + 3 = 27$ bits; then if the received signal is faster than the transmitted signal one, two or three bits are added to the buffer, otherwise the buffer length is reduced accordingly.

2.8.2 Token losses and corruptions

Like the token-bus protocol, the 802.5 standard also includes special procedures for managing anomalous situations such as the corruption or loss of the token, which can occur, for instance, when the token holder fails before releasing the right to transmit. In this case, however, the recovery actions are undertaken only by the active monitor since, from this point of view, the system control is centralized rather than fully distributed as for the 802.4 standard.

Two basic mechanisms are used in the recovery procedures: timers and special control frames. For example, the active monitor can detect a token loss by the expiration of a *valid_transmission-_timer* which is restarted each time a correct frame or token is received by the monitor itself. When this event occurs, the monitor starts a ring purge operation to clear the network and to get rid of any possibly invalid frame and/or token still circulating in the system. The ring is purged by continuously transmitting *purge* control frames until they are received from the monitor's upstream neighbor, then a new token is created and inserted in the ring.

The monitor is also responsible for removing frames that are persistently circulating on the network. This function is performed by means of a *monitor bit* (MB) contained in the header of the data and token frames. The basic idea is that no frame, except for the lowest priority tokens (see Section 2.8.4), can reach the active monitor twice if the ring is working correctly. Thus, when a frame is received by the monitor the first time MB is set to one. All the other stations in the network leave MB unchanged while copying it from the input to the output link. Each frame which has MB set to one and reaches the active monitor again is immediately removed from the ring and the monitor starts the purge procedure.

When the ring has been initialized each station joins the network at its own bootstrap time by carrying out the following procedure. First the new station looks for the presence of an active monitor (see Section 2.8.3) or purge frame to verify that a ring has been built correctly. Then it waits for the first usable token and sends a *duplicate address test* (DAT) control frame to check whether another station in the system exists with the same physical address. If the DAT message returns to its sender with the address recognized bit reset to zero, the sender's address is unique in the network and the station can enter the standby monitor state, that is, the normal working state. Otherwise, two stations with the same MAC address exist in the ring, and since this is an anomalous situation the new station goes back to the by-pass state.

2.8.3   Ring initialization

When the network is booted, stations have to elect an active monitor before the normal transmission operations can begin. In a steady-state condition the active monitor notifies its presence to the other stations by periodically sending out an *active_monitor_present* (AMP) control frame. A station which receives an AMP restarts its *standby_monitor_timer*, since the AMP frame is a signal that the active monitor is operating correctly. At initialization the timer expires since there is no active monitor and the station tries to become the new active monitor. It begins to transmit *claim_token* control frames and continues to do so until one of the following frames is received:

- a *claim_token* frame sent by the station itself
- a *claim_token* frame sent by a station with a higher address
- a *purge* frame
- a *beacon* frame sent by another station (see Section 2.8.5).

In the first case the station has won the contention and becomes the new active monitor by starting the ring purge procedure, otherwise it enters the so-called standby monitor state where it carries out its normal transmit/receive operations and periodically verifies the active monitor behavior by means of the AMP mechanism.

2.8.4   Priority classes

The IEEE 802.5 standard also includes special mechanisms for supporting different message priorities. However, unlike the token-bus approach (see Section 2.6.5) the token ring priority scheme is based on reservation bits rather than on timers.

Each valid token circulating over the ring has an associated service priority P_s encoded in three *priority bits* of a field in the token header called *access control*, so eight priority levels can be used, zero being the lowest priority. Once it has captured the token, a station can only send frames having a priority equal to or greater than the current service priority; when these frames are exhausted or the token holding timer expires the station is forced to pass the token to the following station.

When a station has one or more frames with a priority P_f higher than P_s it can ask to raise the service priority to P_f by setting three *reservation bits* (R_s) in the access control frame of any frame received from its upstream neighbor. In fact, each station maintains, in two variables P_r and R_r respectively, the values of both P_s as contained in the last token received and of the highest reservation found in the frames received during the last token rotation. If the value of P_f is larger than R_r the station can set the reservation bits of the received frames to P_f, otherwise no reservation can be done since more urgent frames need to be sent by the other stations. Before releasing the token each station compares the values of P_r with R_r and P_f (if other priority frames are still queued for transmission inside the station) and possibly raises the service priority when P_r is found to be lower than the maximum between R_r and P_f.

Since this priority scheme cannot work if P_s is not lowered once all the priority frames have been transmitted, the station which raises the service priority is also responsible for restoring it to its original value. This is done by letting the station save the new and old values of the service priority in a pair of variables S_r and S_x respectively, each time P_s is increased.

It is worth noting that a station can raise the service priority more than once before restoring the original P_s value, and these increments can be interleaved between different stations. For instance, a node A could raise P_s from zero to one, then a station B could change its value to four and again A could increment P_f to five. This is why S_x and S_r must be thought of as stacks of values rather than simple variables, and a station which increments the token priority is said to become a *stacking station*.

Obviously a number of different situations can occur on each token visit to a station depending on the relative values of P_f, P_s, P_r and R_r. The actions carried out by the token holder in the most significant cases are summarized in Table 2.4 where the operator $\oplus$ applied to the pair of input operands P_f and R_r returns the larger of the two values or P_f (R_r) when R_r (P_f) is not defined.

The 802.5 protocol has also been designed to recover from anomalous situations caused by the failure of a stacking station. In fact, when such an event occurs the service priority can no longer be lowered by the faulty node and this would prevent the low priority frames from being transmitted. Thus the active monitor also has to look for tokens with a service priority greater than zero that perform

Table 2.4   Actions performed by the token holder to implement the priority scheme.

Conditions	Actions
Frame available and $P_s \leq P_f$	Send frame
(Frame not available or THT expired) and $P_r \geq R_r \oplus P_f$	Send token with $P_s = P_r$ and $R_s = R_r \oplus P_f$
(Frame not available or THT expired) and $P_r < R_r \oplus P_f$ and $P_r > S_x$ (top of stack)	Send token with $P_s = R_r \oplus P_f$ and $R_s = 0$ push $S_r = P_r$, push $S_x = P_s$
(Frame not available or THT expired) and $P_r < R_r \oplus P_f$ and $P_r = S_x$ (top of stack)	Send token with $P_s = R_r \oplus P_f$ and $R_s = 0$ change top of stack $S_x = P_s$
(Frame not available or (Frame available and $P_f < S_x$)) and $P_s = S_x$ and $R_r > S_r$	Send token with $P_s = R_r$ and $R_s = 0$ change top of stack $S_x = P_s$
(Frame not available or (Frame available and $P_f < S_x$)) and $P_s = S_x$ and $R_r \leq S_r$	Send token with $P_s = S_r$ and $R_s = R_r$ pop S_r, pop S_x

more than one rotation on the ring. This is accomplished by means of the monitor bit mechanism described in Section 2.8.2. MB is set to one in each token reaching the active monitor with $P_s > 0$. When a station increases/decreases the service priority or it uses the current service priority to send frames, a new token is then released with MB set to 0. The token is retransmitted with MB unchanged when the station has to transmit only frames with $P_f < P_s$ so that the token is not usable. It follows that when a priority token completes more than one rotation with MB set, no station has been able to send a single frame and in spite of this the service priority was neither lowered nor increased, hence a fault has occurred. The active monitor then discards the unusable token and purges the ring before releasing a new (low priority) token to reach a correct working situation.

2.8.5   Ring fault detection

As mentioned in the previous sections, overall system reliability is one of the main drawbacks of the token ring access method. Hence, special mechanisms have been included in the protocol for reporting errors as soon as they are detected, so that the network manager can start the appropriate recovery operations.

The error reporting scheme is based on *beacon* control frames that are transmitted by any station when a fault is detected. This also involves the concept of the *failure domain* as defined in the 802.5 standard. A failure domain consists of three basic elements: the station which detects and notifies the failure (called the *beaconing* station), its upstream neighbor and the physical link connecting the aforementioned nodes.

When a station detects some anomalous behavior, for example because an AMP frame is not received within a reasonable time period, it can assume that something has gone wrong inside its failure domain (FD), including also its receiving circuits and the transmitting section of its upstream neighbor. Thus the station becomes a *beaconing* node and starts to send beacon frames containing the failure domain it belongs to; FD is specified by means of the two physical addresses of both the station and its predecessor.

In this situation the following events can then occur at the beaconing station:

- A beacon frame is received with the source address equal to the station address: in this case it is likely that the failure has been repaired since the beacon frame has completed a whole rotation on the ring. The station starts to send *claim_token* frames and tries to become the new active monitor.

- A beacon frame is received with the source address not equal to the station address: in this case a failure is being reported by one of the upstream stations, hence the right FD does not include the beaconing node. The station stops sending beaconing frames and starts to behave as a standby monitor looking for AMP frames.

Since the beaconing station needs to know its upstream neighbor's address in order to identify the failure domain, the token ring protocol includes a set of operations for the *neighbor notification*. These mechanisms are based on the A and C bits in the frame status field (see Section 2.8.6). When a frame is broadcast to all the stations in the ring the A and C bits are reset to zero by the sender. Then the first station which receives the message, that is, the sender's downstream neighbor, modifies the A and C bits that are repeated unchanged later on by all the other stations. Hence, when a station receives a broadcast frame with the A and C bits reset it can

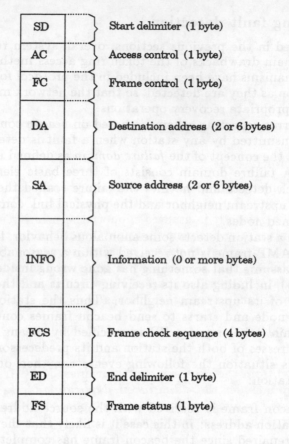

Figure 2.21   Format of the IEEE 802.5 frame.

safely assume that the source address field in the frame contains its predecessor's address.

This notification scheme is started by the active monitor whenever an AMP frame is sent over the ring; similarly each other station working as a standby monitor broadcasts a *standby monitor present* (SMP) frame as soon as possible to pass its own address to the following node.

2.8.6   802.5 MAC frame structure

The general structure of the 802.5 data and control frames is shown in Figure 2.21. The meaning of the fields in the picture are described in the following sections.

Start and ending delimiters (SD and ED)

The frame boundaries are delimited by this pair of fields that are also encoded using non-data symbols. This prevents a length field from being included in the frame as in the 802.4 standard. The ending delimiter also contains an *error bit* which is set to one by the receiving stations when an (FCS) error is found to have occurred during the frame transmission.

Access control (AC)

This field is one byte long and contains the priority and reservation subfields (P_s and R_s), together with the monitor (MB) and token (TB) bits. Therefore it is used to support the priority mechanisms and the monitor management functions described in the previous sections. Note also that the start of frame sequence, consisting of the start delimiter and access control fields, is the same for both tokens and data frames, except for TB which is reset to zero in a token and set to one in the other frames.

Frame control (FC)

This one-byte field is used to distinguish the normal data frames (LLC frames) from the protocol control frames (MAC frames). The control group includes the *claim token*, *duplicate address test*, *active monitor present*, *standby monitor present*, *purge* and *beacon* frames used to control the token ring operations.

Destination and source addresses (DA and SA)

These fields contain the MAC addresses of both the intended destination and the sender of the frame. The address format is the same as that used for the 802.4 and 802.3 frames (see Section 2.6.7).

Information (INFO)

This field contains user or control data. The 802.5 standard does not specify any upper bound to the length of the information sequence; however the overall frame length must be short enough to be transmitted without exceeding the token holding time selected for a station.

Frame check sequence (FCS)

This field is four bytes long and contains the check code used to detect transmission errors in the received frames. As mentioned in the previous sections, the FCS coverage includes FC, DA, SA and INFO but not the AC and FS fields that have to be modified 'on the fly' by the repeating stations without recomputing the FCS.

Frame status (FS)

This field contains the address recognized (A) and frame copied (C) bits. Since these bits are not protected by the FCS field they are replicated twice in the frame status to make this information more robust against transmission errors.

2.9   Fiber optics and FDDI

The earlier MAP specifications did not include any recommendation about subnetworks using physical media based on fiber optics, but recent advances in fiber technology have made this communication technique attractive both from the industrial automation and process control points of view. In fact, it is worth remembering that optical communications offer a very large transmission bandwidth which implies impressive data rates. In addition, fibers are thin and light, and are not affected by electromagnetic interference or corrosive environments as opposed to copper wires, thus they can be considered an ideal medium for applications in factories and industrial plants.

At present industrial fiber optics subnetworks have to be extensively investigated since optical components and devices are still rather expensive, nevertheless some guidelines are given in the appendix to the MAP 3.0 specification concerning the use of the fiber technology in the manufacturing automation protocol context. In practice two methods are suggested for using fiber optics communications in MAP networks: the first is based on the 802.4 access method whilst the second adopts the 802.5 philosophy.

The 802.4H approach extends the token-bus protocol to the fiber medium. Obviously, some architectural differences exist with respect to the 802.4 subnetworks based on coaxial cables mainly because buses are difficult to implement with fiber technology. The solution considered in MAP makes use of a single passive star structure where the signal transmitted by one station is broadcast to all the other stations, thus obtaining a behavior similar to the shared bus. A data rate of 10 Mbps is recommended and no more than 32 stations can be connected to the system because of the power losses introduced by the passive nature of architecture adopted.

When larger systems are needed, the 802.5 token ring must be used. In this case the data rate has been chosen to be 16 Mbps and networks spanning several kilometers can be built because the ring technology is based on point-to-point links and the signal is regenerated inside each station. The reliability problems typical of ring architecture are circumvented by using an additional (redundant) physical medium: in fact, a dual-ring structure is able to tolerate a fault in a link or a station so preventing the whole network from being stuck indefinitely.

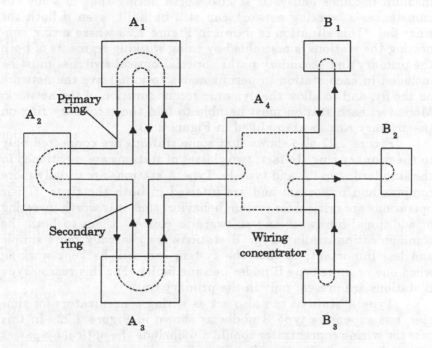

Figure 2.22   Architecture of an FDDI network.

2.9.1   Fiber distributed data interface

The fiber distributed data interface (FDDI) is a standard proposal
developed by committee X3T9 of ANSI. FDDI is designed specifically
for networks based on fiber optics and covers the MAC and physical
layers of the IEEE 802 model, so that it can be used in conjunction
with the 802.2 LLC. Even though FDDI is not taken into account at
present in MAP and TOP, it should be considered as one of the most
relevant alternatives for designing optical LANs, because it was not
obtained by simply adjusting the parameters of an older protocol but
was developed bearing in mind the characteristics that are peculiar
to fibers. In an FDDI network light pulses are obtained by using light
emitting diodes. Since LEDs are not able to generate very strong
signals, point-to-point connections have been adopted to circumvent
the problem of power losses caused by multiple stations coupled to
a shared fiber link. Multimode fibers are used with a wavelength of
1300 nanometers.

The basic architecture of an FDDI network is shown in Figure 2.22. It consists of a pair of counter-rotating rings, called the
primary and *secondary* ring, that can work in parallel. However,
the secondary ring has been provided mainly for backup purposes,
so that the system can go on working correctly when the primary

medium becomes faulty. It is also worth noting that in some circumstances a working network can still be built, even if both the rings fail. This situation is shown in Figure 2.23 where a ring connecting the stations is assembled by using working segments of both the primary and secondary paths. Special optical switches must be included in each station to permit nodes to join/leave the network on the fly, and to allow the dynamic reconfiguration of the network. Moreover, each station must be able to fold the secondary ring on the primary ring as exemplified in Figure 2.23.

Figure 2.22 also shows that some stations are connected only to the primary ring. In fact, two classes of stations are mentioned in the standard: type A and type B. Type A stations are usually more complex and important and are inserted in both the rings. Their operations are critical for system behavior, thus it is worth investing in additional hardware and software to connect them to both the communication media. Type B stations are generally more simple and less important, so that the system can still be kept working when one or more type B nodes become faulty. For this reason type B stations are present only in the primary ring.

Type A stations can also act as wiring concentrators for simpler, less expensive type B nodes as shown in Figure 2.22. In this case the wiring concentrator should also include the optical by-passes to switch out a faulty type B station from the network.

A large network can include up to 500 stations linked by 100 km of optical cable, however it is worth noting that FDDI is attractive in other fields of applications. In particular FDDI can be used in:

- back-end networks
- front-end networks
- backbone networks.

A back-end network consists of a collection of very high performance mainframes or minicomputers, peripheral controllers, communication controllers, file servers, database machines etc. Thus it usually connects type A stations over relatively short distances as shown in Figure 2.24. Note that in this kind of environment performance and reliability are the most important issues.

Front-end networks can span larger distances (usually several kilometers) and consist of a number of simple workstations with reduced performance and reliability requirements. These systems can be implemented by using FDDI type B stations connected to one or more type A nodes acting as wiring concentrators.

Backbone networks are used to interconnect a number of subnetworks offering smaller throughputs and working at lower data rates. A typical example of this situation is shown in Figure 2.24. With the advent of optical communications in the factory environ-

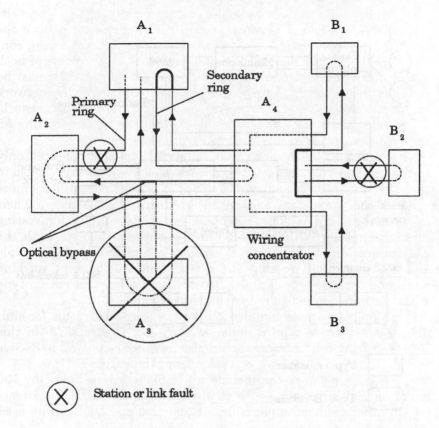

Figure 2.23 Dynamic reconfiguration of an FDDI network.

ment it is not surprising that FDDI can be considered as a possible alternative to the MAP backbone.

The data rate used in an FDDI system is equal to 100 Mbps on each ring, which causes an effective throughput equal to 200 Mbps to be reached when the two rings are operated in parallel, as under normal conditions; the performance is obviously reduced if some fault occurs which forces the network to work with only one active ring.

High data rates require efficient encoding schemes to keep the transmission frequencies as low as possible. For instance, the differential Manchester system encodes each data bit into a two bits symbol, thus a 200 Mbps baud rate would be necessary to achieve the 100 Mbps data rate of FDDI. For this reason a 'four out of five' (4B/5B) encoding scheme has been adopted in FDDI; with this method each group of four bits in the transmitted message is encoded by using a five bits symbol. The scheme efficiency is then increased to 80% and a transmission frequency equal to 125 MHz is required. In this way the costs of the transmitting and receiving equipment

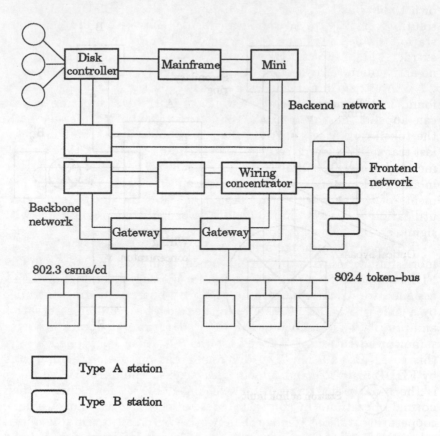

Figure 2.24   Applications of the FDDI networks.

used in an FDDI network can be reduced: in fact a LED and PIN diode pair operating at 125 MHz can be five to ten times cheaper than a similar pair operating at 200 MHz.

In the 4B/5B scheme sixteen symbols are used to encode all the 4 bit data values, six symbols are assigned special control meanings while the remaining ten are illegal for FDDI.

The access method used for the distributed fiber data interface is very similar to the 802.5 approach, however some important differences exist between the token ring and the FDDI MACs.

For instance, the centralized clocking scheme adopted in the 802.5 requires that a 6 bit deep latency buffer be supplied by the active monitor in order to prevent the insertion or dropping of bits in the ring caused by small differences in the reception and transmission frequencies of each station (see Section 2.8). The transmission frequencies and the values of the other parameters (link lengths, number of stations etc.) used for FDDI would lead to a very large number of bits to be included in the latency buffer; instead, each node has its own 10 bit elasticity buffer in accordance with the FDDI distributed solution. In this way a significant benefit has been obtained: each station is able to transmit at its own clock speed, whilst the receiver extracts the phase and the frequency from the incoming signal, and no active monitor is needed to supply the clock to the whole system.

Another important characteristic of the FDDI protocol is found in the token passing method, since the transmitting station can append the token to the stream of transmitted messages. In the token-ring access method the token holder must wait until the last transmitted frame returns before sending the token, thus a single message at a time can be traveling in an 802.5 network. By contrast, in an FDDI system several messages can be moving in different segments of the network at the same time, and this leads to a better utilization of the system bandwidth, especially when long rings with significant latencies are considered.

When the message priority scheme is considered, FDDI shows more similarities with the 802.4 protocol than with the 802.5. In fact FDDI supports four priority classes for messages, the highest being assigned to synchronous traffic. Priority operations are controlled by a timed-token mechanism as in the token bus, and no reservation and priority bits are included in the FDDI frame structure; thus the same considerations developed for the 802.4 can be applied also in this case. In addition, two different kinds of token are supported by FDDI: *restricted* and *unrestricted* tokens. The unrestricted token is the usual right to transmit exchanged by stations during their normal operation. In contrast, a restricted token enables a pair of cooperating stations to hog the network by virtually excluding all the other nodes from the system for the whole duration of a predefined data transfer phase.

2.9.2 FDDI frame format

The basic structure of the FDDI frame is shown in Figure 2.25: it consists of nine fields having the following meanings:

Preamble (P)

This field contains at least sixteen 'idle' symbols and each symbol is 5 bits long but is equivalent to 4 bits of data. The preamble is needed to synchronize the station's clock with the beginning of the frame received on the incoming link.

Start and end delimiters (SD, ED)

These fields are two symbols long and are used to mark the beginning and the end of the frame. Since special non-data symbols are used in both SD and ED no length field is required in an FDDI message.

Frame control (FC)

This field is two symbols (one byte) long and is used to distinguish different frame types. For instance synchronous and asynchronous frames have different FC fields, moreover the length of the address fields is also encoded in the frame control. FC is also used to distinguish restricted and unrestricted tokens from data frames; note that a token consists of only four fields: P, SD, FC and ED.

From this point of view a significant architectural difference exists between the 802.5 and the FDDI stations. In fact, a token ring node recognizes the token by a single bit in the frame header, thus it is able to complement the token bit on the fly, so changing the token frame into the starting sequence of a data frame (see Section 2.8). A full duplex architecture is then required, since the station must be able to send out a bit while receiving another bit from its predecessor. This is no longer true for FDDI because of its symbol-level encoding scheme: when the token is detected by means of the analysis of the FC field a station can suspend its transmission by sending out a sequence of 'idle' symbols to keep its successor synchronized with the data stream. In the meantime the message to be transferred can be assembled and the station circuits set up to enable its transmission. Thus a simpler and less expensive half-duplex architecture can be adopted to implement an FDDI station.

Source and destination addresses (SA,DA)

FDDI addresses can be either 16 or 48 bits long and make use of the same encoding scheme adopted for the 802 MAC addresses.

Information (I)

The information field can contain up to 4500 data bytes; this limit is mainly due to the distributed clocking scheme used in FDDI.

Frame check sequence (FCS)

This field is 32 bits long and is used to detect possible errors that have occurred during the frame transmission. It contains a cyclic redundancy check obtained with the same standard polynomial used in the IEEE 802 MACs.

Frame status (FS)

The frame status is a three-symbol field used to return information to the sender concerning the frame reception status. Thus the transmitter can know whether the destination address has been recognized by the receiver, the frame contents have been copied or some transmission error was detected.

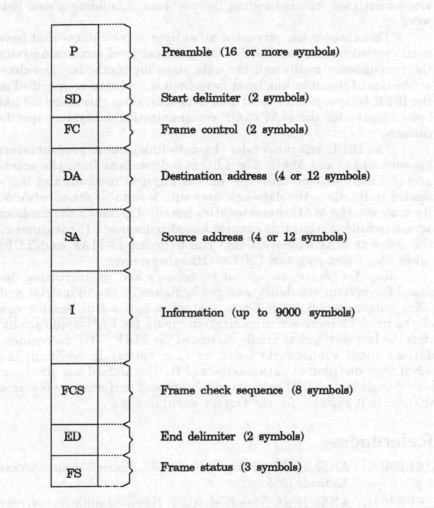

Figure 2.25   Structure of the FDDI frames.

2.10   Conclusions

The OSI physical and data-link layers are mainly concerned with the transmission of messages over a physical medium. The MAP and TOP specifications involve a number of transmission media and channel access control techniques that must be well known to the system designer who is tackling the problem of building a new network.

This chapter has presented an outline of the choices that have been carried out in the MAP/TOP physical level concerning both the transmission media and the data signaling methods. The characteristics of the data-link layer have been introduced as specified in the IEEE 802 project for local area networks, since this standard has been adopted for the MAP/TOP communication subsystem specifications.

The IEEE 802 subdivides the data-link layer in two sublayers known as LLC and MAC. The LLC is independent from the access protocol used to send messages on the physical medium and is intended to interface the data-link user with a suitable set of services. By contrast, the MAC characteristics heavily depend on the medium access technique, thus this chapter has also discussed the features of the different MAC sublayers that can be found in MAP and TOP: token-bus, token-ring and CSMA/CD subsystems.

Rapid advances in optical technology and an increasing demand for system reliability and performance in the industrial and office automation fields indicate that fiber optics will become one of the most attractive communication media for LAN applications; thus the last section has briefly discussed the MAP/TOP recommendations about subnetworks based on fiber optics. In addition, the ANSI fiber distributed data interface (FDDI) standard has also been introduced, since FDDI exhibits reliability and performance features that make it suitable for the factory environment.

References

[IEEE8023]   ANSI/IEEE *Standard 802.5 Token Ring Access Method*, 1985.

[IEEE8024]   ANSI/IEEE *Standard 802.4 Token-passing Bus Access Method*, 1985.

[IEEE8025]   ANSI/IEEE *Standard 802.3 Carrier Sense Multiple Access with Collision Detection*, 1985.

[8802dad]   ISO *Draft Proposed Addendum to ISO DIS 8802-2 Logical Link Control: Acknowledged Connectionless Service*, 14th Draft, June 1986.

[ISO8802/2] ISO *Information Processing Systems - Local Area Networks - Part 2: Logical Link Control*, DIS 8802-2.2, 1987.

[ISO8802/3] ISO *Information Processing Systems - Local Area Networks - Part 3: Carrier Sense Multiple Access With Collision Detection*, DIS 8802-3, 1989.

[ISO8802/4] ISO *Information Processing Systems - Local Area Networks - Part 4: Token-passing Bus Access Method and Physical Layer Specifications*, DIS 8802-4.2, 1989.

[ISO8802/5] ISO *Information Processing Systems - Local Area Networks - Part 5: Token-ring Access Method and Physical Layer Specifications*, DP 8802-5, 1988.

[ChlFra80] Chlamtac I. and Franta W.R. Message Based Priority Access to Local Networks. *Comp. Comm.*, **3**(2), Apr. 1980.

[Tobagi] Tobagi F.A. Carrier Sense Multiple Access with Message Based Priority Functions. *IEEE Trans. on Communications*, **COM-30**, pp. 185-200.

[CiDeVa88] Ciminiera L., Demartini C. and Valenzano A. Industrial IEEE 802.3 Networks with Short Delivery Time for Urgent Messages. *IEEE Trans. on Industrial Electronics*, **35**(1), Feb. 1988, pp. 18-25.

[FDDI] ANSI *FDDI Token Ring Media Access Control*, Draft X3T9.5/83-16, Rev. 8, Mar. 1985.

[CiVa88] Ciminiera L. and Valenzano A. Acknowledgment and Priority Mechanisms in the 802.4 Token Bus. *IEEE Transactions on Industrial Electronics*, **35**(2), May 1988, pp. 307-16.

[ISO7498] ISO *Information Processing Systems - Open Systems Interconnection - Basic Reference Model*, Int. Standard No. 7498, Oct. 1984.

[Zimmer83] Day J.D. and Zimmermann H., The OSI Reference Model. *IEEE Proceedings*, **71**(12), Dec. 1983, pp. 1334-40.

[ISO7776] ISO *Information Processing Systems - Data Communication - High-level Data Link Control Procedures - Description of the X.25 LAPB-compatible DTE data link procedures*, IS 7776, Dec. 1986.

Chapter 3

Network, Transport and Session Layers

3.1 Introduction

As is probably well known, the main role of the network layer is to provide the user with a set of communication facilities in order to transfer data between any pair of stations in the network. In fact, the data-link layer is able to support the delivery of messages only on a point-to-point link established between two communicating machines; it is not concerned with moving information across multiple links, routing messages towards their destination by selecting a suitable path in the network and so on. All these aspects fall under the jurisdiction of the network layer which extends, to some extent, data-link communication capabilities to the whole system, even though it has a complex topology consisting of several different subnetworks.

The service offered to the application processes is further enhanced by the transport and session layers which support a set of functions and mechanisms for achieving reliable in-sequence data delivery and for managing and controlling the dialogue between remote application entities.

Usually the developer of applications for a network such as MAP and/or TOP is not particularly interested in the service offered by the intermediate OSI layers, since application processes are interfaced directly to the top of the OSI protocol stack. At the same time, most device manufacturers are mainly concerned with the physical and data-link layers, in order to design suitable interfaces for connecting their equipment to the network. Nevertheless, in both these cases significant help in achieving good results can be found in understanding the main characteristics of the intermediate layers and the mechanisms governing their behavior. For instance, application designers can benefit from a knowledge of the reasons that led to the implementation of a well-defined set of communication services as well as the basic functions underlying the services themselves, whilst hardware designers can take advantage of including suitable mechanisms for enhancing the performance of the upper layer software and simplifying its implementation at the same time.

The purpose of this chapter is to give some insight into the intermediate protocol layers (network, transport and session) from the MAP and TOP points of view. The reader must be warned that there is no claim that the following sections are a detailed and exhaustive discussion of these protocol layers: only those characteristics that are relevant to MAP/TOP will be considered by following an approach which is more qualitative than quantitative.

3.2 Network layer structure

Communication networks such as those used in MAP and TOP are commonly called *local area networks* (LANs) because they are intended to interconnect computing devices placed inside a single building or a group of buildings. Since the physical area covered by this kind of network is quite small, a number of characteristics make LANs rather different from metropolitan and wide area networks (MANs and WANs). For instance, the network is usually owned and maintained by a single (private) organization, so that it is often called a *private* network. Moreover the network topology is simple (buses and rings are used) and broadcast communications are frequently adopted over a single transmission medium. Given the low distance between any pair of communicating stations, high transmission rates can be used and low transmission error probabilities are not uncommon.

By contrast, WANs concern large (geographical) areas and are often installed, owned and maintained by some public organization. Their topologies are generally complex and not regular, consisting of a mesh of point-to-point links connecting couples of 'neighbor' stations so that a suitable 'path' of concatenated links must be selected in order to enable the communication of a given pair of nodes. Since more than one path can exist between two stations, routing and relaying functions are needed for messages sent over a WAN.

Furthermore, because of the long distances involved and the

heterogeneity of the transmission media used, data rates are significantly lower when compared to LANs, whilst the error probabilities can also be significantly higher.

At first glance it could be argued that the protocol profile for a local area network such as MAP and TOP does not need to include any particular service offered by the network layer, since MAP is based on a shared bus system topology and no particular problem can occur in routing messages to their destinations.

The main reason for having a network layer service in this case can be found in the requirement of interconnecting MAP and TOP with other different systems, consisting of either LANs or wide area networks (such as packet switched X.25 public networks) or both.

As for the other communication layers, the MAP and TOP network service is based on a set of ISO standards designed in the framework of the OSI model. It is worth noting that at the network layer particular attention was paid to distinguishing between *end systems* and *intermediate systems*. Roughly speaking, end systems are those machines that are able to provide communication functions above the network layer: typically end systems can be hosts running application processes either in the factory or in the office environment. Intermediate systems are stations that perform functions belonging to the three lowest layers of the OSI model; thus they are primarily concerned with communications (i.e. routing and relaying the messages towards their final destination). Figure 3.1 outlines the difference between end and intermediate systems; it is worth remembering that the upper layer protocols have end-to-end significance since only the source and destination entities are involved in each data exchange. By contrast, the communication between end systems at the network layer can involve several intermediate systems to forward the messages to their destinations.

In a real situation there can be stations that are both end systems and intermediate systems at the same time; for instance, this is the case for a station which runs some application processes but also performs routing and relaying functions for incoming messages addressed to other destinations.

Figure 3.2 shows the model of the internal organization of the network layer as defined in the ISO standard document [ISO8648] which has been adopted by MAP and TOP. The different blocks in the picture represent the protocol 'roles' that are the functions the network protocols perform to support the OSI network service. In the figure a separate protocol is used for each single role, however this is not a requirement of the standard since the same protocol can fulfill more roles (or even all the roles) included in the network layer. The picture also shows that routing and relaying have been extracted from the upper role; this was done to take into account the peculiar characteristics of intermediate systems that also have to perform those functions which enable the forwarding of informa-

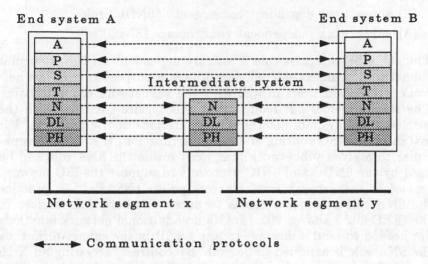

Figure 3.1 Communication protocols involving end systems and intermediate systems.

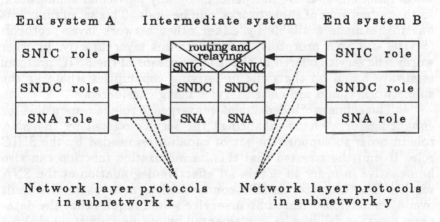

Figure 3.2 ISO model of the network layer.

tion. Thus the network layer architecture for an end system does not necessarily include the region delimited by the two sloping lines. The intermediate system in the picture is attached to two different subnetworks labeled 'x' and 'y', respectively. In this situation the protocols fulfilling the network layer roles can be (and usually are) different for each subnetwork.

As the figure shows, the ISO model is based on the three following protocol roles:

(1) subnetwork access (SNA) role

(2) subnetwork dependent convergence (SNDC) role

(3) subnetwork independent convergence (SNIC) role.

The subnetwork access role is strictly dependent on the particular subnetwork being considered since its main purpose is to offer a network service which fits in well with the subnetwork characteristics. The standard does not require that this service coincides with the service made available at the upper interface of the network. For instance, non-ISO routing and relaying functions (i.e. functions peculiar to a given subnetwork) can exist inside the SNA role and be used by the SNDC and SNIC protocols to support the ISO network service at the network service access points (NSAPs). In practice the SNA role provides a means to access the data-link service: in the IEEE 802.3 and/or 802.4 LANs no additional network functions are needed to send a message to any LSAP in the subnetwork, thus the SNA role is assumed to be null. By contrast, accessing an X.25 geographical network requires specific SNA functions to be carried out by some SNA protocol.

The purpose of the subnetwork independent convergence role is to allow the construction of the (OSI) network service by using a set of functions that are independent on any particular subnetwork, so that a 'network of subnetworks' can be built. This set of functions has to be made available by either other network layer protocols (SNDC and SNA protocols) or the data-link layer directly. In other words, the service offered to the user by means of the SNIC protocol is always based on the same underlying capabilities whatever the subnetwork(s) and associated service being considered.

The subnetwork-dependent convergence role is responsible for enhancing (or even de-enhancing) the service offered by the SNA role in order to support the set of capabilities needed by the SNIC role. It must be stressed that this harmonization function can also be negative in order to obtain an effective degradation of the SNA service. For instance, an ISO connectionless network service built over a connection-oriented SNA service would require that the datagram message delivery be implemented by opening a virtual channel between the communicating stations that are hidden to the network users by the SNDC mechanisms.

3.3   Network service

Usually the user of the network layer (that is the transport layer) is not concerned with its internal structure, since it is only interested in the services that are accessible by exchanging network service data units (NSDUs) through the network service access points (NSAPs). The network service provider is able to support two different service types (connection-oriented and connectionless) and this is also true for other OSI layers, such as the transport and the session layers, as will be discussed later in this chapter.

The MAP and TOP specifications for the network layer are based on the connectionless mode service [ISO8348add1], thus the user is allowed to send each single data unit to a remote NSAP without establishing any communication context (i.e. virtual channel) with it. In this situation more complex functions for error detection and recovery, for instance, have been left to the communication protocols of the upper layers.

It is worth noting that the use of a connectionless service always requires an *a priori* agreement between the communicating users about the type and meaning of the data to be transmitted. By contrast, no dynamic (virtual) association has to be established between the sender and the receiver before transferring any data unit.

Because of the characteristics of the connectionless service the sender has to specify all the information needed to deliver a data unit whenever a new message must be transmitted to some remote entity; this information includes the destination address, the desired quality of service and possibly the options the user intends to select.

Since no logical relationship is maintained by the network layer between different data units each message to be sent can be processed and routed independently from the others. This implies that the messages are not necessarily delivered in the same order as they are passed to the service provider, moreover it is also possible that the network layer does not return any notification to the sender when a message cannot reach its destination because of errors, resource unavailability, data loss, duplications and/or corruptions and so on. When one of these situations occurs the upper layers, in general, and the transport service provider, in particular, are responsible for implementing suitable mechanisms to improve the quality of the service offered to the application processes.

The connectionless mode service is supported by means of two primitives:

- *N_UNITDATA.request* is invoked by the sender when a message has to be transmitted to an NSAP connected to the destination user;

- *N_UNITDATA.indication* is passed to the destination NSAP by the service provider together with the data coming from the sending user.

A set of parameters including the source and destination NSAP addresses and the desired quality of service is associated with each primitive. In particular, the quality of service (QOS) is represented in turn by the parameters shown in Table 3.1.

The transit delay is the time elapsed between the submission of a data request primitive and the delivery of the corresponding in-

Table 3.1   Quality of network service parameters for the connectionless mode.

Connectionless QOS Parameters
Transit delay
Protection
Cost determinants
Residual error probability
Priority

dication to the destination NSAP; the user can specify a maximum value for this time interval that should not be exceeded by the network service provider. The purpose of the protection parameter is to prevent unauthorized listening to and manipulations of the user message by other entities in the network. In particular, it is possible to invoke protection against either passive monitoring or the modification, deletion and addition of data to the user message. The cost determinants are a means for either specifying the maximum communication costs acceptable for the user or for asking the service provider to use the least expensive solution for delivering the message, whilst the residual error probability is a measure of the likelihood that user data units are lost, corrupted or duplicated by the network layer. Finally, the priority parameter allows the service provider to distinguish between different classes of data units according to the degree of relative importance the user assigns them.

3.4   MAP and TOP network protocols

3.4.1   SNA protocol

The roles presented in Section 3.2 must be fulfilled by one or more (discrete) protocols, depending on the characteristics of the system being considered. Typically in each MAP end system the SNA role is covered by the data-link layer, thus a specific SNA protocol is not required. This is true also for TOP when the underlying subnetwork consists of an IEEE 802 LAN. When TOP machines have to be connected to some wide area (public) network, the ISO 8208 protocol [ISO8208] is needed; this standard describes the operation for accessing packet switched networks using procedures and formats conforming to CCITT recommendation X.25.

3.4.2 SNIC protocol

For the SNIC role both MAP and TOP adopt the ISO 8473 [ISO8473] standard, which is a protocol for providing the connectionless-mode network service. The SNIC protocol has to carry out the set of functions which is briefly discussed below. From the point of view of the user the services available are obtained by the cooperation of the protocol servers residing on the different machines in the network. This cooperation is based on the exchange of messages (both data and control information) that in the following are referred to as protocol data units (PDUs).

PDU composition

User data passed to the network layer for transmission have to be assembled into packets before being routed to their destination. The PDU composition function is responsible for building a packet using the data and the addressing information supplied by the user. In addition the SNIC protocol server also inserts into the message other auxiliary (control) information concerning the PDU length, its type and format and the maximum lifetime allowed for the packet itself. Each PDU is assigned a unique identifier to distinguish it among multiple PDUs sent by one user to the same destination.

PDU decomposition

When a PDU is received addressing one of the local NSAPs interfaced to the network service provider, the SNIC entity serves to remove the control information that was used in delivering the message to the destination machine. Thus this function is symmetrical, to some extent, to the PDU composition.

Header format analysis

Addressing and control information is contained in a portion of the packet called the PDU header. At the reception of a message the header is analyzed to determine whether or not the PDU has reached its final destination (this is the case, for instance, for a plain end system). If the destination address corresponds to an NSAP located on the same machine as the SNIC server, the message is passed to the addressed user, otherwise it is forwarded to another station which belongs to the path selected for reaching the destination NSAP.

PDU lifetime control

This function is used to prevent a PDU from circulating indefinitely in the network because of errors, resource unavailability, network congestion and so on. As mentioned above, identifiers are used by the SNIC entities to label PDUs; when a PDU has been passed to the final user its identifier can be re-used by the network layer. Delays experienced by a message in traveling through the network could cause the same identifier to be associated to two different PDUs at a given time, so causing a potential error situation. The solution to this problem is to assign a maximum lifetime to each PDU: if the lifetime expires before the PDU reaches its destination the message is discarded by the network layer. The lifetime mechanism is implemented by means of a counter included in the PDU: the counter is decremented by one or more units (usually each unit corresponds to a 500 ms time interval) each time the PDU is processed by a machine in the network. If the counter becomes zero before the message reaches its final destination, the message itself is discarded by the processing machine and an error is generated.

PDU routing and forwarding

This is another function peculiar to the network layer. Its purpose is to select the path through the network so that each PDU can be forwarded towards its final destination. It is worth noting than when the network topology is complex several alternative routes can exist for reaching the same destination NSAP. In this case the SNIC protocol is responsible for choosing one of the possible paths by also taking into account the desired quality of service. For instance, a longer or slower route can be selected for delivering the PDU if the transfer costs have to be kept as low as possible.

PDU segmentation and reassembly

When a PDU is longer than the maximum size allowed by the underlying service, it must be segmented into a suitable number of smaller PDUs that can fit in the data units delivered by the network. The SNIC protocol is responsible for both segmenting the user message in transmission and reassembling the original message from the received fragments.

PDU discard

PDUs can be discarded by the protocol server for a number of different reasons: for instance a violation of the protocol rules can cause a wrong PDU to be processed or a corrupted PDU can be received. In addition, the lack of local resources such as memory buffers, protocol tables and so on can prevent the network entity from processing a message. Similarly, messages whose header is not correct and/or whose lifetime has expired must be discarded; the same occurs when the selected route is invalid or the destination address is unreachable.

Error reporting

When a PDU is discarded by some entity in the network an error reporting message can be generated and returned to that protocol server which is the real PDU sender. The error message contains information that is useful in identifying the discarded PDU and the type of error which has occurred. For example, the error PDU contains the header of the discarded message and none, all or part of the data field. The reporting function can be enabled/disabled by the network entity which sends a PDU by setting/resetting a special flag in the message itself, however no error message is generated in the case when an error PDU is discarded. It is worth noting that if an error report is not received the sender cannot assume that the PDU has been delivered correctly.

Header error detection

While being transferred from one machine to another the PDU header can also be affected by errors. Thus the network layer provides suitable mechanisms for detecting erroneous control information in the PDU. In particular, a checksum is computed and appended to the header when a PDU is transmitted; when the header is modified (for instance by an intermediate system) the checksum is updated to reflect the changes in the header. Similarly, when a PDU is received by either an intermediate or an end system the checksum is re-computed and compared to the value included in the PDU: a possible mismatch signals an error in the header. It is worth noting that the checksum mechanism covers only the header contents and not the data part of the PDU; this occurs because the protocol is responsible for routing and delivering the user messages and consequently it must protect the control information. By contrast, the integrity of the user data is not guaranteed by the network service, hence the upper layers (i.e. the transport) have to supply their own error detection and recovery mechanisms to protect the user data units.

Security

When a certain degree of protection is invoked by the user with the quality of service parameters the network service provider must support suitable mechanisms for authenticating the sender of the PDU and for assuring data integrity and confidentiality.

Source routing

This function enables the originator of a PDU to specify the path the PDU will take. The selected route consists of both a list of network entities (i.e. addresses of intermediate systems) and an indicator pointing to the next element in the list that has to be used to forward the PDU. The routing information is inserted in the PDU header. When a network entity receives the PDU, it analyzes the routing list; if a match occurs between the element currently in use and the entity's own identifier the list indicator is advanced one position and the PDU is forwarded in order to reach the next station in the path. The ISO standard [ISO8473] distinguishes between two possible types of routing: the *complete source routing* and the *partial source routing*. The *complete source routing* requires that each machine specified in the path is compulsorily visited, and the order specified in the path must be observed. If the specified path cannot be taken the message is discarded. By contrast, the *partial source routing* allows the sending entity to specify a path list that should also be taken in order. In this case, however, the PDU may also visit other intermediate systems not specified in the list, whilst this is not possible for the complete source routing.

Route recording

This function is used to record the path taken by the PDU while it is being routed through the network. When the PDU reaches an intermediate system the identifier of the station is appended to a list containing the identifiers of the visited systems, then the PDU is forwarded to the next network entity in the route. The list is stored in the header of the PDU and it is updated whenever the PDU is received by a new intermediate destination. As for the source route function, there are two variants of route recording: the *complete route record* and the *partial route record*.

Quality of service maintenance

When a PDU is forwarded to an intermediate system a parameter is included in the message header to convey the required quality of service values. In turn each intermediate system can take routing decisions in order to maintain the desired quality of service. When the expected QOS cannot be granted, the routing station can attempt to deliver the PDU at a quality of service different from the desired QOS.

Priority

PDU can be given a priority value, which is stored in the PDU header. When processing a message network entities try to give precedence to those PDUs having a higher priority value. In particular, this allows communication resources in intermediate systems such as buffers, queues and tables to be assigned preferentially to the most urgent messages.

Congestion notification

Congestions can be caused by the unavailability of communication resources in one or more stations in the network, so that the service provider is no longer able to process all the message load offered by the users. When an intermediate system experiences congestion, it can notify the anomalous condition to the final destination of the PDU. This is obtained by setting a flag in the PDU header which is originally reset when the PDU leaves the original sending station. PDUs received with the flag set to one indicate one (or more) congestion point(s) in their route. The actions to be taken at this point (such as informing the sender that a new route should be selected) fall outside the purpose of the standard and are implementation-dependent to some extent.

The SNIC protocol functions listed above are grouped in three classes in the ISO standard document [ISO8473]:

(1) **Type 1** functions must be supported by each implementation.

(2) **Type 2** functions may or may not be implemented. When a PDU is received requiring a type 2 function which is not implemented, the message is discarded and an error reporting PDU is created and returned to the original sender of the discarded PDU.

(3) **Type 3** functions may or may not be implemented. Requests for type 3 functions that are not implemented are simply ignored: the PDU is not discarded and is processed as though the unsupported function(s) had not been selected.

The ISO 8473 standard also specifies two possible subsets of the full SNIC protocol:

(1) The *inactive subset* is in practice a null protocol to be used when the source and the destination of the PDUs belong to the same subnetwork and no SNIC function is needed to support the connectionless service in the subnetwork itself.

(2) The *non-segmenting subset* is used when the size of each PDU fits in the maximum length allowed for the data unit of the underlying service, so that no PDU segmentation is required. In this case the control information contained in the PDU header can be simplified and the protocol overhead introduced in processing messages can be significantly reduced.

Table 3.2 shows the types assigned to the different protocol functions for each protocol subset included in the standard. Missing items in the table mean that the corresponding functions cannot be applied to the protocol subset being considered and this is the case for most functions when the inactive protocol is selected.

Table 3.2   SNIC protocol function types.

Function	Protocol subset		
	Full	Inactive	Non-segmenting
PDU composition	1	1	1
PDU decomposition	1	1	1
Header format analysis	1	1	1
Lifetime control	1	1	-
Routing and forwarding	1	1	-
Segmenting and reassembling	1	-	-
Discard PDU	1	1	-
Error reporting	1	1	-
Header error detection	1	1	-
Security	2	2	-
Complete source routing	2	2	-
Partial source routing	3	3	-
Complete route recording	2	2	-
Partial route recording	3	3	-
Priority	3	3	-
QOS maintenance	3	3	-
Congestion notification	3	3	-

MAP and TOP adopt both the full connectionless protocol and its inactive subset. The latter is used when no internetworking is required and all the destinations can be reached simply by using their data-link addresses; moreover the PDU segmentation/reassembly functions should not be needed when the inactive subset is selected. This is the case for a MAP network consisting of 802.4 segments and for any plain 802.3 TOP system. In this situation each network entity can be reached by using its IEEE 802.2 address and message fragmentation is supported by the transport layer.

When the full protocol is needed (i.e. when MAP and TOP are connected to an X.25 public network) the MAP/TOP requirements include all the (mandatory) type 1 functions. Type 2 functions are not implemented; when a PDU is received requiring a type 2 function a MAP/TOP system behaves as specified in the ISO standard: the message is discarded and an error is reported to its sender. The implementation of type 3 functions is considered optional for end systems, whilst each intermediate system must implement the partial route record mechanism. Finally when a TOP network is connected to an X.25 packet switching network the priority function has to be supported by the intermediate systems.

Figure 3.3 shows the sequence of protocol functions that are carried out when a user message is transmitted by the network layer. First the user data passed to the service provider with an NSDU are assembled into a PDU, then the source route is also recorded in the PDU header if this function has been selected. The next step is the header format analysis: in this phase the PDU destination field is checked to find out to which NSAP the message must be sent. When the security option is required protection information is encoded in the PDU, whilst the lifetime control function enables the lifetime counter to be set correctly. Note that if for any reason an error occurs during one of these steps the PDU is discarded and an error message is generated and returned to the sending user.

The next action consists in assigning the message a route through the subnetwork accessible to the service provider and selecting a new network entity (i.e. machine) to which the PDU will be forwarded. This choice can be affected by the QOS maintenance function, since several alternative routes can be possible, each one corresponding to a different QOS value. Finally, the header checksum is generated to protect the control information against errors and corruptions, and if PDU segmentation is needed the segmentation function is invoked and one or more PDU fragments are appended to the output queue for transmission.

When a PDU is received the SNIC protocol carries out the set of functions shown in Figure 3.4. Received fragments are reassembled if segmentation is used. Once the whole message has been completed the header is checked for errors by verifying the checksum field. As usual, possible errors in both the reassembly and header checking phases cause the PDU to be discarded and an error report PDU to be sent to the original sender. PDUs received correctly are subjected to the same header analysis, security control and lifetime control carried out for the messages that are being transmitted. If none of these checks fails the PDU is either passed to the local user (when the message has reached its final destination) or is resent to the next system in the route. In the latter case the sequence of functions for routing and forwarding the PDU is the same as that used for transmitting a message which has been originated locally, as shown

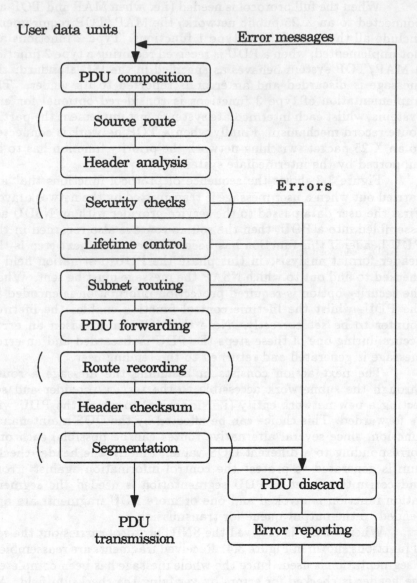

Figure 3.3   Functions carried out by the connectionless protocol for transmitting a PDU.

in Figure 3.4.

3.4.3   SNDC protocol

As mentioned in Section 3.2, the purpose of the subnetwork dependent convergence protocol is to adapt the service provided by the

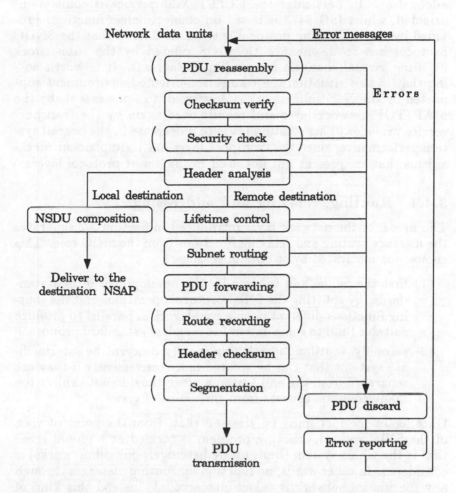

Network data units   Error messages

PDU reassembly

Checksum verify

Errors

Security check

Header analysis

Local destination   Remote destination

NSDU composition   Lifetime control

Deliver to the
destination NSAP

Subnet routing

PDU forwarding

Route recording

Header checksum

Segmentation

PDU discard

Error reporting

PDU
transmission

Figure 3.4 Functions carried out by the connectionless protocol when a PDU is received.

underlying subnetwork to the requirements of the SNIC role. When the SNIC protocol is used on the top of an IEEE 802 subnetwork the 802.2 type I service [ISO8802] (included in both the service classes 1 and 3, see Chapter 2) is perfectly suited to support the ISO 8473 subnetwork independent convergence facilities. In other words the type I connectionless functions are precisely the underlying services required by the ISO 8473 standard, hence in this case the MAP/TOP network layer consists only of the SNIC entity, since no additional SNDC and SNA protocols are needed.

When the SNIC connectionless protocol must be used with

a packet switching network offering the X.25 service some expedients have to be adopted [ISO8473] in order to cover the SNDC role adequately. In particular the CCITT X.25 service is connection-oriented, whilst ISO 8473 is based on connectionless functions provided by the underlying protocol entities. It follows that the SNDC protocol has to de-enhance the QOS offered by the subnetwork by using virtual channels for sending datagrams. It is worth noting that in this situation the connection-oriented environment supported by the X.25 subnetwork is destroyed, to some extent, by the MAP/TOP network layer and rebuilt once again by the transport service provider. This solution leads to a decrease in the overall system performance, since the transport layer has to implement mechanisms that are present but not used in the lowest protocol layers.

3.4.4   Routing, relaying and addressing

The model of the network layer introduced in Section 3.2 separates the message routing and relaying functions from the SNIC role. This choice was motivated by two main reasons:

(1) first the model had to simplify the development of new standards: by splitting the SNIC protocol operations and the routing functions different people could work in parallel to produce suitable (and to some extent independent) standard proposals;

(2) secondly, routing and relaying mainly concern the intermediate systems that can be treated more conveniently if they are separated from the end systems, since they do not exhibit too many common aspects from this point of view.

Once again the fact must be stressed that, from the point of view of the SNIC role, the routing problem is tackled at a global level, that is the whole system (built up by heterogeneous subnetworks) is considered. In other words, no function for routing messages through any specific subnetwork is taken into account; instead this kind of problem is analyzed and solved under the responsibility of the SNA (and/or even the SNDC) role(s).

The dynamic end system (ES) to intermediate system (IS) routing scheme [ISO9542] which is used in MAP/TOP in conjunction with the SNIC protocol has been designed to cope with a number of practical situations. For instance, this standard enables end systems to discover the existence and reachability of intermediate systems that can route the PDUs to their destinations in subnetworks that are not directly connected to the sender.

Similarly, another problem solved by the routing protocol is that of allowing any IS to know the reachable ESs that are connected to the subnetwork(s) and can be reached in some way by the intermediate system itself. Finally, the protocol is also used by each sending ES to select the IS to which a PDU has to be forwarded when several possible alternatives exist. This choice usually involves cost and performance considerations and should lead to selection of the next IS as the one belonging to the most convenient path for delivering the PDU.

On the one hand, the ES to IS routing protocol tries to maintain up-to-date information about the current configuration (i.e. existing and reachable ESs and ISs) for the whole network, thus eliminating the need for specific actions to manually change control data structures such as mapping tables inside each ES and/or IS. In practice each ES can dynamically obtain the addresses of all the ISs that are directly connected to one of its links, while ISs can have the addresses of the ESs in the same subnetwork, even though they can be reached through other intermediate systems.

On the other hand, no standard protocol exists at present for solving the IS to IS routing problem. In this case each MAP/TOP intermediate system maintains a static table containing the addresses of the other reachable ISs; obviously this scheme requires periodic interventions to modify the address table when some change occurs in the network configuration.

Roughly speaking the main goal of routing is to determine the addresses of the systems belonging to a path which has to be traversed in order to deliver a given PDU to its destination NSAP. These addresses are often referred to as *subnetwork attachment points* (SNAPs) in the ISO literature. It is worth noting that whilst SNAPs addresses are subject to encoding rules that also depend on the particular subnetwork being considered, no restriction is imposed, in principle, on the format of the NSAP identifiers, since NSAPs are defined only at the conceptual level as the points for accessing the ISO network service primitives. This can lead to some relevant difficulties in extracting the sequence of SNAPs from the addressed NSAP identifier. To simplify these operations MAP and TOP have adopted a routing model consisting of the three following basic levels:

(1) routing between enterprises

(2) routing between subnetworks within the same enterprise

(3) routing between ESs and ISs within the same subnetwork.

Figure 3.5 puts into evidence the three levels of routing taken into account in the MAP/TOP world. Enterprises are distinct organizations such as corporations and/or government agencies. Each enterprise can have its own addressing domain consisting of one or more subnetworks. In turn each subnetwork consists of ESs and ISs that can be reached by means of the routing conventions used in the subnetwork itself.

The NSAP format selected in the MAP/TOP specifications reflects this three-level routing model and adheres to the ISO stan-

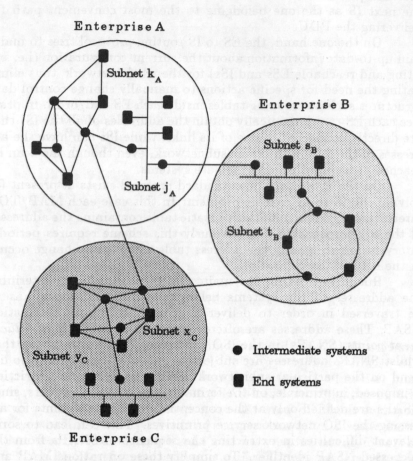

Figure 3.5   Routing levels in a MAP/TOP network.

dard [ISO8348add2] which gives guidelines on how the NSAP identifiers have to be structured. Figure 3.6 shows the basic format of the MAP/TOP NSAP identifier. The enterprise portion enables the network layer to identify each single organization; this NSAP portion corresponds to the ISO *initial domain part* (IDP) which is structured in the 'authority and format identifier' (AFI) and 'initial domain identifier' (IDI) subfields. The AFI mainly contains information about the network authority responsible for allocating values of the IDI and the format used for the IDI itself. The IDI contains the network addressing domain for the remaining part of the NSAP structure called the *domain specific part* (DSP). Figure 3.6 shows that the DSP is subdivided into three subfields. The first of them concerns the IS to IS routing scheme, while the second and third

ISO 8348 NSAP identifier

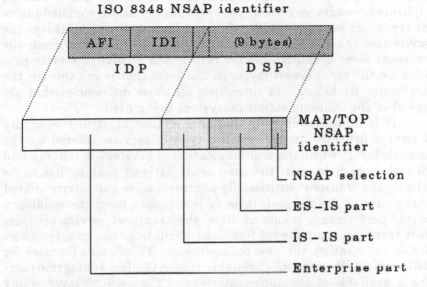

Figure 3.6   Basic structure of the MAP/TOP NSAP identifier.

concern the ES to IS routing and the NSAP selection, respectively. To permit a higher degree of flexibility the DSP is nine bytes long and there is no predefined length and alignment for the IS–IS and ES–IS subfields, but the NSAP selection always requires 1 byte. For instance the IS–IS part can use 6 bytes to identify a given subnetwork while 2 bytes are assigned to the ES–IS subfield for specifying a station in the subnetwork and 1 byte is left to select the NSAP inside the station. Similarly it is possible to have the IS–IS and ES–IS lengths equal to 4 bytes according to any specific organization needs.

3.5   Transport service

The fourth layer of the OSI model was introduced to offer a reliable, in-sequence data transfer service to transport users in general and to the session layer in particular. In fact, whilst the three lowest OSI layers of the OSI architecture are primarily concerned with the data transmission mechanisms for physically transferring information among remote stations in the network, the three upper layers are mainly application-oriented and perform functions that are quite independent of the characteristics of the underlying communication system. Nevertheless, these layers need a reliable means to exchange control and data messages in order to carry out their operations and this support is found in the transport service. The main requirement of the typical transport user is not to be concerned (even marginally) with aspects such as detecting transmission errors, retransmitting lost or corrupted messages, detecting and discarding duplicated packets and so on. All these functions are confined inside the transport layer and hidden from each process which invokes the service through a transport service access point. In other words the transport layer is responsible for raising the quality of service provided by the three lowest layers to the level that is suitable for the user needs, by hiding and correcting all those deficiencies that are typical of the communication subsystem being used.

It is immediately clear that this enhancement in the quality of service depends strongly on the type of services offered by the network layer; when the communication subsystem is reliable and efficient enough to meet the user needs little or nothing has to be done by the transport entities. By contrast, when the service offered to the user of the network layer is inadequate from the reliability and/or performance points of view, the transport service provider must carry out a number of functions to improve the quality of service so as to satisfy the user requirements. This is also the case for MAP and TOP: since an unreliable connectionless (datagram) service is available at the upper interface of the network layer, many error detection and recovery mechanisms have been included in the transport layer, so that the resulting transport protocol is the most complete (and complex) among the different alternatives described in the ISO international standard [ISO8073].

The transport layer has end-to-end significance: users interacting through the transport service are located on different end systems and are allowed to exchange data by either creating suitable virtual channels (connection-mode service) or by sending and receiving transport datagrams (connectionless-mode service). Each user is attached to a transport service access point (TSAP), which is uniquely identified all over the network by the transport layer, and each data transfer operation always occurs between a pair of source and destination TSAPs.

3.5.1   Transport connectionless service

The connectionless service is used neither in MAP nor in TOP: the main reason is that the connectionless primitives are intended to support the transfer of limited and unrelated amounts of data (transport service data units – TSDUs) without opening any virtual association between the sender and the receiver. This also means that no type of relationship is maintained by the transport layer among multiple transport datagrams that are sent from one user to the other since any logical relation among the different TSDUs has to be managed by the user. For instance, a file transfer application built over the connectionless service should be responsible for subdividing the file to be transferred into fragments fitting in the maximum TSDU size, for reordering and then reassembling the fragments on the destination side. The confinement of these functions into the user processes could be inconvenient for full MAP and TOP stations where several different applications can require the fragmentation and sequencing mechanisms.

The connectionless mode service is accessed by means of the two following primitives:

(1) *T_UNITDATA.request*, which allows the user to send a TSDU to a remote interlocutor; besides the data to be transmitted (which cannot exceed 63 488 bytes) the sender must specify its own TSAP address, the destination TSAP and the quality of service required;

(2) *T_UNITDATA.indication*, which is passed to the user by the transport provider when a TSDU is received by a remote sender. The parameters of this primitive are the same as those submitted with the corresponding T_UNITDATA.request.

It is worth noting that the desired quality of service (QOS) is expressed by the user by means of a set of parameters rather than a single value. In particular the OSI standard document [ISO8072dad1] takes into account the parameters described in the following sections.

Transit delay

The transit delay is the maximum time interval the user is ready to accept between the submission of a T_UNITDATA.request primitive and the delivery of the corresponding T_UNITDATA.indication to the remote TSAP.

Protection

This parameter is used to set the degree of protection of user data by the transport provider. The user can require either no specific protection, or protection against passive monitoring (for instance wiretapping) and/or modification, addition and deletion of its TSDU.

Residual error probability

This parameter measures the probability that the user's TSDU is lost, duplicated or corrupted by the transport layer while being transferred to the remote destination.

Priority

The priority value allows the user to specify the importance of a TSDU with respect to the other data units passed to the transport layer. The service provider uses this parameter to change the service order for different user requests and to select the TSDUs to be discarded when some recovery action must be undertaken. Furthermore, high priority TSDUs can have their QOS maintained at the expense of a degradation in the QOS of the lower priority data units.

3.5.2   Model of the connection-oriented service

Connection-oriented services provide the user with a way to establish multiple bi-directional virtual connections with remote interlocutors for the purpose of exchanging TSDUs. Each connection is based on the model shown in Figure 3.7 and is established between two interacting TSAPs; the model consists of a pair of queues connecting the two TSAPs in opposite directions. Queues are an abstract way of describing the exchange of data: each user sends data by means of its output queue and receives messages from the remote interlocutor by extracting information from the input queue in the form of TSDUs. The insertion of an object in a queue is controlled by the transport layer entities, whilst objects are removed under the control of the destination user. The transport server enables its clients to put in the transmission queues only those objects that belong to a restricted set of types, moreover the insertion of objects in the queues is achieved by invoking suitable service primitives. In addition, the number of objects that can be placed in a queue is limited to some extent, regardless of their type, since each queue has a finite capacity; this characteristic of the model results from two main factors: first the user attached to the output side of the queue has its own speed for extracting the TSDUs and this can affect the ability of the sender to place other data in the queue. Secondly, the transport layer processes messages with timings that can vary significantly during the system's lifetime, thus a sort of flow control is needed for the TSDUs submitted on each sender's side.

According to the standard specifications the items listed below can be inserted in the queue on the initiative of the user:

Connection requests and responses

These elements are used to set up the transport connection and to convey the values of a number of parameters representing the quality of service expected by the users, in fact a suitable mechanism is provided by the transport layer for negotiating the QOS for any single connection during the opening phase.

Data units and end of TSDU signals

These elements are generated by a data transfer request. A user's TSDU can be longer than the maximum allowed for a network service data unit (NSDU), thus the transport provider has to fragment the TSDU into smaller pieces that are individually sent on the virtual connection by using different NSDUs. In addition an 'end of TSDU'

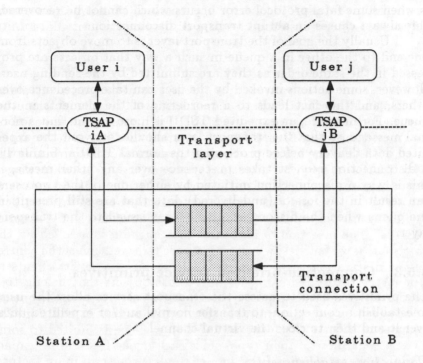

Figure 3.7 Model of a transport connection between a pair of interaction users.

mark must be appended to the data stream so that the receiver can detect the end of the message and distinguish among multiple TSDUs placed in the queue.

Expedited data units

Two different data flows can be supported by the transport service on each connection: *normal* and *expedited*. The expedited flow is used for urgent messages and is based on special delivery rules. Each expedited data transfer request by the user causes an expedited data unit to be put in the queue.

Disconnection requests

Disconnection requests are used to destroy the connection in a unilateral way. Note that when a disconnection primitive is invoked a limited amount of data can also be specified that has to be delivered to the remote user.

Besides the users the transport service provider can also place disconnection items in the queues in some special circumstances, that is when some fatal protocol error occurs which cannot be recovered; this always causes an abrupt transport disconnection.

Usually the goal of the transport layer is to move objects from one end to the other in a queue in such a way that objects are processed in the same order as they are submitted by the sending user. However, some actions invoked by the user can take precedence over others, and this fact leads to a reordering of the elements in the queue. For instance, an expedited TSDU is more urgent that a normal message, so that the transport layer should carry out the expedited data delivery before processing the normal TSDUs. Similarly, a disconnection request takes precedence over any other message; this is why a disconnection initiated by either one of the two users can result in the loss of (undelivered) data that are still present in the queue when the disconnect primitive is issued to the transport layer.

3.5.3   Connection-oriented service primitives

The primitives used to access the transport service allow the user to establish a connection, to transfer normal and/or expedited data over it and then to close the virtual channel.

Connection establishment

The creation of a transport connection is invoked by means of a *T_CONNECT.request* primitive. The user who submits the request must specify its own TSAP address together with the destination TSAP, the desired quality of service and a flag indicating whether or not the expedited data service has to be supported for the new connection. Optionally the user is also allowed to pass a limited amount of data to the transport layer that have to be delivered to the remote interlocutor when it is notified of the attempt to open a new connection. This notification takes the form of a *T_CONNECT.indication* primitive passed from the transport layer to the called user. The latter can accept the connection by using a *T_CONNECT.response* primitive, however some adjustment of parameters is also possible at this point; for instance, the called user can disagree, in general, on the use of the expedited data service; this is not the case for MAP and TOP, where the use of expedited data is mandatory at the transport level. Finally, a *T_CONNECT.confirm* is returned to the initiating user containing the confirmation of the connection establishment.

It is worth noting that the called user can also refuse to open the connection by responding with a *T_DISCONNECT.request* primitive which also contains the reason for the refusal. The disconnection request causes a *T_DISCONNECT.indication* to be returned to the initiating user instead of the *T_CONNECT.confirm*.

In some circumstances connection requests can also be rejected by the transport provider itself, either for internal reasons, such as the unavailability of memory resources, or because of errors found in the communication subsystem. In this case the disconnection indication is generated directly by the transport layer without involving the called user.

Data transfer

The user can send a TSDU by means of a *T_DATA.request* primitive and data are delivered to the other end of the connection with a *T_DATA.indication*. Expedited data are transmitted by means of the *T_EXPEDITED_DATA.request* primitive and received with a *T_EXPEDITED_DATA.indication*. The ISO standard does not put any theoretical limit on the maximum length of a normal TSDU, whilst expedited TSDUs cannot exceed the limit of 16 bytes.

Disconnection

The user who wishes to close a connection invokes a *T_DISCON-NECT.request*, which causes the destruction of the virtual channel and possibly the loss of all the data that must still be delivered in both directions. The remote user is notified of the disconnection by means of a *T_DISCONNECT.indication*. When the connection is closed on the transport layer's own initiative an indication is passed to both users at each end of the virtual channel. The indication always contains the cause of the disconnection; possible reasons can be the lack of local or remote resources of the transport provider, some misbehavior of the transport layer and so on.

Tables 3.3, 3.4 and 3.5 summarize the parameters that are required by each transport service primitive.

Mandatory parameters are marked 'y', while optional values are indicated by the letter 'o'. Dashes in a table row mean that the corresponding parameters cannot be applied to the primitive associated with the columns, moreover the letter 's' is used to denote each parameter appearing in an indication or confirmation which has the same value as the corresponding parameter in the request or response primitive.

Figure 3.8 shows an example use of the transport service primitives. First a connection is opened on the initiative of the user at the left side (station A) of the picture, then normal and expedited data are exchanged using full-duplex mechanisms. Note that the expedited data message in Figure 3.8 is delivered before the second TSDU submitted to the transport layer by the user on station A. Finally a disconnection is initiated by the user at station B that causes deletion of the virtual channel.

Another important point to be stressed concerns the quality

Table 3.3   Parameters of the transport service primitives: connection establishment phase.

Parameter	Service primitives			
	CONNECTION			
	request	indication	response	confirm
Calling address	y	s	-	-
Called address	y	s	-	-
Responding address	-	-	y	s
Exp. data option	y	s	y	s
Quality of service	y	y	y	s
User data	o	s	o	s
Reason	-	-	-	-

Table 3.4   Parameters of the transport service primitives: data transfer phase.

Parameter	Service primitives			
	DATA		EXP_DATA	
	request	indication	request	indication
Calling address	-	-	-	-
Called address	-	-	-	-
Responding address	-	-	-	-
Exp. data option	-	-	-	-
Quality of service	-	-	-	-
User data	y	s	y	s
Reason	-	-	-	-

of service, because the transport layer includes a mechanism for negotiating the QOS which is offered for each virtual channel in both directions. When a user tries to establish a new connection (or, in other words, puts a connection request in an empty queue in Figure 3.7) it is possible to specify both the *desired* and the *minimum acceptable* QOS by means of a set of parameters. At this point the local transport server performs one of the two following actions:

(1) If the minimum QOS values cannot be guaranteed anyway the connection establishment request is refused at once, otherwise

(2) If the desired QOS cannot be granted, the optimal values are lowered but still kept greater or equal to the minimum QOS values. Then a request containing both the (possibly reduced)

Table 3.5 Parameters of the transport service primitives: disconnection phase.

Parameter	Service primitives DISCONNECTION	
	request	indication
Calling address	-	-
Called address	-	-
Responding address	-	-
Exp. data option	-	-
Quality of service	-	-
User data	o	s
Reason	-	y

optimal and minimum values is sent to the transport entity placed on the same station as that where the called user resides.

In its turn the remote entity can:

(1) Refuse the connection if the minimum values requested for the QOS cannot be satisfied or

(2) accept the connection with the proposed QOS values or

(3) lower once again the desired QOS.

Finally, when the initiating user is notified that the connection has been established it is also told what values of QOS parameters have been selected to support the connection.

The transport service standard [ISO8072] does not specify the formats and encodings of the QOS parameters that are used as arguments for the service primitive, since the user's interface to the service is a local matter which falls outside the purpose of the standard itself. Nevertheless, the document contains a list of the parameters and their characteristics since all implementations must agree on the meaning of each QOS element. In practice the following parameters are taken into account:

Connection establishment delay

This is the maximum delay that can elapse between the user request for opening a new connection and the confirmation by the transport provider that the connection has been opened. Note that this time interval also depends on the remote user, who can accept or refuse the connection, as well as the transport layer itself and the communication subsystem.

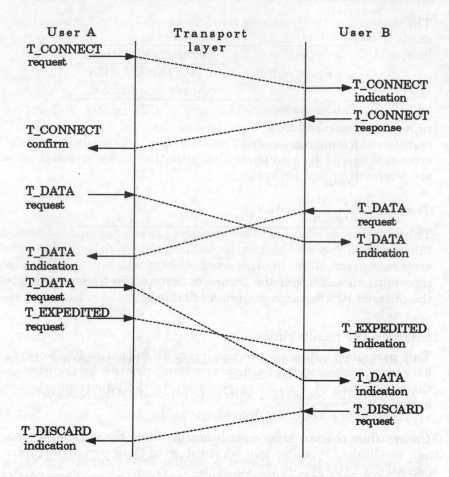

Figure 3.8 Example of data exchange between two transport users.

Connection establishment failure probability

This parameter represents the likelihood that the connection cannot be established within the maximum delay allowed because of problems and errors in the transport or the lower communication layers.

Throughput

This parameter is specified independently for each direction of the connection. It consists of both a maximum value, representing the maximum rate at which the transport layer can accept and deliver TSDUs without taking into account the delay introduced by the sender and the receiver, and an average value which also takes into account the delay introduced by the two interacting users.

Transit delay

The meaning of this parameter is the same as for the connectionless-mode transport service, however a different transit delay value can be specified for each direction of the connection.

Residual error rate

This value represents the number of TSDUs that can be lost, corrupted or duplicated when compared to the total number of TSDUs transferred during a measured period of time. Obviously the residual error rate should be zero in an ideal situation, however small values are tolerated in real networks.

Transfer failure probability

This is the probability that the transport provider is unable to maintain the QOS specified by the throughput, transit delay and residual error rate parameters. In other words the transfer failure probability represents the ability of the transport layer to keep promises about the offered QOS for a given period of time.

Connection release delay

This parameter measures the maximum delay that can be accepted between the invocation of a disconnection primitive by the user and the notification of the closing operation to the remote interlocutor by the service provider.

Connection release failure probability

The meaning of this parameter is similar to the connection establishment failure probability, but it is applied to the disconnection service invocation.

Protection

This parameter is the same as that used in the connectionless-mode transport service.

Priority

This parameter has the same meaning as for the connectionless-mode transport service.

Resilience of the connection

This parameter represents the likelihood that the transport provider begins an abrupt disconnection during a specified time period be-

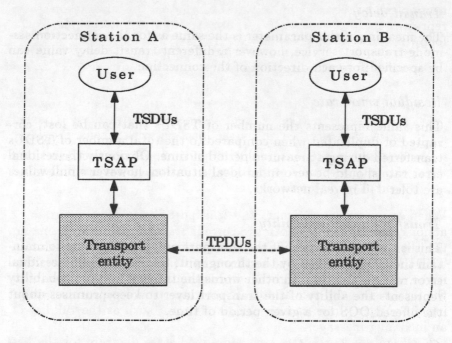

Figure 3.9   Logical relations among users, transport entities, TSDUs and TPDUs.

cause of internal errors or problems in the communication subsystem.

MAP and TOP do not make use of all the parameters listed above, in fact in their case the QOS negotiation does not include the security, throughput, transit delay, priority and residual error rate values. These parameters are always ignored even though they are specified by the user in a connection request or in a confirm primitive.

3.6   Transport protocol

Transport entities residing on different stations must cooperate in order to offer the transport service to users interfaced to the transport layer on each machine in the network. This cooperation is obtained by exchanging data and control messages called transport protocol data units (TPDUs) according to the rules and formats specified by the transport protocol. Figure 3.9 shows the relationships existing between users, the transport entities, the TSDUs and the TPDUs when a transport connection is in progress.

The transport entity implementing the protocol for each connection can be seen as a finite state automaton; the automaton states represent the protocol states, whilst the input events belong to the following three categories:

- service requests and/or responses obtained by the local transport user;
- TPDUs received from the transport entity at the other end of the connection in the form of network service primitives passed to the transport server by the local network service provider;
- events generated internally in the transport layer such as timer expiration signals, special values assumed by auxiliary and control variables and so on.

When an input event occurs the transport entity carries out some actions that depend on both the current state of the automaton and the type of event itself. These actions include the transmission of TPDUs to the remote transport layer by using network service primitives, the exchange of indication and confirmation primitives with the local transport user and other internal operations such as starting/stopping a timer and checking conditions such as the validity of an incoming message.

Figure 3.10 shows a very simplified state diagram for the behavior of the transport entity when a connection is established. Protocol states are represented by circles whilst arrows show the automaton transitions. Each transition is labeled with the event causing the change of the protocol state and the action(s) performed by the transport entity. Each label has the form 'input/outputs' where 'input' is the event associated with the transition and 'outputs' are the corresponding actions performed by the automaton. For instance, when no connection is established both the automata at the involved stations are in the 'disconnected' state; if the user at station A invokes a *T_CONNECT.request* primitive a connection request TPDU (CR) is sent to the transport entity at station B and automaton A enters the 'wait for connection confirm' state. The reception of the CR TPDU causes the protocol machine at B to change its current state from 'disconnected' to 'wait for connection response' while a *T_CONNECT.indication* primitive is passed to the called user. The latter can accept the connection by replying with a *T_CONNECT.response* and the transport entity on B reaches the 'connected' state after sending a connection confirm TPDU (CC) to the initiating transport. Thus the automaton at A can enter the 'connected' state after passing a *T_CONNECT.confirm* primitive to the calling user. By contrast when the reply from the called user is a *T_DISCONNECT.request* primitive the transport entity at B returns a disconnect request TPDU (DR) to the caller and goes back to the disconnected state. The reception of DR by station A has two effects: first a *T_DISCONNECT.indication* is passed to the user, and, secondly, the transport state of the automaton is changed to disconnected again.

In practice the state diagram of the real transport protocol is significantly more complex than the simplified example shown in Figure 3.10, since it must take into account all the possible events and situations that can occur for each state of the automaton. When large automata have to be considered, including several states and transitions, more convenient description techniques must be adopted. The ISO standard [ISO8073] describes the transport protocol by means of state tables like the one shown in Table 3.6. Each column of the table is associated with a different protocol state, whilst input events are mapped onto the table rows. Table items contain conditions and actions to be performed, besides the name of the new state to be reached by the automaton. The meaning of the table is straightforward: when the current state of the automaton is j and the event i occurs the table element (i,j) is identified containing the conditions to be checked, the actions to be performed (for instance send a TPDU or pass a service primitive to the local user) and the new state to be reached. It is easy to verify that Table 3.6 describes the same protocol behavior as the state diagram in Figure 3.10; even though the advantages of the former method are not so evident in this example it is a fact that this description technique based on state tables is clearer and more manageable when the number of states and events grows larger.

The complexity of the transport protocol largely depends on the quality of service supported by the underlying network; the ISO standard mentions three different types of network according to the characteristics of the service offered:

(1) **Type A** networks exhibit an acceptable rate of both residual and signaled errors. In other words the network is able to detect and recover transmission errors in a way that is satisfactory for the user. Note that the term 'satisfactory' always refers to the requirements of the user: the same QOS can be suited to the needs of one class of applications and be inadequate for others at the same time. However, when the network type is 'A' from the user's point of view the transport protocol becomes rather simple because no particular enhancement of the QOS is required.

(2) **Type B** networks have error detection mechanisms that makes the percentage of undetected errors sufficiently small, however the error recovery features cannot be accepted by the application processes.

(3) **Type C** networks are unsatisfactory from both the error detection and recovery points of view; in this case the transport layer has to provide suitable functions for making the data

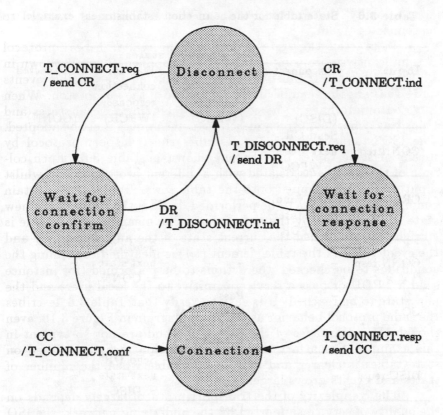

Figure 3.10 Simplified state diagram for the transport connection establishment phase.

transfer service supported by the communication subsystem both reliable and error free.

The ISO standard document [ISO8073] takes into account five classes of transport protocol to cope with the three network types listed above:

(1) **Class 0** is the simplest class; it is suitable for type A networks and maps each transport virtual channel on a different network connection.

(2) **Class 1** is used with type B networks since it includes mechanisms for managing possible network disconnections and/or resets. A one-to-one mapping of the transport channels on the network connections is also performed in this case.

(3) **Class 2** is similar to class 0 because it has to be used with type A networks; in addition, however, the multiplexing of multiple transport channels on one network connection is implemented.

Table 3.6   State table for the connection establishment example.

Input events	Protocol states			
	Disconnected	Wait for connection confirm	Wait for connection response	Connected
	(DISC)	(WFCC)	(WFCR)	(CONN)
CONN.req	Send CR, next state = WFCC	–	–	–
CR	Pass CONN.ind, next state = WFCR	–	–	–
CONN.resp	–	–	Send CC, next state = CONN	–
CC	–	Pass CONN.conf, next state = CONN	–	–
DISC.req	–	–	Send DR, next state = DISC	–
DR	–	Pass DISC.ind, next state = DISC	–	–

In other words a class 2 transport can decide to use a single network connection to support the data traffic concerning two or more transport associations when the QOS requested by the users enables it to do so. Thus a better use of system resources can be achieved without decreasing the overall performance.

(4) **Class 3** is to be used with type B networks and includes error recovery mechanisms similar to those in class 1. Also in this case the multiplexing of multiple transport connections is made available.

(5) **Class 4** is the more complete protocol class and is used with type C systems; it must include error detection and recovery functions because the network service is assumed to be unreliable. This is also the case for the MAP/TOP transport, where the network layer is able to offer only a plain (unreliable) connectionless service.

3.6.1 Transport protocol procedures

Each protocol class has to implement a number of procedures in order to support the transport service, so this subsection is devoted to discussing those functions that are carried out inside the transport layer. For the sake of completeness all the procedure elements included in the ISO standard [ISO8073] are considered in the following, even though only the class 4 protocol is used in MAP and TOP.

Assignment to network connection

Each transport virtual channel must be assigned to one network connection, previously opened by the transport provider. Note that this is not true for MAP and TOP since no virtual connection is supported by the network layer.

TPDU transfer

Another function each protocol class must implement is the exchange of data and control information between remote transport entities. This is obtained by moving TPDUs from one station to the other by means of the network layer data transfer service primitives.

Segmenting and reassembling of TSDUs

This function is needed to allow the transmission of TSDUs without any size limit. The sending transport entity subdivides a long TSDU into an ordered sequence of TPDUs that are individually transmitted over the connection; then the receiving transport entity reassembles all the pieces in the original TSDU before delivering it to the destination user.

Concatenation and separation of TPDUs

Transport protocol data units are transmitted by means of network service data units (NSDUs). The transport provider is allowed to pack multiple TPDUs in a single NSDU in order to achieve better performance. It is worth noting that the sending entity can concatenate TPDUs concerning different connections, whilst the receiver is responsible for separating the protocol data units and assigning them to the proper virtual channel. These functions are supported by each protocol class except for class 0.

Connection establishment

This is the procedure used to set up a new connection. This also includes the mechanisms for negotiating a number of options such as the preferred protocol class (which must be class 4 in MAP and TOP), the maximum TPDU size to be adopted for the connection, the quality of service and so on.

Connection refusal

This function is used when a negative answer has to be returned in reply to an attempt to establish a new connection.

Normal release

This is the procedure carried out by the transport layer to close a connection. There are two variants of normal release: implicit and explicit, the former being used only in class 0. Implicit release means that the transport connection is closed simultaneously to the underlying network connection; in this way the lifetimes of the transport and network virtual channel are strictly related. By contrast, the explicit variant allows the transport layer to close a connection independently of the network connections status; this means that a network channel can be re-used to support different transport connections in different time periods as shown in Figure 3.11.

Error release

This function is used only in classes 0 and 2 to close the transport connection when a disconnection or reset primitive is obtained by the network service provider. In fact, it is worth remembering that classes 0 and 2 are based on a reliable network service; thus when a disconnection occurs at the network level, it is assumed that no further recovery action can be performed and the transport channel is consequently destroyed. On the other hand classes 1, 3 and 4 have to cope with partially or totally unreliable networks, thus a fault at the network level should be handled in a way that is transparent to the transport user, and possibly recovered without causing the release of the transport connection. Hence the transport provider can decide to reassign the transport connection(s) to another network connection or to establish a new network channel when this is needed.

Association of TPDUs with transport connection

This procedure is required to map the contents of the TPDUs, exchanged between a pair of dialoguing transport processes, on the NSDUs and to assign them to the different transport connections.

Data TPDU numbering

This function is not used in class 0. Since users' TSDUs are fragmented into TPDUs, a procedure for numbering the fragments must be provided. The numbering scheme is used for two main purposes: first the receiver uses the sequence numbers to reassemble to original TSDUs in a correct way, for instance by reordering the received

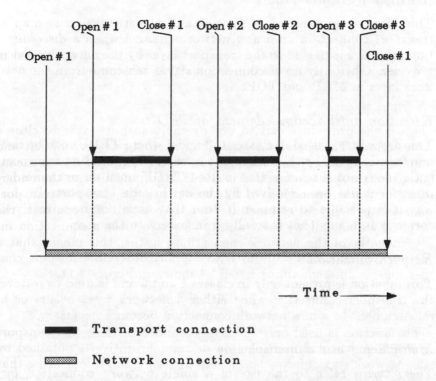

Figure 3.11 Re-use of a network connection to support several transport connections.

TPDUs and by discarding the duplicated fragments. Secondly, the numbering mechanisms are used to implement the TPDU acknowledgment and flow control functions, in fact the transport layer uses a sliding-window acknowledgment scheme that allows multiple TSDUs to be acknowledged at the same time, moreover the same windowing scheme is also adopted for flow-controlling the TPDUs traveling independently in each direction of the connection.

The ISO standard document specifies two possible lengths for the TPDUs sequence numbers, that is 7 and 31 bits, and both are used in MAP/TOP, even though the 31 bits format is the preferred one.

Expedited data transfer

The purpose of this function is to support the transfer of urgent data without observing the delivery rules governing the normal TSDUs. Expedited data are not used in class 0, whilst they must be supported in all the remaining protocol classes.

Reassignment after failure

This function is required in type B and C networks to re-map a transport connection on a new network channel when a disconnection primitive is passed to the transport layer by the network service provider. Obviously no disconnection signal can come from the network layer in MAP and TOP.

Retention until acknowledgment of TPDUs

This procedure is used in classes 1, 3 and 4 where TPDUs can be lost and/or corrupted by the underlying network. The sending transport entity does not discard a transmitted TPDU until an acknowledgment for it has been received by the destination transport. In this way it is possible to retransmit data that have not been received correctly in a way that is totally transparent to the user.

Resynchronization

This function is present only in classes 1 and 3 and is used to restore the transport connection when either a network reset occurs or a reassignment to a new network connection becomes necessary.

Multiplexing and demultiplexing

These terms refer to the use of a single network connection for supporting multiple transport channels; remember that multiplexing/demultiplexing is present only in classes 2, 3 and 4.

Explicit flow control

Flow control is used to adapt the speeds of the transmitting and receiving transport entities in processing data TPDUs. Transport flow control is independent of similar functions possibly performed in the other OSI layers and is used only in classes 2, 3 and 4.

Checksum

The checksum procedure has been introduced to provide additional error detection capabilities by the transport layer. This function is present only in class 4 and the users are able to negotiate its use when the connection is established. When the checksum option is accepted the sending transport appends a checksum parameter to each data TPDU, whose value is computed by summing (modulo 255) the user data bytes. The checksum is recomputed by the transport entity on the receiver side and compared to the one received with the TSDUs in order to detect possible discrepancies caused by transmission errors not detected by the network layer.

Frozen references

Each connection is labeled with a reference number by the service provider at each end of the connection. Reference numbers are then used to associate TPDUs with the connections and are included in the TPDUs themselves when they are exchanged between the dialoguing entities. When a connection is closed the transport layer must 'freeze' the reference number associated with that connection for a suitable period of time. This precaution prevents an incorrect re-use of the reference from occurring, and avoids any TPDUs related to the closed connection still surviving in the network when the reference number is reassigned to a new virtual channel.

Retransmission on timeout

This is another function used only in class 4. Retransmission occurs when no acknowledgment is received for outgoing data TPDUs within a reasonable period of time. The purpose of this mechanism is to recover from TPDU losses, however it also introduces the problem of TPDU duplications when the acknowledgments are simply delayed by the network. Nevertheless, duplicate TPDUs can be detected and discarded by means of the sequence numbering scheme adopted by the transport protocol.

Resequencing

This function is used only in class 4. Its purpose is to reorder the TPDUs that may be misordered by the communication subsystem, so that the source TSDU is reassembled correctly.

Inactivity control

This function is needed in class 4 to detect the disconnections not signaled by the network layer. Since the network underlying the class 4 transport should be considered as unreliable, it follows that disconnection indications can be lost. Thus the transport provider has to monitor the activity on each transport connection; if no traffic is detected during a given period of time it is assumed that the underlying network connection has been broken and must be established again.

Treatment of protocol errors

This function allows the service provider to manage those situations caused by some violation of the protocol rules; this typically occurs when a data or control TPDU is received at one end of a connection which is not correct with respect to the current state of the transport protocol automaton.

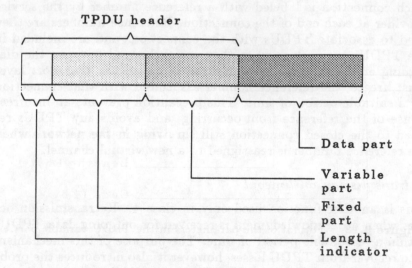

Figure 3.12   Basic format of a transport protocol data unit.

Splitting and recombining

This function is present only in class 4 and enables the service provider to map one transport connection on several different network virtual channels in order to obtain the desired quality of service. For instance, if the desired throughput value is too high to be supported by a single network connection the transport layer can use more connections, each one having its throughput characteristics, and split the data traffic accordingly.

3.6.2   TPDU structure

As outlined in the previous sections, peer transport entities cooperate by exchanging data and control information encoded in TPDUs. Each protocol data unit is structured according to the basic format shown in Figure 3.12.

The message always consists of a header and a data part. The latter contains the data bytes specified by the user, whilst the header is organized into the three following components:

(1) **Length indicator** (LI): this field is one byte long and is used to encode the length in bytes of the whole TPDU header, excluding the LI field itself.

(2) **Fixed part** (FP): this field contains the most important pa-

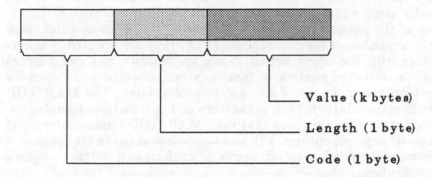

Value (k bytes)

Length (1 byte)

Code (1 byte)

Figure 3.13   Format of the parameters in the TPDU variable part.

rameters used in the TPDU. Obviously the fixed part contents heavily depend on the particular TPDU being considered, however a code subfield is always present that enables the transport layer to distinguish among different TPDU types (i.e. connection requests and responses, data TPDUs and so on).

(3) **Variable part** (VP): this field contains those parameters that are either optional or are seldom used; VP is not necessarily present in each TPDU, however if a variable part exists it must contain at least one parameter. It is worth noting that each parameter appearing in VP can have a variable length but is always structured according to the basic format shown in Figure 3.13.

3.7   Session service

OSI applications can need suitable mechanisms for managing the dialogue between peer processes residing on different stations; these requirements are met by the session layer, whose purpose is to enable the presentation and application entities to exchange data in an organized and synchronized way. In fact, in this context the user is given capabilities for changing the communication mode of a session connection (half duplex and full duplex are the two possible choices), invoking the graceful release of the connection itself, synchronizing and resynchronizing the exchange of data by means of synchronization points and so on.

It is worth pointing out that some applications do not really need all the session services (or even any one of them), since in certain circumstances the functions supported by the transport layer are more than sufficient for the application tasks. In this situation the presence of the session layer can introduce processing and communication overheads that are not compensated for by any really useful enhancement of the quality of service available. This is one of the reasons that caused the session service to be subdivided into a number of functional units (FUs) that are selected in accordance with the user's needs. Some implementations can support only a restricted number of functional units, whilst more complex systems can make use of a complete session layer. The MAP/TOP specifications include both mandatory and optional functional units. Mandatory FUs are those that each MAP/TOP implementor must support anyhow; optional FUs can be present or not in an implementation without affecting its degree of conformance to the standard specifications.

3.7.1   Session connectionless service

The session layer includes both connectionless and connection-oriented services. The former have been added to the original services based on virtual channels to cope with those applications that can not tolerate the processing overhead of establishing a connection when a session service data unit (SSDU) has to be sent to (received from) a remote interlocutor. The main advantage of this solution is that better performance, in general, and response times, in particular, can be achieved in a number of time-critical situations; however this approach also exhibits a significant drawback: none of the typical session capabilities can be offered to the user since session features have been conceived for a connection-oriented context.

As with the transport layer this 'afterthought' of the ISO standardization committee has produced an addendum [ISO8326dad3] to the main standard document [ISO8326] which describes the connectionless service supported by means of the two following primitives:

(1) *S_UNITDATA.request* which is invoked when an SSDU must be sent to a user residing on another station;

(2) *S_UNITDATA.indication* which is passed to the user by the session layer when an SSDU is received from a session entity residing on a remote system.

Neither MAP nor TOP make use of the connectionless primitives, since the communication scheme adopted by the MAP/TOP transport and upper layers is connection oriented.

3.7.2   Session connection-oriented service

Connection-oriented services can be grouped in two main categories usually known as the *confirmed* type and the *not-confirmed* type.

Confirmed services

Confirmed services are those functions offered to the session user that require the cooperation of a remote user for their completion. The originating user submits a request to the session layer which causes an indication to be passed to the remote interlocutor; the response of the called user is returned to the caller to confirm that the service request has been satisfied. Thus this scheme is based on four variants of service primitives: *request, indication, response* and *confirm*. The connection establishment procedure is an example of confirmed service of the session (and transport) layer(s).

Not-confirmed services

Not-confirmed services do not involve any explicit cooperation of the remote user. In this case only two service primitives are needed: request and indication. An example of the not-confirmed service can be found in the session (and transport) normal data transfer functions.

Several session services are similar to those provided by the transport layer: for instance the user is able to open a session connection, transfer data over it and then release the virtual channel. This redundancy of functions is partially due to the connection-oriented communication model: since a virtual connection must be opened before data transfers can occur each layer has to provide suitable services for creating, destroying and managing its own virtual channels. However, it is worth noting that other functions were replicated in order to allow the users of the Nth layer to access useful services provided by the layer $N-1$: for instance an expedited data flow has to be implemented by the session layer (possibly based on the transport expedited data service) if the session users need to exchange expedited messages. It is a fact that this causes a significant overhead in the communication software and affects the overall system performance.

3.7.3 Session connection establishment

Session connections are created by means of the $S\_CONNECT$ primitives that support a confirmed service, since the creation of a virtual channel always requires the approval of the called user.

A connection is always established between a pair of session service access points (SSAPs) used to interface the users (usually presentation processes) to the service provider. The approach followed in this case is very similar to the solutions presented for the transport layer: the connection establishment mechanisms allow the two interacting session users to negotiate the quality of service supported for the connection and the values of a number of attributes associated with the connection itself. The quality of service is selected by the same set of parameters used for the transport connections plus two additional ones:

- session connection establishment delay
- session connection establishment failure probability
- throughput
- transit delay
- residual error rate
- transfer failure probability
- session connection release delay
- session connection release failure probability
- session connection protection
- priority
- session connection resilience
- extended control
- optimized dialogue transfer.

The meaning of the parameters listed above is the same as that discussed in Section 3.5.2 except for the last two items in the list which are peculiar to the session layer. In fact the extended control parameter enables users to invoke a selected set of services, including for instance connection abortion or resynchronization, even though the normal data flow is congested and no further command could be accepted by the service provider. Similarly the optimized dialogue transfer parameter allows the concatenation of several service requests by the session layer.

Attributes associated with the connection are another typical feature of the session layer: they allow the user to control some characteristics of the dialogue carried out on the virtual channel such as the ability to send data (half-duplex or full-duplex transmissions), to invoke a graceful disconnection and/or to use synchronization points.

Attributes are called *tokens* in the ISO standard document [ISO8326]; for each connection the following four tokens are defined:

(1) data token
(2) release token
(3) synchronize-minor token
(4) major/release token.

The data token controls the right to send session protocol data units (SPDUs) on the connection; no ordinary message can be transmitted by the user who does not hold the data token. The release token enables its holder to initiate an orderly connection release procedure in accordance with the user at the other end of the connection, while the remaining two tokens affect the synchronization services as described later in this chapter.

Each token is always in one of two possible states: *available* or *not available*. When the token is not available no restriction is put on the users who are authorized to invoke the corresponding service; in other words unavailable tokens cause both the users at the connection endpoints to be treated in the same way by the session service provider. Thus the data transfer and release services can be invoked by both the users, while none of them can use the synchronization and activity functions.

An available token is always assigned to one of the two users connected by the virtual channel and, consequently, not assigned to the other. In this case the token holder has exclusive access to the corresponding service (i.e. can initiate a graceful release), whilst its remote interlocutor has no right to invoke the same function.

Availability/unavailability of tokens is decided by the connection establishment procedure which also allows for the negotiation of initial assignments for the available tokens. Token management services are then supported by the session provider for changing the assignments dynamically during the connection's lifetime, so that the right to invoke a service can be exchanged between the dialoguing users.

3.7.4 Session data transfer

Each session connection can support four different data flows known as *normal*, *expedited*, *typed* and *capability* data.

Normal data

Normal data are the ordinary way of exchanging information between the communicating SSAPs; as mentioned in the previous section the ability to invoke this service is controlled by the data token, which can be used to implement full-duplex (data token unavailable) and half-duplex (data token available and dynamically exchanged by the users) communications. It is worth noting that each transport connection always supports a full-duplex data transfer, while some applications make use of a half-duplex dialogue scheme. For instance, the MAP manufacturing message service (MMS) discussed in Chapter 6 is based on a client-server model which alternates requests and answers in a natural half-duplex fashion. This kind of data exchange can be elegantly obtained by controlling the right to transmit on the connection established between the server and the client by means of the session token management mechanisms. The normal data transfer of SSDUs is a not-confirmed service that can be invoked with the *S_DATA* primitives.

Expedited data

Expedited data have the same meaning as transport expedited messages. However, session expedited data can be sent irrespective of the current data token assignment: expedited SSDUs are used to carry urgent information and the user must be able to invoke this kind of service even though the right to transmit is currently assigned to the remote interlocutor. The mechanisms governing expedited data delivery can cause some reordering by the session layer in processing normal, typed and expedited data SSDUs; in particular the user is assured that an expedited SSDU which is passed to the session provider will not be delivered after any normal or typed data subsequently submitted on the same connection. The expedited service is not confirmed and can be invoked by using the *S_EXPEDITED_DATA* primitives. As for the transport layer the amount of data transferred with an expedited SSDU is limited; in particular the maximum length of 14 bytes can not be exceeded.

Typed data

The typed data transfer is a not-confirmed service which uses the *S_TYPED_DATA* primitives. Typed data build up an autonomous information flow on the connection that is managed with the same service rules adopted for the normal data SSDUs. However, typed data transmissions do not depend on the availability and assignment of the data token. The purpose of typed data is to provide session users with a means for transferring information out of the normal delivery mechanisms; this facility may be used for exchanging management data and control messages that are recognized and transferred separately from the normal SSDUs by the session layer, even though their meaning is application-defined. Note that no restriction is put on the length of typed SSDUs, whilst this is not true for expedited data.

Capability data

Capability data delivery is a confirmed service activated with the *S_CAPABILITY_DATA* primitives. Capability data enable the user to send and receive limited amounts of data (a capability SSDU can contain up to 512 data bytes) when no activity is currently in progress on the connection (see Section 3.7.8). Thus this service can be requested only when the activity management service has been selected during the connection establishment phase.

3.7.5   Disconnection

A session connection can be closed in three different ways depending on the user choice, the type of service supported by the session layer and the reason for the disconnection.

Abrupt disconnections that are similar to those found in the transport layer can be originated either by the user or by the session service provider itself. In fact the user can obtain the connection destruction whenever an *S_U_ABORT.request* primitive is passed to the local session entity. This user-initiated abort function is a not-confirmed service which causes an immediate disconnection from the remote interlocutor, even if some session protocol data units (SP-DUs) are still traveling on the connection and there are some SSDUs still to be delivered to the dialoguing users. In other words, the abort service can imply losses of data if the initiator is not careful in deciding when this service should be invoked.

In addition there is another type of abrupt disconnection which is initiated by the session layer. The service type is also not-confirmed in this case, however only the *S_P_ABORT.indication* primitive is used since the procedure is started by the service provider. The indication is passed to both users at the connection endpoints to notify them of the destruction of the virtual channel (which implies possible losses of data). In a normal situation provider-initiated disconnections should occur very seldom, because these actions are undertaken when some error is found inside the session layer that cannot be recovered. Typical abort reasons included in the ISO standard are the disconnection of the transport layer (which may no longer be able to grant a reliable service) and errors affecting the session protocol.

Graceful disconnections are typical of the session layer and represent a real enhancement with respect to the type of service offered by the transport entities. In fact the negotiated release function is always supported by the session provider, even when a minimum set of services is selected during the connection establishment phase.

The negotiated release is a confirmed service based on the *S_RELEASE* primitives; confirmation by the remote user is needed because an orderly disconnection requires the cooperation of both users to prevent undelivered data from being lost. The release mechanisms are affected by the state of the release token: when the token is available the token holder can invoke the *S_RELEASE.request*. In this case the receiver who gets the *S_RELEASE.indication* primitive can either accept or refuse the disconnection by responding with an affirmative or negative *S_RELEASE.response*; when the disconnection is refused, the dialogue on the virtual channel continues in the usual way without loosing any SPDU. By contrast, when the release token is unavailable the disconnection cannot be refused and the virtual channel is destroyed when the *S_RELEASE.confirm* is returned to the initiating user.

3.7.6   Token management

Available tokens can be assigned permanently to users when the connection is established, or they can be exchanged between its two endpoints, depending on the requirements of the activities carried out on the session channel. The session layer supports two basic services for claiming and passing tokens. S_TOKEN_PLEASE primitives are used in the former case; they build up a not-confirmed procedure which enables the initiator to ask its interlocutor for one or more tokens that are available and currently assigned to the other side of the connection. When an S_TOKEN_PLEASE.indication is received, the addressed user can either ignore the request or reply by invoking the S_TOKEN_GIVE not-confirmed service to pass the requested tokens. Obviously a token cannot be asked for which is already assigned to the requesting user, nor can a user pass token(s) currently owned by the peer (remote) interlocutor.

Finally, another service exists for transferring all the available tokens to one of the users, which is related to the activity management functions (see Section 3.7.8). The service is activated by the S_CONTROL_GIVE.request and causes an S_CONTROL_GIVE.indication to be passed to the remote user, thus completing the not-confirmed procedure.

Figure 3.14 shows an example of half-duplex data exchange on a session connection: at the connection establishment both the data and the release tokens are assigned to the user on the left side of the picture (user A). When the data transfer phase begins only user A can send normal data, then the right to transmit is passed to user B by means of the token give service; typed and expedited data are transmitted even though the sender is not the token holder. The bottom part of the figure concerns the graceful disconnection procedure: user A initiates the service and waits for a confirmation from B; in the picture the response is positive and the connection is closed, however a negative reply from B would have caused the data exchange phase to be continued.

3.7.7   Synchronization and resynchronization

Data exchanged on a session virtual channel can be structured in a sequence of *dialogue units* as shown in Figure 3.15. Each dialogue unit concerns a piece of work carried out on the connection which is fully 'self-contained' from the communication point of view. In other words all the communication operations inside a specific dialogue unit are completely separated by the dialogue units preceding and following the one being considered. The figure shows that the boundaries of each dialogue unit are marked with *major synchronization points*; each major point delimits the end of a dialogue unit and the beginning of the next at the same time. Data transferred

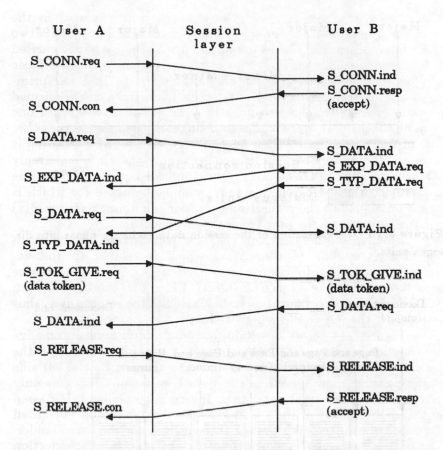

Figure 3.14   Example of half-duplex data exchange on a session connection.

inside a dialogue unit can be structured in their turn by means of *minor synchronization points*. The user can insert minor and major synchronization points in the data flow by using a suitable synchronization service. The session layer implements the mechanisms for numbering and moving points between the two ends of the connections, however the semantic of each point is totally left to the user.

An example of use of synchronization points is shown in Figure 3.16 concerning a simple application for transferring documents. In this case each document to be transferred corresponds to a dialogue unit, while the end of each page in a document is labeled with a minor point.

The synchronization service allows the two dialoguing users to maintain a perfect agreement about the work in progress on the connection, so that if a failure occurs it is not necessary to restart the

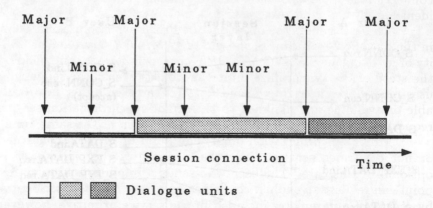

Figure 3.15   Organization of the session data exchange phase into dialogue units.

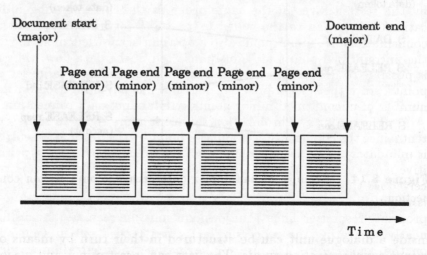

Figure 3.16   Example of use of synchronization points for transferring documents.

dialogue from the beginning. For instance, in the example of Figure 3.16, the receiver can fail to write page n to the backing store. In this case the sender can retransmit either the single page n or a small number of pages including page n, depending on the number of outstanding synchronization points that are still unconfirmed, so saving time and system resources.

The session layer keeps track of the points issued in the data flow by numbering them on each side of the connection. The service provider is able to maintain the same numbering sequence at both the connection endpoints so that synchronization points can be uniquely identified by the dialoguing users.

The user causes the insertion of a minor synchronization point in the data flow by means of the *S_SYNC_MINOR* service. The ability of invoking an *S_SYNC_MINOR.request* primitive is controlled by the state of the synchronize-minor and data tokens: the requesting user must have the right to send data (data token either not available or available and assigned to the minor synchronization service requestor) and hold the synchronize-minor token at the same time.

Minor synchronization points can build up either a confirmed or not confirmed service, since the response of the called user is optional in this case. The user who sends a minor synchronization point can request an explicit confirmation by the remote interlocutor by means of a parameter included in the service primitive, however the receiver can return a response even though the confirmation is not explicitly required.

It is possible to send other minor points while waiting for the confirmation of a previously issued request. Responses are returned by the session layer in the same order as the corresponding indications are passed to the called user. It is worth noting that the confirmation of a minor point also acts as an acknowledgment for all the unconfirmed points previously inserted in the data flow, thus it is possible to use a single response also for confirming a large set of points, since the session provider does not put any limitation on the number of unconfirmed minor points outstanding on a connection.

The major synchronization service is more rigid, to some extent, since the confirmation of a major point by the destination entity is mandatory. The user invoking an *S_SYNC_MAJOR.request* primitive is not allowed to send other data until the confirmation is received for that point; similarly when an *S_SYNC_MAJOR.indication* is received no other action can be performed before sending the appropriate response. Thus a major point must be seen as a means for neatly separating the processing activities carried out in sequence on the connection. The use of the major synchronization service is controlled by the assignments of both the minor-synchronize and major/activity tokens. If the former is available it must be assigned together with the latter to the user who initiates the service. Moreover the confirmation of a major point also acknowledges all the unconfirmed minor points previously sent on the connection.

Resynchronization is a service which allows the dialoguing users to put the connection into a correct and known state. This form of re-initialization always occurs without closing the current session connection and is used to re-establish communications when errors or anomalies are discovered, either caused by the interacting users or originating inside the session layer itself.

When the resynchronization service is invoked the assignments of the available tokens and the value of the synchronization point serial number are usually changed: the users must agree on the new values to be adopted and this is done by exchanging suitable parameters with the resynchronization primitives. The service type is confirmed and the *S_RESYNCHRONIZE* primitives are used. Once the resynchronization request has been passed to the session layer the user cannot initiate any other service (except for the *S_U_ABORT* abrupt disconnection) before receiving the service confirmation. Similarly, the reception of an *S_RESYNCHRONIZE.indication* prevents the called user from continuing the dialogue on the connection before sending an appropriate response.

Actually, three different forms of resynchronization are available that can be selected by specifying a 'resynchronization type' parameter in the *S_RESYNCHRONIZE.request*:

(1) abandon resynchronization

(2) restart resynchronization

(3) set resynchronization.

The abandon variant is intended for putting the connection into a completely new state; in fact the synchronization point serial number can be set to a value greater than the number of the last point issued on the connection by the session layer. In practice the service initiator signals to its interlocutor the wish to discard the work being carried out and to continue the session by starting a new task from the beginning.

The restart option allows users to go back and restart the work from an agreed point; the latter is selected among the synchronization points (both acknowledged and unacknowledged) that have been exchanged on the connection. However, it is worth noting that the restart point cannot be earlier than the last confirmed major point, since the major synchronization is used to close a dialogue unit definitely.

The set variant allows the requesting user to set the new value of the synchronization point number: any valid value can be specified, no matter whether the point has already been issued on the connection.

3.7.8   Activity management

Activities are another tool offered by the session layer to structure the dialogue between two communicating users. In this case the basic idea is to organize a session into a sequence of tasks that are logically independent and unrelated. Figure 3.17 shows how the activity concept can be applied to the simple example of document transfer introduced in Figure 3.16.

In the picture it is assumed that the application processes were designed to transfer several documents from one station to another

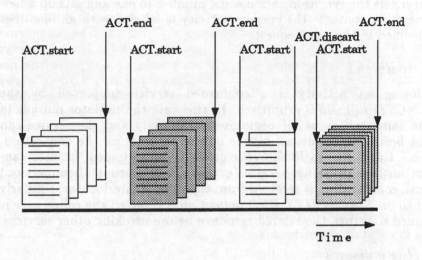

Figure 3.17 Example of multiple document transfer using activities.

during the same session. Each document corresponds to one different activity; the session layer enables the user to mark the beginning and the end of an activity so that each document can be uniquely identified and distinguished at both the ends of the connections. Each activity is logically and physically separated from the others; moreover there is no way for the session users to go back and resume the dialogue inside an activity which has already been completed.

The application can use the minor and major synchronization mechanisms inside an activity; for instance, each document can be structured into dialogue units (i.e. chapters) and dialogue units include minor synchronization points (i.e. for separating pages). Since the end of an activity definitely concludes a piece of work, the activity end mark also carries the meaning of a major synchronization point; in other words no major point can be used to synchronize the dialogue inside an activity which was concluded at an earlier time.

The session layer supports a number of primitives for managing activities that can be started, suspended, resumed, discarded and closed. The use of these management primitives is restricted to the availability and assignment of the major/activity token.

Activity start

Starting an activity is a not-confirmed service implemented by the *S_ACTIVITY_START* primitives. The initiating user must hold the activity/major tokens, moreover the data and synchronize minor tokens are required if they are available. Note that it is not possible to start a new activity when another one is in progress on the connection; when the *S_ACTIVITY_START.request* is processed the session layer sets the synchronization serial number to one and sets up a new operating context: the current activity is labeled with an identifier specified in the user request.

Activity end

Closing an activity is a confirmed service supported by the *S_ACTIVITY_END* primitives. In this case the initiator must hold the same tokens as for beginning an activity and the service can not be invoked if an activity is not in progress on the connection. Once the *S_ACTIVITY_END.request* has been issued the user cannot initiate any other service (except for an abrupt disconnection) until confirmation is received from the remote interlocutor; similarly when an *S_ACTIVITY_END.indication* is received the called user is forced to return the related response before invoking other services.

Activity discard

The work carried out inside an activity can be abandoned definitely by means of the discard confirmed service option. This is done by using the *S_ACTIVITY_DISCARD* primitives; the initiating user must specify the reason for discarding the work and wait for remote confirmation. When the service is completed the initiator is assigned all the available tokens and can start a new activity. This service can be useful when the dialoguing users realize that the work currently in progress is not worth continuing; for instance a more recent version of a document might become available while an older version is being transferred. In this case the application can decide to abort the transmission of the out-of-date document and to start the transfer of the updated version.

Activity interrupt

An activity can be interrupted when more urgent work has to be carried out. This can be done by invoking the activity interrupt confirmed service. The *S_ACTIVITY_INTERRUPT* primitives allow for suspension of the current activity without discarding any work already done; an interrupted activity can be resumed later when the two users agree. The service initiator must specify the reason for the interruption; at a given time there can be several interrupted activities on the session connection but only one activity in progress.

Activity resume

This service is not confirmed and allows the user to restart an activity which was interrupted at an earlier time. The initiator issuing the *S_ACTIVITY_RESUME.request* primitive must specify the identifier of the activity to be resumed, together with the value of the synchronization serial number to be used. This allows the remote interlocutor to restart the work from a specific arranged point inside the activity. It is worth noting that an activity suspended on a connection can also be resumed on another virtual channel; in this case the user must also pass the old session identifier to the service provider.

3.7.9   Exception reporting

The exception reporting service allows users to be notified when some error or problem occurs, either in the session layer or in the applications themselves. In practice there are two types of error reporting, depending on whether the service initiator is the session layer or the user.

(1) **User-initiated exception reporting**: in this case the user can send an exception signal to the remote interlocutor by means of the *S_U_EXCEPTION_REPORT* primitives. Errors notified with this mechanism are typical of the application processes and do not involve the communication system. For instance, the application receiving a document can fail to write it to the backing store; in this case the sender can be informed by means of a user-initiated report containing the reason for raising the exception. The report indication causes the sender to remove the error condition; thus it can decide to resynchronize (i.e. to retransmit the document), to abort the connection or to discard/interrupt the current activity.

(2) **Provider-initiated exception reporting**:   this not-confirmed service is used by the session provider to inform both the ends of the connection about possible errors or malfunctions inside the session layer.   Only the *S_P_EXCEPTION_REPORT.indication* primitive exists, which is passed to the users; when it is received the user process can try to remove the error conditions by undertaking one of the following actions: resynchronization, disconnection, activity discard and activity interrupt.

3.8   Session functional units

As mentioned in Section 3.7 the services supported by the session layer have been structured into a set of functional units (FUs). In general the use of an FU can be negotiated by the users when a new connection is established. At present the ISO standard document [ISO8326] includes the following functional units:

- kernel

- negotiated release
- half-duplex
- duplex
- expedited data
- typed data
- capability data exchange
- minor synchronize
- major synchronize
- resynchronize
- exceptions
- activity management.

The kernel functional unit cannot be negotiated, since it supports the basic services needed for opening a connection, transferring data over it and then closing the virtual channel. All the other FUs can be selected or not according to the user requirements. An implementation which is in conformity to the standard must support the kernel FUs, together with either the half-duplex or full duplex FUs or both of them. The MAP and TOP specifications require the kernel and duplex FUs, whilst the resynchronization is optional in MAP/TOP and its implementation is left up to the manufacturer.

Table 3.7 shows the services included in each FU and distinguishes confirmed and not-confirmed services. It is worth noting that the standard also mentions session subsets; a subset is a combination of the kernel FU with any other functional unit(s), provided that the selection of the capability FU implies also the activity FU, while the exception reporting implies the half-duplex FU. In this way it is possible to define subsets of the session service that are compatible with the older versions of the ISO standard.

3.9   Session protocol

The ISO standard [ISO8327] describes the session protocol by means of state tables similar to those introduced for the transport layer. Even though several states (that is large tables) have been used in this case because of the relevant number of services provided by the session entities, the protocol itself is less complex when compared to the transport procedures and does not contain any mechanism which appears particularly significant.

Session entities cooperate according to the rules of the session protocol by exchanging session protocol data units (SPDUs). Each SPDU is transmitted and received by using the data transfer services offered by the Transport OSI layer. A single SPDU can be mapped on a corresponding normal TSDU or multiple SPDUs can be concatenated to fit in one TSDU in order to achieve a better usage of the

Table 3.7 Session functional units and associated services.

Functional unit	Services	Confirmed yes/no	Required tokens
Kernel	Connection	y	
	Normal data	n	
	Orderly release	y	
	User abort	n	
	Provider abort	n	
Release	Orderly release	y	release
	Give token	n	
	Please token	n	
Half-duplex	Give token	n	data
	Please token	n	
Duplex			
Expedited	Expedited data	n	
Typed data	Typed data	n	
Capability data	Capability data	y	
Minor synchronize	Minor synchronization points	y,n	synch-minor
	Give token	n	
	Please token	n	
Major synchronize	Major synchronization points	y	major/ activity
	Give token	n	
	Please token	n	
Resynchronize	Resynchronization	y	
Exceptions	User exception report	n	
	Provider exception report	n	
Activity management	Activity start	n	major/ activity
	Activity end	y	
	Activity resume	n	
	Activity interrupt	y	
	Activity discard	y	
	Give token	y	
	Please token	y	
	Give control	y	

communication resources. Three classes of SPDUs are mentioned in the standard:

(1) class 0 concerns those SPDUs that can be either mapped one to one on a TSDU or concatenated with other class 2 SPDUs;

(2) class 1 refers to those SPDUs that cannot be concatenated and are always mapped one to one on the transport messages;

(3) class 2 contains the SPDUs that are always concatenated with others protocol data units.

Furthermore, two different types of concatenations can be adopted: basic concatenation always applies to a pair consisting of one class 0 and one class 2 SPDU, whilst the extended type concerns the concatenation of one class 0 unit with one or more class 2 SPDUs. Extended concatenation is optional in MAP and TOP and can be refused during the negotiation phase at the establishment of the connection.

If the transport layer supports the expedited data transfer service the session provider can use this facility to carry out its protocol operations. In particular the most urgent SPDUs can be mapped onto the transport expedited flow: this means that the abort services (both provider-initiated and user-initiated), the session expedited data and some control SPDUs can take precedence over the other messages that make use of the normal transport data flow.

3.10   Conclusions

Distributed applications such as those developed in the MAP and TOP environments need a number of communication facilities in order to exchange data among processes residing on different stations in the network. The quality of the service offered by the lowest OSI layers (namely physical and data-link) is often insufficient to satisfy the communication requirements of the application entities. The gap between the service quality offered at the data-link upper interface and the QOS demanded at the application level is bridged by the intermediate OSI protocol layers, and in particular by the network, transport and session layers.

The network layer is responsible for transferring units of data between any pair of stations in the network. Since the overall system can be composed of several heterogeneous subnetworks, each one having its own low-level protocols and characteristics, the network service provider has to cope with problems such as: routing and relaying messages within a given subnetwork and/or through different subnetworks; forwarding data units to the next host belonging to the route a given message has to take; and harmonizing the service offered to the transport entities so that each user of the network layer can access the same set of (OSI) services, independently of its point of attachment to the network.

Several protocol roles have been identified inside the network layer that can be fulfilled by one or more (discrete) network protocols. This chapter has introduced those aspects of the network layer that are relevant and interesting from the MAP/TOP point of view; in particular the ISO connectionless internet protocol has been presented, since this standard has been adopted to support the network connectionless service in this framework.

Our discussion has also tackled the typical problems solved by the transport layer. It has been shown that the MAP/TOP transport protocol is particularly huge and complex, since the MAP/TOP transport layer has to enhance significantly the quality of service offered by the underlying subnetwork. Users interfaced at the transport service access points can have faith in a reliable, in-sequence data transfer service supported by using a connection-oriented approach. By contrast, only an unreliable datagram service is accessible at the top of the network layer, so that the transport service provider has to implement a number of error detection and recovery mechanisms in order to improve the communication functions offered to the user. This is why the ISO class 4 transport protocol has been included in the MAP and TOP protocol profiles; the class 4 protocol was explicitly conceived to be used with type C subnetworks offering unsatisfactory communication services from the error detection and recovery points of view.

The session layer adds several dialogue management capabilities to the transport service. In particular the users are able to control and modify the state of some attributes (such as the right to transmit or to invoke a graceful disconnection) of the communications carried out on session virtual channels by invoking a set of primitives supported by the session service provider. The session service also incorporates mechanisms for synchronizing the exchange of data between a pair of dialoguing users and for structuring the dialogue into separate activities that are also managed by the session layer itself. This chapter has introduced all the main features of the ISO session standard and discussed the characteristics of the session subset which is used in MAP and TOP.

References

[ISO8648]   ISO *Information Processing Systems – Open Systems Interconnection – Internal Organization of the Network Layer*, IS No. 8648, 1988.

[ISO8348add1]   ISO *Information Processing Systems – Data Communications – Network Service Definition – Addendum 1: Connectionless-mode Transmission*, IS No. 8348/Add.1, 1987.

[ISO8208]   ISO *Information Processing Systems – Open Sys-*

tems Interconnection – X.25 Packet Level Protocol for Data Terminal Equipment, IS No. 8208, 1988.

[ISO8473]   ISO *Information Processing Systems – Data Communications – Protocol for Providing the Connectionless-mode Network Service*, IS No. 8473, 1988.

[ISO8802]   ISO *Information Processing Systems – Local Area Networks – Part 2: Logical Link Control*, DIS 8802-2.2, 1987.

[ISO9542]   ISO *Information Processing Systems – Telecommunications and Information Exchange Between Systems – End Systems to Intermediate Systems Routing Exchange Protocol for Use in Conjunction with the Protocol for Providing the Connectionless-mode Network Service (ISO 8473)*, IS No. 9542, 1988.

[ISO8348add2]   ISO *Information Processing Systems – Data Communications – Network Service Definition – Addendum 2: Network Layer Addressing*, IS No. 8348/Add. 2, 1988.

[ISO8072]   ISO *Information Processing Systems – Open Systems Interconnection – Transport Service Definition*, IS No. 8072, 1986.

[ISO8072dad1]   ISO *Information Processing Systems – Open Systems Interconnection – Transport Service Definition – Addendum 1: Connectionless-mode Transmission*, IS No. 8072/Add. 1, 1986.

[ISO8073]   ISO *Information Processing Systems – Open Systems Interconnection – Connection Oriented Transport Protocol Specification*, IS No. 8073, 2nd ed., 1988.

[ISO8326]   ISO *Information Processing Systems – Open Systems Interconnection – Basic Connection Oriented Session Service Definition*, IS No. 8326, 1st ed., 1987.

[ISO8326dad3]   ISO *Information Processing Systems – Open Systems Interconnection – Basic Connection Oriented Session Service Definition – Addendum 3: Connectionless-mode Session Service*, Dad. 3 to IS No. 8326, 1988.

[ISO8327]   ISO *Information Processing Systems – Open Systems Interconnection – Basic Connection Oriented Session Protocol Specification*, IS No. 8327, 1st ed., 1987.

Chapter 4

The Presentation Layer

4.1 Introduction

It is well known that when equipment from different vendors or manufacturers has to exchange data, problems arise, since a different representation is often assumed by the different machines.

In order to exemplify this fact, let us consider data transfer between a one's complement unit and a two's complement machine. When a 16 bit integer is correctly transferred, the semantic content of the information is interpreted differently by the two units. As an example the bit pattern 0fff (hexadecimal) is valued as -15 (decimal) on the one's complement unit whilst its value is -16 (decimal) on the other device.

The responsibility for handling data and preserving their meaning has been assigned to the presentation layer [ISO8822] [ISO8823], which provides a common method for representing the information the devices wish to intercommunicate. The method used is based on the availability of a common language, called *abstract syntax*, which is used to describe the data format for each application. Rules are also available to translate the abstract description of data into a transfer code, which will be transferred effectively between the remote applications. Such rules constitute a *transfer syntax*. In more detail: an abstract syntax is defined as the set of rules for the formal specification of data which are independent of the encoding technique used to represent the data themselves. A typical example of an abstract syntax can be a set of data type definitions or a BNF grammar. An example of an abstract description of data using the C language is given in the following:

```
struct{
char Name ,
char Surname,
integer Exa-given,
integer Exa-left
} student
```

In this case, the C structure contains a data type definition, 'student', related to a course attendee and represents an abstract description of a particular data element used in a specific application. This approach gives an abstract description of the item 'student' directly manageable by the applications. To transfer this information to a correspondent remote application, the concrete syntax rules have to be adopted to generate the bit pattern associated with abstract description. Table 4.1 shows an example of such rules applied to the abstract description shown above; in this case a type and length for the coded item has been introduced, so that the receiver is made aware of the semantic meaning of the received data element. If the receiver knows the conventional order used to transmit type, length of data field and information, it can rebuild the correct meaning of the information, according to the abstract description, independently of the data representation used by its own processing unit. Even if the sender and the receiver have different data representations, it is possible for the presentation layer to understand what the data mean and store them correctly in memory. In this case the *struct* type is coded using the hexadecimal value 10 followed by the total length of the structure; furthermore, each element included in the record is described individually: the *char* type is represented by the hexadecimal value 1, whilst the *integer* value is described by the hexadecimal value 3. Figure 4.1 shows the byte stream transferred on the wire.

The method of describing syntax is also a standardization matter, and the Abstract Syntax Notation 1 specified by ISO [ISO8824] represents one of the most common examples. The purpose of ASN.1 is to provide designers of upper layer protocol standards and applications with an effective technique for abstract syntax specification and coding rules for data transfer [ISO8825]. In other words, ASN.1 may be seen as a general language capable of describing data structures for protocols and applications. Although the previous example for the 'student' data type description and coding is simple, it provides

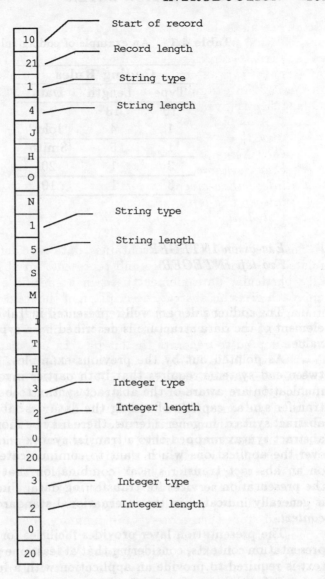

Figure 4.1 The byte stream obtained from the 'student' data type, using a suitable transfer syntax.

a basic approach to describe how the ASN.1 works.

Referring to the previous example, the information item 'student' will be described in ASN.1 as follows:

student::= SEQUENCE
{ Name VisibleString,
Surname VisibleString,

Table 4.1 An example of coding rules.

Coding Rules		
Type	Length	Data
10	13	
1	4	'John'
1	5	'Smith'
3	1	20
3	1	10

Exa-given INTEGER
Exa-left INTEGER
}

The coding rules are well represented in Table 4.1, where each element of the data structure is described by a type, a length and a value.

As pointed out by the previous examples, data transfer between end systems requires that both parties involved in the communication are aware of the abstract syntax to be used and of the transfer syntax capable of coding the data described by the chosen abstract syntax. In general terms, there may be more than one single abstract syntax mapped onto a transfer syntax and vice versa, however the applications which want to communicate must first agree on an abstract/transfer syntax combination that can be used by the presentation services for transferring data. Such a combination is generally indicated in the international standard as *presentation context*.

The presentation layer provides facilities for the definition of presentation contexts, considering that at least one presentation context is required to provide an application with a fully defined environment for the transfer of data.

When a presentation service user wants to define a presentation context, they must select an abstract syntax, from those available, whilst the service provider will try to identify a transfer syntax capable of supporting that abstract syntax and supported also by the open system to be reached by the data. For the purpose of determining a mutually acceptable transfer syntax, a *negotiation mechanism* is supported by the service provider at the time of the presentation connection establishment. Moreover, for the correct definition of the context, it is necessary that both the service users and the service provider have knowledge of the abstract syntax chosen, which is made known through a specific identifier to the presentation protocol, to be provided by the context. The service provider also has to know the transfer syntaxes associated with each specific abstract syntax through their names. During the negotiation process for the definition of the context, the initiator supplies to the remote corresponding entity a list of supported transfer syntaxes, which may be seen as library modules describing data structures associated with specific applications, the responder may then select any one of them.

A question may arise when there is the opportunity to have different transfer syntaxes instead of a single set of encoding rules. The fact is that different transfer syntaxes may be required by the application the system is involved in; in some cases, for example, a syntax using encryption is required, whilst in others, for example, data compression plays a more important role. To this purpose Figure 4.2 shows an optimized byte string for the 'student' data type using a different set of coding rules.

The users of the presentation layer are both the application layer protocol, which is based on the transfer of basic data elements termed *application protocol data units* (APDU), and user applications, characterized by specific protocols which are, usually, based on a set of several *user protocol data units* of different types. The set of APDUs and each set of UPDUs represent an abstract syntax associated with the corresponding protocol. Hence two application entities will be able to communicate only if an agreement of the abstract syntaxes to be used during the communication takes place before starting the data exchange process. In practice, the abstract syntax defines the types of each UPDU used in the protocol, which means that it identifies the general nature of the information contained in the UPDU such as the different categories of information and the way they are combined.

The application entities will inform the presentation layer of the set of abstract syntax agreed on, whilst the presentation layer will determine which transfer syntax is to be used for the chosen abstract syntaxes.

The basic functions carried out by the presentation layer are the following:

- *negotiation of the transfer syntaxes*: it provides the presentation service context definition
- *translation to and from the transfer syntax*: this function has no impact on the presentation protocol structure, being contained in the presentation entity

The negotiation of a transfer syntax is handled by the presentation layer when an application entity specifies an abstract syntax for which a specific transfer syntax is required. In this case the presentation entity activates the negotiation, which, if successful, provides the association of an abstract syntax with a compatible transfer syntax so that a specific presentation context is available.

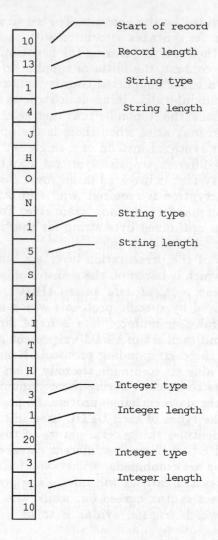

Figure 4.2   The byte stream obtained from the 'student' data type, using an alternative transfer syntax capable of supporting a compression algorithm.

MAP/TOP systems use the basic presentation services required to establish a presentation connection, transfer normal data and release the connection. Other services may be introduced if supported by the session layer according to the requirements of the different applications available.

In the following a general overview of the ISO specification for the presentation layer is given, together with a description of the ASN.1 aspects related to data representation and coding.

4.2 Presentation layer services

Table 4.2 lists the presentation layer services classified into functional areas related to connection establishment, connection termination, context management, information transfer and dialogue control. It can be noted that most of these services can be directly mapped onto the corresponding session services.

The service specifications are based on the definition of a set of functional units, which constitute the basic implementation blocks for the layer designer. Each functional unit includes a group of services needed to make available a specific function the implementor wants to introduce in the layer. Some of the functional units are optional, in this case the presentation service user will specify suitable parameters in order to negotiate those presentation functional units needed for the communication requirements.

Two categories of functional units are introduced in the International Standard:

(1) **Session functional units**, which include:

    (a) the kernel functional unit

    (b) the half duplex functional units

    (c) the duplex functional unit

    (d) the expedited data functional unit

    (e) the minor synchronize functional unit

    (f) the major synchronize functional unit

    (g) the resynchronize functional unit

    (h) the activity mangement functional unit

    (i) the negotiated release functional unit

    (j) the capability data functional unit

    (k) the exceptions functional unit

    (l) the typed data functional unit.

(2) **Presentation functional units**, which include those services provided by the presentation layer and are composed of:

    • the kernel functional unit

    • the context management functional unit

    • the context restoration functional unit.

The reader can get further information about the services provided by the session functional units in Chapter 3, where the session layer is treated in detail.

It should be noted that the kernel functional unit is introduced in both the functional categories, since it supports the basic protocol elements required for the establishment of a presentation

Table 4.2   List of presentation services.

Presentation services		
Service primitive	Type of service	Description
Connection establishment		
P_CONNECT	C	Connection establishment
Connection termination		
P_RELEASE	C	Connection release
P_U_ABORT	U	User initiated abort
P_P_ABORT	U	Provider initiated abort
Context management		
P_ALTER_CONTEXT	C	Context definition and deletion
Information transfer		
P_TYPED_DATA	U	No token control
P_DATA	U	Subjected to token control
P_EXPEDITED_DATA	U	Expedited data
P_CAPABILITY_DATA	C	Capability data
Dialogue control services (see Session)		
P_U_EXCEPTION_REPORT	U	
P_P_EXCEPTION_REPORT	U	
P_TOKEN_GIVE	U	
P_TOKEN_PLEASE	U	
P_CONTROL_GIVE	U	
P_SYNC_MINOR	C	
P_SYNC_MAJOR	C	(see session services)
P_RESYNCHRONIZE	C	
P_ACTIVITY_START	U	
P_ACTIVITY_RESUME	U	
P_ACTIVITY_END	C	
P_ACTIVITY_INTERRUPT	C	
P_ACTIVITY_DISCARD	C	

connection, for the transfer of data and for the release of the presentation connection. The context management functional unit and the context restoration functional unit are optional, this means that their use may be negotiated at the time when the presentation connection is opened. The context management functional unit supports services for context addition and deletion, whilst the context restoration functional unit provides services to restore contexts previously suspended; these service can be used only when the session activity management functional unit is selected or when both the session synchronization (minor or major) and the session resynchronization functional units are selected. However this functionality is available only when the context management functional unit is selected. Hence the kernel functional unit includes services for:

- *Connection establishment,* which allows users to establish a presentation connection; parameters are exchanged between users so that suitable characteristics for the service may be selected; they include the presentation functional units available, the initial set of presentation contexts, the attributes of the session connection and the abstract syntax to be used in the default context. As shown in Table 4.2 the service is confirmed (C).

- *Connection termination,* which allows both an orderly release of a presentation connection – so that the involved entities are aware of the fact that communication is being terminated – and a forced termination of the connection (abort services) – data can be lost in this case, since termination is carried out by only one of the entities involved in the process. It should be noted that, whilst orderly release services are confirmed ones (C), the abort services are unconfirmed (U).

- *Information transfer services* allow data to be transferred between presentation users over a connection previously established. Data with dialogue control, capability data and expedited data are options which can also be supported by these services.

These services represent the minimum set of functions to be guaranteed for an implementation of the presentation layer.

There are a number of presentation service primitives that map directly onto a corresponding session primitive without any modification being required; they can be found in the *dialogue control services* and include the primitives provided for the optional functions of:

- token control
- synchronization control
- exception reporting

- activity management.

These include all the session functional units previously introduced. These primitives do not generate any presentation protocol data units and, usually, the parameters associated with such primitives are inserted in the user data field of the corresponding session primitive.

Functional units typical of the presentation layer are the following:

- *Context management*: this functional unit provides services to define presentation contexts on the agreement of both the presentation users involved in the communication other than the service provider. An identifier is assigned to the defined presentation context, which is valid within the connection environment only. The service also allows the presentation context to be deleted from the set of contexts available for the connection.

- *Context restoration*: this functional unit adds further presentation layer functionalities when the session activity management functional unit is selected or when both the session synchronization (major or minor) and the session resynchronization functional units are selected. Its availability depends upon the activation of the context management functional unit.

4.2.1   Service parameters and procedures

Figure 4.3 and Figure 4.4 present the time diagrams of the presentation services. Their relationship to the session services is pointed out in Figure 4.4, where the protocol data units associated with the presentation services are also reported.

The p-connect service is characterized by the parameters shown in Table 4.3. The result of the operation activated by this service is a presentation connection for two application entities identified in the parameter list. Among the parameters shown in Table 4.3, the *responding presentation address* is used only if a presentation address other than the *called presentation address* has to be used when re-establishing the connection after failure. The *multiple defined context* parameter is used when the presentation user intends to use multiple contexts; if this parameter is absent then the defined context set is composed of only one element.

The *presentation context definition list* parameter is used at the time of connection establishment to insert one or more presentation contexts in the defined contexts set, which consists of a list containing one or more items each composed of a presentation context identifier and an abstract syntax name. The list of contexts represents the set of contexts which can be used on the connection.

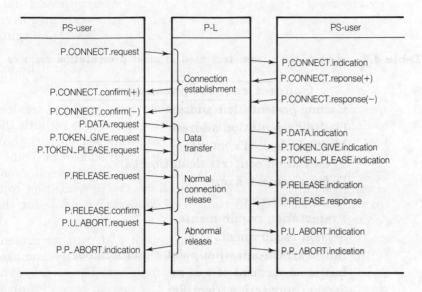

Figure 4.3 Basic presentation services.

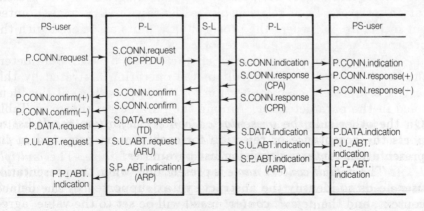

Figure 4.4 Presentation services and related session services.

Table 4.3   List of the parameters used in most presentation services.

Connect request parameters
Calling presentation address
Called presentation address
Multiple defined contexts
Presentation contexts definition list
Default context name
Quality of service
Presentation requirements
Session requirements
Initial synchronization point serial number
Initial assignment of tokens
Session connection identifier
User data

On the other side the *presentation context definition result list* reports the acceptance or rejection for each context proposed in the presentation contexts definition list parameter.

The *default context name* is present only when the presentation user needs to identify the abstract syntax supported by the default context, and the *default context result* will be set to the value 'agree' in the indication, response and confirm primitives only if the provider can support the requested default context.

The *result* parameter is provided by the responding presentation service user or presentation service provider and indicates the result of the connection operation. The symbolic values which indicate the status of the operation are the following: *acceptance* of the connection, *user-rejection* and *provider rejection*.

The connection process requires that the service provider transfer the following parameters without modifying them:

- calling presentation address
- called presentation address
- responding presentation address
- presentation context definition list
- default context name
- initial synchronization point serial number
- initial assignment of tokens
- session connection identifier
- user data parameter
- quality of service
- user data.

The other parameters specified by the presentation requirements, session requirements quality of service and multiple defined context service parameter are negotiated between the service user and the service provider which, moreover, can modify the values specified in the request. If the presentation service user sends a p-connect response in which the 'accept' result is indicated, then the p-connect confirm primitive is issued and the presentation connection is established. If the p-connect response contains 'reject' as a result of the operation, then the p-connect confirm primitive is sent with a result of 'user reject' and the connection is not established. If the p-connect confirm cannot be accepted by the service user then the user itself may issue a p-u-abort service request, so that an abrupt release of the connection is forced.

The *p-u-abort* service is used to force a non-negotiated release of the connection, hence any one of the users may initiate the transaction at any time and the corresponding user will be informed of the connection termination. The effects of this operation are destructive in the sense that the operation sequences started by a previous transaction will not be saved.

Similar to the previous primitive is the *p-p-abort* service, the difference being the fact that the initiative for the connection termination is taken by the service provider for internal reasons. Even this service is destructive, since previously initiated services are immediately aborted.

The *p-typed-data-service* allows the user to transfer data out of the token mechanism, using the defined context set or the default context, if the defined context set is empty; the interpretation of these kinds of data is left to the application. On the other hand, the *p-data* service gives the user access to the *s-data* service of the session layer, even in this case the interpretation of data is an application matter.

As previously pointed out the *p-alter-context-service* provides presentation context management facilities; in particular it allows the creation of presentation contexts and their insertion within the defined context set; the deletion from the list is also supported. The effects of this service are not destructive. The parameters used by this service primitive are the following:

- presentation context definition list
- presentation context deletion list
- presentation context definition result list
- presentation context deletion result list
- result data.

The *presentation context definition list* allows contexts to be defined and added to the defined context set. As in the connection request service, each item in the list is composed of two elements, a presentation context identifier for the local environment and an abstract syntax name. The local identifier and the syntax name are provided by the requesting user.

The *presentation context deletion list* contains presentation contexts that have to be removed from the defined context set, whilst the *presentation context definition result list* indicates the acceptance or rejection of each of the context definitions proposed in the context definition list parameter. The *presentation context deletion result list* indicates the acceptance or rejection of each item deletion proposed in the context deletion list parameter. The modifications requested by the service user for the defined context set are active only when the responder issues the response, or when the initiator receives the confirm primitive.

4.3   Model of the presentation layer

Figure 4.5 shows the architecture of the presentation layer. It should be noticed that the *presentation protocol machine* (PPM) interacts with the presentation service user through a *presentation service access point* (PSAP) using the service primitives introduced in the previous paragraphs. The presentation service primitives will cause or be the result of *presentation protocol data units* (PPDUs) exchanged between the remote PPM by using a session connection. These protocol exchanges are carried out by using services made available by the session service layer. In some cases, as pointed out in the previous paragraphs, presentation service primitives will directly cause or be the result of session service primitives.

It should be noted that presentation connection end points are identified in end systems by an internal implementation dependent

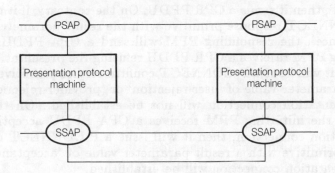

Figure 4.5   A model for the presentation layer.

mechanism so that the presentation service user and the presentation entity can refer to each presentation connection directly.

4.3.1   Connection establishment

The connection establishment procedure is used to establish a presentation connection between two presentation entities. In particular it is used by a PPM when a P-CONNECT request primitive is received. The protocol procedure is based on the following three protocol data units:

(1) CP: presentation connection protocol data unit

(2) CPA PPDU: accept presentation connection protocol data unit

(3) CPR PPDU: reject presentation connection protocol data unit.

When a P-CONNECT request service primitive is passed from the user to the PPM so that the connection establishment can be initiated, a CP protocol data unit containing the presentation data values and the proposed protocol parameters needed for the operation is sent to the remote entity.

If the initiating PPM cannot establish a presentation connection as a consequence of a failure that has arisen in the session layer, then a P-CONNECT confirm service primitive with a result parameter value of 'provider-rejection' is passed to the user and the connection is not established. The responding PPM may refuse the proposed presentation connection as a consequence of bad parameters included in the CP PPDU; in this case the PPM sends back to the initiator a CPR PPDU with a reason parameter included. If the responder is not refusing the connection, then it sends a P-CONNECT indication service primitive to the user.

If the responding PPM receives a P-CONNECT response service primitive from the user, with a result parameter set to 'user-rejection', then it sends a CPR PPDU. On the contrary, if it receives a P-CONNECT response primitive with the result parameter set to 'acceptance', the responding PPM will send a CPA PPDU. If the initiating PPM receives a CPR PPDU refusing the presentation connection, it will issue a P-CONNECT confirm service primitive with a result parameter value of 'user-rejection' or 'provider-rejection' and the presentation connection will not be established. On the contrary, if the initiating PPM receives a CPA PPDU accepting the presentation connection, then it will issue a P-CONNECT confirm service primitive with a result parameter value of 'acceptance' and the presentation connection will be established.

4.3.2   Forced release of the connection

The procedure for the abnormal release of the connection is used at any time to force the release of the presentation connection. It is invoked by the P-U-ABORT service or in response to a protocol error or to the reception of an invalid PPDU. The procedure uses the following PPDUs:

- ARU: abnormal release user protocol data unit
- ARP: abnormal release provider protocol data unit.

When a presentation connection is currently active or a CPA PPDU has been sent without a CP PPDU or a CPR PPDU being received, and the PPM receives a P-U-ABORT request service primitive, it sends an ARU PPDU and the presentation connection is released.

When a PPM receives an unrecognized or unexpected PPDU, or an unexpected session service primitive, it will issue a P-P-ABORT indication service primitive and, if possible, send an ARP PPDU. The presentation connection will be released.

If a PPM receives an unrecognized or unexpected PPDU containing an invalid PPDU parameter value or an unrecognized or unexpected PPDU parameter, including data values that cannot be managed in the corresponding abstract syntax, it will issue a P-P-ABORT indication service primitive and send an ARP PPDU, as a consequence the presentation connection will be released.

When a PPM receives an S-P-ABORT indication session service primitive, it will issue a P-P-ABORT indication service primitive and the presentation connection will be released. IF an ARU PPDU is received by the PPM, it will issue a P-U-ABORT indication service primitive and the presentation connection will be released. On the contrary, when an ARP PPDU is received, the PPM will issue a P-P-ABORT indication service primitive and the connection will be released.

4.3.3   Context alteration

The context alteration procedure is used to modify the defined context set. In particular it negotiates the definition of one or more new presentation contexts to be added or deleted from the defined context set. The procedure is based on the following PPDUs:

- AC: alter context protocol data unit
- ACA: alter context acknowledge protocol data unit.

When a P-ALTER-CONTEXT request service primitive is received by a PPM, it will send an AC PPDU. This will be received by a PPM which has the role of acceptor; the PPM may itself refuse some or all of the proposed presentation context additions. Subsequently it will issue a P-ALTER-CONTEXT indication service primitive, in which it will mark those elements which have been refused using the value 'provider-rejection'.

When a P-ALTER-CONTEXT response service primitive is received by the accepting PPM, it will send an ACA PPDU indicating the acceptance or rejection of each proposed presentation context addition and of each proposed context deletion in the request.

The presentation contexts proposed for addition in the response service primitive and marked with 'acceptance' will be added to the defined context set and will be available for use from the time of receipt of the response. They may also be used for presentation data values contained in the user data parameter of the ACA PPDU. The presentation contexts proposed for deletion and marked with 'acceptance' will be deleted from the defined context set and no longer be available for use from the time of receipt of the response, and will not be used for presentation data values contained in the user data parameter of the ACA PPDU.

When an ACA PPDU is received by the requesting PPM, it passes a P-ALTER-CONTEXT confirm primitive to the user. On receipt of an ACA PPDU, the requesting PPM adds the presentation contexts accepted in the ACA PPDU to the defined contexts set. The presentation contexts accepted for deletion in the ACA PPDU are deleted from the defined context set and no longer available for use from the time of receipt of the ACA PPDU.

4.3.4   Information transfer

The information transfer procedure is used to send presentation data values originating from P-DATA, P-TYPED-DATA, P-CAPABILITY-DATA, and P-EXPEDITED-DATA request service primitives and P-CAPABILITY-DATA response service primitives. The procedure uses the following PPDUs:

- TD: presentation data protocol data unit

- TTD: presentation typed data protocol data unit
- TE: expedited data protocol data unit
- TC: capability data protocol data unit
- TCC: capability data acknowledge protocol data unit.

If a P-DATA request service primitive is received by a PPM, it sends a TD PPDU to transmit, according to the agreed transfer syntaxes, the presentation data values contained in the P-DATA request service primitive. When a remote PPM receives a TD PPDU, it issues a P-DATA indication service primitive containing these presentation data values obtained from the PPDU.

The same approach is used when typed and expedited data are involved. When typed data are considered, the session typed data functional unit must be available at the session layer.

If a P-CAPABILITY-DATA request service primitive is received by a PPM, it sends a TC PPDU to transfer data contained in the P-CAPABILITY-DATA request service primitive. When a PPM receives a TC PPDU it issues a P-CAPABILITY-DATA indication service primitive containing the data just received to the user. If the accepting PPM then receives a P-CAPABILITY-DATA response service primitive, it must send a TCC PPDU to transfer data according to the selected transfer syntaxes. When a PPM receives a TCC PPDU, it issues a P-CAPABILITY-DATA confirm service primitive containing the received data to the user.

4.3.5   Activity management

The activity management procedure is used to make available to the presentation user the activity management functionalities provided by the session layer. In this way a PPM may support the P-ACTIVITY-START and P-ACTIVITY-RESUME request and indication service primitives, the P-ACTIVITY-END, P-ACTIVITY-INTERRUPT and P-ACTIVITY-DISCARD request, indication, response and confirm service primitives.

When the context restoration functional unit is selected, the activity management procedure affects the defined context set.

4.3.6   Synchronization and resynchronization

The synchronization and resynchronization procedures are used to make available to the presentation service user the synchronization and resynchronization facilities provided by the session layer. In particular, the resynchronization procedure has influence on the defined context set when the restoration functional unit has been selected.

4.4 Abstract syntax notation one

Information to be transferred by the lower layers of the communication architecture are typically simple in their structure, so that they are usually represented by a simple sequence of binary octets. A significant example is given by the frame structure defined for the IEEE 802.4 standard (token-bus, see Chapter 2). When higher level layers are considered, parameters and data to be transferred become more complex; an example is given by information managed by system and user modules placed at the application layer. A typical example is the data structures required by an electronic mail system or a distributed store system where each transaction involves complex elements composed of many fields, some of which are optional or to be set to default values. What the application wants is to preserve the meaning of the information to be transferred to a remote user. This cannot be done at the lower and intermediate levels of the communication system, whose main purpose is to provide pure transfer services for octet strings. Hence this property has been introduced at the presentation layer in such a manner that each value to be transferred is completely described using an abstract notation without determining the representation of the value. Even if a data element is defined to be of a specified type, this does not mean that it has the same representation: a variable of type *integer* in one computer may have a different syntax in terms of the number of bits and position of the sign bit, for example, from an *integer* type in another computer. This means that even if the information components are of the same type, their structure may be different. Associated with the abstract notation, therefore, there is a corresponding coding method that converts each field in the information unit, defined according to the abstract notation, into the associated concrete syntax form. It is, then, the latter which is transferred between the application entities, so that the exchanged information unit has a common meaning to both entities.

According to the ASN.1 standard [ISO8824], every object to be transferred must be defined through the use of three basic elements: a *type*, which refers to the collection of potential values the object may assume, a *length* to identify the octet number for the data field, and a *value*, which is a specific instance of the type. A type may be composed of a sequence of simpler types, so that it becomes easy to build new complex types, defined as *constructed types*, suited to a wide spectrum of applications. Each type is given a *tag*, which may also be specified by the user.

A single tag may be defined for more than one type since no conflict arises when different contexts are considered. On the contrary, when more occurences of a single type have to be distinguished from each other, the user can assign them different tags. Four classes of tag are specified in the standard. The most important is the *uni-*

versal class, which is only used for a single or a structured type, such as, for example, *integer* or *sequence*, specified in the international standard. *Application* class tags are assigned to types by other standards and can be assigned to only one type. *Private* tags are not used by standards, they are made available for user needs. The last class is represented by the *context-specific* tags, which are interpreted in the context in which they are used. It should be noted that tags were introduced for machine use and not for human readers. However, even readability may be improved when certain types must be distinct.

4.4.1   Language elements

A context-free grammar can describe the structure of ASN.1 types as shown in Figure 4.6. In this grammar the terminal symbols are written in capital letters. All production rules have the following form:

definition ::= rule

The starting symbol of the grammar is ModuleDefinition and alternatives within a rule are given using the | symbol as a separator.

The first production allows a module, containing all specifications for data structures involved in a specific application or the complete set of protocol data units (PDUs) related to a particular protocol entity, to be defined as a *module*:

ModuleName ::= Name DEFINITIONS "::="
BEGIN ModuleBody END

Name is used to identify the module containing the type definitions, hence it must be used only once, so that type definition duplication can be avoided. It should be noted that if a module contains type descriptions for data structures of an ISO standard, such as FTAM, or MOTIS, the module name is specified according to the following schema:

ISOnumstd-idstd

where *numstd* is the number of the international standard, composed of four digits, whilst *idstd* is a suitable acronym for the international standard; as an example, to specify the file transfer access and management standard the term FTAM is used: in this case the module name is ISO8571-FTAM.

The body of the module contains all the type definitions and assignments for that application.

When a type or a value defined in another module has to

ModuleDefinition ::= Name "DEFINITIONS ::= BEGIN" ModuleBody "END"

ModuleBody ::= AssignmentList | Empty

AssignmentList ::= Assignment | Assignmentlist Assignment

Assignment ::= Name "::=" Type

Type ::= ExternalType | BuiltinType

ExternalType ::= Name "." Name

BuiltinType ::= PrimitiveType | ConstructedType | TaggedType

PrimitiveType ::= Integer | Boolean | BitStr | OctetStr | Any | Null | ObjId

ConstructedType ::= Sequence | SequenceOf | Set | SetOf | Choice

TaggedType ::= Tag Type | Tag "IMPLICIT" Type

Integer ::= "INTEGER" | "INTEGER" "{" NamedNumberList "}"

Boolean ::= "BOOLEAN"

BitStr ::= "BITSTRING" | "BITSTRING" "{" "NamedBitList" "}"

OctetStr ::= "OCTET STRING"

Any ::= "ANY"

Null ::= "NULL"

ObjId ::= OBJECT IDENTIFIER

Sequence ::= "SEQUENCE" "{" "ElementListType" "}" | "SEQUENCE {}"

SequenceOf ::= "SEQUENCEOF" Type | "SEQUENCE"

Set ::= "SET" "{" ElementListType "}" | "SET {}"

SetOf ::= "SETOF" Type | "SET"

Choice ::= "CHOICE" "{" AlternativeTypeList "}"

Tag ::= "[" Class UnsignedNumber "]"

Class ::= "UNIVERSAL" | "APPLICATION" | "PRIVATE" | Empty

NamedNumberList ::= NamedNumber | NamedNumberList "," NamedNumber

NamedNumber ::= Name "(" UnsignedNumber ")" | Name "(" "-" UnsignedNumber ")"

NamedBitList ::= NamedBit | NamedBitList "," NamedBit

NamedBit ::= Name "(" UnsignedNumber ")"

ElementListType ::= ElementType | ElementTypeList "," ElementType

ElementType ::= NamedType | NamedType "OPTIONAL" | NamedType "DE-FAULT" Value

NamedType ::= Name Type | Type

AlternativeTypeList ::= NamedType | AlternativeTypeList "," NamedType

UnsignedNumber ::= Digit | UnsignedNumber Digit

Digit ::= "0" | "1" | "2" | "3" | "4" | "5" | "6" | "7" | "8" | "9"

Empty ::=

Figure 4.6   BNF grammar for ASN.1.

be used, an external reference is possible according to the following rules:

> *ExternalType ::= Name "." TypeName*
> *ExternalValue ::= Name "." ValueName*

where *TypeName* represents the name of the type defined in the external module *Name* and *ValueName* is the name of the value.

A type or a value can be defined according to the following rules:

Table 4.4   ASN.1 primitive and constructed types.

ASN.1 Types	
c Type	c Description
Primitive types	
BOOLEAN	true or false
INTEGER	arbitrary length value
BITSTRING	sequence of 0 or more bits
OCTETSTRING	sequence of 0 or more bytes
NULL	no type
OBJECT IDENTIFIER	object name
ANY	union of all types
Constructed types	
SEQUENCE	ordered list of types
SEQUENCE-OF	ordered list of a single type
SET	unordered collection of types
SET-OF	unordered collection of a single type
CHOICE	a type taken from a given list

$$TypeDefinition ::= TypeName \text{ ``::='' } Type$$
$$ValueDefinition ::= ValueName\ Type \text{ ``::='' } Value$$

where *TypeName* must be different from the native types of the ASN.1 notation which are shown in Table 4.4, where they have been classified as *primitive* and *constructed* types. Primitive types represent the basic elements of the language which can be used to build up other more complex types composed of basic and other constructed types.

BOOLEAN is a primitive type with two distinguished values, TRUE and FALSE, and can be used to define a logical variable. The INTEGER type represents the whole positive and negative numbers including zero as a single value. An integer variable can assume values without any limitation. However, distinguished values can be specified for an integer variable which may have more than two states:

$$color ::= INTEGER\ \{white(0),\ green(1),\ red(2),\ yellow(3)\}$$
$$DayOfTheMonth ::= INTEGER\ \{first(1),\ last(31)\}$$

BITSTRING is a primitive type whose distinguished values represent an ordered sequence of zero or more bits, there is no limitation for the string length, which, in general, could be different from a multiple of eight:

Operation ::= BITSTRING {read(0), write(1), execute(3), delete(4)}

The bits in the string are set to 1 or 0 depending on whether the corresponding action is allowed or not.

The BITSTRING type can be used to describe a bit map as an ordered collection of logical values, to express the state of a binary condition associated with each element of the sequence:

NetworkNodes ::= BITSTRING {first(1), last(24)}
- - node j is alive if bit j is set to one, dead in the other case

A double hyphen is used to introduce a comment, which in ASN.1 is often used to specify that information not supplied by the language; a typical example is shown by the maximum size of a SEQUENCE OF type, which cannot be expressed directly by the language, hence a comment may be added to the declaration in order to specify the length of the data structure. In order to overcome these problems and other bugs contained in the original standard, new specifications have been introduced, they are indicated as *addenda*.

Other strings can be defined in ASN.1 using the OCTET STRING type, which specifies an unlimited string composed of bytes. It is also possible to specify subsets of octet values using predefined types, reported in Table 4.5, such as *PrintableString* which includes all those values specified in Table 4.6, and *NumericString*, which includes the ten digits 0 through 9 and the space. It should be noted that Videotex, Teletex and Graphic string types have also been introduced. The standard also states that when suitable subsets are not available between those included in the predefined set, comments may be used to describe the character subset needed.

Another basic type is ANY, which can be considered as the union of all the ASN.1 types so that a variable declared this way may contain any value, whilst the primitive type NULL describes a null value, and is used to specify the effective absence of an element of a sequence, which will not be transmitted in case of data transfer.

The last type mentioned in the table is the *object identifier*, which refers to specific identifiers to be used for those libraries which intervene when a suitable abstract syntax and associated coding rules have to be chosen by remote entities for data transfer.

The value corresponding to such a type is obtained by an *object identifier tree* whose root corresponds to the International Standards Organization (ISO) and vertices refer to administrative authorities which are responsible for the definition of the values to be assigned to the arcs coming out from their respective vertices. Those values

Table 4.5   List of character set types.

Character set type	
Universal class number	Type name
18	NumericString
19	PrintableString
20	TeletexString
21	VideotexString
22	IA5String
26	VisibleString
25	GraphicString
27	GeneralString

Table 4.6   Characters which can appear in the PrintableString type.

Printable string	
Name	Graphic
Capital letters	A,B,...Z
Small letters	a,b,...z
Digits	0,1,...9
Space	(space)
Apostrophe	'
Left parenthesis	(
Right parenthesis	)
Plus sign	+
Comma	,
Hyphen	-
Full stop	.
Solidus	/
Colon	:
Equal sign	=
Question mark	?

Table 4.7 ISO assignment of the object identifier components values.

Object identifier		
Value	Identifier	Authority
0	ccitt	CCITT
1	iso	ISO
2	joint iso-ccitt	common agreement

Table 4.8 ISO assignment of the object identifier components values for the second level of the tree.

Object identifier	
Value	Identifier
0	Standard
1	Registration-authority
2	Member-body
3	Identified-organization

are numeric elements and represent the object identifier value components. An ordered sequence of those values builds up a unique identifier for one of the objects sited at the end of the tree path. In other words, starting from the root of the object identifier tree, each value component identifies an arc of the tree. Table 4.7 gives the arc values of the first level of the tree starting from the root, whilst Table 4.8 gives the values for the arcs starting from the ISO vertex. Going on, the arcs coming out from the 'standard' vertex refer to the specific international standard identified by the number of the international standard itself. Below this, a single arc exists if the standard includes a unique part, otherwise there are as many arcs as there are parts, each one identified by the effective number of the part. The subsequent arcs are defined by the specific part of the international standard. An example is given by the following object, *iso standard 8571 part 4 ftam-pci(1)*, which is represented by the following codes:

1 0 8571 4 1

In this code the last digit, 1, is the arc value assigned by the *ftam* international standard, *part 4*, for the object *ftam-pci* also defined there.

Table 4.4 also reports the so-called constructor types, which allow more complex types to be defined by using the primitive ones. The first constructor mentioned in the table is the type *sequence*, which defines an ordered sequence of other types. Its function can easily be compared to the *structure* type used in the C language. As an example, let us consider the definition of a complex data structure which identifies a user in a computing system; when the C language is used, the following definition may be used:

structure {
user_name char,
password char,
account integer
} user

whilst using ASN.1 types it becomes:

user ::= SEQUENCE
{ userName VisibleString,
password VisibleString,
account INTEGER
}

Hence the SEQUENCE type describes a sequence whose types may differ and whose order is significant. Any type may be included in the sequence, in particular even other constructed types may be used in the definition block.

When a collection of variables, whose type is the same and whose order is important for the preservation of the information semantic content, has to be defined, a SEQUENCE-OF type is used. It can be compared to an array definition used in C or Pascal; however, there is a difference since, whilst the array definition specifies the size of the object, this is not done for the ASN.1 SEQUENCE-OF type. However, this problem has been solved in an addendum to the standard. Any type may be used in the definition, also constructor types, as shown in the following example:

```
allUsers ::= SEQUENCE OF
{ user
}
```

The SET type represents a fixed and unordered list of types; it resembles the SEQUENCE type, in fact the only difference is that the latter is an ordered list of values, whilst the SET type states a free order. Such types allow a data structure to be defined without introducing any limitation for the order to be used when transmitting the information. The SET-OF type specifies an array data structure, where the order of the elements belonging to it is insignificant. It should be noted in the following example that, since no order is specified, equal-type variables may be sent to the receiver without it being able to assign the correct semantic to the whole data structure. To avoid this problem, a *tag* is used in the context of the data structure to distinguish the different variables so that the correct semantic of the information may be reconstructed. The tag is reported as an integer number in square brackets. The following example shows the use of the SET and SET-OF type:

```
employee ::= SET
{
name [0] VisibleString
surname [1] VisibleString
address [2] VisibleString
country [3] VisibleString
}
```

For the SET-OF type:

```
staff ::= SET OF employee
```

The CHOICE type is used to describe a variable extracted from a collection. Even in this case a context specific tag is used to completely describe the variable chosen, so that the receiving entity can correctly rebuild the information. As an example, let us consider the following definition, which specifies part of the remote operation protocol, giving the description for the application protocol data units involved in the communication:

Remote_Operations_APDUs DEFINITIONS ::= BEGIN

ROSEapdu ::= CHOICE {
[1] Invoke,
[2] ReturnResult,
[3] ReturnError,
[4] Reject }

Invoke ::= SEQUENCE {
invoke/id INTEGER,
Operation_value Op_Value,
Argument ANY OPTIONAL }

Op_Value ::= INTEGER {
ConfirmedEventReport (1),
UnconfirmedEventReport (2),
ConfirmedGet (3),
ConfirmedSet (4),
ConfirmedAction (5),
ConfirmedCompare (6),
UnconfirmedSet (7),
UnconfirmedAction (8) }

ReturnResult ::= SEQUENCE {
invoke/id INTEGER,
result ANY OPTIONAL}

ReturnError ::= SEQUENCE {
invoke/id INTEGER,
error Error,
result ANY OPTIONAL}

Error ::= INTEGER {
TooManyParameters (1),
NonExistentOperation (2),
ParameterLimitExceeded (3),
OperationError (4) }

Reject ::= SEQUENCE {
invoke/id CHOICE { INTEGER, NULL },

```
      problem CHOICE {
      [0] IMPLICIT GeneralProblem,
      [1] IMPLICIT InvokeProblem,
      [2] IMPLICIT ReturnResultProblem,
      [3] IMPLICIT ReturnErrorProblem }}

      GeneralProblem ::= INTEGER {
      unrecognizedAPDU (0),
      misTypedAPDU (1),
      badlyStructuredAPDU (2) }

      InvokeProblem ::= INTEGER {
      duplicateInvocation (0),
      unrecognizedOperation (1),
      mistypedArgument (2),
      resourceLimitation (4),
      initiatorReleasing (5),
      invalidLinkedId (6) }

      ReturnResultProblem ::= INTEGER {
      unrecognizedInvocation (0),
      resultResponseUnexpected (1),
      misTypedResult (2) }

      ReturnErrorProblem ::= INTEGER {
      unrecognizedInvocation (0),
      errorResponseUnexpected (1),
      unrecognizedError (2),
      UnexpectedError (3),
      misTypedParameter (4) }

      END
```

The name of the module is Remote_Operations_APDUs and gives
the abstract description of the PDUs involved in the protocol implementing the Remote Operation Service. In this case the ROSE
protocol data unit may be of four different types. Only one of them
is valid for a specific action required by the protocol, as indicated
by the CHOICE constructor. In other words, if an *invoke* protocol
data unit must be sent to the remote entity, the first type is chosen,
which defines a protocol data unit composed of three elements: an
invoke identifier, the operation code of the action required (specified
in this case as a type Op_Value, defined immediately afterwards in
the module as an integer field) and an argument field which contains
the parameters needed by the operation itself.

In another case a *ReturnResult* type protocol data unit must
be sent to the remote entity; it can be seen in the event that, in

this case, the protocol data unit includes only two elements: the invoke/ID and the result field. It should also be noted that each element of the choice type is tagged; this is made necessary by the fact that the receiver cannot know *a priori* which type will be chosen by the transmitting entity, hence the only way to make it known is to provide an identifier for each type included in the choice structure that will be interpreted by the receiving entity.

Another useful type available in ASN.1 is the so-called *generalized time* which includes a string representing the calendar date with a four digit representation of the year, two digits representing the month and two digits for the day without any separators; this string is immediately followed by another string composed of the time of the day. Hence the string 149210081403.23 means 3 minutes, 23 seconds after 2 p.m., on the eighth of October 1492. In this way a standardized approach for time date is guaranteed. For historical reasons another type has been maintained, it is the *universal time* which uses a six byte string for the year, month and day, followed by a four or six character string for the time, depending on the precision required.

In order to take into account the fact that some fields in a generic data structure may have default values or may be not included in the current instantiation of the data, the keywords DEFAULT and OPTIONAL are used. If one of them is present, the encoding rules ensure that the encoding for a sequence or a set type is the same for the corresponding type without the optional or default elements. In particular, for a default element a value is also specified in the declaration; it will be used by the receiver to set the correct value for that element even if no transmission has occurred from the sending entity. To this purpose, it should be noted that if any field belonging to a SEQUENCE or SET type is declared to be optional, some fields of the data structure may be transmitted, and others not, without the receiving entity being able to decide which element corresponds to the information layout. As has already been pointed out previously, the use of a tag solves this problem, since a new identifier is introduced for typing all the information items transferred between the communicating entities.

A tagged type is a new type which maintains the semantics of the original type, but has a different identifier so that another instantiation of the original type is forced. This approach allows encoding schemes to distinguish the two different types. A tag is completely specified by two different elements: a *class*, and a *number*. Four classes are available. The *universal* class refers only to the types defined in the ASN.1 international standards, in fact they are agreed by ISO and CCITT, and cannot be used by others. The *application* class refers only to the types contained inside a single module definition, hence once a specific application tag has been used, it cannot be duplicated for another type in the same module. The *private* tag may be used by the implementors for their applications, whilst in the last case the *context specific* tag is used within the scope of a local environment (within another type, such as a sequence, set or choice type). It should be noted that, in this case, there is no limitation in the use of the tag, since it is sufficient that each new tag is not duplicated within the environment where it has already been defined. If two different environments are considered, then a duplication is possible, since the scopes of the two environments are disjointed.

When tags are used each item of information transferred to the destination includes a tag and a type specification, this leads to an increase in the amount of data to be moved on the network; in order to avoid redundant information being sent, a mechanism is introduced based on the reserved word IMPLICIT which is inserted after the tag. In this case only the tag is coded and sent without the type being specified. The following example shows the use of the reserved words introduced above:

> *employee ::= [PRIVATE 4] IMPLICIT SEQUENCE {*
> *name [0] IMPLICIT OCTET STRING,*
> *surname [1] IMPLICIT OCTET STRING,*
> *address [2] IMPLICIT OCTET STRING,*
> *country [3] IMPLICIT OCTET STRING,*
> *married [4] IMPLICIT BOOLEAN DEFAULT FALSE*
> *age [5] IMPLICIT INTEGER OPTIONAL*
> *}*

In this case each item is still represented by a type, a length and a value, but all the types are tags; in particular the outer level type is described by a private class tag, whilst all the others are context specific.

The advantage of this will become more apparent in the following paragraph where the encoding and decoding rules associated with ASN.1 are examined.

4.4.2 The transfer syntax

The previous section introduced ASN.1 as a language to be used for the definition of abstract syntaxes. A particular abstract syntax, defined using that notation, describes a set of data structures related to a specific application, which may be a standard module such as FTAM or Network Management, or the whole data environment of a user developed application such as a flight management system. The application layer modules may then define the types of information which must be transferred by using presentation services.

This paragraph introduces the rules for translating the abstract syntax, which describes the format of the information into machine manageable code. The set of rules applied to the abstract

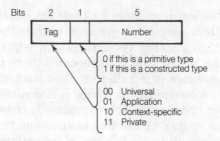

Figure 4.7   Bits organization of the tag.

syntax allows a transfer syntax to be defined for the values of the various types contained in the abstract syntax and the same rules apply to the concrete syntax to rebuild the abstract syntax that is usable by the applications. It should be noted that these rules are applied at the time of communication by the presentation service provider; on the presentation layer, in fact, lies the responsibility for negotiating the appropriate abstract and concrete syntaxes, in order to make information transfers possible.

Given a generic type of the ASN.1 notation, the coding mechanism is based on the following elements:

- an *identifier*, composed of one or more octets
- a *length field*, composed of one or more octets
- a *data field*
- an *end of data field*, when length is not specified; it includes one or more octets.

It should be noted that when the field length assumes a specific value, defined in the specifications, an *end of contents flag* is required to signal the end of the information block related to the type considered. Figure 4.7 reports the first byte organization; it specifies the information type as a tag. The two most significant bits indicate the *class* of the tag, whilst bit 5 indicates if the type is *primitive* (bit 5 is set to 0) or *constructed* (bit 5 is set to 1), and the other 5 bits contain the *tag number*, if it is lower or equal to 30 decimal (i.e. 11110 binary).

When the tag number exceeds the limit given above, further bytes are associated with the first, so that an unlimited range is available. In this case, the five bits belonging to the first byte are coded as a sequence of logical ones, whilst the following bytes, except the last one, have their most significant bit set to one and the other seven available for the number representation; the last byte has the most significant bit set to zero, so that the end of the octet sequence is signaled, and the other seven bits are also used for number representation. Hence the tag number is represented as an unsigned binary integer, having the most significant seven bits in the second

Table 4.9   End of contents representation.

End of contents		
End of contents	Length	Contents
00	00	absent

octet and the less significant part in the last byte of the sequence, where the most significant bit is set to zero.

As has been pointed out before, the length field may assume two different configurations: the former is based on the explicit indication of the bytes number involved in the object representation, the latter is based on the signaling that the end of data is given by the use of an end flag. The explicit length indication includes a short and long form for the representation of the length value. The short form consists of a single octet in which bit seven is set to zero and bits six to zero encode the length value (which must be lower than 127 decimal) as an unsigned binary value. When the length value exceeds 127, an initial octet followed by one or more octets must be used. The initial octet has bit seven set to one, whilst bits six to zero encode the number of subsequent octets as an unsigned binary integer. Hence the length value is coded in the subsequent octets as an unsigned binary integer, with the first subsequent octet being the most significant eight bits of the value. As an example the value 205 can be coded as follows:

10000001 11001101

In this case the first octet says that one more byte is following; this byte contains the value to be coded.

When an end-of-content flag has to be used, the length field is composed of a single octet having bits seven to one and all others set to zero. In this way the content can be coded with an end of contents flag at the end of the data sequence. It should be noted that the standard considers end-of-content as a primitive type, without contents, whose tag is universal and with number 0, as shown in Table 4.9.

The contents octet consists of zero or more octets, according to the type associated with the value. In the case of a boolean value, the contents consist of a single octet and a value TRUE can be encoded as specified in Table 4.10.

It should be noted that the tag is characterized by the class *universal* and number 1 as shown in Figure 4.7.

When integers are considered, contents include one or more octets. If more than one byte is used, then the integer is a two's

Table 4.10   A boolean representation.

Boolean		
Boolean	Length	Contents
01	01	FF

Table 4.11   Bit string representation using a primitive type.

Bit string		
Bit string	Length	Contents
03	05	044141414130

complement binary number having the high significant bits in the first octet and the low significant bits in the last octet of the sequence.

Bit strings are encoded in ASN.1 according to both primitive and constructed types. In the former case an octet is used to specify the type, the second octet is used to indicate the number of unused bits of the last octet belonging to the string, whilst the subsequent octets contain the effective bit sequence; the number of unused bits is in the range zero to seven. The constructed type allows the creation of a string composed of substrings, as pointed out in Table 4.12, where a bit string is shown as a constructed type. The structure of the corresponding primitive type is also given in Table 4.11. In both cases the universal tag is used; the string to be coded, using the hexadecimal representation is '414141413'H. It should be noted that the first byte of the contents sequence specifies the number of unused bits.

Octet strings are also encoded in both the primitive and constructed type, in the latter case an end of contents flag is used. A null value is encoded as shown in Table 4.13.

A sequence value is a constructed elements composed of one data value from each of the types listed in the ASN.1 definition of the sequence type; it should be noted that the encoding of a data value may, but need not, be present for a type which was declared to be optional or default. The following example will clarify the coding process:

employee ::= SEQUENCE {
name [0] OCTET STRING,
surname [1] OCTET STRING,
country [3] OCTET STRING,

Table 4.12   Bit string representation using a constructed type.

Bit string				
Bit string	Length	Contents		
23	80	Bit string	Length	Contents
		03	02	004141
		03	03	04 414130
EOC	Length			
00	00			

Table 4.13   Null representation.

Null		
Null	Length	Contents
00	00	absent

married [4] BOOLEAN,
age [5] INTEGER
}

The value {name 'Peter', surname 'Bush', country 'Great Britain', married TRUE, age 34} is coded according to the example shown in Table 4.14.

A sequence-of value differs only in the fact that the structure includes a unique type for all the elements which may belong to the sequence.

The approach for encoding a set type corresponds to that followed for the sequence type, the difference lies only in the fact that, whilst a sequence has an ordered organization, a set value can be composed as an unordered collection of values related to the types listed in the ASN.1 definition, without regard to the order specified in the definition itself.

The encoding of a choice type must be the same as the chosen type, hence a real encoding for it does not exist, since it always coincides with the structure of the data being transferred. In order to describe the approach the following example specifies two different choices for the type color:

color ::= CHOICE {
flag BOOLEAN,

Table 4.14   A sequence type structure representation.

Sequence				
Octet string	Length	Contents		
30	13	Octet string	Length	Contents
		04	05	'Peter'
		04	04	'Bush'
		Boolean	Length	Contents
		01	01	FF
		Integer	Length	Contents
		02	01	22

```
number INTEGER
}
```

Hence the type color will be coded as a boolean type or as an integer, according to the selection valid at the current time.

Tagged types are the means to solve ambiguity in the type definition. In particular, as has been pointed out previously, universal tags are used in the international standard to define application-independent types that must be distinguishable from all other types. An application tag allows a data type to be defined inside a specific presentation context, so that it can be totally distinguished in its representation from all other types defined for that context, the following example defines an application wide type:

```
employee ::= [APPLICATION 9] SEQUENCE {
name [0] OCTET STRING,
surname [1] OCTET STRING,
country [3] OCTET STRING,
married [4] BOOLEAN,
age [5] INTEGER
}
```

Context specific tagged types are used to distinguish the members of a set or other constructed types:

```
employee ::= SET
{
name [0] VisibleString
surname [1] VisibleString
address [2] VisibleString
country [3] VisibleString
}
```

Table 4.15   Coding of an IA5 string.

Type ::= **IA5string**		
IA5 string	Length	Contents
16	05	'Peter'

Table 4.16   A IA5 string representation using a constructed type.

Type ::= **[APPLICATION 9] IA5string**				
[APPICATION 9]	Length		Contents	
69	07	IA5string	Length	Contents
		16	05	'Peter'

Since the order used to transfer the information specified in the type *employee* is unknown, the use of a tag helps the receiver to rebuild the correct structure of the information.

When the implicit keyword is not used in the definition of the tagged type, the encoding is constructed and the contents octets must contain the complete encoding of the base type. On the contrary, if the implicit keyword was used in the definition, then the encoding must be constructed only if the base encoding is constructed and the contents octets are the same as the contents octets of the base encoding. Table 4.15 shows the coding of the string 'peter' without the explicit keyword for the tag being used. If a tagged type has to be used, then the tag defines a constructor type as shown in Table 4.16.   If the implicit keyword is used, the tag defines a primitive type as shown in Table 4.17.

The object descriptor type allows the definition of a human readable string identifying an object; the same authority which assigns the object identifier to an information object usually also indicates the object descriptor.

In the following an example of the coding mechanism to generate a concrete syntax from an abstract description of a specific type is given. The abstract notation gives a description of the 'division' data type as follows:

Division_Structure ::= [APPLICATION 0] IMPLICIT SET {
ident [0] IA5String,
Division_num Teleph_num,
Date_found [1] Date,
Name_of_Resp [2] Name,

Table 4.17   A IA5 string representation using the IMPLICIT keyword.

Type ::= [APPLICATION 9] IMPLICIT IA5string		
IA5 string	Length	Contents
49	05	'Peter'

>   *employers [3] IMPLICIT SEQUENCE OF employee_Detail*
>   *}*
>
>   *employee_Detail ::= SET*
>   *{*
>   *name*
>   *date_of_birth [0] Date*
>   *}*
>
>   *Name::=   [APPLICATION   1]   IMPLICIT   SEQUENCE*
>   *{*
>   *given_name IA5String*
>   *family_name IA5String*
>   *}*
>
>   *Division_num ::= [APPLICATION 2] IMPLICIT INTEGER*
>   *Date::= [APPLICATION 3] IMPLICIT IA5String –*
>   *YYMMDD*

The value assigned to the abstract definition of the *Division_Structure* type can be formally described using ASN.1 as follows:

> *{ Denom = ' Production ', Division_num = 100,*
>   *Date_of_found = '860609',*
>   *Name_of_Resp = { given_name = 'Dave',*
>   *family_name = 'Smith'}, employers = {{{given_name =*
>   *'Mark', family_name = 'Dark'}, Date_of_birth = '601111'},*
>   *{{given_name = 'John', family_name = 'Red'},*
>   *Date_of_birth = '621111'}}}*

The representation in octets of the record value stated above is shown in Figure 4.8. The values of identifiers, lengths and the contents of integers are shown in hexadecimal digits per octet. The values of the contents of characters and strings are shown as text, one character per octet.

Transfer code								
Division_Str	Length				Contents			
60		Ident	Length			Contents		
		A0	0C	IA5String	0A		'Production'	
		Division_num	Length			Contents		
		42	01			64		
		Date_Of_found	Length			Contents		
		A1	8	Date	Length		Contents	
				43	6		'890609'	
Name_of_resp	Length				Contents			
	0F							
		Name	Length			Contents		
		61	0D	IA5String	Length		Contents	
				16	4		'Dave'	
				16	5		'Smith'	
[3]	Length				Contents			
A3	32	SET	Length			Contents		
		31	30	Name	Length		Contents	
				61	2E	IA5String	Length	Contents
						16	4	'Mark'
						16	4	'Dark'
				Date_of_birth	Length		Contents	
				A0	20		Contents	
						Date	Length	Contents
						43	6	'601111'
		SET	Length			Contents		
		31	17	Name	Length		Contents	
				61	15	IA5String	Length	Contents
						16	5	'John'
						IA5String	Length	Contents
						16	3	'Red'
				Date_of_birth	Length		Contents	
				A0	20	Date	Length	Contents
						43	6	'621111'

Figure 4.8   Bit string representation using a constructed type.

4.5   Conclusions

In this chapter the presentation layer has been examined, pointing out its main functions dealing with the manipulation of data structures, their description in terms of abstract types and their representations according to the requirements to be satisfied for achieving efficient transfer activities. Data types and values can be described using the ASN.1 notation, which supports primitive types such as boolean, integer, bit string and octet string, and also constructed types, for complex data structures. ASN.1 also defines a transfer syntax so that data can be transferred unambiguously.

MAP and TOP support the basic functionalities such as connection establishment and release. Multiple contexts management are also devised. Data representation is obtained using the ASN.1 specification for format descriptions. Different abstract syntaxes for file transfer, network management, directory service and message transfer have already been defined.

References

[ISO8822]   ISO 8822 *Connection Oriented Presentation Service Definition*, 1988.

[ISO8823]   ISO 8823 *Connection Oriented Presentation Protocol Specification*, 1988

[ISO8824]   ISO/DIS 8824 *Specification of Abstract Syntax Notation One (ASN.1)*, 1986.

[ISO8825]   ISO/DIS 8825 *Specification of Basic Encoding Rules for Abstract Syntax Notation One (ASN.1)*, 1986.

Chapter 5

Basic Application Protocols

5.1 Introduction

At the application layer a set of programs oriented to user needs is made available. These programs operate by using the presentation services when communication activities have to be supported. Some of these applications are so common that suitable standards have been developed. A typical example is given by message and file transfer services, for which specific protocols have been developed to avoid a situation where each developer might implement tools that were unable to work with each other.

Three building blocks are introduced in this chapter. They represent a special class of applications, since their services are necessary for the correct operation of other application tools. One of these deals with *connection* management and is referred to as the *association control service element* (ACSE), whilst another is related to the *management* of the *network* operations. The last one provides a way to find the network addresses of people and services available on the network, it is called the *directory service*.

Network management [ISO7498/4] plays a basic role in the network environment, being responsible for collecting information and for providing reports on the usage of the network media by the network devices and resources, so that correct network operations

199

can be guaranteed.

As is well known, a network's primary activity is to deliver information from one side of the network to another, in this case the transport responsibility of each network component is clear. In fact, *de facto* and formal standards have rapidly emerged for each type of information transmission, so that rules for information exchange between network devices have been specified in detail.

The management responsibilities of a network component are less obvious: for example if an error arises in one piece of network equipment, it should inform its network of the problem so that specific mechanisms may take suitable actions to overcome it. In a heterogeneous network, it is difficult to control efficiently the various network stations unless some sort of standardized procedure is used. For example, it is important, when operating connection oriented protocols, that the recovery timers are set to a realistic value for the current traffic conditions. It is more difficult for an individual station to determine the correct value to be used for its timers than it is for a centralised manager to monitor the network traffic and supply the suitable values when the condition changes. Hence information related to the use and performance of each network device and resource must be transferred to an individual network manager in order to allow for network planning, accounting and configuration. For this purpose the single device should also facilitate the tracking and changing of the network configuration, cooperating directly with the network manager.

Information types involved in the management process can be summarized and classified as follows:

- **maintenance data**: used by technicians in order to carry out problem detection and diagnosis for preventive maintenance
- **operation data**: used by the network operators to provide for performance monitoring, network access and configuration
- **planning data**: used by network planners to develop network design and modeling, also for simulation purposes.

It should be noted that the internal management of a station is not standardized; in fact what the standards describe are methods of describing objects to be managed within stations such as timers, counters, events, and their values or states. A protocol for the transfer of this information between management processes is also specified, so that remote management interactions can be easily generalized.

In large systems such as networks the need for *directory capabilities* arises from the desire to isolate the user of the network from the frequent changes which may characterize the system activity. Typical examples are represented by the two following cases:

- different kinds of objects may enter or leave the network without warning, and objects may move either as a single entity or in a group

- the connectivity of the objects will change over time, and this is particularly true when network nodes are considered.

This can usually be solved by placing a level of indirection between users and the objects with which they are dealing. This implies that users refer to objects by name, rather than by, for example, address. For this purpose, the directory provides the required mapping functions.

Another aspect is the requirement to provide a more user friendly view of the network without being involved in complex mechanisms to retrieve information or find objects. In this case the directory provides specific solutions, such as aliases to refer to the same object using different identifiers or simple mechanisms such as the 'yellow-pages' to find objects using some attributes related to the objects to be accessed.

Both MAP and TOP specifications address these topics. In particular, network management for multi-vendor networks appears to be a basic point for the interoperability of different devices. Hence, even if stable ISO standards for the complete spectrum of this capability are not currently available, MAP specifications and the *TOP Network Management Application Profile* refer to available ISO and IEEE documents, supplementing as necessary to provide a basic level of functionality.

For directory services, the MAP specifications and the *TOP Directory Service Application Profile* refer to the *National Bureau of Standards* (NBS) *Stable Implementation Agreements*, which are derived from harmonized ISO and CCITT standards.

5.2 Association control service element

This module, placed at the application layer, was introduced by ISO after it was realized that the various application modules available had the same functional requirement in terms of connections (at this layer they are called *association*), to be established for supporting communications. Hence, instead of introducing the same service primitives in all applications, which would have meant replicating the same functionality in all the modules, it was decided to make a single point available where this functionality could be found and used by all applications. This module is called the *association control service element* (ACSE). Figure 5.1 shows the application layer in the MAP/TOP protocol profiles, pointing out that all modules at that layer use association management services made available by ACSE [ISO8649/2], [ISO8650/2]. In this way ACSE services provide a standard mechanism to establish and terminate associations between standard and private applications. Hence an application program, which is generally indicated as an *application entity* (AE)

Table 5.1   ACSE service primitives.

OSI ACSE Primitive	Description
A-ASSOCIATE request	Request for association establishment
A-ASSOCIATE indication	Indication of an association request
A-ASSOCIATE response	Response to the association request
A-ASSOCIATE confirm	Confirm for the requested association
A-RELEASE request	Request for the release of the association
A-RELEASE indication	Indication of a release request
A-RELEASE response	Response to the release request
A-RELEASE confirm	Confirm for the requested release
A-U-ABORT request	Abrupt release request from the user
A-U-ABORT indication	Abrupt release indication
A-P-ABORT indication	Abrupt release indication from the service provider

and is known through its *application entity title*, may establish an association with a remote application entity known through its application entity title.

If we consider the ACSE primitives, it should be noted that those functions can be also available using the presentation service primitives directly. However, the reason why they have been introduced at the application layer is that a sort of functional symmetry has to be maintained for all upper layer operations. This means that if the transport, session and presentation layer use specific primitives to manage connections, then the application layer also has to operate according to the same scheme. A further argument is represented by the fact that special functions will soon be introduced at this level, such as authentication which is a typical application

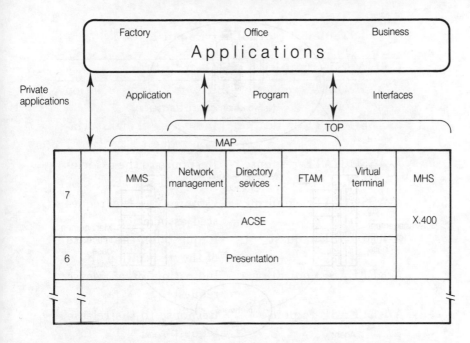

Figure 5.1 The application layer and the ACSE module.

procedure. This functionality will be available at the association establishment time. Table 5.1 lists the ACSE primitive services. An association may be established by the *A-ASSOCIATE* service, which is confirmed and allows the definition of all those parameters needed to describe the association. The A-RELEASE service supports a negotiated termination of the association, whilst *A-U-ABORT* provides an abrupt interruption of the connection requested by the user. Also, the service provider may decide to destroy the association and this is done by the use of the *A-P-ABORT* service. This service is used by the service provider when, for example, a local or remote transport connection failure occurs.

5.3 Management architecture

The network management architeture is based on five elements, which are described in Figure 5.2:

The first element, the *network manager application*, consists of a specific application devoted to management purposes; it can be located in a single node or distributed on more than a single site. It also includes an operator interface, so that management mechanisms can be controlled directly by a network operator, who can read and alter data, exercise control over the whole network and access reports related to management operations. In most cases the network

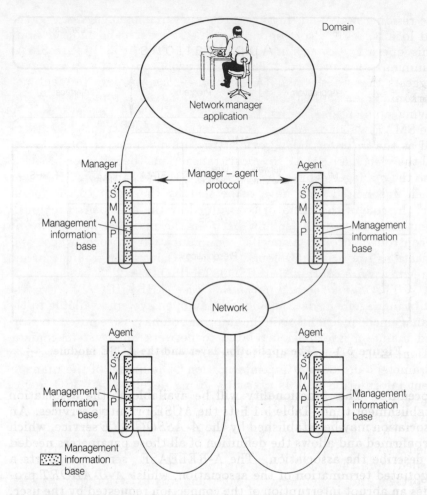

Figure 5.2   Architectural scheme and components of network management.

manager application is a simple command line interface to the process responsible for management mechanisms. Enhanced solutions include an expert system requiring very little interaction with the human operator. It should be noted that these items have not yet been addressed by standardization activity, hence MAP/TOP management specifications do not give suggestions about the development of the application which is, then, left up to the implementor's initiative.

The second and third elements, named the *manager* and the *agent*, are two processes whose interaction allows management mechanisms to be implemented. A basic component of an agent or manager entity is the *system management application process* (SMAP), which collects management information from the different layers on the residing node and, further, exchanges management data, gathered locally, with a corresponding process located in another node. This operation is accomplished using a specific SMAP-to-SMAP communication protocol. The model proposed in the specification suggests that those SMAPs which have one or more resident network manager applications be *manager* SMAPs, whilst others not having applications are called *agent* SMAPs. In this architecture the SMAP which originates a transaction for data transfer is indicated as the *initiator*-SMAP, whilst the other process involved is called the *responder*-SMAP. In most transactions the initiator-SMAP is also the manager, whilst the responder-SMAP is an agent. However, when unsolicited data have to be sent by the agent to the manager, the role of the initiator is assumed by the agent. As previously mentioned, data transfer flow between the manager and the agent is controlled through a specific communication protocol whose specifications are being developed by the ISO working groups; current agreements are contained in [ISO9596] [ISO9596/2].

The *management information base* (MIB) [IEC/JTC1] is the set of management data included in an open system available to the management mechanisms. The information base is required to store and maintain information related to network and system configuration, such as current and historic performance, failures, security parameters and accounting information. The model of the management information base is presently being developed by ISO; hence the work is still in a preliminary state and several member bodies have proposed that the OSI directory model be adopted.

The MAP/TOP network management subcommittee has identified a set of activities in specific functional areas so that information needed from the various layers could be chosen and defined since, at present, no layer management standards exist for the network, transport, session, presentation and application layer modules. In particular for the lower two layers (the physical and data-link) the management information from the IEEE 802 layer management standard [IEEE802/1] has been selected.

To meet organizational needs for flexibility, the MAP/TOP management environment has been partitioned into a number of domains. A domain, which is the fifth basic element of the management architecture, is composed of a set of agents which refer to the same manager. In other words, the manager's domain contains all the agents which deliver notifications to it; however, an agent may belong to more than one domain as Figure 5.3 points out. In that case the *i*-domain contains the *i*-manager, the *i*-agent(a) and the *i*-agent(b), whilst the *j*-domain includes the *j*-manager along with the *j*-agent(c) and the *i*-agent(d). The *i*-managed-object[a,k] is handled by both the management domains.

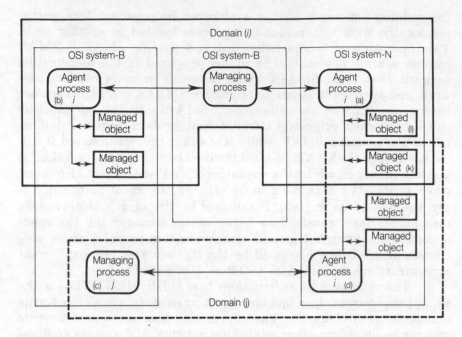

Figure 5.3   The network management environment and domains.

5.3.1   Network manager application

The *network manager application* can have a number of functions associated with it. According to ISO specifications [ISO7498/4] five functional areas have been identified, as listed below:

- configuration and name management (CM)
- performance management (PM)
- fault management (FM)
- security management (SM)
- accounting management (AM).

Only the first three areas have been addressed in the MAP/TOP management specifications, being the most important aspects on an operational basis:

- **configuration management**: allows access and control of the logical and physical configuration of the system
- **performance management**: ensures control of the network and node performances
- **fault management**: allows detection and diagnosis of failures using specific tests handled by the manager.

These functions can be distributed in any number of network manager applications over the network or in the same node as an alterna-

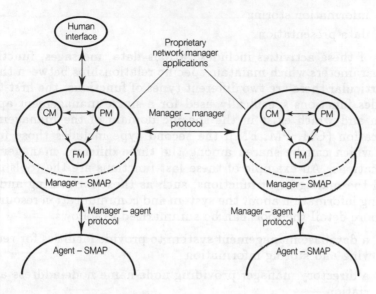

Figure 5.4   Manager-to-manager and manager-to-agent communication.

tive. For the sake of simplicity it is supposed that all the three functions are included in a single application located in a single node.
Figure 5.4 shows two manager–agent couples, which can exchange
information through a generic manager–manager protocol.

In this case the network manager applications include the management functions previously introduced. Each function interacts
with the agents to extract information about the system, monitor the
current state, access communication resource parameters for tuning
operations and so on. Management mechanisms are implemented via
the transfer of different message types obtained using the manager–
agent protocol. Figure 5.4 showed how a management application
can be partitioned: the management application is generally located in the network manager node, and the agent represents the necessary mechanisms to be assigned to each node in the network so
that information can be treated locally and then transferred to the
manager. In particular an agent SMAP supports all basic mechanisms to accomplish control and monitoring functions on network
resources, while management policies are left to the network management applications. In general such policies are developed by the
network operators, which use management tools made available by
the network management application. In the MAP/TOP management specifications the network management application provides
the following operating activities:

- data collection
- data processing

- information storing
- data presentation.

Each of these activities includes various data, messages, functions and parameters which maintain specific relationships between them. In particular there are two different types of functions: the first type includes functions specifically used for a single management application and which exist in the specific domain of the management application (CM, PM, FM); the second type includes those functions which can be shared among the three different management applications. An example of these last functions are the tools used by all the management functions, such as those for storing and retrieving information about the system and communication resources. For more detail the tools can be summarized as follows:

- a database management system to provide facilities for retrieving and storing information
- a directory manager providing node-name node-address association
- network services providing file transfer and graphics capabilities
- facilities for reading/writing parameters.

Data to be processed have also been categorized into two classes: data for *administrative* purposes and *real-time* data. These latter are used to manage the running of the system and can be monitored and changed on the fly, thus having an immediate effect on the system state. The administrative data refer to all the system aspects not related to real-time needs. A typical example is represented by the software version running on a specific node in the network.

5.3.2   System management structure

A MAP/TOP system which can participate in MAP/TOP management is shown in Figure 5.5. MAP/TOP management is obtained by means of functions provided by *systems management*, *N-layer management* and *N-layer operations*.

The whole system is controlled through the *systems management functions*, which provide mechanisms so that system parameters can be adapted to changing environmental conditions. Such mechanisms allow local environment access and, cooperating with remote peer systems, the management of the various physical resources involved in the communication process and in the network.

The systems management functions are supported by the *system management application process* (SMAP), which is local to the system and has access to the whole system capabilities and parameters, being able to manage all aspects of the system both individually and in a coordinated way. In particular, in the MAP/TOP

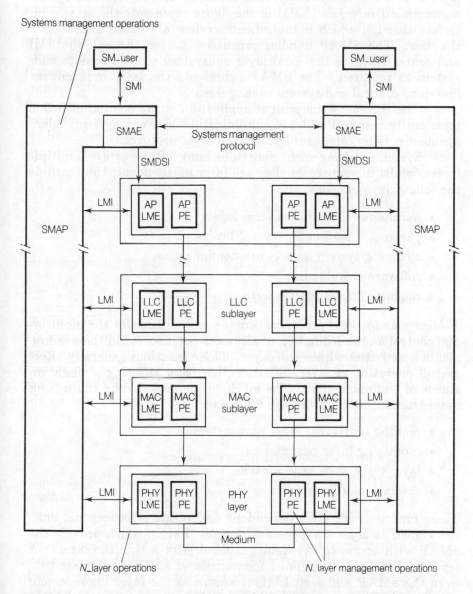

Figure 5.5 The layered architecture and the network management components.

context, the system management application process can manage the layer protocol entities providing mechanisms operating on a single layer or in a coordinated approach across several layers. The *system management interface* (SMI) in the figure represents the service interface through which management services are made available to the user. The SMAP handles primitives passed through the SMI and routes them to the local layer subsystem or to a remote end-system as required. The SMAP represents the layer independent functions of local end-system management.

The *systems management application entity* is an application layer entity responsible for communication between systems management entities, and uses application layer protocols.

Systems management functions may often involve multiple layers, whilst in some cases they are layer independent; they include the following operations:

- parameter change in several layers
- parameter reading in several layers
- changing system or network configuration
- software downloading
- requests for diagnostic tests.

N-layer management functions provide mechanisms for the monitoring, control and coordination of all resources involved in the communication activities within a *N*-layer. These functions generally affect overall operation of layer entities rather than affecting a single instance of communication. The mechanisms provided by the *n*-layer management functions are the following:

- reading individual layer parameters
- modifying layer parameters
- layer tests, such as loopback
- activation of layer services.

These functions are layer dependent and reside in conceptual entities known as *layer management entities* (LME), which provide the SMAP with access to the manageable objects within the layers. A separate LME type is defined for each layer and the interface between the SMAP and each LME is known as the *layer management interface* (LMI), across which LM-primitives are passed to the LMEs. When a user request identifies a local mangement entity, the SMAP routes it to one of the LMEs. At the LMI a LM-primitive is generated which contains a subset of the information contained in the original SM-primitive.

The *N-protocol operation* provides those management functions which are required to agree on a particular set of parameters used for an instance of communication. Actions carried on by *N*-protocol operations are local to the instance of communication and they are processed together with the normal activity of the communication protocol supported by the layer. Examples of management data processed within an *N*-protocol are:

- parameters associated with connection establishment related to a single instance of communication

- parameters used during a communication instance, which modify the environment in which the communication instance is operating

- parameters used for connection release which handle information related to the instance of communication being released

- reports of errors and performance processed during the operation of the instance of communication.

Like OSI assumptions, MAP/TOP specifications have defined systems management as an application, so that most management functions are performed using layer 7 communication facilities. However, taking into account the whole characteristics of MAP applications, different solutions have been introduced. In particular, the system management application entity may use a specific *link service access point* (LSAP), usually called the *management link service access point* (MLSAP), when the full seven layer connection oriented facility is not available. In this case, systems management protocols may use the connectionless services made available by the data link layer. Figure 5.6 shows both the solutions.

5.3.3 Management mechanisms

An SM-user request can identify either local or remote management entities. A request naming a local entity is routed by the SMAP to one of the LMEs, whilst, if a remote entity is indicated, an additional mechanism is involved in order to transfer the information to a remote SMAP for delivery to the remote LME. Hence MAP specifications define two different approaches for the management mechanisms: a local approach, which is simple in its implementation, since it does not require specific operating protocols and information to be processed is locally available, and a remote approach, which involves a general purpose management protocol.

Three elements defines a management mechanism:

- **Attributes**: these include counters, timers and thresholds which can be read, set and reset by the manager. Both local and remote attributes can be accessed by the manager.

- **Actions**: these are directives to a layer subsystem to take specific actions, such as state modification, initialization, or a test activation. Actions can be carried out locally and remotely.

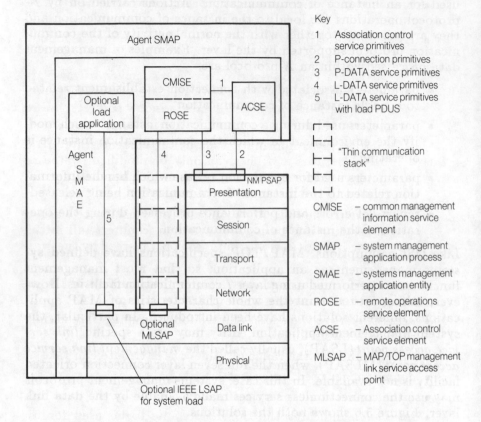

Figure 5.6   Management interface, full and reduced profiles.

- **Events**: these interactions are initiated by the responder system and not by the SM-user. They are notifications to either a local or remote SM-user that a local event of some significance has occurred. Examples are: an event counter has passed a preset value threshold, a significant type of protocol error has occurred or a particular user request has been received.

Attributes, actions and events are described in the MAP/TOP specification by means of a template, which is then used for the description of specific items. For attributes the template has the following structure:

- *Name*: identifies the mechanism as described by means of the abstract syntax notation
- *Description*: gives general information about the object
- *Requirement Reference*: defines the functional area involved by the object (configuration, performance or fault management)

- *Standard Reference*: indicates what standard defines the parameter, if it is already defined
- *Class*: indicates one of three different classes defined as follows:
  - *characteristic*: read-only or read-write parameters; this attribute can be accessed by the manager to alter the configuration of the system; usually it is readable and writable by the manager; timers, window and retry values belong to this class
  - *status*: gives information about the current state of the resource; this attribute can only be modified by the resources themselves, not by the manager, hence it is usually read-only with respect to the manager
  - *statistic*: this attribute contains information referred to a certain time period, for example, counters fall in this category; statistic attributes can only be read by the manager
- *value type*: indicates a constraint for the structure of the attribute, such as integer on 16 or 32 bits
- *access*: refers to the access allowed for the manager, read-only, read-write, write-only
- *range*: indicates the range of values the attribute can take
- *default value*: used for characteristics only
- *initial value*: used for statistics only
- *threshold*: indicates the threshold name to be used for the current statistic.

The *threshold* mechanism can be associated with all attributes. As an example let us consider the counter *StatCount*, the threshold is defined as *StatCountThld*, which is the threshold name reported in the *threshold* field of the template describing the attribute StatCount.

Agents use thresholds to generate *event notification messages*, which are sent to the manager when the statistic attribute used to trace the specific event reaches the threshold specified for it. In order to implement such operation, the agent maintains an internal count for the occurrences of the event, and when the counter reaches the associated threshold, the message is sent to the manager and the counter reset. The agent maintains an internal counter, which is unavailable to the manager, for each threshold. As shown in the flow chart shown in Figure 5.7, when the threshold is 0 then no event count is performed and so no event message can be notified.

For actions the template is characterized by the following fields:

- *Name*: identifies the mechanism as described by means of the abstract syntax notation

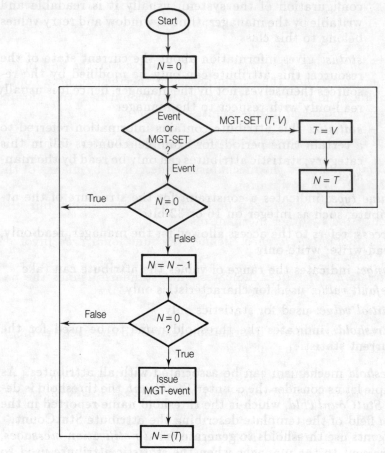

Event = Occurence of event to be counted

N = Counter variable

MGT-SET (T, V) = MGT set value of threshold T to value V

Figure 5.7   Threshold operation scheme.

- *Description*: gives information on the operation
- *Requirement Reference*, defines the functional area involved by the object
- *Standard Reference*: indicates what standard defines the parameter, if it is defined
- *Class*: action
- *Action arguments*: parameters needed to carry on the operation
- *Action results*: this parameter is reported at the end of the operation, when the action has been specified to be a confirmed action; in fact, if the action is unconfirmed, this parameter is not taken into account.

In case of events the template has the following form:

- *Name*: identifies the mechanism as described by means of the abstract syntax notation
- *Description*: events can be triggered on thresholds, but also generated by other mechanisms
- *Requirement Reference*: defines the functional area involved by the object
- *Standard Reference*: indicates what standard defines the parameter, if it is defined
- *Class*: event
- *Event information*: information related to the event is included for use by the manager.

In order to exemplify an attribute description, a counter for the retransmitted transport protocol data unit (TPDU) [ISO8073] is considered:

- *Name*: NumberTPDURetransmitted
- *Description*: the counter is incremented each time a TPDU is retransmitted
- *Requirements reference*: performance management (determination of congestion), fault management (validation of underlying services)
- *Standard reference*: ISO 8073 Section 6.19 and 12.2.1.2.j
- *Class*: statistic
- *Value Type*: Counter16 (non-negative increasing integer, which, unless specified otherwise, wraps to 0 when incremented beyond 65 535)
- *Range*: 0..65 535
- *Initial Value*: 0

- *Threshold*: none.

The following example refers to an event description; the transport layer has been chosen for it:

- *Name*: transportThresholdEvent
- *Description*: refers to a common event triggered when any Transport Threshold is reached.
- *Requirement Reference*: fault management (fault notification), performance management (congestion notification)
- *Class*: event
- *Event information*:
  - threshold-ident – identifies the threshold which triggered this event
  - destinationReference – identifies the destination
  - sourceReference – identifies the source
  - callingTSAPID – identifies the calling TSAPID
  - respondingTSAPID – identifies the responding TSAPID
  - reasoncodeDRTPDU – reason code from the DRTPDU sent or received
  - reasoncodeERTPDU – reason code from ERTPDU sent or received
  - TPDU – the TPDU sent or received which caused the event to occur.

An example for the action description refers to the system management and corresponds to the operation which allows a manager node to be defined:

- *Name*: addManagerName
- *Description*: a manager name and the associated MAC address are added to the managerName table. Existing entries with the same name are overwritten
- *Requirements Reference*: configuration management (Registration – delivery of events)
- *Standard Reference*: none
- *Class*: action
- *Action arguments*:
  - manager name
  - Manager MAC Address
- *Action Result*: success – failure.

5.3.4 Management services and protocol

The MAP/TOP architecture for management requires that management interactions between managers and agent occur at the application layer, as also specified by the OSI standard. In this case services made available by the connection oriented association control service element [ISO8649/2] (ACSE) and the remote operation service element [ISO/DP9072/1] (ROSE) are used to transfer *common management protocol data units* (CMPDU). Since MAP networks include reduced protocol profile systems such as MiniMAP, bridges and MAP/EPA nodes, the concept of the *thin communication stack* is introduced, so that information exchange could always be performed at the application layer. In this case, in fact, a lower layer has to be accessed directly, so the OSI functions in the missing layers, such as segmentation and reassembly, which are typical transport functions, must be handled by using the support provided by the stack. It has the responsibility of bridging the gap in the OSI model between the application layer, to which the SMAP belongs, and the OSI (N)-layer service being used. Such a solution should guarantee minimal connection oriented or connectionless services for the layer above the data-link. The extreme case is represented by the unavailability of the thin stack; in this case, MAP management specifications introduce the possibility of mapping the remote operation application protocol data units (ROAPDU) onto the data-link services made available at the management link access point (ML-SAP). Protocols for the management operations correspond to the common management information protocol [ISO9596] [ISO9596/2] (CMIP), which provides request/replay services. The management transactions are generated by an initiator SMAE and carried on by a responding entity in a remote system. Further, an unsolicited event report service is also provided, in this case the system defined as *responder* operates as an event generator, whilst the *initiator* works as a collector of information produced by the events in the remote systems. Services suported by the CMIP are listed in the following. They can be separated into four main categories:

- *Data manipulation services*: allow management data to be processed, and include two different services:
  - *M-[CONFIRMED-]GET*: provides the capability for retrieving data from the management information base
  - *M-[CONFIRMED-]SET*: provides the capability for modifying data in the management information base.
- *Event reporting services*: since the managing and managed systems must be aware of events generated asynchronously or on a periodic basis, event reporting services are available; these services may be activated or deactivated, but do not require specific mechanisms, such as polling, to retrieve data

about events. Both confirmed and unconfirmed services are provided:

- — *M-[CONFIRMED-]EVENT-REPORT*: allows a system to report information about events to its manager.

- *Direct control services*: provide the capability to request a remote system to perform some action which can permanently alter the state of a resource in the remote system, or carry on some transient behavior:

  - — *M-[CONFIRMED-]ACTION*: which allows the invocation of an action.

- *Association related services*: which allow a connection to be established at the application layer:

  - — *M-INITIALIZE*
  - — *M-TERMINATE*
  - — *M-ABORT*.

The association related services assume the availability of the association control service element (ACSE), whilst the other services use the *remote operation service element* (ROSE) to provide the transaction-oriented service needed by the system management application entity. Four protocol data units are supported by the ROSE:

- *ROIV-PDU* (invoke PDU): represents the invocation of an operation to be performed by an invoked ROSE user. The PDU contains an identifier *invokeid*, which is used to correlate the invoke request to the corresponding response, and an *operation code* used to specify the operation to be performed, followed by *parameters* strictly related to the operation itself.

- *RORS-PDU* (return result PDU): is used by an invoked ROSE user to replay the initiator user with the *results* of the requested operation; the PDU contains an *identifier*, which relates the PDU itself to the corresponding request (ROIV-PDU) previously sent by the initiator user, and an *argument* to qualify the information about the performed operation. This PDU is used by the management service only when a *confirmed* service has been requested.

- *RORE-PDU* (return error PDU): is used by an invoked ROSE user to report information about the unsuccessful completion of an operation previously requested by the initiator user. The PDU contains an *identifier* to correlate the response to the invoke request previously received, and an *error code* to describe the failure followed by an *argument* to qualify the reason for the failure. This PDU is used only when a *confirmed* service is requested.

L_DATA request/indication	
Sender LSAP (MLSAP)	Reserved LSAP for the exclusive use of the SMAE on the sending system
Destination LSAP (MLSAP)	Reserved LSAP for the exclusive use of the SMAE on the destination system (MLSAP)
L_SDU	Choice of ROIVapdu, RORSapdu, ROERapdu, RORJapdu

Figure 5.8 Mapping of a generic ROSE PDU onto the L-DATA service.

- *RORJ-PDU* (reject PDU): is used to reject a request sent by an invoking user as a consequence of a problem that arises because of the service user or the service provider. The PDU contains a *problem code* describing reasons for rejection.

It must be pointed out that all management services, with the exclusion of the association related services, may operate using either a *connection* oriented or a *connectionless* mechanism: the ROSE makes it transparent to its user, since it can specify what kind of approach must be used, taking into account the available underlying services.

Services from the underlying layer

The association control service element (ACSE) [ISO8649/2] provides the services to handle the association at the application layer; the primitives handling the association establishment and release are summarized in the following:

- *A-ASSOCIATE*: establishes the association
- *A-RELEASE*: negotiated release of the association
- *A-ABORT*: forced termination of the association due to user request
- *A-P-ABORT*: forced termination of the association requested by the service provider.

The presentation layer [ISO8822] makes the P-DATA service element available to transfer the ROSE protocol data units, while the datalink, when only connectionless services can be used due to the lack of intermediate layers, makes the L-DATA service element available to transfer the ROSE PDU. When connectionless services are required, the association establishment and information related are statically known. Figure 5.8 reports the mapping of a generic ROSE PDU onto the L-DATA service.

5.4   The directory system

Features of computer networks for industrial automation and process control are different, to some extent, from those found in other application fields such as distributed computing centers or office automation. A distinctive feature of industrial applications is the need to connect to the network a number of simple microcomputer based stations, where no mass storage (disks, for instance) is envisaged because of either cost or environmental problems. It turns out that one of the requirements for a suitable object location handler is that it should avoid overloading the main memory of smaller stations with a huge database used to perform the mapping between the name and specific attributes of the referenced object.

Furthermore, a closer look at the structure of the specific application software shows that a simpler solution can be devised. Industrial control is a typical example of an 'embedded application' environment where the interactions between a process and the other elements within the system are determined *a priori* by the programmer (or a group of programmers) of the application. Hence it differs from other applications where each process, in general, can communicate with any other task in the system. It turns out that the interactions of each process with other tasks are limited and, consequently, the amount of information to be stored in each node in order to facilitate the location of the object is also small, since each node only needs to know the attributes (such as the address) of the objects referenced by processes running on the node itself.

The need to store only small mapping tables on simple hosts can be satisfied in different ways. A classical solution is represented by a central name server placed in a host equipped with mass storage devices and able to manage the whole database required to describe any object in the network. Of course, a pure centralized solution incurs a performance penalty caused by the need for accessing the name server to implement any form of access to any object in the network. Hence some form of caching is necessary in the host where requests are issued.

Dynamic caching tries to minimize the memory occupation of the portion of the database cached, because only the mapping table entries referring to the most frequently used objects are copied from the central name server tables. However, the problem of updating the different copies cached in different hosts when an object is moved from one node to the other (or host address is changed) arises. Every approach must deal with the problem of ensuring the consistency of the distributed copies. Unfortunately this leads to a loss of efficiency in the location service and, moreover, complicates implementations.

Another important point about the software for industrial control is that the different processes are allocated taking into account the I/O characteristics of the different nodes. For example, if a process x has been designed to control the machine y, then it can be allocated only on node z, because it is the only one connected to y (note that, in order to achieve fault tolerance, z may be an intrinsically fault tolerant system, since the required proximity between I/O and CPU-memory subsystems allows the user to implement redundancy at the local level). It turns out that, in order to achieve fault tolerance, the application cannot be moved around just for the sake of load balancing or performance optimization; hence the system is quite static. Anyway, some mechanisms for process migration must be provided, because the programs performing some general management functions can be executed on different network stations. Fortunately, in most cases, object migration occurs rarely so that the efficiency of this operation does not influence the overall system performance.

The alternative to avoid inconsistencies among the different copies of the database used to locate the objects is to cope with them. Fortunately the local mapping tables used to locate the objects have the ability to discover whether an entry is correct or not by simply trying to access the object. It turns out that the inconsistencies (or better, the discrepancy with the current physical location of the object) are automatically detected whenever the table entry is used for access, because a wrong destination is reached, and the system will inform the requesting entity of the access failure. In the following, two directory service configurations are examined: in the first case the MAP/TOP directory system is described [MAP], while the subsequent paragraph examines the MiniMAP Dictionary [MAP], pointing out the solutions adopted for real-time requirements of the MiniMAP applications.

5.4.1 The MAP/TOP directory system

Directory services support user references to network objects in such a manner that additions, deletions and changes may succeed without the physical location in the network environment being known to the user. The directory system structure takes much from database organization without involving all the mechanisms provided for them. The main difference relies on the fact that for directory systems the expected update rate is much lower than the query frequency. For this purpose, it should be noted that the update frequency depends on the object dynamics rather than on the dynamic of the network. Another aspect is that when an update is to be performed, no instantaneous global commitment is required, in contrast with what happens for distributed databases. Moreover, as has been pointed out in the previous paragraph, transient conditions, where both old and new versions of the same information are available, can be accepted and suitably handled by the directory system.

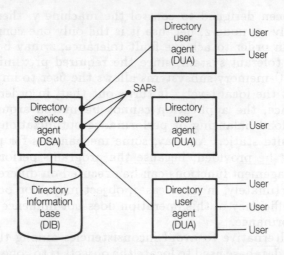

Figure 5.9   A directory system organization.

The model

In general terms the *directory* is composed of a collection of cooperating systems holding a logical database of information which describes a set of objects belonging to the real environment [ISO9594/1] [ISO9594/2]. The users of such a system include both people and computer programs which can read or modify that information, or part of it, subject to having permission to do so. A user can access the directory by the operations of a *directory user agent* (DUA), which is generally considered to be an application process and provides services to access information contained in the *directory information base* (DIB), as shown in Figure 5.9.

Services are quite simple and include modification and retrieval mechanisms. Access points to the DUAs are provided by the directory as pointed out in Figure 5.9. The directory is composed of one or more processes named *directory system agents* (DSAs) each of which may provide one or more access points to a directory user agent. Figure 5.10 shows a directory system composed of some DSAs which give rise to a distributed directory system, since DSAs may be located on different nodes. It should be noted that a DSA and a DUA may also reside on different physical nodes so that specific protocols [ISO9594/5] have to be used to obtain mutual remote interactions. A set of DSAs together with zero or more DUAs belonging to a single organization, such as a public telecommunications administration or a private administration, form a single environment, which is called a *directory management domain* (DMD).

Objects in the system are organized into classes, each one representing an object family which is characterized by specific attributes. An object class may be an object of another object class

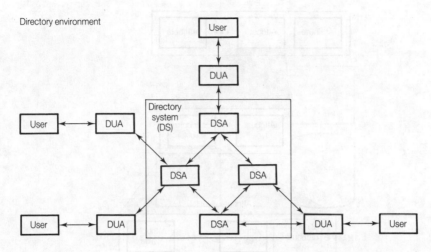

Figure 5.10 A distributed directory system configuration.

and, in this case, the objects belonging to the subclass are also considered as members of the parent class. Any object in the system is described by an *entry* in the DIB which is unique for each element. In other words, an entry fully represents an object belonging to the network. A mechanism is also introduced so that users are allowed to refer to a specific object by using different names: this is based on the use of the so-called *alias entry*. Figure 5.11 shows the structure of an entry.

The DIB structure has been planned according to the requirements of flexibility and performance, hence a tree structure has been adopted, called the *directory information tree* (DIT), which perfectly maps on the hierarchical relationship commonly found among objects; a typical example is represented by an employee who works for a department belonging to an organization sited in a particular country. A structural scheme of a DIT is also shown in Figure 5.12, where a simple example is considered.

The DIT is characterized by the following elements:

- the **vertices**, which are the entries of the DIB; in fact object entries may be either leaf or non-leaf vertices; it should be noted that alias entries are always leaf vertices and the root can be viewed as a null object entry;

- the **arcs** define the relationship between vertices. Referring to Figure 5.12 an arc from vertex 1 to vertex 2 means that the entry at 1 is the immediately *superior entry* of the entry at 2 and that the entry at 2 is the immediately subordinate entry at 1;

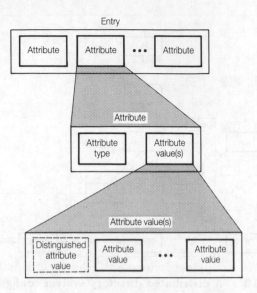

Figure 5.11   Structure of an entry.

- **naming authorities** associated with the entries, which control the subordinate entries for the object represented by each entry;
- **the root**, which represents the highest level of naming authority for the DIB.

Directory entries

Figure 5.11 points out the entry structure, which includes the elements listed below:

- *attribute*: represents the information of a particular type concerning an object and appearing in an entry describing the object in the DIB [ISO9594/6]
- *attribute type*: that component of an attribute which indicates the class of information given by an attribute
- *attribute value*: a particular instance of the class of information indicated by an attribute type
- *attribute value assertion*: a proposition, which may be true, false, or undefined, concerning the values of an entry
- *distinguished value*: an attribute value in an entry which has been designated to appear in the relative distinguished name of the entry.

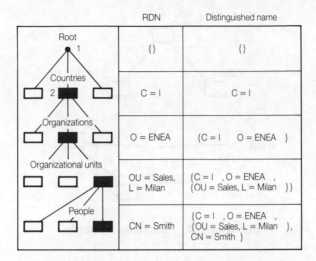

	RDN	Distinguished name
Root ●1	{}	{}
Countries 2	C = I	C = I
Organizations	O = ENEA	{C = I O = ENEA }
Organizational units	OU = Sales, L = Milan	{C = I , O = ENEA , {OU = Sales, L = Milan }}
People	CN = Smith	{C = I , O = ENEA , {OU = Sales, L = Milan }, CN = Smith }

Figure 5.12   An example directory hierarchy with definition of distinguished names.

An entry consists of a set of *attributes*. Each attribute provides a piece of information about the object to which the entry corresponds. As an example, for the attributes which may be present in an entry, naming information can be considered, such as the object's personal name, and also addressing information such as a telephone number. As shown in Figure 5.11, an attribute consists of an *attribute type* and the corresponding *attribute values*. In some cases the attribute types are or will be internationally standardized, while other types will be defined by national administrative authorities and private organizations. At most one of the values of an attribute may be indicated as a *distinguished value*; this value will take the part of the *relative distinguished name* of an entry.

An *attribute value assertion* (AVA) is a proposition which may be true, false or undefined, concerning the values of an entry. An attribute type and an attribute value are involved in the proposition. The value is undefined when the attribute type is unknown, the matching rule for equality comparisons is not defined, or the value does not conform to the data type of the attribute syntax. On the other hand, the AVA is true if the entry contains an attribute of that type, one of those values matches the value introduced in the proposition. The AVA is false in all other cases.

Names

In general terms a *directory name* is a construct that identifies a particular object from among the set of all objects [ISO9594/2]. A name must be unambiguous, that is, denote just one object. How-

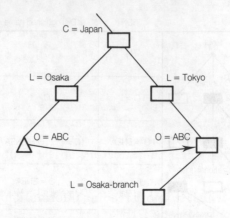

Figure 5.13   Aliasing example.

ever, a name need not be unique, that is, be the only name that unambiguously denotes the object, in fact more names may be used to identify the same object.

Each entry in the DIT has a unique *relative distinguished name* (RDN), which consists of a set of attribute value assertions, each of which is true, concerning the distinguished value of the entry.

The *distinguished name* (DN) of a given object is defined as the sequence of RDN of the entry which represents the object and those of all its superior entries in descending order. In the case of the root entry the name is defined as a null sequence, while the distinguished name of an alias entry is defined to be the sequence of RDN of the alias entry and those of all of its superior entries in descending order. Figure 5.12 shows the relationship between the relative distinguished name and the distinguished name. It should be noted that the vertex at the first level in the tree is characterized by an RDN composed of a single value assertion, as happens for the second level, while in the third the entry is characterized by a sequence of two attribute value assertions (D=Sales, L=Milan). In the column of the distinguished name, it can be noted that each entry in the signed path is characterized by its own distinguished name.

Particular attention has to be given to alias names, which provide a basis for alternative names for an object. Specifically an *alias name* for an object is a name where at least one of the RDN is an alias entry. Hence by aliases an object is permitted to have multiple immediate superiors. Alias entries cannot have subordinate entries, thus an alias must always be a leaf entry in the DIT as shown in Figure 5.13.

Service definition

Directory services are made available to the user through *access points* to the DUA as shown in Figure 5.9. Taking into account the various operations which can be performed on the directory data base, the access points have been defined according to the type of actions they can support. Hence, considering the directory as an object, a number of types of *ports* are available, each one associated with a specific interaction between the directory and a DUA [ISO9594/3]. In particular the directory object supports three kind of ports:

- *read-ports*: which support reading information from a particular named entry in the DIB
- *search-ports*: which allow an extensive exploration of the DIB
- *modify-ports*: which enable the modification of entries in the DIB.

In the same way a DUA object may be defined by taking into account that, from the viewpoint of the directory, the same ports are accessed by the DUA as a consumer of the services provided by the directory.

For the read port the following services are available: *read, compare, abandon*; for the search port the *list* and *search* services are provided, while *add_entry, remove_entry, modify_entry, modify_RDN* services are supplied by the modify port.

Each operation in the directory environment is based on the availability of arguments which qualify the action to be performed. The basic components are listed in the following:

- *service controls*: define constraints for the provision of the service and, in particular, they are based on the elements listed below:
  - *options*: this parameter may indicate that the chaining mechanism, rather than referral (see the following paragraph) is preferred to provide the service, or that the chaining approach is prohibited. Another value is used to indicate that copied information can be used instead of original ones, when a distributed directory is available
  - *priority*: three values are provided, low, medium and high, and indicate the priority of the requested service
  - *time limit*: this indicates the maximum elapsed time, in seconds, within which the service should be provided. If this constraint cannot be satisfied, then an error is reported to the requestor. If this parameter is omitted then no time limit is implied
  - *size limit*: this is used for the search and list operations and indicates the maximum number of objects to be re-

turned; according to the MAP specification the limit has been set to 20.

It should be noted that certain combinations of priority, time limit and size limit may result in conflict: a typical example is given by a short time limit, which could conflict with low priority, or a high size limit which could conflict with a low time limit.

- *security parameters*: they govern the operations of various security features associated with the different directory operations. In particular the most important elements are the following:

  - *certification path*: the certificate is used to identify the originator's distinguished name and verify the signature on the argument or result

  - *name*: it is the distinguished name of the first intended recipient of the signed argument or result

  - *time*: indicates the intended expiry time for the validity of the signature, when signed arguments are used

  - *target protection request*: this parameter indicates the requestor's intent regarding the degree of protection to be provided for the result. Two levels of protection are provided; a null value indicates that no protection is required, while the 'signed' value indicates that the directory is requested to sign the result, supposing that the directory itself may provide that facility.

- *requestor distinguished name*: it indicates the requestor of a particular operation, since it identifies the user directly. It must be present only if a signed result is required.

Another important parameter is represented by the *entry information selection* element which indicates what information is being requested from an entry in a retrieval service. An *attribute types* component specifies the set of attributes about which information is requested, in particular three options are available: if the *select* option is assumed then the attributes involved are listed and information about each specific attribute in the list can be returned if the attribute is present and access rights are valid; if the *all attributes* option is selected, then information is requested for all the attributes associated with the entry.

The *information type* component specifies if both the attribute type and attribute value are requested or the attribute type information only is needed.

Selected information from a specific entry is conveyed by an *entry information* parameter, which includes a *distinguished name* of the entry, a *from entry* element indicating whether the information has been obtained by the original entry (in this case the value TRUE is returned) or a copy of it (a value FALSE is returned).

In order to retrieve a specific set of objects, a *filter* is used, expressed in terms of assertions about the presence of values of certain attributes of the entry so that the objects to be retrieved can be directly accessed. A filter can be considered as a logical expression of elementary assertions, each one related to the presence of a value of an attribute of a particular type in the entry under test. Each logical operation is referred to a specific attribute also defined by a specific attribute type, and any assertion about the value of such an attribute is evaluated if there is accordance between the attribute type specified for the assertion and the type of the value. Assertions about the value of an attribute are evaluated using the matching rules associated with the attribute syntax defined for that attribute type. Assertions include the following cases:

- *equality*: this assertion is true when there is a value for the attribute which is equal to that proposed in the assertion
- *substring*: this assertion is set to true when the substring is contained in the value assumed by the attribute in the entry
- *greater or equal*: is true when the relative ordering, according to the algorithm chosen for such an operation, places the supplied value after any value of the attribute
- *less or equal*: is true when the relative ordering places the supplied value before any value of the attribute
- *present*: this is true when the attribute indicated is present in the entry
- *approximate match*: this is true if, according to locally defined approximate matching algorithms, a value of the attribute matches that which is asserted.

Directory read function

Two different operations are provided: a simple *read* and a *compare* operation. A read operation allows information to be extracted from a specified entry, or it may also be used to verify a distinguishing name, which means to point out whether or not the object exists in the database, given its distinguishing name. The following arguments qualify the read operation:

- *object*: identifies the object entry from which the information has to be obtained
- *selection*: this parameter defines what information is to be evaluated among the various attributes which are associated with the entry
- *common argument*: specifies the service controls applied to the request as already discussed in the previous paragraph.

The information obtained from the operation is reported in the *entry result* parameter, while the result of the operation is reported in the *common result* parameter.

When a value has to be compared to the value of a particular attribute type in a particular object entry, a *compare* operation may be used. The following parameters are involved:

- *object*: identifies the name of the particular object entry concerned with the operation

- *purported argument*: identifies the attribute type and the value to be compared with that in the entry

- *matched result*: contains the result of the comparison, and is set to true if the values were compared and matched, otherwise it is set to false

- *common argument*: specifies the service control applied to the request.

A specific service, called *abandon* has been introduced to allow the directory user the ability to abandon the operation previously initiated. It is characterized by a single argument, the *invoke identifier*, which identifies the operation to be abandoned.

This operation can only be used for the read, compare, list and search operations. A DSA may abandon an operation locally. If the DSA has chained or multicast the operation to other DSAs, it can, in turn, request them to abandon the operation.

Directory search function

Two search operations are available: a *list* command and a *search* operation. The list operation is used to obtain a list of the immediate subordinates of an explicitly identified entry. Among the different parameters the most important are the following:

- *object*: identifies the name of the object entry whose immediate subordinates have to be extracted

- *subordinate*: this parameter conveys information about the immediate subordinates, if they exist, of the named entry

- *limit problem*: this parameter indicates whether the time limit, size limit, or an administrative limit has been exceeded

- *unexplored*: this parameter indicates whether regions of the DIT were not explored; this information can be used by the DUA so that further access can be carried out using other access points if needed.

When a portion of the DIT has to be examined for entries of interest, then the search operation may be used. The arguments, in this case, are:

- *base object*: it identifies the object entry relative to which the search operation is going to be used
- *subset*: indicates whether the search is to be applied to the base object only (which means that only the first sublevel of the DIT is of interest to the operation) or all subordinates of the base object (which means that the whole subtree will be of interest to the search operation)
- *filter*: this argument is used to eliminate those entries from the search space which are not of interest for the aims of the search; in this way only information about entries which satisfy the conditions expressed by the filter will generate information to be returned
- *entry*: this parameter conveys the requested information from each entry which satisfies the conditions expressed by the filter.

The *common result* parameter indicates the result for each operation.

Directory modify operations

These operations include four actions, all of which can modify the directory entries: *add entry, remove entry, modify entry* and *modify RDN*.

The *add entry* operation is used to add a leaf entry to the DIT, in fact in its present form the service is intended to be used to add entries which will remain as leaves, such as entries for people or application entities. This service has no facility for controlling the physical placement of the entry, in fact the general directory service only supports adding an entry to the same DSA in which the immediate superior resides. The arguments associated with the operation are the following:

- *object*: identifies the entry to be added. The identifier of the immediate superior of the actual entry can be obtained directly from the name of the object by removing the last RDN belonging to the entry to be created
- *entry*: this argument contains the information which represents the entry to be created, including the attributes of the RDN.

The *remove entry* operation is used to remove a leaf entry, including alias entries, from the DIT. This service, like the add entry operation, only supports removing an entry which is in the same DSA in which the immediate superior resides. The *object entry* parameter identifies the entry to be deleted from the DIT.

An entry previously created may be accessed for corrections and changes by the *modify entry* operation, which provides the following actions:

- *add a new attribute*: this defines a new attribute to be added to the entry specified in the argument; if the attribute already exists, an error is generated

- *remove an attribute*: the argument refers to an attribute to be removed from the specified entry

- *add attribute values*: the argument specifies an attribute to which a sequence of values has to be added to the already existing ones

- *remove attribute values*: specifies one or more attribute values to be removed from the attribute specified in the argument.

An argument named *object* identifies the entry to which the modification, should be applied, while the *changes* argument conveys an ordered sequence of modifications, each one being considered as an atomic action. In this way, if any of the individual modifications fails, then a suitable error is generated and the entry is left in the state it was prior to the operation.

The relative distinguishing name of a leaf entry in the DIT may be changed using the *modify RDN* operation. In this operation the *object* parameter identifies the entry whose RDN is to be modified, while the *new RDN* argument specifies the new RDN of the entry. If an attribute value in the new RDN does not already exist in the entry, it is normally added to the entry itself and, in particular, if the *delete old RDN* flag is set, then all attribute values not included in the new RDN are completely deleted. On the other hand, if the flag is not set, then all old attributes remain in the entry, but not as a part of the RDN.

5.4.2 Distributed directory model

In the previous paragraph the abstract service description has been introduced, without being involved in the implementation details for those services. The specification of the abstract directory object does not address the physical realization of the directory and, in particular, it does not address the specification of the directory system agents (DSAs) through which the services are provided, and which contain the directory information base (DIB). Beside that, the specifications do not consider whether the DIB is centralized and stored in a single DSA or distributed over a number of DSAs [ISO9594/4].

Directory distribution

It should be noted that each entry in the DIB is administered by a unique DSA's administrator which has the authority to control and administer that entry. Even if copies are not supported by the directory system, it is nevertheless possible to replicate information according to two different approaches:

- a bilateral agreement between the DSAs involved, so that mechanisms to maintain and manage the replicated information can be fully specified

- copies of an entry may be acquired by storing locally a copy of an entry which results from a request using a dynamic mechanism.

The originator of the request will be informed if the information returned in response to a request has been obtained from a copy or not. In any case the originator may ask, using a suitable parameter in the request, that the information be obtained from an original entry instead of from a copy.

Each DSA in the directory system maintains a part of the whole DIB, which may be described as a subtree of the whole directory information tree (DIT). The subtree may contain one or more *naming contexts*. In general terms, a naming context may be described as a partial subtree of the DIT, which starts at a vertex and extends downwards to leaf and/or non-leaf vertices. The starting and ending vertices constitute the border of the naming context, and non-leaf vertices can be considered as the starting point of another naming context.

As illustrated in Figure 5.14, a DSA's administrator may control a set of naming contexts that are completely disjointed; in fact it can be noted that the contexts do not share the same superior entry. The DSA maintains the sequence of RDNs which leads from the root of the whole DIT to the initial vertex of the subtree constituting the naming context. This sequence of RDNs is called the *context prefix*. In order to control the administration of the whole contexts located in the different DSAs, each DSA's administrator may delegate administrative authority for any immediate subordinates of any entry held locally to another DSA. In this case the DSA which delegates authority is called a *superior* DSA, while the context that holds the superior entry is called the *superior naming context*. Figure 5.14 gives an example where a DIT is logically partitioned into five naming contexts, named c1, c2, c3, c4, and c5, which are physically distributed over DSA1, DSA2, and DSA3. According to the configuration illustrated in the example it can be easily understood that the physical allocation of the naming contexts may be chosen referring to the real requirements for the network organization. Certain DSAs may be planned to contain those entries which represent higher level naming domains, such as the organizational structure of a large company, while the other DSAs may be used to handle those naming contexts representing primarily leaf entries.

It should be noted that, even if the physical mapping of the DIT into DSAs is potentially arbitrary, the information location and management is simplified if the DSAs are configured to maintain a small number of naming contexts. When a user or a program needs

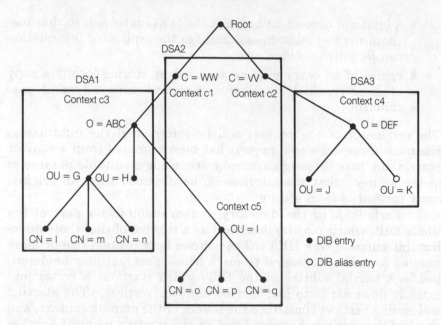

Figure 5.14   Interrelationship between contexts.

information about a network object, the user or program submits a request to be processed by the DUA on the basis of the available information which is, in particular, the presentation address of at least one DSA, which will be contacted initially. The interaction between the user and the distributed directory must succeed transparently without the user being aware of the location of the object to be accessed. Hence, from the user's viewpoint the directory is virtually located in a single DSA. This fact is satisfying only if each DSA can identify and eventually interact with all the DIB fragments held by other DSAs. To this purpose, two types of information have to be supported by each DSA:

- **directory information**, which is the collection of entries related to the naming contexts for which the administrator of a specific DSA has administrative authority

- **knowledge information**, which represents the naming contexts handled by a particular DSA and describes also how it fits into the whole DIT hierarchy. This information is used by the *distributed name resolution* process for locating the DSA which has administrative authority for a particular entry for which a name was specified.

Hence a naming context is uniquely identified when a context prefix, constituted by a sequence of RDNs leading from the root of the DIT to the initial vertex of the naming context, and a collection of knowledge references are given. In particular, a naming context must contain the following knowledge references:

- internal references which define the internal structure of the part of the DIT belonging to the naming context
- subordinate and non-specific subordinate references to other naming contexts.

Since the directory must ensure that each entry can be reached by every DUA in the system, then a *reference path* composed of a sequence of references must be available at each DSA, so that all naming contexts within the directory can be addressed. In order to make the directory able to operate, a minimum amount of information constituted by a minimal set of references must be available. For this purpose each DSA maintains the following information:

- *subordinate knowledge*, which is represented by a reference to those DSAs which handle naming contexts subordinated to the context held by the administrative authority. In this way, starting from the root, each naming context may be reached since a reference path exists for any of them.
- *superior knowledge*, which is a reference path to the root context.

The root context represents an exception to the rule introduced above. In fact, since the autonomy of different countries or large organizations must be preserved, the root context cannot be assigned to a unique physical entity represented by a specific DSA. Hence the solution adopted introduces the concept that, for the resolution process, the root context is also to be maintained by those DSAs which have administrative authority for naming contexts that are immediately subordinated to the root. Looking at Figure 5.14, it can be seen that all those DSAs belong to the first level of the tree. Thus each first level DSA in the naming context hierarchy must be able to simulate the functionality of the root DSA. This can be obtained only if the DSAs involved in the mechanism have a complete knowledge of the root naming context, which means that the root context has to be replicated into each first level DSA. In this case administrative authority on the root context will be available at all the DSAs which hold the root naming context. The first level DSA will also maintain a reference path to each other first level DSA, and all other DSAs will have a superior reference path to any arbitrary first level DSA.

Every DIB entry may be reached by each DSA in the directory system when each DSA has got knowledge about the entries which it itself holds, other than about subordinates and superiors. Hence the following types of knowledge reference must be available for a DSA:

- *internal reference*: consists of the RDN associated with a DIB entry and an internal pointer to where the entry is stored in the local DIB. The DSA exercises control over the entries stored locally by use of the internal references.

- *subordinate reference*: consists of an RDN related to an immediate subordinate DIB entry, a distinguishing name (application title) of the DSA to which administrative authority was delegated and the presentation address of the DSA.

- *superior reference*: consists of the distinguishing name (application entity title) of a DSA holding the superior entry of the naming context and the presentation address of that DSA. Each DSA not containing contexts of the first level maintains one superior reference which relates the context prefix with the fewest number of RDNs. When a new non-first level DSA is introduced in the system, it must have a minimal amount of knowledge, which is represented by the superior reference. Subordinate references and cross references will provide additional information. On the other hand, when a first-level DSA is added it must acquire the root context and inform the other first-level DSA of its presence.

- *cross reference*: is based on a context prefix, a distinguishing name (application entity title) of the DSA which has the administrative authority for that naming context and the presentation address. This reference is used to increase the time response of the distributed name resolution process, thus it can be considered as an optional solution.

- *non-specific subordinate reference*: it includes the distinguishing name (application entity title) of a DSA which holds one or more immediately subordinate naming contexts and the DSA presentation address. This type is optional and is used for those cases in which a DSA is known to contain subordinate entries, but the RDNs of those entries are not known.

A distributed directory may offer a high degree of performance with an acceptable level of consistency, if the knowledge base is suitably maintained by the administrator. Specific procedures are used to maintain and extend the knowledge related to each DSA. In more detail, if the knowledge base changes, then the DSA transfers information related to it to the DSAs which have references to the base. In this way the superior, subordinate and non-specific subordinate references can be maintained in the system; in addition, the DSA may request cross references so that performance can be considerably improved.

DSAs interactions

The directory object has been described in terms of one or more DSA objects cooperating for the implementation of the directory services. These last are modelled in terms of ports, each one able to support a specific set of directory services. Figure 5.10 illustrates the distributed directory model, being composed of a DUA object and several DSA units. DSA objects have to support the distribution of the DIB and suitable predefined interactions so that distributed services are made available to the user. Access to DSAs is obtained through externally visible ports, which can be classified into two types: *service ports* and *distributed service ports*. The service ports of a DSA object are identical to those of the directory object: *read, search* and *modify* ports; they constitute an access point through which the directory services are made available. The distributed service ports support interactions between cooperating DSAs, and are indicated as *distributed_read, distributed_search* and *distributed_modify*.

Given a distributed DIB, users must have their service request satisfied independently of the access point at which the request was submitted. This means that, in order to be able to satisfy the request, any DSA involved in the process must have some knowledge of where the requested information is placed in the distributed environment and must return such knowledge to the requestor, whether this be a DUA or another DSA.

Three types of interactions between DSAs have been defined:

- *chaining*: this mode of communication may be used by one DSA to transmit a remote operation to only one other DSA, when the former has specific knowledge about naming contexts held by the latter. Chaining may be used to contact a DSA pointed to in a cross reference, subordinate reference, or a superior reference. Figure 5.15 illustrates the mechanism.

- *multicasting*: this mode of communication is used by one DSA to pass on an identical remote operation in parallel or sequentially to one or more other DSAs as shown in Figure 5.16. This operation is a consequence of the fact that the first DSA involved in the directory request processing does not know the complete naming contexts held by the other DSA. In this case the same remote operation is passed to the other DSA, according to a parallel or sequential approach. Usually, during name resolution, only one of the DSAs will be able to continue processing the remote operation; all of the other DSAs will return an 'unable to proceed' service error.

- *referral*: a referral is returned by a DSA in its response to a remote operation which it had been requested to perform either by a DUA or another DSA. The referral contains a knowledge reference, which may be either a superior, subordinate, cross

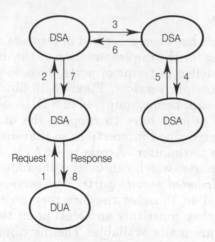

Figure 5.15   Access obtained using the chaining mechanism.

or non-specific subordinate reference. The referral received by
the DUA or DSA may, then, subsequently be used to chain
or multicast the original operation to other DSAs. Alternatively, the DSA receiving the referral may, in turn, pass it back,
included in its response. Figure 5.17 shows the mechanism.

5.4.3   The MiniMAP object dictionary

As discussed in Chapter 2, the OSI seven layer model was introduced so that heterogeneous systems could be interconnected and integrated in a single communication environment. The results of the
architecture in terms of functionalities have been obtained against a
disadvantage in terms of response time. In order to overcome this
problem the MiniMAP [MAP] architecture has been introduced in
the MAP specifications. This architecture is designed to sacrifice
some of the functions available in the full seven layer architecture
for improved performance. Advantages in terms of performance are
desirable for those applications which require a fast response time
and low overhead, as is often the case in the process control and
industrial automation field where programmable controllers, robots
and other time-critical equipment are used.

To achieve this aim the MiniMAP architecture uses only
three layers: the physical, the data-link and the application layer. A
special node based on an Enhanced Performance Architecture supports both the three layers and the standard seven layer model, so
that an effective connection between the full MAP backbone and the
reduced architecture based subnetwork can be obtained.

Given the particular characteristics of a subnetwork based on
a reduced architecture, in place of the MAP directory system, the

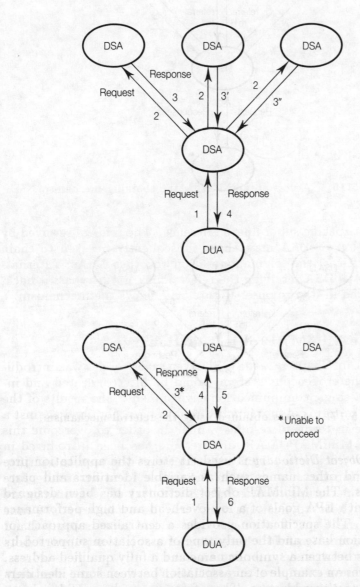

Figure 5.16   Access obtained using the multicasting mechanism.

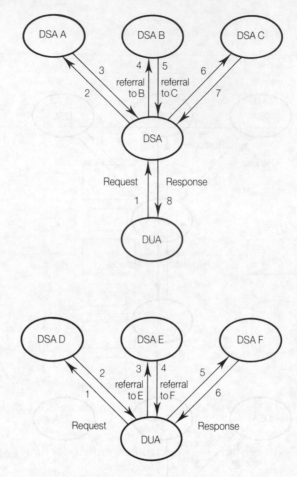

Figure 5.17   Access obtained using the referral mechanism.

MiniMAP Object Dictionary is used. It stores the application process titles and other names such as variable identifiers and parameter names. The MiniMAP object dictionary has been designed to comply with EPA goals of a low-overhead and high-performance subnetwork. The specification provides a centralized approach for the information base and the only type of association supported by the system is between a symbolic name and a fully qualified address. Table 5.2 gives an example of an association between some identifiers and their respective addresses. These features can be considered as a subset of the possibilities offered by the full MAP directory system, where name-to-group-of-names and name-to-attributes associations are also supported. Services defined for the MiniMAP dictionary are intended to be used on a logical segment composed of multiple physical segments, and restrictions on logical segment size are intended

Table 5.2 Address mapping in the DIB.

Name	MAC address	SAP address
Process1	1200003405	10
Variable1	1200003405	11
PLC	1200003406	12

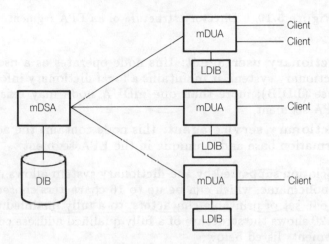

Figure 5.18 Model of a directory system for an EPA architecture.

to be provided through network management facilities supplied by
bridges.

The model

The EPA dictionary system consists of a *dictionary information base*
(DIB), a *local dictionary information base* (LDIB), a *dictionary service agent* (mDSA), a *dictionary user agent* (mDUA) and one or
more clients who represent the users of the dictionary system. Figure 5.18 gives a scheme of the relationship between the elements
mentioned above.

The DIB maintains the current dictionary information and
access to it is performed by the mDUA, which operates as an intermediate agent between the user and the DSA. Figure 5.19 reports a
typical directory structure of an EPA segment.

The system is based on three different types of nodes:

- **no dictionary services available**: in this case the node does
  not support any dictionary service, thus hard-coded addresses
  must be used for communication

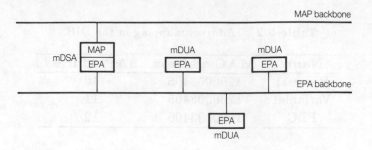

Figure 5.19   Directory structure of an EPA segment.

- **dictionary user agent**: this node operates as a user of the dictionary system; it maintains a local dictionary information base (LDIB); more than one mDUA node may exist in the EPA segment

- **dictionary service agent**: this node contains the actual information base and is unique in the EPA segment.

The association supported by the dictionary system allows mapping of a symbolic name, which can be up to 16 characters chosen by the full ISO 646 set of printable characters, to a fully qualified address. Figure 5.20 shows the structure of a fully qualified address composed of the elements listed below:

- *MAC address*, which represents the physical address on six octets

- *LSAP*, which is the data-link service access point represented on a single octet

- *ASID*, which is the application specific identifier represented by an eight byte string.

Figure 5.21 presents some configurations for the use of an mDUA, or mDSA, and it can be seen that a MiniMAP mDUA may be located on a MiniMAP node while a MiniMAP DSA would typically be located on a MAP/EPA node. It should be noted that both the MiniMAP mDSA and the MiniMAP mDUA are located at the application layer of the end system.

The DIB structure

Figure 5.20 describes the DIB structure, which is composed of a symbolic name and a fully qualified address; the DIB is maintained by the mDSA, which is the only administrator of the DIB in the logical segment. All updates of the information contained in the DIB reach the mDSA through the mDUA and each update is accomplished only if the access rights are correct.

Symbolic name	Fully qualified address			
	MAC address		LSAP	Application-specific ID
Gage 1	49 00 01 11 00 00		04	7
Gage 2	49 00 02 10 00 00		04	6
Sensor 1	48 01 04 10 00 01		03	1
Sensor 2	48 01 05		03	1

DIB

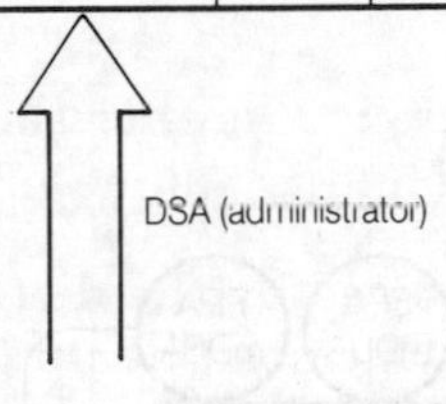

DSA (administrator)

Figure 5.20   Logical structure of the DIB.

Each mDUA maintains a local data base which only contains data of local interest. It should be noted that the LSAP identifier used in the DIB is the access point directly available to the application process identified in the same information unit. A MAC address is stored as a six byte item and is characterized by a 48-bit destination station address according to the IEEE 802.4 standard definition. The least significant bit, which is also the first bit transmitted, indicates whether the address is an individual (if set to 0) address or a group (set to 1) address. The next bit says whether the 48-bit address is locally administered or belongs to a global environment. If the MAC address is composed of all ones, then the predefined broadcast address is indicated; in this case all the EPA nodes are addressed at the same time.

The interactions between a mDUA and a mDSA are based on the fact that only an LSAP is available for the dictionary operations, moreover the LSAP has to be configured to support *request without response* types of service, which means a simple datagram service. Table 5.3 lists operations available to the user. They are divided into *request* and *indication services*. A *request* primitive indicates that a service of the $n-1$ layer is being used; hence if the user of the mDSA protocol wants to issue a *query DIB entry* operation, a *query DIB entry request* primitive must be used. An *indication* primitive says

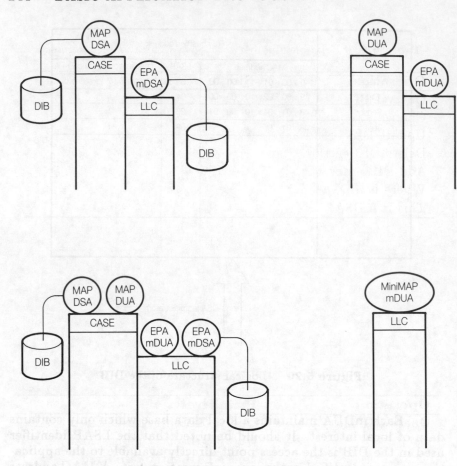

Figure 5.21   Physical allocation of the mDSA and mDUA on the network nodes.

that if a service of the $n+1$ layer is being invoked, then if a *query DIB entry request* protocol data unit is delivered from the LLC, the user will detect a *query DIB entry request indication* primitive.

Table 5.4 reports the relationships between the operations and the associated primitives.

The protocol

Actions in the object dictionary system are atomic, this means that each action corresponding to a received PDU must be successful or no external change may be acquired. As an example, if multiple objects have to be added to the dictionary, none of the elements will be inserted if an error occurs during each adding operation. Multiple requests may be handled by the system since each operation is uniquely identified by the *request identifier* contained in each PDU;

Table 5.3 Relationships between operations and LLC services.

Operation	Single destination	Broadcast
Query DIB entry	*	
Change physical address	*	
Update DIB broadcast		*
Delete DIB entry	*	
Add DIB entry	*	
Where Is mDSA		*
This Is mDSA		*

Table 5.4 List of protocol service primitives.

Operation	Primitives
Query DIB entry	Query DIB entry request_req
	Query DIB entry request_ind
	Query DIB entry result_req
	Query DIB entry result_ind
Change physical address	Change physical address request_req
	Change physical address request_ind
Acknowledgment	Acknowledge_req
	Acknowledge_ind
Update broadcast	Update broadcast_req
	Update broadcast_ind
Delete DIB entry	Delete DIB entry request_req
	Delete DIB entry request_ind
Add DIB entry	Add DIB entry request_req
	Add DIB entry request_ind
Where Is mDSA	WhereIsmDSA_req
	WhereIsmDSA_ind
This Is mDSA	ThisIsmDSA_req
	ThisIsmDSA_ind

in this way any response may be associated with the correct request. Simple context management is also provided, based on the identification of the source *link service access point* (LSAP), which has the value of 18 in hexadecimal representation. If the PDUs received do not have such identification they are discarded or logged into an appropriate file. In the following the most important operations are described:

Query DIB Entry

This operation allows an mDUA to request object dictionary information of the mDSA by the submission of a name rather than a physical address; in this case an mDUA issues a request to the mDSA, which also supports a mechanism for tagging the response in such a manner that the requesting mDUA can distinguish between multiple outstanding requests. The mDUA requests DIB information by using a name in the PDU, which is used by the mDSA to identify the entry, extract the information and subsequently build and send the response.

Change Physical Address

When a node or a subprocess is relocated, the mDSA's DIB must be updated to reflect such changes; this operation allows an authorized node to change the physical attributes of either a single name, all the names associated with a given LSAP, or all names associated with a given node. After a change has occurred, it is propagated by the mDSA, using the broadcast mechanism, to all nodes connected to the local network. After a request has reached the mDSA, this latter provides for the continuance of the operation and then sends back an acknowledgment to the originating mDUA, immediately followed by an update operation which is broadcast on the network. This approach allows transparent changes to occur in the LDIB owned by each mDUA in the network.

Delete DIB Entry

This operation requires that the mDSA's DIB is capable of being updated to reflect such changes. When this operation is used, an authorized node can delete a DIB entry of either a single name, all names associated with a given LSAP, or all names associated with a given node. Hence, when the request is received, the mDSA performs the operation and, if successful, an acknowledgment is sent back to the requestor; after that, an update operation is broadcast on the network so that the various local DIBs owned by the mDUA in the network can also be modified.

Add DIB Entry

When an mDUA issues a request to the mDSA, this latter performs the action and then acknowledges the addition.

Where Is mDSA

This operation requests the location of an mDSA; this is particularly important when a new mDUA is added to the network, in this case the node must be able to request the location of the mDSA; the answer to this request is represented by the primitive *This Is mDSA*.

This Is mDSA

This service is invoked when an mDSA is first powered up, when the location of the mDSA has changed, or in response to a PDU asking what the address of the mDSA is (Where Is mDSA primitive).

5.5 Conclusions

Some of the application modules located at the application layer have been examined. In particular, the ACSE functions have been considered. The ACSE module supplies the primitives required to handle associations to all other applications.

Network management has also been described, pointing out those aspects considered in the MAP and TOP specifications. In particular, remote management mechanisms and protocols have been discussed.

As a basic application support, directory service has been analyzed, describing a hierarchical system in which objects can be located by various attributes, according to the approach suggested by the results currently available from the standard organizations working on this subject.

References

[ISO7498/4]   ISO/DIS 7498/4, *OSI Management Framework*, July 1988.

[ISO9595/1]   ISO/DP 9595/1, *Management Information Service Definition, Part 1, Overview*, June 1987.

[IEC/JTC1]   Information Processing System, Open Systems Interconnection, Management Information Services, *Structure of Management Information*, ISO/IEC JTC 1/SC21 N2687.

[ISO9595/2]   ISO/DP 9595/2, *Management Information Service Definition, Part 2: Common Management Service Definition*, June 1987.

[ISO9596]   ISO/DP 9596/1, *Management Information Proto-col Specification, Part 1: Overview*, December 1987.

[ISO9596/2]   ISO/DP 9596/2, *Management Information Proto-col Specification, Part 2: Common Management In-formation Protocol*, December 1987.

[IEEE802/1]   Draft IEEE Standard 802.1, Part B, *Systems Ma-nagement*, Rev. M, January 1987.

[IEEE802/1L]   Draft IEEE Standard 802.1, Part B, *Systems Mana-gement, System Load Protocol*, Rev. B, May 1987.

[ISO/DP9072/1]   Working Document for DP 9072/1, *Remote Ope-rations, Part 1: Model, Notation and Service Defi-nitions*

[ISO/DP9072/2]   Working Document for DP 9072/2, *Remote Ope-rations, Part 2: Protocol Specification*.

[IEEE802/3m]   Draft IEEE 802.3 *Layer Management*, Rev. H, May 1987.

[ISO8073]   Transport Protocol Specification.

[ISO8649/2]   ISO DIS 8649 OSI: *Service definition for common application service elements – Part 2 – Association Control*, March 1986.

[ISO8650/2]   ISO DIS 8649 OSI: *Protocol specification for com-mon application service elements – Part 2 – Asso-ciation Control*, March 1986.

[ISO8822]   ISO 8822/3 OSI: *Presentation Service/Protocol Specification*.

[MAP]   MAP Task Force, *Manufacturing Automation Pro-tocol, Version 3.0, Implementation Release*. War-ren, MI, General Motors Technical Center, 1987.

[ISO9594/1]   ISO IEC DIS 9594/1, *Information Processing Sy-stems – Open Systems Interconnection – The Di-rectory – Part 1 – Overview of concepts, models and service*, Nov. 1988.

[ISO9594/2]   ISO IEC DIS 9594/2, *Information Processing Sy-stems – Open Systems Interconnection – The Di-rectory – Part 2 – Models*, Nov. 1988.

[ISO9594/3]   ISO IEC DIS 9594/3, *Information Processing Sy-stems – Open Systems Interconnection – The Di-rectory – Part 3 – Abstract Service Definition*, Nov. 1988.

[ISO9594/4]   ISO IEC DIS 9594/4, *Information Processing Sy-stems – Open Systems Interconnection – The Di-rectory – Part 4 – Procedures for Distributed Ope-rations*, Nov. 1988.

[ISO9594/5]   ISO IEC DIS 9594/5, *Information Processing Systems – Open Systems Interconnection – The Directory – Part 5 – Protocol Specifications*, Nov. 1988.

[ISO9594/6]   ISO IEC DIS 9594/1, *Information Processing Systems – Open Systems Interconnection – The Directory – Part 6 – Selected Attribute Types*, Nov. 1988.

Chapter 6

Manufacturing Message Specification

6.1   Introduction

The Manufacturing Message Specification (MMS) [ISO9506] is a protocol lying in the application layer of the ISO–OSI reference model, and is intended to support communication and interworking of programmable manufacturing devices.

In particular, MMS supports the communication between the application tasks controlling the operations of the manufacturing plant. The type of application tasks that could take advantage of the MMS services are those that need to exchange data messages (usually short) and synchronization messages used to coordinate the application activities (i.e. the plant activities). The latter aspect is peculiar to MMS, as it is not covered by other protocols lying in the same layer, such as file transfer or electronic mail. The coordination functions required include:

- access control to limited resources;
- definition of some events that are relevant for the application (alarms, for example) and definition of actions to be performed upon the occurrence of an event;

- up/down-loading of part programs and control of their execution.

The exchange of short data messages and a simplified form of file transfer are also included in the MMS in order to obtain a single communication environment supporting all the operations required by the application tasks. It is worth noting that not all the application tasks require the use of MMS in a general architecture for CIM, because the tasks devoted to higher level administrative functions usually perform query and update operations on data bases, thus they do not require the functions offered by MMS. In general, tasks performing functions from level three and below in the model presented in Chapter 1 could take advantage of the mechanisms offered by MMS; however this is only a coarse classification and several exceptions are possible.

The real environment requiring MMS functionalities is the shop floor, because the coordination of application tasks needs a synchronization of operations that cannot be implemented using asynchronous data base updates used by higher level entities. Therefore the devices that may gain most advantage from MMS functions are: cell or area sub-process controllers, robot controllers, numerical machine controllers, PLCs and other types of programmable controllers.

It is important to note that a whole class of automation devices are not included in the previous list: intelligent actuators and sensors. The reason for this is that the relative complexity of the MMS protocol calls for computer capabilities far exceeding those of the microcontrollers usually used to build intelligent sensors and actuators. Another reason is that networks used to interconnecting controllers to field devices should be designed to cope with jitter requirements higher than those taken into consideration by the MMS designers.

The area of networks interconnecting field devices is covered by an IEC standard project, called FIELDBUS, currently under development. Though still in its definition phase, FIELDBUS will probably include some of the MMS services, and it will provide an easy interconnection with networks running MMS in their application level.

6.2   Protocol basics

All the interactions between two MMS entities is based on the *client-server model*. The client entity sends a confirmed service request to the server, which is responsible for generating a response (possibly negative) to the received request. Figure 6.1 depicts the interactions between the two MMS entities; each entity includes an MMS Protocol Machine (MMPM), which in turn comprises a sending and a receiving section. Alternatively, in principle the client may also send

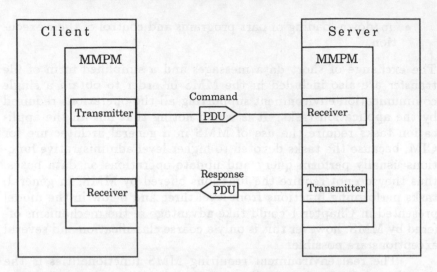

Figure 6.1   Interaction between client and server MMS entities.

an unconfirmed service; in this case, no response is requested from the server.

The MMPM implements only those functions required for exchanging protocol data units (PDUs) between the two entities, but it does not provide any function for the execution of the service. Thus the server must include one (or a group of) application task(s), referred to as a Virtual Manufacturing Device (VMD), which executes the function required by the incoming service request and prepares the response, which will be sent to the client via the two MMPMs.

The assumption of the client-server model leads to a behavior of the MMS entities that is asymmetric. In fact, it is likely that some entities may act only as servers; in this case they do not generate any message unless a client entity request them to do so, except unsolicited status reports. The server MMS entity may be seen as a slave, because it only reacts to client stimuli.

Single manufacturing machines may assume the server-only configuration, whilst the computer supervising a group of machines may assume the client-only configuration. In this case the supervisor can read the status and set the control parameters for each individual machine, by requesting them to perform specific MMS services.

It is also possible for an MMS entity to act as both server and client. In this case the same entity can send requests for service while processing other requests received from other entities. A typical situation where this configuration is required can be found in systems (or sub-systems) composed of peer machines that need to coordinate their operations with no centralized control; therefore, each of them needs service from other machines to know their status, for example, and offer the same type of services to the other machines.

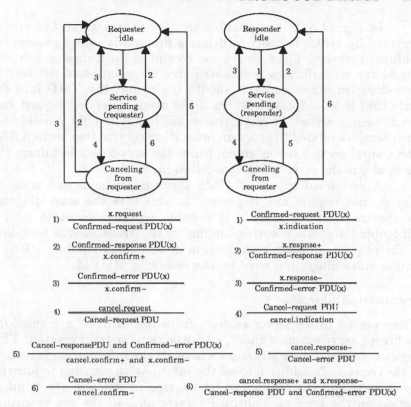

Figure 6.2 State diagrams for the execution of each confirmed service invocation.

The operations performed by each MMPM to implement a confirmed service can be described by the two state diagrams in Figure 6.2, describing the behavior of the client and server MMPM, respectively. It is important to note that the diagrams in Figure 6.2 refer to a single instance of service invocation. Multiple concurrent service invocation instances may be active at the same time, each of them evolves according a separate state machine of the type shown in Figure 6.2.

The input and output actions associated with each transition in Figure 6.2 are associated with numbers whose meaning is shown in the lower part of the figure; the event shown above the horizontal line is an input operation, while output operations are shown below the line. Operations denoted with capital initials correspond to interactions with the other MMPMs, whilst the others refer to interactions with the user above the MMPM. The operations suffixed with a + denote positive responses or confirmations, while those suffixed with − denote the negative ones, caused by detection of errors or unavailability of resources.

In Figure 6.2, it is possible to note that a *Cancel* service is provided by MMS, in order to delete a previously issued request for confirmed service. The server, upon receipt of the Cancel.indication, should try to perform a non-destructive cancellation of the service procedure; in other words, it should try to put the VMD into the state that it would have been in if the original service request had never been received. Destructive cancellation is only possible for some services related to program invocation control (see Section 6.5). The Cancel service is confirmed, hence the server should inform the client about the result of the cancellation.

A restricted subset of MMS services are non-confirmed, as they do not require any response. In this case the state diagram for the transmitting MMPM is reduced to only one state with a self-looping transition corresponding to the transmission reception of the request and the transmission of the corresponding PDU; a similar state diagram is used by the receiving MMPM.

Transaction objects

Whenever an MMS server receives from the MMPM a request for confirmed service from a client, a transaction object is created. This object contains a data structure where all the information is related to the request. In addition to all the information required to identify the request and the client, the transaction object also stores information on the type of confirmed service and all the pre-execution and post-execution modifiers which are used to change the meaning of the request and whose usage will be explained in Sections 6.8 and 6.9.

A transaction object is destroyed when the corresponding response is sent to the client.

6.2.1   Application association

The MMS uses a connection-oriented protocol, hence, before any confirmed or non-confirmed service could be executed, it is necessary to establish an environment between the client and the server. Such an environment is referred to as an application association (or AA), which is also often known as a dialogue.

The ability to initiate operations to establish an AA is not related to the role (client or server) played by the initiator, as it is possible for the entities at both ends of the AA to send both responses and requests.

The mechanism to establish an AA is the ACSE A_ASSOC process (see Chapter 5) and it is not worth describing in detail here. What is interesting is the set of parameters, whose values are negotiated in this phase, as the environment set-up is required in order to make sure that a sufficient level of resources are available for communication at both ends of the AA.

One of these parameters is the maximum number of outstanding requests, that is the maximum number of transaction objects that can be active at any time. The value of this parameter limits the number of requests for confirmed service, which are received on the AA, and are still awaiting a response, at any one time. This mechanism may also be seen as the implementation of a flow control function at the application level, because no other request for confirmed service can be sent to the other end of the AA if the number of unanswered previous requests equals the value of this parameter as negotiated during the environment set-up phase. This simplified flow control mechanism is very useful when the MMS has to be used in a reduced protocol profile (such as MiniMAP), because, in this case, it is not possible to rely on flow control mechanisms implemented by the intermediate layers of the full OSI stack of protocols.

It is possible to negotiate two distinct values for the maximum number of outstanding requests for the two ends of the AA. In this way it is possible to choose the best suited parameters, even when the two systems participating in the AA have different levels of resources available for communication. For example, a simple automation device may have a small memory and it should use a low value for the maximum number of outstanding service requests; its communications with the controller, implemented in a larger computer, can be performed without imposing the same restrictions on the controller, as a different value for the maximum number of outstanding requests may be selected for the second partner.

Another parameter negotiated during the set-up phase is an upper limit to the level of nesting in the MMS variable definition (see Section 6.7). As it is possible to manipulate structured variables, it is necessary to limit the level of nesting of the structure definition, because the higher the nesting level, the larger the memory used for storing this definition. A single value for this parameter is negotiated for both parties.

Other negotiated parameters are the following ones:

- *version number*: the common compatible MMS version between the version numbers of the two parties;
- *conformance building block*: the largest set of conformance building blocks (see Section 6.3.1) supported by both parties;
- *services supported*: the largest set of services supported by both parties.

6.3 Virtual manufacturing device

Unlike other OSI protocols, MMS defines not only the behavior of the two peer level entities involved in a message exchange, but also partially defines the external behavior of the application tasks sitting on top of an MMS entity.

In particular, the protocol definition, briefly described in the previous section, covers only the message transfer operations, whilst the service definition is based on the description of the behavior of objects (such as variables, semaphores, events and jobs) that are implemented by the MMS user (i.e. application tasks) on the server side, as shown in Figure 6.1.

It turns out that the external (i.e. visible from remote stations) behavior of the application is partially standardized in the MMS service definition.

The Virtual Manufacturing Device (VMD) plays a key role in the MMS service definition, because the implementation of an MMS server must map the external behavior of a VMD onto the functionalities of a real manufacturing device. Therefore a single robot, programmable controller or tool machine may be seen on the network by a client application program through the behavior shown by the associated VMD. Of course, the view of the same device available to the local application processes is in general different, and it is not relevant for the MMS, as it deals only with the view from a remote station.

There is no provision in MMS for creating or destroying a VMD, thus the activation or deactivation of the process or set of processes implementing a VMD should be performed through management operations not included in MMS.

VMDs are logically independent from each other, even when a single station implements more than one VMD. Also their addresses are separated, because each VMD is associated with a distinct set of service access points at the presentation layer.

The structure of a VMD includes:

- exactly one executive function

- zero or more program invocations (see Section 6.5) with the associated domains.

The executive function is that part of a VMD which actually executes actions on the VMD objects related to the execution of the incoming requests for MMS services. Thus it is the real 'brain' of a VMD, and a fully functional executive function exactly corresponds with the existence of a VMD. The relationship between the executive function, the MMPM and the local application processes is shown in Figure 6.3; whilst the executive function manipulates the VMD objects on behalf of the remote client, the local application processes may also change the state of the same objects through local operations. The concurrent access of the executive function and the local application is in general controlled by the local operating system.

In addition to all the subordinate objects that can be included in a VMD, there is also a set of attributes associated with each VMD as a whole. In order to understand the meaning of some VMD

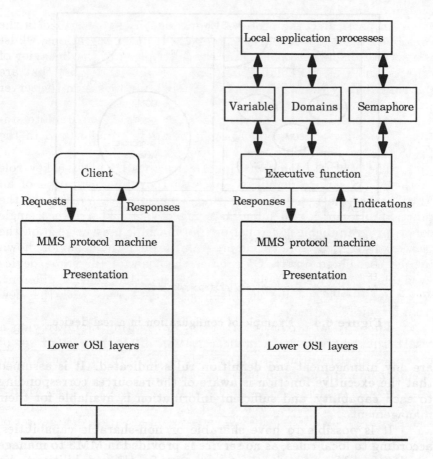

Figure 6.3   Structure of a VMD.

attributes, it is necessary to define some other MMS objects.

The relationship between the real device, VMD, domains and other MMS objects is described in Figure 6.4. Each real device may implement more than one VMD, however the virtual devices are always considered independent from each other; in fact they have associated disjoint sets of service access points to the underlying presentation layer. Domains may be shared among different program invocations, but no object can be shared between two VMDs.

Capabilities

The real device modeled through the VMD may be seen as a collection of resources which can be used individually or as a part of a set of resources. A capability is a resource or set of resources of the real device, which can be associated with a character string. No standard definition is given for the behavior of capabilities, nor

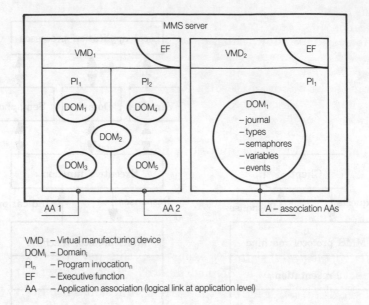

VMD – Virtual manufacturing device
DOM$_i$ – Domain$_i$
PI$_n$ – Program invocation$_n$
EF – Executive function
AA – Application association (logical link at application level)

Figure 6.4   Example of configuration in a real device.

are any management and definition rules indicated. It is assumed that the executive function is aware of the resources corresponding to each capability, and sufficient information is available for their management.

It is possible to have sharable or non-sharable capabilities, according to local rules, as no service is provided in MMS to manage capabilities. Moreover, it is not necessary for the capabilities to be distinct, as it is possible to have capabilities encompassing one or more other capabilities.

Domains

A domain is an object that includes all the resources required to perform a particular aspect of a coordinated control or monitoring application. An example of domain in the robot environment is a robot arm, which is composed of all the resources for the operation of the real arm, including the data and code for the control program.

A domain may include:

- a set of capabilities
- subordinate MMS objects that cannot exist if the domain does not exist
- information: code and data areas which can be used for a program execution.

Domains may be static, when they are ever present within the VMD, or dynamic, when they may be created and destroyed. In the latter case it is possible to down/upload the domain contents from another station. When a domain is created, all the subordinate MMS objects are created too; while the destruction of the domain leads to the destruction of the subordinate objects. Note that subordinate MMS objects may also be created during the lifetime of a domain, in addition to those created with the domain; these objects are destroyed with the associated domain.

The set of VMD attributes includes:

- *executive function*;
- *vendor name*;
- *model name*;
- *revision*;
- *list of abstract syntaxes supported*: this parameter refers to abstract syntaxes as defined in ASN.1 (see Chapter 4);
- *logical status*: describes the current functional level of the executive function (more details are given in the following);
- *list of capabilities;*
- *physical status*: describes the overall state of the capabilities in the VMD (more details are given in the following);
- *list of program invocations*: includes all the program invocations currently defined for the VMD (program invocations are described in Section 6.5);
- *list of domains*: includes all the domains defined for the VMD;
- *list of transaction objects*;
- *list of upload state machines*: includes the state of all the state machines governing the operations of domain uploading currently active;
- *list of subordinate objects*;
- *additional information*: attribute to be defined in companion standards (see Chapter 10).

Four values are possible for the logical state of the VMD:

- *STATE-CHANGES-ALLOWED*: when in this state, the VMD is able to perform all the services defined;
- *NO-STATE-CHANGES-ALLOWED*: when in this state, the VMD is able to accept only requests for service regarding the application association set up and closure, and those intended to get the different object attributes or to read object contents; in this case, only monitoring operations can be carried out, while it is not possible to control the state of MMS objects; this state can be used to model a real manufacturing device

that is currently under local control, thus it can be used from a remote station only for monitoring purposes;

- *LIMITED-SERVICE-PERMITTED*: the VMD supports only the services used to close an application association and to get status and identification information on the VMD; in this case, the VMD is not available on the network for monitoring operations either;

- *SUPPORT-SERVICE-ALLOWED*: all the services defined for the VMD can be executed, with the exception of services controlling the execution of program invocations in the VMD; in this case the VMD can participate in both monitoring and control applications, with the limitation that it is not possible for a remote station to activate or de-activate part programs.

The physical state of a VMD is related to the status of the hardware composing the real device, and it may assume one of the following values:

- *OPERATIONAL*: the VMD is able to perform all its intended tasks, as no problem is reported;

- *PARTIALLY-OPERATIONAL*: hardware malfunctions limit the number of operations that can be performed by the VMD;

- *INOPERABLE*: the problems are so severe that they prevent the execution of any real useful work;

- *NEEDS-COMMISSIONING*: a local (probably manual) operation is required before any of the intended tasks could be executed.

6.3.1   Conformance building blocks

MMS defines a relatively large class of objects that can be included in a VMD; each class has an associated set of services. Thus the implementation in a VMD of the whole set of services for all the types of objects defined by MMS can give rise to problems when the resulting VMD has to be run on a relatively small machine (a programmable logic controller, for example) with limited memory space and CPU speed. Moreover, the implementation of the whole set of MMS services could not be required by the application activities executed by the VMD, resulting in a waste of implementation effort and run-time resources.

To overcome this problem, standard subsets of services are defined, these standard subsets are referred to as *conformance building blocks*.

Two types of conformance building blocks are defined:

- Vertical building blocks
- Horizontal building blocks.

The first type defines which classes of MMS objects are actually supported by the VMD; for those objects not supported, all the associated services are not implemented. The second type indicates which subset of services, among those related to a specific class of objects, is implemented by the VMD.

Therefore it is possible to tailor the implementation of MMS services to the needs of the application to be run. In particular, it is possible to implement small standard versions of MMS supporting only a limited set of services, to be run on machines with limited capabilities.

6.4 Domains

A definition of the main features of a domain has already been given in Section 6.3. Here a more detailed description of the operations and attributes of a domain will be presented.

The following are the most relevant attributes of a domain:

- *name*: identifies the domain;
- *list of capabilities*;
- *state* (described below);
- *MMS deletable*: indicates whether or not the domain is dynamic (i.e. deletable);
- *sharable*: indicates whether or not the domain can be shared among different program invocations (see Section 6.5);
- *list of subordinate objects*: the list includes all the currently active jobs defined within the domain scope; the lifetime of the subordinate objects cannot exceed the domain lifetime;
- *list of program invocations*: the list includes all the program invocations currently defined over the domain.

The domain can be in one of five states:

- *LOADING*: this state indicates that the domain is being loaded;
- *COMPLETE*: this state is reached when the last segment of the domain has been loaded, but the command closing the upload sequence has not been issued yet;
- *READY*: when the upload sequence is closed by the appropriate message, this state is reached;
- *INCOMPLETE*: this state is reached when the upload sequence is closed before all the segments of the domain have been received;
- *IN-USE*: the domain is in this state if one or more program invocations are defined which use the domain.

6.4.1 Loading domains

The services controlling the loading process of the domain contents allow two classes of operations:

* *downloading*: the domain contents are loaded to the VMD, where the domain is also created;
* *upload*: the contents of an existing domain are offloaded from the VMD and saved in a filestore.

In both of these cases, it is necessary for a station with a filestore to be involved in the domain loading operation. Three configurations are possible:

* the filestore is internal to the VMD participating in the domain loading;
* the filestore is located in the client entity requesting the domain loading operation;
* the filestore is located in a third party, distinct from both the client requesting the domain loading operation and the VMD acting as a server.

Moreover, the operation can be initiated by both ends of the association; that is, it is possible for a VMD to initiate the upload operation to a filestore located at the other end of an AA.

The third configuration listed above gives the possibility of using networks with cheap configurations, where only one station hosts a filestore, while the others do not (diskless stations).

The operations required to download a domain, with the filestore located in the client, are shown in Figure 6.5. The client entity requests the download operation and the creation of the domain, by issuing a InitiateDownLoad.request. Then the server gets control of the data transfer, and issues a DownLoadSegment.request whenever it is ready to receive a new domain segment; the client replies by sending the segment contents with the DownLoadSegment.response.

Once the segment marked as the last one has been received, the server sends a TerminateDownloadSequence.request, which is acknowledged by the corresponding response. Finally, the server issues the InitiateDownLoad.response to conclude the whole download service execution.

The same operation can be initiated by the MMS entity where the domain has to be created, as shown in Figure 6.5; in this case, the RequestDomainDownload.request instructs the client to initiate a downloading sequence.

The operations for uploading a domain are not much different; Figure 6.6 shows this sequence. The main difference from Figure 6.5 is that now the client controls the data transfer. Another difference is that domain download causes the domain creation, while the upload

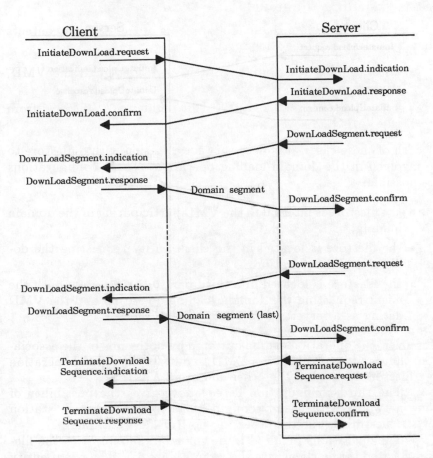

Figure 6.5 Time diagram for domain downloading operation with the filestore located on the client station: the operation is initiated by the client.

operation does not change the domain status. A domain may be destroyed (if deletable) by using the DeleteDomain service.

The sequence of operations for up/downloading a domain to or from a filestore located in a third party requires the use of additional services illustrated in the following. The typical downloading sequence is shown in Figure 6.7. The client initiates the domain transfer by sending to the server a LoadDomainContent.request; this action causes an exchange of messages as in Figure 6.5, where the server requests the third party to initiate a download sequence. The upload from a third party works in similar fashion; the main difference is that the client sends a StoreDomainContent.request, and the server requests the third party to initiate an upload sequence.

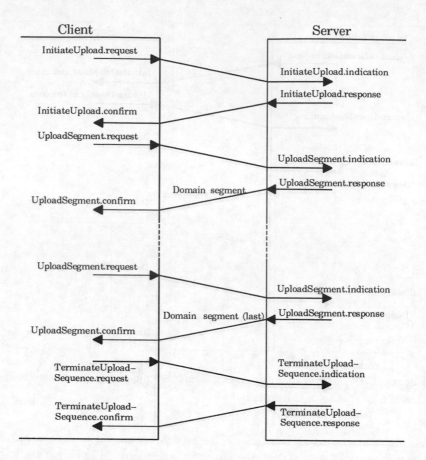

Figure 6.6   Time diagram of a domain uploading operation, with the filestore located on the client station: the operation is initiated by the client.

Of course, when the filestore is located in the same station as the VMD including the domain, no up/download sequence of messages is necessary; the messages exchanged are request and response for the services LoadDomainContent or StoreDomainContent.

6.4.2   Note on files in MMS

The operations for loading a domain correspond to a file transfer to or from a VMD. As other standards cover this type of operation (see Chapter 7), it is important to see whether or not the use of files in MMS duplicates the functions provided by other protocols.

First of all the MMS services deal only with the transfer of the file content. The method of accessing the file consists of pro-

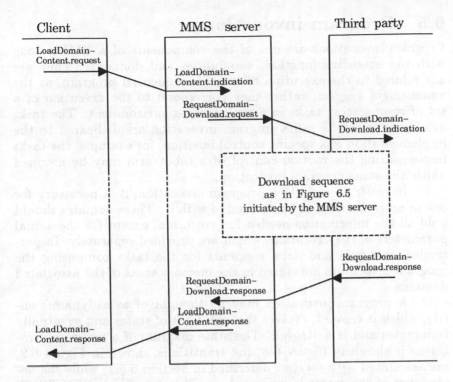

Figure 6.7 Time diagram for domain downloading operation from a filestore located in a third party.

viding a string of characters to be interpreted by the filestore, but the contents of the string are totally ignored by MMS. In this way, the MMS entities are completely unaware of the directory structure of the filestore. Furthermore, file attributes are not considered by MMS services.

Another relevant difference with specialized protocols for file transfer is that the file can be accessed only in sequential mode and, when a file transfer is initiated, the whole file is transferred. Moreover, the internal file structure (division in logical records) is not considered in MMS, because it is assumed that the applications participating in the file exchange are already aware of it. On the other hand, the domain content is usually a binary file ready to be loaded into memory.

In conclusion, the services for up/downloading the domain contents provide a simple way to support remote programming of manufacturing devices, without implementing a whole specialized protocol for file transfer, such as FTAM (see Chapter 7).

6.5   Program invocations

Program invocations are one of the components of a VMD, along with the executive function, capabilities and domains. They are not related to the execution of a single sequential program, as the name might suggest; rather they correspond to the execution of a set of co-operating tasks in a multitasking environment. The tasks associated with the same program invocation are dedicated to the implementation of a specific control function; for example, the tasks implementing the motion control of a robot arm may be grouped under the same program invocation.

In order to execute a program invocation, it is necessary for one or more domains to be associated with it. These domains should hold all the information needed for execution, except for the actual parameters of the execution, which are provided separately. In particular, the code and data segments for the tasks composing the program invocation are stored in the memory areas of the associated domains.

A program invocation may be thought of as a dynamic entity, which is created, evolves through a set of states and eventually terminates and is destroyed. The state diagram of a program invocation is shown in Figure 6.8; the transitions, shown in Figure 6.9, are associated with services described in Section 6.5.1, while the description of the states is given below. The state NON-EXISTENT is added to indicate the situation of a program invocation that has not been created yet.

- *IDLE*: this state indicates that the program invocation is created but not activated yet; hence it is known to the system, but it does not perform any action;
- *RUNNING*: this state indicates that the program invocation is executing; the real meaning of execution is defined internally by the VMD; in particular, this state is not necessarily connected to the running state of the tasks composing the program invocation, as defined by the local multitasking operating system; in general, the execution is associated with changes in the subordinated domains, caused by the program invocation;
- *STOPPED*: this state is reached when the program invocation terminates its execution, either because of normal completion or because a client has stopped the execution; while in this state, the associated domains do not change;
- *UNRUNNABLE*: when the program invocation reaches this state, it can no longer be executed; this state just precedes the program invocation destruction;
- *STARTING*: this is a transitory state that is reached when a Start.indication has been received, but not yet acknowledged;

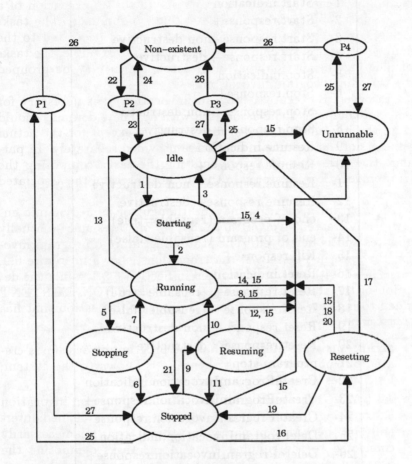

Figure 6.8   State diagram of a program invocation.

1-	Start.indication
2-	Start.response+
3-	Start.response—non destructive
4-	Start.response— destructive
5-	Stop.indication
6-	Stop.response+
7-	Stop.response— non destructive
8-	Stop.response— destructive
9-	Resume.indication
10-	Resume.response+
11-	Resume.response— non destructive
12-	Resume response— destructive
13-	end of program (reusable=true)
14-	end of program (reusable=false)
15-	Kill.response+
16-	Reset.indication
17-	Reset.response+ (reusable=true)
18-	Reset.response+ (reusable=false)
19-	Reset.response— non destructive
20-	Reset.response— destructive
21-	program stop
22-	CreateProgramInvocation.indication
23-	CreateProgramInvocation.response+
24-	CreateProgramInvocation.response—
25-	DeleProgramInvocation.indication
26-	DeleteProgramInvocation.response+
27-	DeleteProgramInvocation.response—

Figure 6.9   Events causing state transitions for a program invocation.

while in this state, the VMD may perform initialization procedures required to prepare the program invocation to be executed;

- *STOPPING*: this is a transitory state that is reached when a Stop.indication has been received, but the corresponding response has not yet been issued;

- *RESETTING*: this is a transitory state between STOPPED and IDLE states, which can be reached only by program invocations that are designated as *re-usable* when they are created; a re-usable program invocation may be stopped and then started again, going through the IDLE state; the subsequent executions are all independent, in the sense that the execution is always started from the beginning, unlike the resume operation;

- *RESUMING*: this a transitory state between the STOPPED and RUNNING state; while in this state the VMD may execute procedures for resuming the execution from the state reached when the program entered the STOPPED state; the program invocation stays in this state for the time between the receipt of a Resume.indication and the issue of the corresponding response;

- *P1, P2, P3* and *P4*: these are transitory states where the program invocation stops, while waiting for some response; no special action may be performed by the VMD on a program invocation in one of these states.

The state changes of the program invocation can give rise to action to send an asynchronous notification of this state change to the user that created the program invocation. This operation is enabled only if an attribute of the program invocation specifies that it should be monitored.

The notification mechanism is implemented, by means of an event condition object (see Section 6.9) activated whenever the program invocation exits the RUNNING state. The event activation triggers the execution, with no acknowledgment, of an event enrolment object, referring to an event action object that specifies a Get-ProgramInvocation service; the response to this service will be sent to the user that created the program invocation. Other attributes of a program invocation specify the execution arguments, which are not interpreted by MMS, but which are seen as a string of bytes. The real meaning of this information should be known to the program invocation itself.

6.5.1   Services

The services associated with program invocations are the following ones:

- *CreateProgramInvocation*: creates a new program invocation object, the initial state being IDLE;

- *DeleteProgramInvocation*: deletes an existing program invocation (if deletable); to execute this service the program invocation should be either in the STOPPED or in the UN-RUNNABLE state;

- *Start*: causes a transition from the IDLE to RUNNING state (through the STARTING state) of an already existing program invocation;

- *Stop*: causes the transition from the RUNNING to STOPPED state (through the STOPPING state) of an already existing program invocation; the negative result of this service execution may be non-destructive (e.g. the stop operation cannot be completed but the execution can be resumed) or destructive (e.g. the program cannot be stopped or resumed); in the former case the program invocation goes back to the RUNNING state, in the latter it goes to the UNRUNNABLE state;

- *Resume*: causes a transition from the STOPPED to the RUN-NING state (through the RESUMING state) of an already existing program invocation;

- *Reset*: causes a transition from the STOPPED to the IDLE state (through the RESETTING state) of an already existing program invocation; this service can be successfully executed only by a program invocation that has been defined as re-usable, when it was created;

- *Kill*: causes a transition to the UNRUNNABLE state from any other state (except for NON-EXISTENT and P1-P4), determining the abnormal termination of the program invocation;

- *GetProgramInvocationAttributes*: provides the client with the values of the attributes of a program invocation object.

6.6   A simple example

In this section we begin to develop a simple example of an application of the MMS, using the objects presented in the previous sections of this chapter; in Section 6.11 the example will be completed with the inclusion of objects that will be presented in the following sections.

So far, the MMS objects presented are more related to configuring MMS for an application, rather than to supporting the actual application operations, such as inter-process synchronization and communication. The latter type of problem is dealt with by the object types described in the following sections.

The example is a simple quality control cell composed of a measuring machine with the associated conveyors and robots for machine loading and downloading. A sketch of the layout is shown in Figure 6.10. The measuring machine M receives pieces from two different sources, through conveyors A and B; two robots, R1 and R2, are used to load M with pieces coming from either conveyor, with each robot dedicated to a specific conveyor. A third robot R3 is used to download the measured piece from M and to put it on either conveyor C or conveyor D, according to whether or not it passed the control.

Each robot and the measuring machine has a separate controller; conveyors C and D are controlled by the same PLC, while conveyors A and B have separate controllers. In addition to the machine controllers, there is another computer dedicated to the cell control functions; the activities of the cell controller include up/downloading of programs or data, monitoring of the operations and alarm handling.

All the computers controlling the machines and the whole cell are interconnected through a network with MMS available as an application layer protocol.

The first type of problems to be solved are related to establishing a configuration for the MMS object suitable for our example, and in particular:

- VMD definition
- domain definition
- program invocation definition.

The VMD is a model of an MMS server available for the remote MMS entities, and usually is related to a real manufacturing device. In our example, the machine, the robots and the conveyors are all MMS servers, because the cell controller may send them requests for monitoring or reconfiguration purposes.

Thus it is possible to use one VMD for each real device (the measuring machine, the three robots and all four conveyors). It is interesting to note that two different VMDs are used for conveyors C and D, though they are both controlled by the same PLC; this choice reflects more the manufacturing configuration than the network configuration, and it is allowed in MMS.

The two VMDs will be treated as two totally distinct MMS entities; this choice improves the clarity of the application and improves flexibility, because a possible evolution to a configuration with two separated PLCs will not involve any change to the application programs. However, it may introduce some penalty in memory occupation, because two VMDs need two separated executive functions and separated AA; the relevance of the increase in memory size due

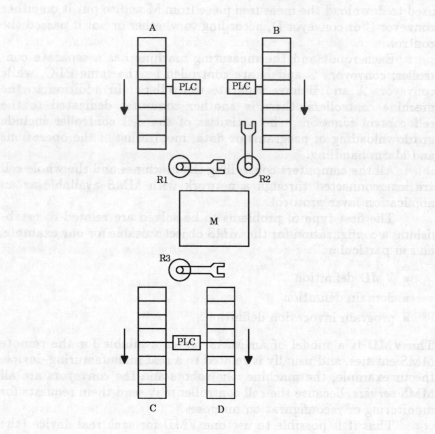

Figure 6.10 Sketch of the layout of a simple quality control cell, composed of a measuring machine (M), three load/unload robots (R1, R2, R3) and four conveyors (A, B, C, D).

to multiple VMDs is strongly dependent on the specific MMS implementation used.

Domains represent complex objects, which include several different types of resources. In fact, other MMS objects can be associated with a domain, as well as information to be stored in the memory of the system implementing the VMD. We now focus our attention on the latter aspect of domains to introduce them in our example.

There are two main types of memory objects: programs and data sets. For example, in the machine M it is possible to have: a domain including the control program, another domain with the part program related to the specific type of piece, a calibration data domain, a probe data domain and a statistical data domain.

The data domains are all used by the control and part programs; the rationale of having this information in separated domains is to obtain more flexibility than in a configuration where both programs and data are in a single domain. In fact, domains can be up/downloaded (by the cell controller in our case) so that it is possible to change the calibration domain associated with a part program, without re-loading the whole set of programs and data, and keeping all this information in separate files.

All the domains mentioned above for the machine M can be deletable, with the exception of a control program, which should be permanent, as it represents the control program that is usually stored in the ROM of the controller. Of course it is possible to modify the control program by loading another domain with a new version and using the latter, instead of the permanent one, in the program invocation implementing the machine operations.

Other devices in our example can have a simpler domain configuration. The PLCs can contain only one program and one data domain for each VMD, and the same configuration can be used for the three robots, as their activity is fixed (loading or unloading the machine M).

In the VMD related to machine M it is possible to have several domains of the same type (for example several probe data sets) present at the same time. Then, the activities of the machine should be defined by creating a program invocation object, defined on a set of existing domains; this object selects one control program, one part program, one probe data set, one statistical data set and one calibration data set out of those potentially available in the VMD. Only the domains selected for a program invocation may contribute with their memory objects to the program execution; all the other domains are active only in the sense that the other MMS objects included may be used by a client, but the program or data set of the domain is not used by the local program.

In our example, only one program invocation is necessary for each VMD. The cell controller can create these program invocations by selecting the domains to be used among those already present (loaded or permanent) in the VMD; in a similar way it is possible to re-configure the application if a change in the probe, part program or calibration data is necessary.

6.7 Variables

A variable is a component of a VMD that accepts or provides a value of a specific type. The MMS objects related to variables are only meant to describe how the real variable is to be accessed, but there is no object holding the data value of the variable. In order to access the value of the real variable, the local VMD should make use of two operations, V-Put and V-Get, which use the appropriate MMS objects and the VMD state to write or to read the value of the real variable.

As the variable related objects in MMS do not contain a value, it is possible that an MMS variable does not correspond to any real variable, but its value is obtained by executing a procedure generating a value for that MMS variable (in this case the variable must be read-only), or the write operation on a variable may correspond to the activation of some system function.

As it is possible to have structured variables, it is necessary that access to MMS variables should either be complete or fail; it must not be possible to obtain partial access. This is not sufficient to ensure that the value of the variable always represents the value it should assume at some point in time, with no internal inconsistency; in fact, while a remote user is reading a structured variable, a local user can write it so that portions of the value read refer to the value before the local write operation, while others already have the new value. To avoid this situation it is necessary to enforce non-interruptible access to the variables; this feature is optional in MMS and the manufacturer should state whether or not it is implemented, and the constraints under which it is implemented.

The two basic types of variable used by MMS are:

- unnamed variables
- named variables.

These variables may then be combined to obtain more complex and structured sets of variables that fall into one of the following categories:

- named list of variables
- scattered access objects.

6.7.1   Unnamed variables

Unnamed variables are the basic type of variables in a VMD. In fact, it is not possible to create or to destroy an unnamed variable, as they are an essential part of the VMD architecture.

There is no name (i.e. identifier) associated with a variable of this category, thus they are distinguished by using an address in a logical space associated with the VMD; it is worth pointing out that the address seen by the MMS is not necessarily the same address as that where the real variable is actually stored, but it only gives an indication of where the associated variable can be found. Nonetheless, the underlying real variable should be a real variable, and not a computed one.

Most of the current computers associate addresses with basic units of memory that are, in general, all equal. However, each unnamed variable, although it is the basic component and has an associated address, also has its own type; therefore, unnamed variables are, in general, of different types, and they can also be structured variables with a structure as complex as any other variable.

The services that can be used with an unnamed variable are the following ones:

- Read: this confirmed service returns the value of the addressed variable
- Write: this confirmed service may be used to assign a new value to the addressed variable
- InformationReport: this non-confirmed service may be used to inform another MMS user of the current value of a variable
- GetVariableAccessAttributes: this confirmed service returns the attributes of the variable object.

6.7.2   Named variables

Named variables associate an identifier with the accessed variable; this may be used for two main purposes. The first one is to describe a variable whose address either does not exist (a computed variable) or is not made available outside the VMD. The other is to create a dynamic mapping between sets of unnamed variables and a named variable, in order to build a new variable with a more complex structure; all the unnamed variables included in the same named variable must be located at contiguous addresses. The constraint on the contiguity does not apply to named variables whose address is not known or unavailable.

Moreover, named variables provide a method to associate application-dependent names to unnamed variables, so that the application program can access these variables with no need to know the corresponding VMD address. It is also possible for different application tasks to define different named variables for the same VMD (that is, on the same set of unnamed variables), in order to obtain different, application-oriented views of the VMD variables.

The mapping between named and unnamed variables may be dynamic as, in general, named variables may be created and destroyed; that corresponds to creating or destroying the mapping onto the underlying unnamed variables, since the value of a named variable is always defined in terms of unnamed ones.

Although it is possible to delete a named variable, it is possible to make some important named variable permanent by indicating in a suitable attribute that it is not MMS deletable; in this case, the delete service fails when used on these named variables.

The services associated with named variables are the same as those for unnamed variables with the addition of the following ones:

- DefineNamedVariable: this confirmed service is used to define a new named variable
- DeleteVariableAccess: this confirmed service deletes a named variable (if deletable).

6.7.3   Scattered access

Named variables provide a means to group several contiguous unnamed variables into a more complex data structure which retains all the characteristics of an MMS variable. Scattered objects represent a further step in the same direction, as they may be used to group several different MMS variables under a single name; the main difference from named variables is that some of the constraints applicable to the latter type of variables are removed:

- it is not necessary for all the components to be unnamed variables, they can also be named variables or other scattered access objects;
- it is not necessary for all the components to be located at contiguous addresses in the logical address space of the VMD.

A typical situation is represented by the example in Figure 6.11, where a scattered variable is composed of named and unnamed variables located at non-contiguous addresses.

The access to a scattered variable has the same properties of access to an unnamed or named variable; in particular, the access is either completed or fails. Moreover, it is possible to implement indivisible access to scattered variables.

Sometimes it is necessary to access a scattered variable only to get or alter the value of one of its components, thus it would be nice to obtain or give the value of the desired component only. In order to allow this type of access, each component has a name associated

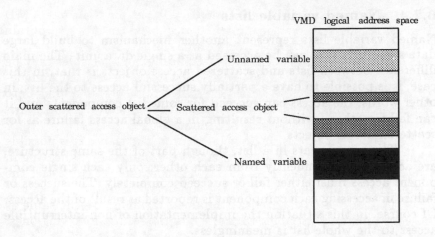

Figure 6.11 Example of location of the components of a scattered object within the logical address space of the VMD.

with it which identifies it within the scattered object; some components, such as named variables and scattered objects, also have a name on their own, but it is different, in general, from their name as components of a larger scattered variable. It is interesting to point out that the components of the scattered objects may be accessed either using their own names (or addresses, in the case of unnamed variables) or by using the scattered object name and the component name. In either case, the same variable is accessed.

It is also possible to use a subset of an unnamed variable, named variable or scattered access object as a component of a scattered access object, rather than the whole variable; in this case, an alternate access needs to be specified (see Section 6.7.8).

The operations allowed on a scattered access object are Read, Write and InformationReport, as defined for unnamed variables (Section 6.7.1) plus the following ones:

- DefineScatteredAccess: this confirmed service creates a scattered object;
- GetVariableAccessAttribute: this confirmed service returns an external description of the scattered object;
- GetScatteredAccessAttribute: this confirmed service returns the actual value of the scattered access object attributes;
- DeleteVariableAccess: this confirmed service deletes a scattered access object (if deletable).

6.7.4   Named variable lists

Named variable lists represent another mechanism to build large data structures that can be accessed as a single data unit. The main difference between lists and scattered access objects is that, in this case, it is possible to have a partially successful access to the list; in other words, the access can succeed for some list components and it can fail for others, without resulting in a global access failure as for scattered access objects.

The components in a list, though part of the same structure, are accessed independently from each other; only each single component access must either fail or succeed completely. The success or failure in accessing each component is reported as result of the access. Of course, in this situation the implementation of non-interruptible access to the whole list is meaningless.

To build a list it is possible to use the same type of components as for scattered objects: unnamed variables, named variables and scattered access objects. Thus it is not possible to define named variable lists composed by other named variable lists (while it is possible to define scattered access objects composed of other smaller scattered access objects). Also in this case, the components of a named variable list may be defined as subsets of already existing variables, by using an alternate access specification (see Section 6.7.8).

The operations allowed on a named variable list are Read, Write and InformationReport, as defined for unnamed variables (Section 6.7.1), plus the following ones:

- DefineNamedVariableList: this confirmed service creates a new named variable list;
- GetNamedVariableListAttributes: this confirmed service returns the value of the attributes of a named variable list;
- DeleteNamedVariableList: this confirmed service deletes a named variable list.

6.7.5   Type definition in MMS

All the MMS variables (including the unnamed ones) have an associated type, thus it is necessary to provide a mechanism to specify types in MMS messages. The type of a variable, whenever needed, can be specified by using one of the following methods:

- by referencing the name of one of the basic classes (for simple types only);
- by referencing the name of a user type already defined;
- by giving the full description of the type.

6.7.6 Basic classes

Most of the basic classes are borrowed from those defined for ASN.1 (see Chapter 4). In particular, the following are basic classes with the same definition as for ASN.1:

- *boolean*
- *bit string*
- *integer*
- *unsigned*
- *real*
- *octet string*
- *visible string*
- *generalized time.*

The full specification of a variable type is not limited to a reference to a class name, but it should also include, in some cases, a parameter specifying the size of the variable, when this information cannot be derived from the basic class referenced. For example, the octet string and integer classes can include types of different size, while for the boolean class no size parameter is required, as all the variables in this class are 1 bit long. The class *real* needs three size parameters: the base (2 or 10), the size of the exponent (in octets) and the size of the mantissa (in octets).

In addition to the classes listed above, three new basic types are introduced by MMS:

- *floating point*: this class defines a type with values representing positive and negative numbers, zero, both infinities (positive and negative) and Not a Number (NaN), as defined in the ANSI/IEEE standard 754 for binary floating point numbers [IEEE754]; the size parameter specifies the number of bits used for the whole representation and the number of bits used for the exponent;
- *binary time*: this class defines a binary representation of time, which may or not include the date, as specified in the size parameter;
- *BCD*: this class consists of a sequence of decimal digits from some character set; the size indicates the number of digits in the sequence.

6.7.7 Type description

The type specifications making use of either a reference to an already defined type or describing the type in the message itself imply that there should be a method to define the structure of the type. For types already defined, this definition should be transmitted whenever a remote user needs to know the structure of the type. For types described in the message itself, the need for this definition is obvious.

Besides simple types, a variable type may be either an array or a structure (with the same meaning as in the C programming language).

The array definition is given by:

- an indication as to whether or not the array is packed, that is storage optimization mechanisms are used for the array;
- the number of elements, as the index is always an integer and its lowest value is always 0, as in the C language;
- the type specification of one element of the array.

The specification of a structure requires the following information:

- an indication as to whether or not the structure is packed, that is storage optimization mechanisms are used for the structure;
- a list of components, where each item specifies:
  - the component name
  - the type specification for the component.

In summary, the specification of a type may be described by the ASN.1 abstract definition in Figure 6.12.

Note that the field *type specification* in Figure 6.12 has the same format as the whole structure. Therefore, the type definition may be recursively composed by other type definitions.

It turns out that a type definition may be seen as a tree (the type tree), where the root is the whole type, the leaves are always the simple types of all the components in the type structure and the intermediate nodes (if any) represent all the arrays and structures composing the whole type. An example of a type tree is shown in Figure 6.13, which defines a structure including in its components some arrays.

There is no pre-defined limit imposed by the standard to the nesting in a type specification, however some practical limitations always exist, because more nesting means more resource (memory) consumption to store the type definition. In order to cope with implementations with different amounts of resources available for this purpose, the two MMS users participating in an application association negotiate the maximum nesting level allowed for variables to be dealt with during the association, as seen in Section 6.2.1.

6.7.8   Alternate access

Variables or scattered access objects may be complex data structures, while, in general, the operations that need to be performed on them

```
TypeSpecification::= CHOICE {
  typeName          [0]   ObjectName
  array             [1]   IMPLICIT SEQUENCE {
    packed              [0]   IMPLICIT BOOLEAN DEFAULT
                                  FALSE,
    numberOfElements  [1]   IMPLICIT Unsigned32,
    elementType       [2]   TypeSpecification
    },
  structure         [2]   IMPLICIT SEQUENCE {
    packed              [0]   IMPLICIT BOOLEAN DEFAULT
                                  FALSE,
    components          [1]   IMPLICIT SEQUENCE OF
          SEQUENCE {
          componentName       [0]   IMPLICIT Identifier
                                        OPTIONAL,
          componentType       [1]   TypeSpecificcation
          }
    },
  -- (simple type specifications follow)
    . . .
    . . .
    . . .
  }
```

Figure 6.12   Description of the type specification parameter, by using ASN.1 notation.

are limited to reading or updating only a part of the whole data structure. Whenever a read or write is performed on a variable or scattered object, the whole contents of the data structure must be sent over the network, even though only part of it is really involved in the read or update operation.

This may be detrimental for communication efficiency; thus MMS provides a method to specify the access to only a subset of the referenced variable, the so-called *alternate access*, which can be inserted in a request whenever access to the whole variable is not needed.

Of course, alternate access specifies the subset of the whole variable following the definition of the underlying type tree. In fact, the alternate access definition consists of the selection of a suitable

```
{structure{ FALSE,
        {{ "field1",
          {array {
          FALSE,
          13,
          boolean}
          }
        },
        {"field2,{unsigned}},
        {"field3",
          {array {
          TRUE,
          25,
          integer}
          }
        }
      }
    }
}
```

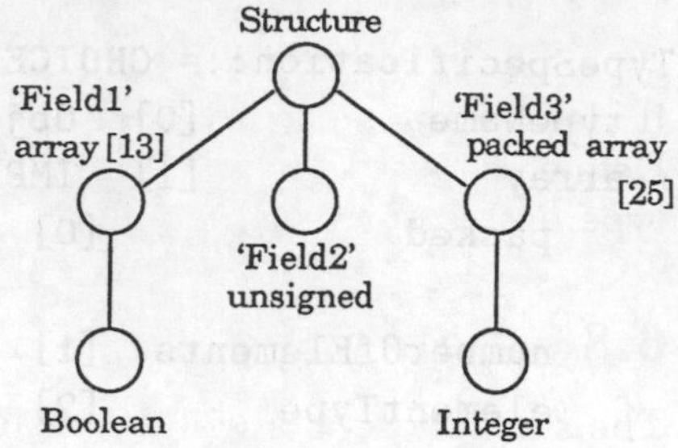

Structure

'Field1'
array [13]

'Field2'
unsigned

'Field3'
packed array
[25]

Boolean

Integer

Figure 6.13   Type tree (right) associated with the variable defined on the left.

subset of the type tree. In particular, it is possible to exclude any sub-tree and, if the root of the sub-tree is an array, it is possible to specify a sub-range for the index that defines the subset to be accessed.

The alternate access can also be used to define new types whose associated tree is obtained by pruning an already defined type tree; with this operation a type name is associated with the pruned type tree, so that variables with that structure may be defined. For example, from the type tree in Figure 6.13 it is possible to derive a type composed of only the first two components of the structure.

6.7.9   Services

Only a few operations are defined for type manipulation:

- *DefineNamedType*: defines a new named type;
- *DeleteNamedType*: deletes an existing named type (if deletable);

- *GetNamedTypeAttributes*: provides the values of the attributes of an existing named type.

It is worth noticing that Read, Write, DefineNamedVariable, DefineScatteredAccess, and DefineNamedVariableList all use the type descriptor parameter.

6.8 Semaphores

The semaphore is an MMS entity that may be used to impose controlled access to a part of the VMD. Using terminology borrowed from operating systems, the semaphore may be used to implement a conditional critical region, as defined in [Brin73]. The same mechanism may also be used to synchronize the operations of different application tasks, as the permission to take control of the semaphore may be granted or denied according to the state of the computation of the cooperating tasks.

It is important to point out that the reason why a client is requesting the control of a semaphore is not known to the VMD; in other words, the VMD cannot establish a relationship between a specific semaphore and the controlled subset of resources. This avoids the VMD enforcing any protection on the subset on the basis of the semaphore status, unlike in operating systems. This point may be better illustrated by an example. Assume that only one VMD client at a time should be allowed to access a particular variable A; as it will be seen later, it is possible to use a semaphore object with only one token to implement this condition. However, a VMD client that receives a deny to control the semaphore (i.e. another client is accessing the variable A) can access all the variables and cannot be stopped by the VMD, as the latter is not aware of the relationship between the semaphore operations and those on the variable A. The enforcement of access through the use of semaphore should be done at the application task level, by making sure that requests for accessing the variable A are never sent when the task does not control the semaphore.

A semaphore has a set of tokens associated with it. In order to take control of the semaphore, it is necessary for a request to find a token available; therefore, the number of tokens is the maximum number of requests that can contemporaneously take control of the semaphore, or the maximum number of users that are allowed to be in the associated critical region.

Each new request for taking control of the semaphore generates a new semaphore entry. If the new entry finds a token available, then it gets the ownership of the token, otherwise, the entry is inserted in a waiting list. Whenever a token is released by one of the owners, the first entry in the waiting list (if any) becomes the owner of the token.

Two different types of semaphores are defined by MMS:

- token semaphores
- pool semaphores.

In the first type, all the tokens are identical, thus the requests are for any available token. Vice versa, each token in a pool semaphore has a name, and the requests are for a specific token; therefore, an entry becomes a token owner only if a token with the requested name is available. This implies also that when a token is released the waiting list is scanned and the first entry (if any) requesting the free token is selected as the new token owner.

The semaphore entries have some parameters that influence the behavior of the semaphore; the most interesting ones are listed below.

- *Priority*: the waiting list is organized in an order that depends on entry priority (the actual ordering rule is an internal matter for the VMD) and, within the same priority class, in First Come First Served order; thus it is possible to implement urgent requests for the semaphore, which can be inserted at the head of the queue, as the semaphore behavior does not allow the preemption of one of the token owners;

- *Maximum waiting time*: this optional parameter indicates the maximum time this entry can be in the waiting list; once the corresponding time has expired without acquiring a token, the entry should be cancelled and the client notified; this parameter may be useful in order to avoid endless waiting;

- *Maximum control time*: this optional parameter specifies the maximum time the entry is allowed to hold a token; this parameter may be used to avoid the situation where an entry controlling a token will never release it;

- *Relinquish if connection is lost*: this boolean parameter indicates whether or not the semaphore entry should release the token (if any is owned) if the application association with the client which generated the entry is lost;

- *abort on time out*: this boolean parameter specifies whether or not the AA with the client which generated the entry must be aborted upon the expiration of the control timeout.

The semaphore entry also has a state following the rules illustrated by Figure 6.14.

- *NON-EXISTENT*: this state is used just to indicate that the entry does not exist;

- *QUEUED*: a request to take control of the semaphore generates an entry with this state, if the control of the semaphore cannot be granted;

- *OWNER*: this state is entered whenever the entry is assigned the ownership of a semaphore token;

- *HUNG*: this state is reached from the OWNER state when some critical event occurs; the associated token is not released in this state, and a preemptive TakeControl request puts back the entry in the OWNER state.

Note that the diagram also includes local actions of the VMD in order to cope with a critical situation without relying on remote clients, which could not take appropriate actions because they have either crashed or are unable to communicate.

An event condition (see Section 6.9) is associated with each semaphore; this event is triggered whenever a critical condition occurs (control timeout or waiting timeout expiration). Using this mechanism, the client can program actions to cope automatically with these critical situations.

Two types of semaphore entries are allowed: simple and modifier. The entries in the first class are generated by normal requests to take control of the semaphore. Those in the second class are generated by requests for any service with a suitable modifier parameter set; these requests are not served when they are received, but their execution is dependent on the semaphore status. When a modifier entry takes control of a token, then the associated service request is executed; once the response is ready to be sent to the client, the token is immediately released, without any action from the client. Simple semaphore entries generate a positive response whenever they get the control of a token; when in control, an explicit request of the client to release the semaphore is required, in order to free the owned token.

The mechanism of modifier entries allows the client to program a pre-defined number of actions, whose execution is delayed until a token is available in the semaphore. Thus it is a way of implementing straightaway the synchronization of operation among different tasks.

6.8.1 Services

The operations defined on semaphores are the following:

- TakeControl: requests control of the semaphore; a response is generated when either the semaphore is available (positive response) or the entry is cancelled because of waiting time out expiration, association abort or local action (see Figure 6.14);
- TakeControl (preemptive): this service does not create a new entry, but assigns new values to an entry in the HUNG state and puts it back in the OWNER state;
- RelinquishControl: this service is used to release a semaphore acquired at some earlier time; this operation is not required for modifier type entries;
- DefineSemaphore: creates a new semaphore;

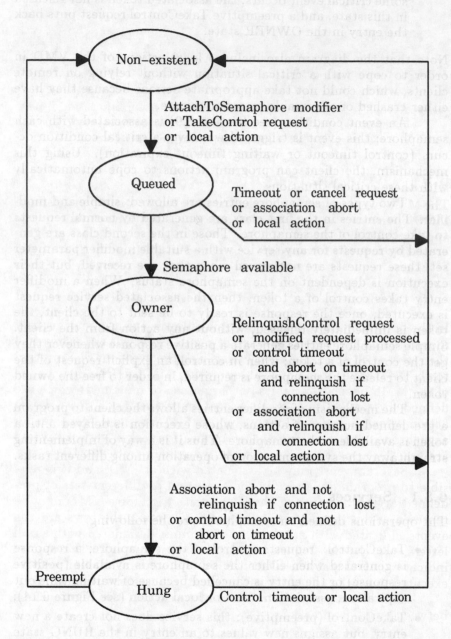

Figure 6.14 State diagram of a semaphore.

- DeleteSemaphore: drops a semaphore object;
- ReportSemaphoreStatus: provides information on the status of a token semaphore;
- ReportPoolSemaphoreStatus: provides information on the status of a pool semaphore;
- ReportSemaphoreEntryStatus: provides the values of the attributes of all the semaphore entries;
- AttachToSemaphoreModifier: creates a modifier semaphore entry and puts it in the QUEUED state; this service is the counterpart of TakeControl for modifier entries.

6.9 Event management

The MMS events provide a mechanism to execute a list of pre-defined MMS operations upon the occurrence of a situation relevant to the application tasks.

Two types of events are considered in MMS:

- monitored
- network.

In the first case, the condition that may fire the event is continuously monitored by the VMD, sampling at regular intervals the state of all the relevant objects. The entity triggering the event may be internal to the VMD (i.e. it is not visible to other MMS users), or it is one of the MMS boolean variables (either named or unnamed) which are defined in the VMD. A monitored event is the model for a VMD action, which is relevant for the application, and should generate an asynchronous notification to other application tasks. Network events are fired by a specific request issued by a client to the VMD.

Several events may be associated with a VMD, and it is possible to program dynamically the execution of different sets of pre-defined actions for each of them. The situation for a VMD may be represented by the matrix in Figure 6.15, where the rows are the events indicated with numbers, the columns, designated with small letters, are the pre-defined actions and the crosses in the matrix indicate that the action identified by the column label should be executed upon the triggering of the event indicated by the row label.

Three types of objects are used to express the relationships between events and actions:

- Event condition objects: describe the type of event;
- Event action objects: describe the actions that may be executed;
- Event enrolment: relate actions and events (their function is similar to that of crosses in Figure 6.15).

Events	Actions				
	a	b	c	d	e
1	X		X		
2		X			X
3	X	X		X	

Figure 6.15   Matrix showing the associations between events (rows) and actions (columns).

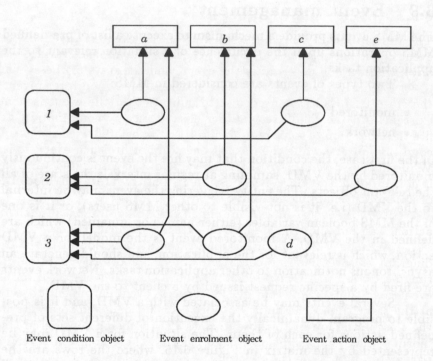

Event condition object   Event enrolment object   Event action object

Figure 6.16   Description of the contents of the matrix in Figure 6.15, by using MMS event objects.

The configuration described by the matrix in Figure 6.15 is shown in Figure 6.16. Note that the action *d* does not have any associated action object, and there is one enrolment object labeled as *d*; this notation is used because it is possible to have enrolment objects including the description of the action to be performed, rather than referencing an event action object.

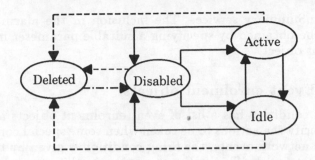

Figure 6.17   State diagram of a monitored event.

6.9.1   Event condition objects

The description of the characteristics of the event is given by an event condition object. This object specifies the boolean variable (if any), whose value determines the event, and the state of the event.

Figure 6.17 shows the state diagram of a monitored event; the state DELETED is used just to indicate that the event is non-existent. All the solid arcs can be selected, in any combination, to fire the execution of some enrolment object associated with the event condition object, while the dashed ones cannot fire such executions. While in the state DISABLED, the value of the associated variable is not sampled; therefore, it is possible to exit this state only because of an explicit enabling action.

Network events have a simplified state diagram, because their actions can only be triggered by an external explicit request.

A single VMD operation may cause a transition in the state diagram of several event condition objects; a priority parameter, ranging from 0 to 127, is used to establish the order of execution of event condition objects that need to process event enrolment objects at the same time. The highest priority should be given to events in the class 0, the lowest to those in class 127 (64 being considered the 'normal' class). In addition to the priority, there is also a severity parameter, indicating the effect of the actions related to the event on the controlled process; its influence on the execution of the actions is not specified by MMS and should be determined by the VMD implementor.

Monitored events also have other parameters specifying the period of sampling for the associated variable, and the time of the last transition to IDLE and to ACTIVE states.

Some monitored events may be defined as alarms. There is no special meaning associated with alarms, as the MMS cannot be aware of the characteristics of the controlled process, hence it cannot take any particular action upon the occurrence of an alarm. The only purpose of the alarm definition is to include the state of the event in a summary report, that can be obtained by invoking the

GetAlarmSummary service. The inclusion in the alarm summary can also be obtained by specifying a suitable parameter in an event enrolment object.

6.9.2   Event enrolment objects

An event condition has a list of event enrolment objects associated, which specify the actions to be taken when some special condition occurs. For network events, the firing condition is given by the receipt of a request for the TriggerEvent service; in this case, all the associated event enrolment objects are processed. Monitored events are more complex, as each associated event enrolment object can specify any set of solid arcs (except for those leading to the DELETED state, which can only be selected altogether) in Figure 6.17 as execution condition. Thus, whenever a possible firing transition occurs, the list of event enrolment objects is scanned and the enrolment objects, including the transition that has just occurred in their execution condition parameter, are selected for processing.

As shown in Figure 6.16, two different types of enrolment object exist: modifier and notification.

Modifier event enrolments

An instance of this type of event enrolment object is created whenever a request for confirmed service is received, with a special modifier field set. In this case, a transaction object is created for the request of service; in addition, an event enrolment object is also created, with a reference to the transaction object and to the event condition object referenced in the modifier field.

The execution of the confirmed service is delayed until a transition in the associated event condition triggers the processing of the corresponding event enrolment object. The whole process is shown in the time diagram shown in Figure 6.18.

After the response to the modified service request has been issued, the event enrolment object is deleted. It turns out that modifier event enrolment objects may be used to program only 'one-shot' operations, as the same operation will not be executed again upon the occurrence of the same condition, unless a client re-programs the operation by issuing a modified request.

In order to avoid overly long waiting times or deadlocks due to VMD crashes, it is possible to specify a maximum waiting time for the modifier enrolment object. If this time expires and the object has not been processed nor is being processed, a negative response is issued for the modified request of service.

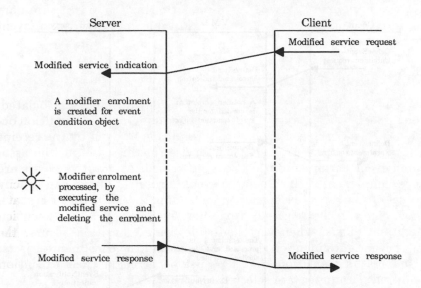

Figure 6.18   Time diagram of the messages generated to program and process a modifier event enrolment object.

Notification enrolments

The creation and destruction of notification event enrolment objects should be done by using suitable confirmed services, thus, once created, the programming of the associated action has to be considered permanent. In other words, the action associated with a notification enrolment is executed every time the same event occurs, as long as the enrolment object is not deleted or updated.

The action associated with a notification enrolment is to provide a response to a confirmed service specified by an event action object. As the action is just a response to a confirmed service, the time diagram of the messages exchanged as a consequence of notification processing is significantly different from that for modifier enrolments. Figure 6.19 shows such a diagram; after the enrolment creation, the triggering of the event enrolment processing produces the operations, local to the VMD, that are necessary to provide a response message, as if a request for the service specified in the associated event action object had been received. After all the parameters for the response have been computed, all the data are sent to the enrolled client, by using an EventNotification service primitive.

It is also possible for a notification enrolment not to reference any event action object, when the client creating the enrolment object needs only a notification that the triggering condition has occurred, and no other action should be taken by the event processor.

In the diagram of Figure 6.19, the notification of the event

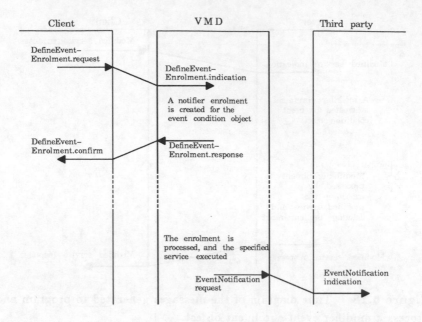

Figure 6.19   Time diagram showing the messages exchanged to create and to process a notifier event enrolment object, without acknowledgment.

triggering remains unacknowledged, as the EventNotification is a non-confirmed service. It is possible, though not mandatory, to send acknowledgments of the notification, but such messages do not have any particular effects.

This is the simplest mode of operation for processing a notification enrolment object. More complex modes are allowed for monitored events only, and they include mandatory acknowledgments for the notification. Note that all the mechanisms described in the following provide a level of acknowledgment higher than an MMS confirmation, because they involve the MMS client to some extent.

Each enrolment object has two parameters that are used in the acknowledge procedure for the notification: the alarm acknowledge rule and the acknowledgment event condition reference. The first parameter indicates what type of acknowledgment mechanism should be used; the reference to alarms is used because all the enrolments specifying mandatory acknowledgment are included in a summary of the state of alarm enrolments. The time diagram for the operations with acknowledgment are shown in Figure 6.20. The AcknowledgeEventNotification service is confirmed, thus a response is needed.

The possible values for this parameter are the following ones:

- *NONE*: indicates that no acknowledgment is required, but that

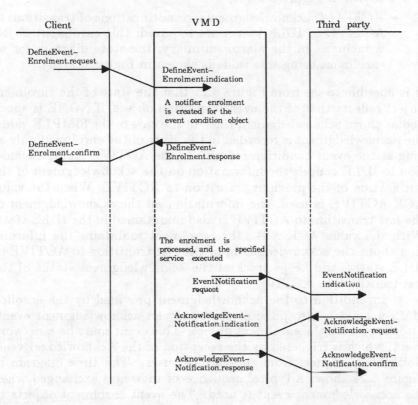

Client VMD Third party

DefineEvent-
Enrolment.request

DefineEvent-
Enrolment.indication

A notifier enrolment
is created for the
event condition object

DefineEvent-
Enrolment.confirm

DefineEvent-
Enrolment.response

The enrolment is
processed, and the specified
service executed

EventNotification
request

EventNotification
indication

AcknowledgeEvent-
Notification.indication

AcknowledgeEvent-
Notification. request

AcknowledgeEvent-
Notification.response

AcknowledgeEvent-
Notification.confirm

Figure 6.20 Time diagram showing the messages exchanged to process
a notification event enrolment object, with acknowledgment.

it is allowed, thus the messages exchanged can be as those
shown in Figure 6.19; the enrolment is not included in the
alarm summary; the state diagram of an enrolment using this
value is shown in Figure 6.21(a);

- *SIMPLE*: the acknowledgment is allowed, but not required, for
  enrolments triggered on a transition to the ACTIVE state and
  it affects the state of the enrolment object; acknowledgments
  of notifications of transitions to the IDLE state do not affect
  the state of the enrolment; this enrolment is included in the
  alarm summary; the state diagram for enrolments using this
  value is shown in Figure 6.21(b);

- *ACK-ACTIVE*: acknowledgment for notifications of a transition to ACTIVE are required; those for transitions to the
  IDLE state are allowed but do not influence the state of the
  enrolment; this enrolment object is included in the alarm summary; the state diagram of an enrolment using this value is

shown in Figure 6.21(c);

- *ACK-ALL*: acknowledgments for notifications of transitions to ACTIVE or IDLE states are required; this enrolment object is included in the alarm summary; the state diagram for an enrolment using this value is shown in Figure 6.21(d).

It is possible to see from Figure 6.21 that the state of the enrolment object reflects that of the event condition object, if NONE is specified as alarm acknowledgment rule. In the case of the SIMPLE value, the acknowledgment is recorded in the state of the enrolment only as long as the event condition remains in the ACTIVE state; a transition to IDLE cancels the information on the acknowledgment of the notification of the previous transition to ACTIVE. When the value ACK-ACTIVE is used, the information on the acknowledgment of the last transition to ACTIVE is also maintained in the IDLE state. With the value ACK-ALL, the enrolment maintains the information about the acknowledgment of the last transition to ACTIVE or IDLE states, and keeps track of the acknowledgment status of the last transition to ACTIVE.

In addition to the acknowledgment provided by the enrolled MMS user, it is also possible to specify an acknowledgment event, associated with the enrolment object. This event must be a network event, which is triggered by the reception of the AcknowledgeEventNotification request from the enrolled user. The time diagram in Figure 6.22 shows a typical sequence of messages exchanged when the acknowledgment event is used. The event enrolment objects to be processed when the acknowledgment event is triggered may be of any type allowed in a network event, and they are programmed by the MMS users and not pre-defined by the standard. The meaning of the acknowledgment event triggering is that the original enrolment object has been processed, the notification has been sent and the enrolled user has acknowledged this notification; hence, the actions programmed upon the triggering of the acknowledgment event should reflect this meaning.

The use of both notification acknowledge and acknowledgment event allows the user to program a sequence of operations (service executions) arbitrarily complex. In fact, one of the enrolment objects associated with the acknowledgment event may trigger another event, with enrolments specifying their own acknowledgment event. Of course, the applications programmers should make sure that the sequence of messages triggered by an event will terminate in a finite time and will not cause a traffic congestion.

6.9.3   Event action objects

The description of the actions that should be executed as a consequence of processing notification event enrolment objects is held in

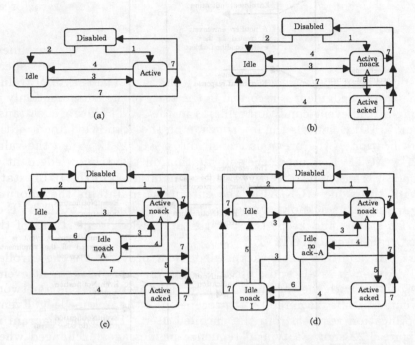

Figure 6.21   State diagram for an event enrolment object, according to the acknowledgment rule selected: (a) NONE, (b) SIMPLE, (c) ACK-ACTIVE and (d) ACK-ALL. The conditions causing state transitions are as follows:

(1) Event enabled, with the monitored variable TRUE or local defined event pending.

(2) Event enabled, with the monitored variable FALSE or local defined event pending.

(3) Monitored variable becomes TRUE or local event detected.

(4) Monitored variable becomes FALSE or local event detected.

(5) Reception of an acknowledge event notification for current state and time of transition.

(6) Reception of acknowledge event notification for ACTIVE while in IDLE state, with time equal to last transition to ACTIVE.

(7) Event disabled.

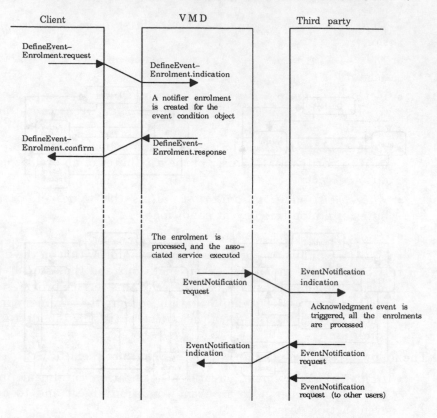

Figure 6.22   Time diagram showing the messages exchanged to process a notifier event enrolment object, with an associated acknowledgment event condition.

the event action object.

The core information is the confirmed service to be executed when an enrolment object referencing the action object is processed. The action object also stores all the parameter values for the specified confirmed service, with all the possible modifiers (including that generating a modifier enrolment object).

The result of the service specified will be sent to the enrolled user as a part of the event notification, when one of the associated enrolments is processed.

The action objects may or may not be deletable.

6.9.4   Services

It is possible to divide the services into three classes, according to the type of objects they are operating upon.

The services associated with event condition objects are the following ones:

- *DefineEventCondition*: causes the creation of an event condition object;
- *DeleteEventCondition*: deletes an event condition object (if deletable);
- *GetEventConditionAttributes*: this confirmed service is used to obtain the values of the attributes of an event condition object;
- *ReportEventConditionStatus*: this non-confirmed service is used to notify an MMS user of the attributes of an event condition object;
- *AlterEventConditionMonitoring*: alters the values of attributes of a monitored event condition;
- *TriggerEvent*: triggers a network event;
- *GetAlarmSummary*: provides summary information on the attributes of the monitored event conditions and the associated notification enrolments; a parameter of this service provides a mechanism to filter the information, so that the summary includes only the attributes of the objects satisfying the filtering conditions.

The following services operate with the event enrolment objects.

- *DefineEventEnrolment*: creates a notification enrolment object and attaches it to an event condition object and to an event action object;
- *DeleteEventEnrolment*: deletes one or more notification enrolments;
- *AlterEventEnrolment*: modifies some attributes of a notification enrolment;
- *GetEventEnrolmentAttributes*: obtains the values of the attributes of one or more enrolments;
- *ReportEventEnrolmentStatus*: this non-confirmed service notifies an MMS user of the status of an event enrolment object;
- *EventNotification*: notifies the enrolled client that the service associated with its enrolment has been executed; the result of the enrolled service execution is included in the notification;
- *AcknowledgeEventNotification*: acknowledges the receipt of the notification, according to the rules explained in Section 6.9.2;
- *GetAlarmEnrolmentSummary*: provides summary information on the status of the enrolment objects selected according to the acknowledging rules specified in Section 6.9.2; it is possible to specify filter conditions to obtain information on only the objects satisfying such conditions.

The services operating on event action objects are the following ones:

- *DefineEventAction*: creates a new event action;
- *DeleteEventAction*: deletes an existing event action (if deletable);
- *GetEventActionAttributes*: provides the values of the attributes of an event action;
- *ReportEventActionStatus*: notifies an MMS user of the state of an event action object.

6.10   Other entities

6.10.1   Journals

The MMS journal provides a facility to record and retrieve information, stored in chronological order, that keeps track of the history of the values of variables and event states, along with operator annotations. The standard does not specify whether the journal contents are stored on a disk or kept in memory, as these decisions are left to the implementor.

The journal entity is defined by using two types of object:

- journal object
- journal entry object.

The first one is used to maintain the journal name and the indication of whether or not it may be deleted by an MMS user.

Each journal object has an associated list of journal entries. The attributes of this type of object include both the information field associated with a single record operation, and a time stamp and order of receipt, which are used to identify the chronological order of the different journal entries.

One of the following three types of information can be stored in a single journal entry:

- *ANNOTATION*: the entry contains a textual comment (probably originated by an operator), which can be used to document some condition which occurred or action that was taken during the application execution; this field is a string of no more than 255 characters;
- *EVENT-DATA*: the entry contains a reference and the status of an event that has been recorded; it is also possible to have the references and the values of one or more variables; this type of entry can be generated as the consequence of processing an enrolment object;
- *DATA*: the entry contains references and values of one or more variables.

The operations allowed on a journal are listed below:

- *CreateJournal*: creates a new journal object with an associated empty list of entries;
- *DeleteJournal*: deletes a journal object (if deletable); all its associated entries are lost;
- *InitializeJournal*: clears all or part of one or more journals, by deleting a set of journal entry objects;
- *ReadJournal*: retrieves one or more entries from a specified journal;
- *WriteJournal*: adds one or more entries to the contents of a specified journal;
- *ReportJournalStatus*: returns the number of current entries in a journal, and an indication of whether the journal is MMS deletable.

6.10.2 Operator communication

The operator station entity in MMS provides mechanisms for exchanging data with a display or data entry device. The type of information exchanged is strings of non-interpreted characters (i.e. special characters or escape sequences are not recognized by MMS); the interpretation or the correct generation of these strings is left to the real device constituting the real operator station.

No mechanism for data flow control is defined for an operator station; however, the operation station object provides in its attributes an indication of the state of data buffers that may be used by the VMD clients to decide whether or not data can be input or output to the operator station.

Additional mechanisms that guarantee the integrity of multiple transaction operations on the same operator station may be implemented locally, as a part of the VMD.

The operator stations may be for data entry only, for data display only, or for data entry and display.

The only two types of services allowed are:

- *Input*: gets a string from an operator station; it is possible to specify a prompt string to be displayed to request the input, and a maximum time for which the request can wait for input data;
- *Output*: puts a list of character strings into the output buffer of an operator station.

6.11   Completing the example

In this section the simple example given in Section 6.6 is completed with the introduction of the other MMS objects discussed in the second part of this chapter. These are more oriented to solving the

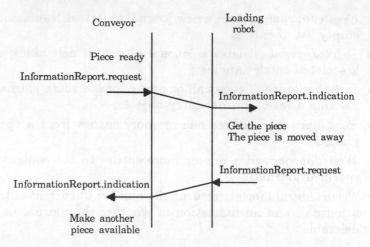

Figure 6.23   Synchronization between robot and conveyor with *InformationReport* service.

problems of communication and synchronization of the activities of the application programs.

Synchronization occurs in two types of situation in the cell in our example: between conveyors and the associated robots, and in the coordination of operations around the machine M. The former is simpler, as only a pair of devices are involved, while the latter should take into account all the robots and the measuring machine.

The coordination of robot and conveyor activities may be solved in different ways, by using MMS objects. Probably the most straightforward method uses non-confirmed services to convey the synchronizations signals. The most likely candidate for this usage is the *InformationReport* service, which can be used by the conveyor to inform the robot that a new piece is ready to be picked, and by the robot to inform the conveyor that the piece has been moved away in a position that allows a new piece to be moved safely to the output position. As the *InformationReport* is used to transmit the value of a variable, it is also necessary to define a boolean variable in the conveyor and another in the robot, to indicate whether or not the other machine is allowed to perform an operation. The whole synchronization operations are shown in Figure 6.23.

Another method for solving the robot–conveyor synchronization problem is based on the use of events. In this case, we use a somewhat more complex mechanism (it depends on the specific implementations considered), but the operation of the application program is simplified and the flexibility is enhanced.

Two event condition objects are needed, one located in the robot VMD, the other in the conveyor VMD. The first one goes to the *ACTIVE* state whenever the robot grasps a new piece and moves

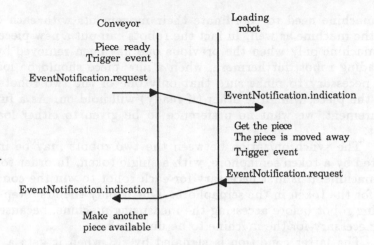

Figure 6.24 Sequence of operations in the robot–conveyor synchronization using events.

it away from the conveyor at a distance such that another piece on the conveyor can be safely moved to the exchange position; when the piece is placed in the measuring machine, the event state goes to *IDLE*. The other event goes to the *ACTIVE* state whenever a new piece has reached the exchanged position, so that it can be grasped by the robot, and it returns to the *IDLE* state once the piece has been removed by the robot.

Both event condition objects are based on a locally defined variable, hidden to other MMS entities, but manipulated by the local application programs. A single event action object is associated with each of the two events; no confirmed service needs to be specified, because the *EventNotification* itself carries information on the occurrence of either event. Also, a single event enrolment object is required for each event, both activated on the *IDLE* to *ACTIVE* transition of the event; the enrolment in the robot VMD is addressed to the conveyor, and the enrolment in the conveyor VMD is addressed to the robot. The sequence of operations is shown in Figure 6.24; it looks quite similar to Figure 6.23, however, it should be noted that, in this case, the application program does not have to know which MMS user should receive a notification of the event. Thus, if it is necessary to inform some other machine (for example the one that loads the conveyor with pieces) of the movement of the objects, it is just necessary to introduce a second event enrolment object with a reference to the AA already established with the other machine; the event management mechanism provided by MMS will also send a notification to this new machine involved in the synchronization.

The coordination of the operation of the three robots and the measuring machine is more complicated. The two robots loading the machine need to coordinate their movements with each other and the machine as well. In fact the robots can put a new piece into the machine only when the previous one has been removed by the unloading robot; furthermore, when a new piece should be loaded, it is necessary to make sure that only one of the two robots will load the piece, while the other (if ready) will hold on. As a further requirement, we want no preference to be given to either loading robot.

The synchronization between the two robots may be implemented by a token semaphore, with a single token. In order to load the machine, it is first necessary for each robot to win the competition for the token in the semaphore. This is only the first step for a loading robot before accessing the measuring machine, because it is also necessary for the machine to be unloaded.

The latter condition is signaled by R3 when it gets a piece from the machine in a position such that another one can be loaded. The occurrence of this situation may be signaled by an MMS event, with two enrolment objects, one per loading robot, triggered on the IDLE to ACTIVE transition. However, in this case the situation is not as simple as in the robot–conveyor synchronization, as shown by the following possible sequence of operations:

(1) R1 requests and gets the control of the semaphore, then it waits for the machine to be unloaded;

(2) R3 unloads the machine and sends an *EventNotification* to both R1 and R2;

(3) R1 loads the piece and relinquishes control of the semaphore;

(4) R2 gets control of the semaphore and processes the *EventNotification* received from R3, this leads to loading a second piece on the machine, as R2 is not aware of the operations performed by R1 in response to the same *EventNotification.indication*.

Moreover, it is not always possible for R3 to know which robot will load the next piece, because it might happen that, when R3 unloads the machine, both robots are waiting for a piece from the conveyor, hence a selective notification of the event occurrence cannot be used. Another possibility is that the robot owner of the semaphore token will hold the token until the *EventNotification.indication* is received from R3; however, if the loading robot is faster than the measuring process and the unloading robot, then it will continuously load pieces, because the notification for the unloaded machine is received when it is again ready to load a piece.

A possible solution to the problem is the use of acknowledgments for the notifications of events (see Section 6.9). In particular, it is possible to use the SIMPLE acknowledgement rule using, for each event enrolment object, the state diagram in Figure 6.21(b).

Hence the sequence of operations performed by either loading robots are as follows:

(1) request the semaphore (i.e. send a *TakeControl.request*);

(2) get the *TakeControl.response*, if positive go to step 3, otherwise something is not working properly;

(3) look for an *EventNotification.indication* from R3 in the input queue, if any, or wait for a new one;

(4) get the *EventNotification.indication*, then read with the *Get-AlarmSummary* service the status of all the enrolment objects for the event;

(5) according to the enrolment status read perform one of the following actions:

    (a) if the event is in the IDLE state (all the enrolments are in the IDLE state), then go to step 3;

    (b) if there is at least one enrolment in the ACTIVE-ACKED state (see Figure 6.21(b)) go to step 3, because the event occurrence has already been handled by the other robot;

    (c) if all the enrolments are in the ACTIVE-NOACK state, then send an *AcknowledgeEventNotification.request*, wait for the response and load the piece on the machine, because this is the first robot to respond to the event; after the loading operation is terminated, relinquish the semaphore and notify M that it can start its operations.

Note that the operations listed above are correct, because the events with acknowledgments are included in the alarm summary (though they cannot be considered alarms from the application point of view); the alarm summary is read while controlling the semaphore, hence the other robot cannot acknowledge the event while the first one is reading the alarm summary. Finally, R3 is allowed to unload the machine only when the latter notifies it that the measuring cycle is terminated; in turn, the machine is allowed to start a measure only when the robot loading the piece signals that the cycle can be started.

Finally, it is necessary to define some variables in the different machines; we will not go into details in specifying all the variables to be used, instead only a sketch of the configuration will be given. First, it is possible to have several variables describing the characteristics and the status of each VMD; for example, the machine M may have variables describing the number and types of axes, with an indication of the type coordinates used, the reference system and the units of measurement for the coordinates.

Other variables may be associated with the domains; in fact, the domain structure allows the program and data sets to be up

or downloaded in a VMD, but it does not give access to their contents. Thus it is possible to define a set of variables associated with
program domains describing their general features, such as the control algorithms used (for a control program) or the type of piece to
be measured (for a part program). Domains containing data sets
also need variables that allow remote application programs to read
or modify the data values stored in the domain; this happens, for
example, to statistical, calibration and probe data domains, whose
contents should be accessible, at least partially, to the application
programs running in the cell controller.

6.12   Conclusions

The MMS provides a standard model for interactions among different application processes, located in different nodes of the network.
The model describes the behavior of a set of abstract entities (such as
VMDs, variables, semaphores, program invocations), which can be
used to implement the commonest mechanisms for communicating,
synchronizing and controlling the execution of cooperating application tasks. It also defines the set of standard operations (services)
that can be applied to these abstract entities.

As the behavior visible over the network of different entities
is fully defined, the scope of the ISO DIS 9506 covers application
layer functions and the lower levels of the application itself. In fact,
the definition of the protocol machine, given in part 2 of [ISO9506],
deals only with environment establishing and with the mechanism
for passing up and down requests, indications and responses, without
dealing with the information conveyed with these messages.

On the other hand, the service definition, described in part 1
of [ISO9506], imposes some constraints to such information, because
it describes the behavior of the objects receiving and generating the
messages processed by the protocol machine. For example, the result
of a Read service on an MMS variable must convey the value of the
last successful Write service performed on the same variable (provided that no local write operation took place); this is a 'semantic'
constraint on the data values carried by the messages used to implement two different transactions (Write and Read), which appear to
be uncorrelated for the protocol machine.

In fact, the actual execution of the service operation is performed by the Executive Function, which sits on top of the protocol
machine and manipulates application variables and objects. The
Executive Function may be thought of as implementing a sort of interface between the application and the protocol stack. It is possible
to envisage an implementation of the Executive Function, by using
a collection of routines, like many multitasking operating system
kernels available today.

The MMS is a real complex standard, when the full implementation of all the entities (i.e. the Executive Function) is considered. However, the definition of a set of conformance building blocks allows the manufacturer to obtain standard implementations, even when the full set of services is not implemented. This is a very important point, because implementations with reduced functionalities are possible for simple manufacturing devices that do not need all the MMS functionalities and cannot run efficiently (or economically) a full MMS.

Finally, some remarks on the problems that are still open with MMS. First of all, although possible, the MMS does not enforce time and space consistency of the VMD state; in fact, as seen in Section 6.7, non-interruptible access of the variables is not mandatory, hence different clients may access the same variable at the same time, with different results, and the value obtained may also not represent the state assumed by the corresponding real variable (as a whole) at any point in time.

The second problem is related to obtaining bounded service execution times, which are very useful in real-time applications. At present, the position of MMS on top of a full OSI layer does not allow this problem to be solved straightway; on the other hand, the MiniMAP usage of MMS is not standard.

Work is currently in progress on an attempt to solve these and other MMS related problems.

References

[ISO9506]   ISO DIS 9506, *Manufacturing Message Specification, Part 1 & 2*, 22 December 1988.

[IEEE754]   ANSI/IEEE Std. 754, *Binary Floating-Point Standard for Microprocessors*, IEEE Computer Society, 1985.

[RoboCS89]   ISO TC 184/SC 1/WG 3, *Robot Companion Standard to MMS*, Working Draft N. 6, February 10, 1989.

[ProcCS89]   ISO TC 184/SC 5/WG 2 N. 181, *Companion Standard for Process Control*, June 1989.

[NCCS89]   ISO TC 184/SC 1/WG 3, *Companion Standard for Numerical Control*, working draft, Feb. 1989.

[PLCCS89]   IEC SC 65A/WG 6/TF 7, *Companion Standard for Programmable Logic Controller*, working draft, Jan. 1989.

[ProdCS88]   ISO TC 184/SC 5/WG 2 N. 141, *Production Management Companion Standard*, Aug. 1988.

[Brin73]   P. Brinch Hansen, *Operating System Principles*, Prentice-Hall, Englewood Cliffs, 1973.

Chapter 7

Companion Standards to MMS

7.1   Introduction

The interaction model provided by the core MMS, illustrated in Chapter 6, is very general. While this characteristic makes MMS flexible enough to be used in several different application environments, it also represents a limitation for the interoperability of devices from different manufacturers. In fact, important aspects of the specific application field are left unspecified, and then are implemented according to particular, manufacturer-dependent specifications. Furthermore, the generic features of MMS do not closely model typical objects that are useful in specific manufacturing fields for implementing distributed applications; hence, only limited support for the application programs is provided by MMS protocol.

For example, if a pressure transducer has to be used in a process plant, it is interesting to know whether there is a variable in the corresponding VMD giving the unit of measure of the pressure value, and if there is a domain encapsulating such variables, and so on. Another problem is the use of standardized names for some MMS objects, so that it is possible to use the same application programs, regardless of the manufacturer, providing the devices are attached to the network.

Filling this open space in the standards is the goal of *companion standards* (CS), which are under development (as this text is written). In particular, the goal of a companion standard is to define:

- a model for both the communications and the internal logical structure of a VMD;
- possible additional, application-specific attributes, and their semantics, for each class of MMS objects (some attributes are already reserved by MMS for this usage);
- possible additional, application-specific services, or modifications of those defined in the core MMS;
- possible new classes of objects, that may obtained from those defined in MMS by specializing them;
- standard configurations of MMS and CS objects, and their semantics, for a specific application field; the standard names for these objects are also specified;
- new conformance classes and building blocks relevant to the specific field.

Each application area in manufacturing has its own culture and terminology, hence the development of the Companion Standards is now carried out by different organizations, working in specific areas, with the coordination of ISO. The following is a list of the Companion Standards under development, with the name of the organization responsible for each of them:

- Robot Message Specification, developed by RIA [RoboCS89]
- Process Control Message Specification, developed by ISA [ProcCS89]
- Numerical Control Message Specification, developed by EIA [NCCS89]
- Programmable Controller Message Specification, developed by IEC [PLCCS89]
- Production Management Message Specification, developed by ISO [ProdCS88].

It is worth noting that other manufacturing areas, such as semiconductors and avionics, have chosen not to use MMS, for historical reasons. At the time this book was written, the first four companion standards in the list above have already produced tentative final documents (see References), though no final decision has been taken by the standard body. Therefore, the contents of these draft documents will be illustrated in the rest of this chapter. The Production Management Companion Standard is the only one that has not yet produced a draft document, hence it could not be discussed in this chapter.

7.2 Robot companion standard

7.2.1 The robot model

The model of the robot considered in the Robot Companion Standard to MMS [RoboCS89] is a standard representation of the robot acting as an MMS server. In other words, the objective of this standard is to define a model of the real robot that can be seen over the network by a remote MMS user acting as a client. Therefore the features described in this section should be implemented in a robot connected to the network, and they are used by a remote client of the same robot.

Communications with this standard robot can take place in one of the four configurations shown in Figure 7.1. In the first one (Figure 7.1(a)), only one remote MMS user can be a client for the robot; this does not imply that the whole network is composed of only two stations, but that the application programs are configured so that only the user programs residing on a specific station need to access information and to send commands to the robot. In this case, the implementation of the MMS protocol machine in the robot can be simplified, because even just one association will be able to implement this configuration, though several associations are allowed for the same client–server pair.

The second configuration (Figure 7.1(b)) shows several possible clients for the same robot. In this case, while monitoring operations (which require only readings) are allowed in parallel for all the clients, it is necessary to coordinate the control operations of the different clients, so that only one of them at a time may acquire control of the robot, in order to avoid incorrect and possibly dangerous operation. This implies that some mechanism should be implemented, so that the different clients can perform control operations only in mutual exclusion; this mechanism is based on the use of an MMS semaphore. Moreover, the server must be able to keep several MMS associations open at the same time, leading to an increased complexity of the MMS protocol machine as compared to the previous case.

In the third configuration (Figure 7.1(c)) the robot is the client, while other devices (such as loading/unloading devices) are servers; this configuration, though possible, will no longer be considered, because the companion standard only deals with robots acting as servers, hence it is out of the scope of this chapter.

Finally, the configuration in Figure 7.1(d) shows a system where several robots may act, at different times, as either clients or servers of each other. This configuration has the same synchro-

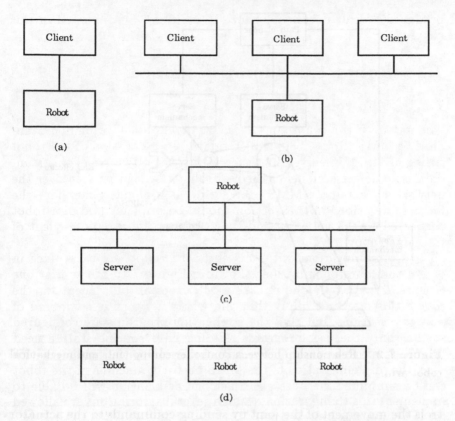

Figure 7.1   Possible configurations: (a) single client, (b) multiple client, (c) robot client, (d) peer robots.

nization problems of the second one, because each robot may have several clients; the only difference is that, in this case, both the client and the server parts should be implemented on the same machine, while this feature is not required in the previous configurations.

Looking inside the robot, as defined in [RoboCS89], it is composed of one or more *robot arms*, a *controller* and by a set (possibly empty) of *separated devices*, the latter are independent of any arm in the system, such as the interlock system.

In turn the robot arm is seen as composed of several types of devices. The physical arm is modeled as a set of mechanical *joints* and *links*, a pair of links and the associated joint is a robot *axis*; each joint is driven by an actuator. A controller is associated with each physical arm, to form a *logical robot arm*; in the following only the logical robot arm will be considered. The controller includes two types of devices: the *servomechanism* and the *path planner*. Their relationship with the physical arm is shown in Figure 7.2.

One servomechanism is associated with each joint, as it con-

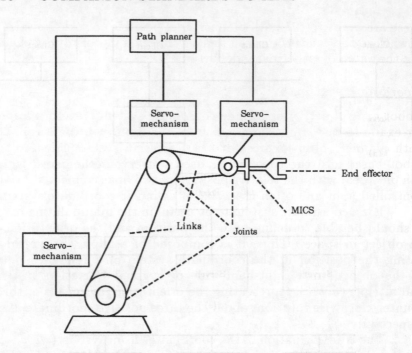

Figure 7.2   Relationship between controller components and mechanical robot arm.

trols the movement of the joint by sending commands to the actuator and receiving feedback information from sensor(s) associated with the joint. A typical servomechanism will implement a closed-loop control algorithm for controlling the speed and the position of the joint, by reading the position from an encoder and the speed from a tachometer and sending commands to the joint motor.

Higher level control activities are performed by the path planner, which is responsible for translating a given trajectory of the end effector carried by the robot arm into a set of commands for the servomechanisms. Note that the path planner has to control the whole arm movement required to obtain a given trajectory of the arm tip, hence it should translate the tip trajectory into a set of commands for each servomechanism associated with a joint, in order to obtain coordinate movements for all the links composing the robot arm. Speed and acceleration of the end effector are also controlled by the path planner, through the feedback information received from the different servomechanisms.

The speed and acceleration are indicated, in this robot model, by specifying a programming value, indicating the default speed or acceleration, and an override multiplying factor, that can be used to modify the default speed or acceleration. As both types of speed and acceleration parameters are referred to the end effector, because these are input to the path planner, it is possible to scale upward or downward the execution speed and acceleration uniformly, by changing the value of either override factor.

Coordinate systems

Robot control activities include coordinate system transformations, for example, the transformations from the input coordinates of the path planner (often expressed in a Cartesian system fixed to the robot base) into the coordinates used by servomechanisms, which can only deal with the relative position of two links connected by the controlled joint and often use polar or cylindric coordinate systems.

For a coordinate system to be useful in the manipulating robot it should be able to define both the position and the orientation of an object in space. Thus, it is composed of a triple (x, y, z) indicating the position in the coordinate system of a reference point of the object, in a right-hand rule orthogonal Cartesian system, and a triple (a, b, c), representing the orientation, by means of three counter-clockwise rotations about the three positive coordinate axes, respectively.

The transformation of the coordinates from system (x', y', z', a', b', c') into another system (x, y, z, a, b, c) can be expressed by the following simple formulas:

$$
\left\{
\begin{aligned}
x &= x' + x_0 \\
y &= y' + y_0 \\
z &= z' + z_0 \\
a &= a' + a_0 \\
b &= b' + b_0 \\
c &= c' + c_0
\end{aligned}
\right.
$$

where (x_0, y_0, z_0) represent the position of the origin of the system (x', y', z', a', b', c') with respect to the other system, and (a_0, b_0, c_0) represent the rotations of the system $(x', y', z', a', b' c')$ with respect to the other system.

The different coordinate systems are chosen in a robot so that they are fixed with respect to different parts; hence it is possible to have coordinate systems that are in either a fixed or movable relative position. In the latter case, the values of the parameters $(x_0, y_0, z_0, a_0, b_0, c_0)$ are time-varying, and need to be continuously re-computed from the values obtained by the joint position sensors.

The standard coordinate systems are shown in Figure 7.3. It should be noted that:

- the origin of the *Base* system is placed in a user-defined point in the robot base;

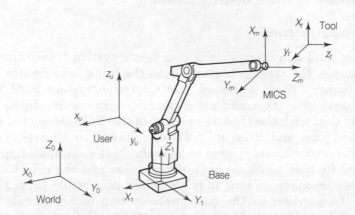

Figure 7.3   Relationships among the different coordinate systems.

- the origin of the Mechanical Interface Coordinate System (MICS) is placed in a user-defined point in the mechanical interface that is provided at the arm tip to install the tool;

- the *World* coordinate system is fixed with respect to the floor, note that the Base system may not be in a fixed position with respect to the World system, if the robot base is mounted on a movable device (e.g. a track);

- the *Tool* coordinate system is placed with the origin at a point of the tool, the Z_t axis as shown in Figure 7.3 and the other two axes perpendicular to each other and to Z_t, so that they form a right-hand system, but the position of X_t and Y_t with respect to the arm may be defined by the user;

- the *User* coordinate system is a right-hand orthogonal cartesian reference system, placed and oriented according to user conventions (the axes in Figure 7.3 are just an example of a possible definition); it is usually employed to provide an alternative coordinate system with respect to the Base.

7.2.2 Mapping to MMS objects

The structure of the robot VMD strictly follows the model outlined in the previous section. Each arm is mapped to a different domain, with standardized names R_ARM_1, R_ARM_2, etc. In order to describe the joint and servomechanism configuration other attributes are added to those defined in the core MMS for domain; the list of robot-specific attributes is shown in Figure 7.4. Note that the

Attribute: Local control (TRUE, FALSE)
Attribute: Device power on (TRUE, FALSE)
Attribute: Device calibrated (CALIBRATED, NOTCALIBRATED, CALIBRATING)
Attribute: Number of joints - integer
Attribute: Base-world - pose
Attribute: Servomechanism
   Attribute: MICS-base - pose
   Attribute: List of joints
      Attribute: Joint type (REVOLUTE, PRISMATIC)
      Attribute: Calibrated (CALIBRATED, NOTCALIBRATED, CALIBRATING)
      Attribute: Joint brakes (TRUE, FALSE)
      Constraint: Joint brakes=TRUE
         Attribute: Brakes on (TRUE, FALSE)
      Attribute: Upper bound - floating point
      Attribute: Lower bound - floating point
      Attribute: Joint servo
         Attribute: Actual joint value - floating point
         Attribute: Moving enabled (TRUE, FALSE)
      Attribute: End effector
      Attribute: ID number
      Attribute: Tool descriptor
      Attribute: Tool-MICS - pose
   Attribute: Path planner
      Attribute: User-base - pose
      Attribute: Desired tool-user - pose
      Attribute: Speed factor - floating point
      Attribute: Programmed speed - floating point
      Attribute: Acceleration factor - floating point
      Attribute: Programmed acceleration - floating point

Figure 7.4   List of the robot arm domain attributes.

constraint clause, in the figure, is used to discriminate different sets of attributes that should be included only if the value of some other attribute has a particular value. In other words, they describe the different alternatives of a variant data structure (like variant records in Pascal).

Besides the general information, such as the calibration state, whether the robot is powered, and the constants for the Base-to-World coordinate transformation, the attributes describe the controller and physical arm parameters all grouped in the servomechanism attribute; this, in turn, is organized in a list of joints, the end effector and the path planner. For each joint, the type, the calibration state, the presence/absence and the state of brakes are described, along with information on the associated servomechanism, including the limit positions, the current one and whether the movement is enabled.

The end effector section provides user-defined information about the tool used, along with the Tool-to-MICS coordinate transformation. The path planner section is composed of the User-to-Base coordinate transformation, the target position of the tool with respect to the User coordinate system, and the default values for speed and acceleration, together with the associated values for the override factors.

A token semaphore with a single token is associated with each robot arm domain, so that only the token owner is entitled to perform all the operations that can result in a state transition of either the robot VMD or the program invocations associated with the domain. In this way, only one client at a time can control the robot arm motion, as it is the only client allowed to request services such as Start, Stop, Resume and Kill (see Section 6.5).

To obtain this feature, the robot companion standard extends the semantics of some of the MMS core services, such that a conformant implementation of the standard must check for the ownership of the token by the client, before serving its request. This introduces a conditional service procedure not present in the core MMS, where semaphores are defined, but their status does not influence service execution on other objects.

The control semaphore associated with a robot arm domain must have the standard name R_CTRL; the name is also always the same in a multiple-arm robot, because the R_CTRL name is local to each arm domain.

In a robot, program invocations may be of three types: CONTROLLING, CONTROLLED and NORMAL. Several CONTROLLED program invocations can be bound to a single CONTROLLING one; this relationship, introduced in the robot companion standard, indicates that services operating on the CONTROLLING invocation may result in state changes in the CONTROLLED ones. As already noted in Chapter 6, a program invocation can be used to model a set of cooperating application tasks, hence it is able to model asynchronous concurrent activities. However, the internal organization of the concurrent activities would be hidden to the remote user if a single program invocation were used. In contrast, the CONTROLLED–CONTROLLING invocations allow the remote user to configure the application program, by establishing and removing the binding between CONTROLLING and CONTROLLED program invocations present in the VMD, and keeping visible the state of each individual program invocation.

The CONTROLLING program invocation is assumed to be the application program with a high-level control of the robot arm

Attribute: Error code - integer
Attribute:
Control (CONTROLLING, CONTROLLED, NORMAL)

Constraint: Control=CONTROLLING
 Attribute:
List of references to controlled programs

 Attribute: Program location - string
 Attribute: Running mode (FRE-RUN, CYCLE-LIMITED,
        STEP-LIMITED)
 Constraint: Running mode=STEP-LIMITED
  Attribute: Remaining step count - integer
 Constraint: Running mode=CYCLE-LIMITED
  Attribute: Remaining cycle count - integer
Constraint: Control=CONTROLLED
 Attribute:
Reference to the controlling program invocation

Figure 7.5   Additional attributes of program invocations.

movement. A robot arm is programmed to perform cyclical operations, where each cycle is composed of several steps. If the operations should be executed until they are terminated when an explicit command is received, the CONTROLLING program invocation is said to be FREE-RUNNING. If the operations should be limited to a particular number of cycles, the program invocation is CYCLE-LIMITED. Finally, if the operations are not really cyclical, they should be terminated after a given number of steps, and the program invocation is STEP-LIMITED. Figure 7.5 shows the additional program invocation attributes introduced by the robot companion standard; it is possible to see that, in the case of a CONTROLLING invocation, the type of execution is specified, along with the remaining number of cycles or steps to be performed, in the case of CYLCE-LIMITED or STEP-LIMITED operations.

The distinction between CONTROLLED, CONTROLLING and NORMAL program invocations also leads to a modification of the state diagram presented in Figure 6.5. In particular, the state IDLE is modified as shown in Figure 7.6. The arrows to and from other states are the same as in Figure 6.5.

There are two stable states indicating whether the invocation is bounded to other ones in a CONTROLLING–CONTROLLED relationship (IDLE Selected) or is NORMAL (IDLE Deselected). The other two are transit states waiting for the conclusion of a selection or de-selection operation. The Select service is a new one, and its effect

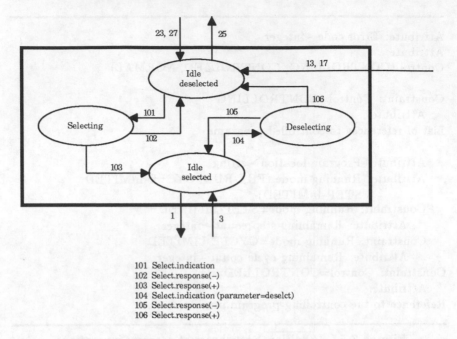

101 Select.indication
102 Select.response(−)
103 Select.response(+)
104 Select.indication (parameter=deselct)
105 Select.response(−)
106 Select.response(+)

Figure 7.6   Modification to the IDLE state of a program invocation.

is to establish or destroy (parameter=Deselect) a binding between a CONTROLLING and its CONTROLLED program invocations.

Note that only selected invocations can be activated, while NORMAL ones cannot. It turns out that the only way to execute program invocations is to create a group of them with one CONTROLLING and one or more CONTROLLED invocations.

The presence of CONTROLLING program invocations also influences the robot state defined by the companion standard. This state provides application-specific information on the VMD situation, in addition to the logical and physical state defined in Section 6.3.

The robot state diagram is shown in Figure 7.7 with the list of the events causing the transitions. The different states have the following meaning:

- IDLE: no CONTROLLING program invocation is defined within the VMD in this state; the IDLE state is normally reached at power-up, unless a permanent CONTROLLING invocation is created during the initialization;

- LOADED: the robot movement is not enabled, but there is at least one CONTROLLING program invocation defined, however, they are not bounded to any CONTROLLED program invocation; in particular, the R_ARM program invocation (the one controlling the robot movements) has no CONTROLLING

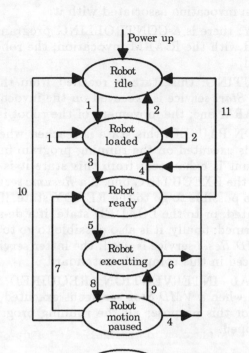

Figure 7.7 State diagram of the robot VMD.

1.	Load	A controlling program is loaded
2.	Clear	A controlling program is removed
3.	Select	One program is selected
4.	Deselect	A program is de-selected
5.	Program start	A selected program is started
6.	End of execution	The robot motion is halted
7.	Program reset	The robot is returned to the READY state
8.	Pause	The robot motion is temporarily halted
9.	Continue	A paused robot resumes its operations
10.	Clear (abort)	Same as 2, except the program has not completed
11.	Clear (abandon)	Same as 2, except the program has not started
12.	Emergency action	The robot goes in a state where manual intervention is required

program invocation associated with it;

- READY: there is a CONTROLLING program invocation associated with the R_ARM invocation; the robot movement is disabled;

- EXECUTING: this state is reached from the previous one when a *Start* service is executed on the invocation controlling the R_ARM one; the movement of the robot is enabled;

- MOTION PAUSED: this state is reached when either a *Stop* service is executed on the running program invocation or the step count is exhausted; from this state it is possible to get back to the EXECUTING one, if a *Resume* service is executed; it is also possible to go to the READY state, if a *Reset* service is executed, or to the LOADED state, if a de-select operation is performed; finally, it is also possible to go to the IDLE state if a *VMD Reset* service is used; the latter service is a new one introduced in this companion standard;

- MANUAL INTERVENTION REQUIRED: this state is reached when a *VMD Stop* service is executed, which is introduced for this purpose; all the running program invocations are stopped.

7.2.3   Other standard objects

The robot companion standard defines a set of objects with standard names, as shown in Table 7.1.

In addition to the R_ARM domain, two other standard domains are introduced: one related to calibration and the other to the safety equipment and operations. Other domains can also be present, with a description of the associated devices (if any), such as loading/unloading equipment; in fact, the standard defines a minimum set of objects that should exist in the VMD, but it does not impose any limitation on the introduction of other user-defined objects.

The R_ARM program invocation, associated with the domain with the same name, contains just the program to control the robot movement, as it is a CONTROLLED one. Another program invocation is required to take control of the operation, by using R_ARM; this user-defined program invocation should include the program with a high-level description of the robot operations, prepared in any language, which is executed by using the primitives provided by the program in R_ARM. Hence the R_ARM program invocation may be seen as providing a library of robot arm operations that can be used by a user program included in another program invocation whose name is not defined in the standard.

The R_CAL is a CONTROLLING program invocation, hence it can take control of the robot operations by also using the R_ARM

Table 7.1 List of robot specific standard objects.

Domains

Name	Meaning
R_ARM	Model of the robot arm
R_CAL	Associated to the calibration procedure
R_SAFE	Associated with safety equipment

Program invocations

Name	Meaning
R_ARM	Manipulates the robot arm
R_CAL	Performs calibration procedure

Types

Name	Type	Meaning
R_PIS	Array	(x,y,z) position in space
R_OS	Array	(a,b,c) rotations in space
R_PSE	Structure	Pose given as (R_PIS, R_OS)
R_EEF	Structure	Description of a tool

Semaphores

Name	Type	Meaning
R_CTRL	Token	Robot control semaphore

Event conditions

Name	Meaning
R_RVS	VMD state change
R_SIV	Safety interlocks violated
R_RLC	Robot control changed
R_ARM	Robot arm operating

Event actions

Name	Meaning
R_STC	Robot status changed
R_ARM	Robot arm operating

Table 7.1   (*cont.*)

Named variables

Name	Type	Meaning
R_VPWR	Boolean	Robot power on
R_VUOM	Boolean	Millimeters used as unit
R_CAL	Boolean	Resources calibrated
R_VLOCAL	Boolean	Local control
R_VSAFEV	Boolean	Safety interlocks violated
R_DPWR	Boolean	Device power on (domain specific)
R_DCAL	Integer8	Device calibrated (domain specific)
R_DLOCAL	Boolean	Device local control (domain specific)
R_NJ	Integer8	Number of joints (R_ARM specific)
R_JT	Array	Joint description (R_ARM specific)
R_JCAL	Array	Joint calibrated (R_ARM specific)
R_JBK	Array	Joint brakes on (R_ARM specific)
R_JBD	Array	Joint bounds (R_ARM specific)
R_AJV	Array	Actual joint values (R_ARM specific)
R_TUB	R_PSE	User to base transformation (R_ARM specific)
R_TTM	R_PSE	Tool-to-MICS transformation (R_ARM specific)
R_TBW	R_PSE	Base to world transformation (R_ARM specific)
R_ATUP	R_PSE	Actual tool user point (R_ARM specific)
R_CTUP	R_PSE	Desired tool to user pose (R_ARM specific)
R_AMBP	R_PSE	MICS to base transformation (R_ARM specific)
R_SF	Floating point	Speed factor (R_ARM specific)
R_PSTU	Floating point	Programmed speed (R_ARM specific)
R_EEFU	R_EEF	Tool in use

invocation; it plays the same role as the program describing robot operations, with the difference that it should be activated whenever calibration is required. As calibration is an operation that is dependent on the specific robot but independent of the specific application, the program performing calibration is fixed, unlike the application program.

The named variables used are, in almost all cases, a replication of the attributes of the VMD, domains and R_ARM domain in particular. This gives the possibility of accessing these values not only through the services reading these attributes, but also with Read and Write (when possible) services.

Finally, four event condition objects are defined:

- R_RVS: is reset when the robot VMD exits the EXECUTING state, hence it may be used to notify the controlling client that the robot is no longer moving;

- R_SIV: is associated with the VMD attribute indicating whether or not a safety interlock has been violated; it may be used to inform all the interested MMS users of the occurrence of a safety violation;

- R_RLC: is activated whenever the attribute indicating whether the robot is under local control changes value; it may be used to indicate a change from local to remote control (or vice versa);

- R_ARM: is activated when the R_ARM program invocation leaves the state RUNNING; it indicates that the control program is no longer in execution.

The two standard event actions are not connected, through any event enrolment object, to any of the four event conditions; this allows both configurations using the events (or some of them) and those not using them. The decision is left to the user, who can also define the recipient of the notifications and the type of acknowledgment required.

However, in general, R_STC, which provides the VMD status in the notification, can be useful as an event action to be connected to event conditions R_RVS, R_SIV and R_RLC, as these are activated upon the occurrence of specific VMD state changes; while R_ARM action, reporting in the notification the attributes of the R_ARM program invocation, should be connected to the R_ARM event condition, as the latter is activated upon the exit of the corresponding program invocation from the state RUNNING.

7.3   Numerical control companion standard

7.3.1   NC model

The model of the machine defined in the NC companion standard is much simpler than that defined for the robot by the corresponding standard. First, the only possible configurations allowed include single and multiple clients for the NC, while the multi-peer configuration is not taken into consideration explicitly.

An NC controller is seen as being composed of a set of *controlling processes*; each of them includes programs and data structures to perform the control operation on a specific *device*.

How all the controlled equipment should be subdivided into devices is up to the user. This decision may be almost mandatory in the case of simple systems that are organized in a single device; when the controller is associated with more than one simple NC machine, real alternatives arise. For example, a system composed by a turning machine and an associated tool changer can be modeled either as a single device or as a pair of devices, one associated with the turning machine, the other with the tool changer. Which solution is best depends on the level of awareness that the designer wishes to give to the remote user about the internal organization of the NC machine.

Each device can be turned on or off independently, hence each of them has its own state. Therefore the organization of devices is also dependent on the possibility of the remote user individually controlling the states of the different devices. The three states allowed are: POWER OFF, READY and NOT READY. A device switches between the first two states whenever it is turned on or off; the third state is reached from READY when some error occurs, and the device gets back to READY when the error is recovered.

Two classes of NC controllers are considered: *attended* and *unattended*. The former operate under the control of a local operator, while the latter are under the control of a remote user. The implication on communication is that a remote MMS client is only allowed to initiate a data transfer (including downloading) if the NC controller is attended; otherwise, the remote client can also control the execution of the controlling processes of the different devices in the NC controller. Attended systems operate in *local control* mode, while unattended ones operate in *remote control* mode; mode switching can only be caused by local actions.

7.3.2   Mapping to MMS objects

Domains

An NC VMD should be composed by one or more non-deletable domains that give an internal image of the physical devices used. Moreover, other loadable data and program domains are usually present to implement the whole data base for a controlling process. The domains and other objects defined for NC VMDs are listed in Table 7.2.

In particular, other types of domains include: data on the equipment setup, data on the tools available, data on the fixtures available, statistical data collected by the machine, data on the probes available and diagnostic data and programs.

Program invocations

A controlling process is a program invocation defined on the device domain, with the addition of other program and data domains. No particular addition is introduced by this companion standard to the state diagram introduced by the core MMS. It is possible, though not usual, for several controlling processes to use the same device domain, or for several device domains to be associated with the same controlling process; in the latter case, there is a single controlling process for several devices.

Semaphores

The possibility of having more than one possible client for the standard NC, leads to the introduction of a control semaphore, modeled by a token semaphore, as defined in the core MMS, with only one token. Only the token owner is entitled to perform control operations, such as modifying the state of the controlling processes.

Of course, if the machine is attended or there is a single client, the semaphore is no longer needed, because in the former case, control operations are not allowed at all, while in the latter, no conflict can arise.

Events

An NC system should be provided with the ability to inform a remote MMS user that some alarm condition has occurred or ceased within the system. This feature is implemented by using an MMS event configured as follows. Though several alarm conditions may occur, only one event condition object is used, specifying a monitored event connected to either an internal condition or to the state of the boolean variable N_ALARM_REFERENCE.

The associated event action specifies a Read operation of the N_Alarm variable as confirmed service. In this way, the EventNotification message issued as a consequence of an alarm state change will include:

- an alarm number, specifying the type of alarm
- a unit code, indicating which unit within the NC system generated the alarm state change

Table 7.2 NC standard objects (... stands for an additional non-standard string).

Domains

Name	Meaning
N_DEV_...	Device domain
N_PRG_...	Program domain
N_TLD_...	Tool data table
N_FXD_...	Fixture data table
N_SET_...	Setup data table
N_SPD_...	Statistical data
N_PRG_...	Probe data table
N_DGN_...	Diagnostic data
R_CAL	Calibration domain

Program invocations

Name	Meaning
R_CAL	Calibration process

Named variable lists

Name	Meaning
N_INF	List of basic information var.
N_PRINF_...	Controlling process description
N_DEVINF	Device description

Semaphores

Name	Type	Meaning
N_CONTROL	Token	Control semaphore

Events

Name	Meaning
N_EC_Alarm	Alarm event condition
N_EA_Alarm	Alarm event action
N_EE_Alarm	Alarm event enrolment

Table 7.2   (*cont.*)

Named variables

Name	Type	Meaning
N_Store	Structure	Description of the NC store
N_Remote	Boolean	Mode of operation
N_Remote_CMD	Boolean	Variable for switching to local
N_INF_...	Not defined	Basic information on the NC
N_INF_Alarm_Condition	Boolean	Alarm active
N_PRINF_...	Not defined	Description of a controlling process
N_Alarm	Structure	Alarm description
N_Alarm_Summary	Array	Alarm table
N_Num_Alarm	Unsigned8	Number of alarms
N_ALARM_REFERENCE	Boolean	Alarm variable
N_NumAxes	Unsigned8	Number of axes (device specific)
N_AXO	Array	Axes offset table (device specific)
N_MIR	Array	Mirror table (device specific)
N_ROT	Array	Axis rotations (device specific)
N_SCF	Array	Scale factors (device specific)
N_NumBLD	Unsigned8	Number of block delete levels (device specific)
N_BLD	Array	Block delete table (device specific)
N_FRL	Array	Maximum feed rates (device specific)
N_FRO	Array	Feed overrides (device specific)
N_OSP	Boolean	Optional stop (device specific)

Table 7.2   (*cont.*)

N_RPO	Structure	Rapid override (device specific)
N_DEV_STATE	Unsigned8	Device state
N_DEVINF_...	Not defined	Device information (device specific)
N_DEVINF_CAL	Boolean	Device calibrated
N_Power_On	Boolean	Power on (device specific)

- a severity code
- a string of characters with a short explanation message related to the alarm state change
- the current alarm state
- the occurrence time of the notified event.

The enrolment object, connecting the alarm condition to the alarm action, is permanent (i.e. NOTIFICATION), and specifies the ACK-ACTIVE acknowledgment rule. With this choice, all the services of the core MMS related to alarms will include this enrolment object in their operations; furthermore, it is always possible to check whether or not the last alarm activation has been acknowledged.

Named variables and lists

Variables are divided into NC specific and device-domain specific; the former have names unique for the whole VMD, while the latter have unique names for a specific device domain. The domain provides a specific name space for its variables, which allows different domains to hold variables with the same name without ambiguity, as the full variable name is composed of the domain and the variable names.

NC specific variables are intended to provide all the information related to the VMD as a whole, hence they include state information, replicating some of the values that can also be obtained by reading the attributes of the VMD. Moreover, there could be variables giving information on the controlling processes, as well as variables related to alarm processing. Some variables in the latter category have already been mentioned; in addition, there is a variable giving the number of alarms that can be generated by the NC system, and another variable containing a summary of all the alarms defined for the VMD.

Domain-specific variables provide information related to each device modeled with a separate domain in the NC system. Therefore, they provide some general data, such as axis position (offset and rotation), but they also represent some data related to the type of work to be done. In particular, N_MIR gives a table of entries, one per axis, specifying whether or not the coordinates in the part program for the axis should be mirrored with respect to a specific point, if so, the center of this mirroring operation is also given.

N_NumBLD and N_BLD are related to the block delete capability used for preparing part programs. It is possible to prefix a portion of a part program with a block code, so that the block of program is executed according to whether the corresponding block code is enabled. N_NumBLD specifies the number of block delete levels supported by the device, while N_BLD is an array of booleans specifying whether or not each block delete level supported is enabled.

The operation speed is another parameter that can be controlled, by using standard variables. In fact, it is possible to control the maximum feed rate, an override factor for the feed rate and an override value for the movement.

The three named variable lists defined are just used to group together all variables of the same type, in order to obtain all their values with a single read. The three lists are defined for basic information variables, variables describing controlling processes and device information variables.

7.4 Programmable controller companion standard

7.4.1 Programmable controller model

The internal organization of a programmable controller (PC), as seen by a remote station through the PC companion standard, is depicted in Figure 7.8. There are three major components:

- *Main processing unit*: this part includes both the CPU(s), the memory and the interfaces to the other subsystems;

- *Remote I/O stations*: in some cases, the field devices to be controlled by the PC are spread over a relatively wide area; consequently, not all the I/O devices are located close to the processing unit, and some of them are implemented in separate boxes interconnected with the processing unit by a special communication system (possibly a network, different from that interconnecting the PCs); it turns out that the PC itself can look more like a distributed system than a single device;

- *Peripherals*: devices controlled by the PC, they may be permanently or non-permanently attached to the system.

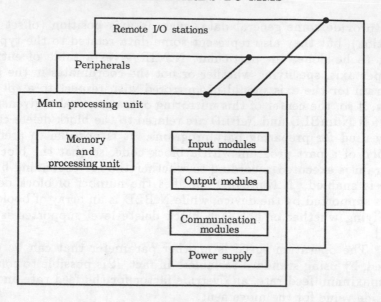

Figure 7.8   Model of the internal structure of a programmable controller.

The communication mode assumed for the PC includes both configurations where non-PC devices act as clients of one or more PC servers, and the peer-to-peer communication between several PCs, where each of them may act as both client and server.

A PC should be able to provide the following types of operations:

- Device verification
- Data acquisition
- Control
- Synchronization between application programs
- Alarming
- Operator interface
- Program management and control
- Recipe manipulation
- Programming, debugging and process verification
- Protection and connection management.

Some of the items listed above are quite self-explanatory, but some others deserve further clarification.

Device verification

This class of function has the goal to provide the possible PC clients with enough information about internal status to assess whether or not the PC is able to perform a given function in the automated system.

A key function in this context is the ability to provide the client with the internal state of the PC. For this purpose, two types of information are defined in the companion standard: *health* and *status*. Both types of information are provided for the whole PC and for each subsystem represented by a box in Figure 7.8 (namely: processing unit, memory, input, outputs, communication and power supply).

The *health* parameter can assume one of the following three values:

- *good*: indicates that the whole system or subsystem is working correctly and no fault occurred;

- *bad*: faults have occurred that impose severe limitations on the operations performed by the system or subsystem, which should be considered out of order;

- *warning*: for the whole PC, this value indicates that at least one subsystem is a *warning* condition, but none is in *bad* health; for a specific subsystem, it indicates that some fault has been reported, but this does not prevent the execution of all the functions of the subsystem, though some limitations should be expected.

Of course, the actual semantic of each of the health values is determined by the PC manufacturer; as the interpretation of what is the set of faults leading to a *warning* or *bad* health value is determined by the implementors of the companion standard in the specific PC. Therefore, the health value should be evaluated in connection to the actual, associated meaning, provided by the PC manufacturer.

The *state* is a list of flags, each one indicating whether or not a particular option is in effect. Typical information carried by such flags indicates if the PC is in local control (its automation functions cannot be altered by a remote MMS user), if the inputs or the outputs are disabled (for debugging), if the memory is protected (cannot be altered by a user), if the primary and the secondary power supply are working, and so on.

Data acquisition

PCs should be able to provide a client with the values of data accumulated internally and coming from a variety of sources. This type of operation is supported through the use of MMS variables.

A constraint imposed by the companion standard for the PC is that access to variable values must be *uninterruptible*, that is it is necessary to implement exclusive access to the variable contents. This feature is only optional for the core MMS (see Section 6.7) and becomes mandatory for the PCs. Exclusive access to variables implies that it is not possible for two clients or a client and a local process to access the same variable (or part of it) at the same time; in this way, it is possible to avoid a situation where components of a structured variable are simultaneously read and written by two different processes, so that the values read for some variable components refer to the situation before the update, and others already carry the updated values.

Four techniques are considered for data transfer, although for two of them the distinction is not clear:

- Polling: the client reads the values of the variables, the MMS service used is Read;

- Unsolicited data acquisition: the server sends data to the client with no external solicitation, the MMS service used is InformationReport;

- Programmed data acquisition: also in this case the server sends data to the client without any solicitation; according to the standard, the difference with unsolicited data acquisition is given by the programmability of this operation, although it is not clear how unsolicited data acquisition can be implemented, if it is not programmed; the basic MMS service used is again InformationReport;

- Configured data acquisition: the server sends data to the client upon the occurrence of a particular transition of an internal MMS event condition (see Section 6.9); the EventNotification service carries the result of a Read operation performed on a set of variables; the UnsolicitedReport service is also used to notify the client of PC state changes that could avoid event condition occurrence, so that the client is aware that data might never come.

Control

As data acquisition is the key activity for monitoring an automated industrial plant, control is the function that allows the information system to drive the controlled process through a desired set of states, by sending commands and reading feedback information.

The control activity can be implemented by a PC according to one of the following techniques:

- Parametric control: the application program implementing the control function runs continuously (until it is stopped or some fault occurs); it is possible to change the values of parameters of the control algorithm, in order to tune the control activities;

- Interlocked control: control operations are explicitly requested by a client, through appropriate services; the server performs the requested control action and, upon termination, sends back to the client a set of data with the results of the operation performed, then it goes back to wait for a new request.

Parametric control is perhaps more common, as the control functions are coded in an application program and then executed, even though some synchronization with other devices is often requested. Interlocked control implements a sort of *one-shot* operation that terminates sooner or later, and it is activated only on the request of a client (often a cell or sub-process controller) and is limited to a specific control operation.

Recipe manipulation

A recipe is a set of programs or data structures (or both) required for making a product, by using the process controlled by the PC. In other words, a recipe plays the same role for the PC as a part program does for numerical control machines.

The operations required for recipe manipulation are not different from those used for managing any other data or program up/downloading and execution control.

Protection and connection management

The core MMS standard does not include any mechanism for protection against thorough or aimless misuse of a VMD, leaving the companion standards with the possibility of introducing such mechanisms. The companion standard for PCs is the first that takes into account protection issues, by introducing an authentication mechanism and an access right data base, which are both used to check whether the service requested by a client violates protection rules.

The authentication is performed upon the establishment of an application association. If the association is initiated by a client, the PC server authenticates the client and grants it a set of rights (i.e. services that can be requested by the client); such rights are stored in a specific data base, where each possible client identifier is associated with a specific set of access rights. The access right data base is implemented within the PC VMD. The rights granted upon opening an application association are valid for all the services requested during the lifetime of the association.

Authentication is required in order to make sure that the client is really what it pretends to be. A client is authenticated on the basis of the AE-title (i.e. name of the client application entity) provided in the parameters of the association management services, and, optionally, by using passwords.

The simple AE-title is sufficient, when it is assumed that the communication system cannot be tampered with, to generate an Initiate service request with an AE-title forged by an intruder. Authentication based on AE-titles only may be used when attempts to misuse the PC are caused only by design errors or faults; in this case, the AE-titles are sufficient, as they are generated by trustable software.

Passwords become necessary if either protection against masquerades is required or the AE-title is not sufficient to identify the client. An example of the latter case is an application program interfacing the network to an operator console; in this case, the authentication of the application program is not sufficient, as it is also necessary to authenticate the human being sitting at the console. The first authentication can be performed on the basis of the AE-title, while the second requires password(s).

If passwords are used, they are stored in the access right data base of the PC, along with the associated AE-title and set of access rights.

It is worth noting that if the application association is initiated by the PC, no authentication is required, unless the other partner is another PC; in the latter case, the rights granted to the called partner are those associated with the AE-title used in the Initiate request.

The introduction of authentication mechanisms requires the use of additional parameters in the services involved in the association establishment. In particular, Initiate requests addressed to a PC should carry the password(s) values, if required. The corresponding response will also carry the set of access rights granted (if any).

The access right data base is also an additional attribute of the PC VMD introduced by this companion standard. Of course, the values stored in such a data base can only be obtained by those clients with the right to use the corresponding services.

7.4.2   Mapping to MMS objects

Domains

PCs use domains for modeling the application software they should execute, thus it is important to look first at the structure of an application program, as considered in the standard.

The internal organization of a PC application program is shown in Figure 7.9. The different blocks are organized in a hierarchical structure, with the outer blocks in the higher levels and the inner ones in the bottom. The outmost block represents the whole application program, and includes several inner blocks, each one associated with a subsystem (processing unit, input, output) or with global information (global definitions and access paths to the internal MMS variables). In turn, the processing unit (PU) subsystem includes declaration and program blocks; the program can also be seen as composed of function calls and function block instantiations (a function block is a piece of code and associated data that

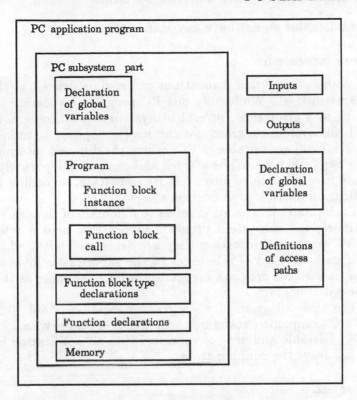

Figure 7.9   Structure of an application program.

implements a typical control block, such as PID, so that the control program can be built up of interconnecting instances of such blocks, as in a block diagram; for more details see Section 7.5.1).

The domains may be declared at one of the three hierarchical levels. The PC level corresponds to the outer block in Figure 7.9, hence a domain of this type includes the whole application program and associated MMS objects required for its execution. The subsystem level corresponds to the next inner level, and domains of this type may include the programs and data for a subsystem, the definition of global variables and data types, or access paths to the MMS variables. Elements are at the lowest level; domains containing elements may include declarations of functions, variables, types or function blocks, or programs. Domains at this lowest level also hold a reference to the associated domain at the subsystem level.

Standard names are defined for the domains. The PC name used as the VMD name should be used for a domain at the PC level. The names P_ACCESS and P_GLOBAL are used at the subsystem level to identify the domains containing access paths to network visible PC variables and global declarations, respectively; while the name of the subsystem should be used for the corresponding domain.

Element domains do not have any standard name.

Program invocations

As for domains, program invocations can also be defined at the PC or subsystem level. While only one PC program invocation can be executing at a given time, several subsystem invocations can run in parallel. Subsystem program invocations (as opposed to monolithic PC invocations) are suitable in PCs where the different internal subsystems can (and need to) be started and controlled separately from a remote user, as each of them has its own state, according to the state diagram illustrated in Section 6.5.

Each program invocation refers to a domain of the same level; furthermore, the subsystem program invocations hold a reference to the PC program invocation they are associated with, while PC invocations hold a list of references to the subordinate invocations. The names used for program invocation will be the same as those of the associated domain.

The state diagram of a program invocation is not modified by the PC companion standard. All the program invocations are reusable, deletable and are not monitors (i.e. no notification is sent when they leave the running state).

Other objects

Both named and unnamed variables are considered by the standard; the use of the latter is limited to scalar values, with sizes of 1, 8, 16, 32 or 64 bits. No standard named variable is defined.

The events are used for implementing alarming functions and configured data acquisition. The event enrolments should use the ACK-ALL acknowledgment rule, in order to both remember the acknowledgments received and be included in the alarm summary. The associated event action specifies a Read service referring to a set of variables organized in a structure.

7.4.3   New objects introduced

Interlocked control requires the introduction of a new class of objects not present either in the core MMS or in the other companion standard. This new object should be used to support the synchronization of activities and data exchange between client and server application programs that is required by interlocked control.

The new object is called *gate*. The interlocked control operations follow the scheme shown in Figure 7.10. The client application program requesting an interlocked control function sends a DataExchange.request to the gate; this operation leads to the activation of the associated control function in the server, which uses the data sent by the client in the service request. The response to the DataEx-

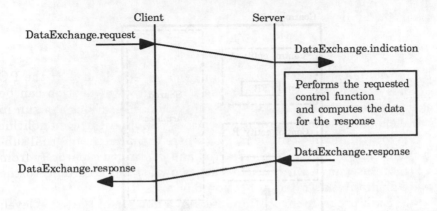

Figure 7.10   Time diagram of the operations for interlocked data exchange.

change service, if positive, is generated when the control function execution terminates, and includes a set of data describing the results of the operation.

The attributes of a gate include the name, a list of types describing the data expected from the client, a list of types describing the data sent in response by the client and the state of the gate. The latter refers to a simple state diagram of a gate, composed of only two states: *IDLE* and *PROCESS*. When in the former state, the gate is ready to receive a request for data exchange, whilst the other state indicates that a request is being processed (i.e. the response has not been sent yet).

7.5   Process control companion standard

The process control companion standard is aimed at defining how the core MMS should be used in the fields of control of both continuous and batch industrial processes. Although batch production often deals with discrete parts, it has been included in the same companion standard as continuous processes, because it can be seen as being composed of streams of (discrete) materials that are processed while flowing through the plant.

However, the standard does not explicitly addresses the problem of using this companion standard in batch processing, as the basic model provided uses typical elements that can be found in the process control environment. Hence some further activity could be expected in order to also cover batch production. In the rest of this section, reference will be made to process control only.

Control unit

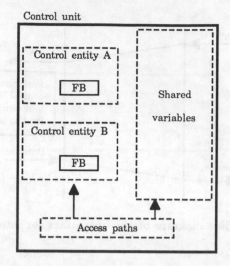

Figure 7.11   Model of a process control system.

7.5.1   Model of a process control system

The remote view of a process control system is based on a model whose fundamental elements are shown in Figure 7.11.

The *control unit* represents the whole remote VMD; it is composed of one or more *control entities*, each one dedicated to performing regulatory activity on a specific subset of the whole process controlled by the VMD. In turn, each control activity is composed of one or more *function blocks (FBs)*, which are normally interconnected in order to implement a more complex operation on the process variables.

Each control entity is defined according to process characteristics, so that it includes a well defined and almost self-contained set of operations; nevertheless, communication among different control entities is, in general, necessary. *Shared variables* provide a means to define global data structures accessible by all the control entities; moreover, function blocks can also expose some of their internal variables, so that other function blocks (even those external to the control entity) can access them, by using *access paths*.

7.5.2   Function blocks

A functional block diagram of an FB in shown in Figure 7.12. The function block is able to execute a specific operation, and it includes both the algorithm to be executed and the internal variables with the connection with the other function blocks.

Internal variables are normally hidden to the outside world, unless they are exposed by defining an access path to them. The

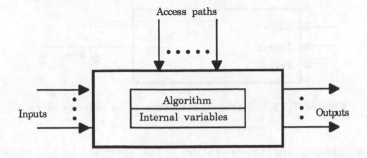

Figure 7.12   Functional block diagram of a generic function block.

definition of an access path takes the following form, and should be declared when the function block is defined in the application program:

$< access\ path\ name >:$ $< control\ unit\ name > .$
$< control\ entity\ name > .$
$< variable\ name >$

The access path name can then be used to access the variable whose name is at the end of the path definition; the names of the control unit and control entity are used to avoid any ambiguity and to direct the search of the variable location. An access path may also be used to access shared variables defined in another control unit; in this case, only the name of the control unit and that of the variable are required to define the access path.

The standard defines broad classes of function blocks, and imposes common parameters for each of such classes; however, the user is allowed to define his/her own function blocks within a defined class, provided that the function block matches the general characteristics prescribed. The classes defined are as follows:

- *measurement blocks*: used to make a process variable available for inspection; these are input blocks used to read a value of a process variable, hence, in general, they include conversion and calibration activities; three different types of blocks are defined according to whether the variable to be read is analog, digital or symbolic; the latter type is used to model a string of characters input from an operator console.

- *output blocks*: used to control an output point of the control system; they are duals of the measurement blocks; also in this case the function block definition takes different forms according to whether the output variable is analog, digital or symbolic.

- *regulatory blocks*: used to drive and keep the value of one analog process variable to a prescribed set point, the algorithm for

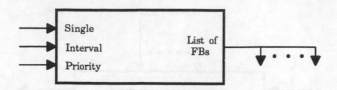

Figure 7.13   External structure of an activity block.

implementing this operation is not specified by the standard.

- *limit blocks*: used to enforce limit values for the set point and output of a control entity.

- *alarm blocks*: used to manage alarms; the block takes an analog variable as input and activates alarms whenever the input value exceeds one of the two limits imposed by two block inputs, or changes its value with a rate (positive or negative) exceeding the limit rates imposed by another pair of input parameters; the alarm state is reset when the input variable gets out of a dead band defined by another input parameter.

In addition to the above listed blocks, the standard also defines *activity blocks*, whose function is to control the execution of the other function blocks in the same control entity. A graphical representation of an activity block is shown in Figure 7.13. The *single* parameter is a boolean value; a transition from false to true causes the activation of all the outputs of the blocks, which in turn leads to the execution of the associated function blocks. If the *single* parameter is tied to false, and the *period* value is not zero, the outputs are activated periodically, with the specified period. Finally, the *priority* parameter provides a value to be used for scheduling the function block execution; higher priority activity blocks and *the associated function blocks* should be executed first, whilst the others are only executed if higher priority activities are not ready to run. Note that the FBs activated by an activity block may be in turn activity blocks, so that it is possible to implement complex activation strategies by interconnecting several such blocks.

An example showing the use of some of the blocks discussed is shown graphically in Figure 7.14; the figure represents a very simple control entity performing closed-loop control of a single process variable. The activity block periodically activates the measurement and output blocks, in order to provide a correct sampling period for the input and output variables. The regulatory and limit blocks are not directly tied to the activity block, hence they are executed whenever they receive a new computed input, in accordance with the evaluation rules of the block diagram.

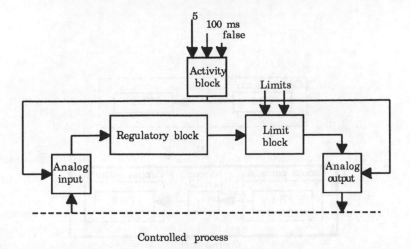

Figure 7.14 Example of function blocks used to implement a control activity performing closed-loop control of a single analog process variable.

7.5.3 Communication model

With the model shown in Figure 7.11, communications take place between function blocks. There are four possibilities, all shown in Figure 7.15. The simplest case is the communication between FBs within the same control entity; in this case, it is possible simply to connect the output of one FB to one input of the other. In the case of communication between FBs in the same control unit, but belonging to different control entities, it is not possible directly to connect the two blocks, as their internal variables are not accessible across control entity boundaries, unless shared variables are used. When the FBs are placed in different control units, it is necessary to use the network services to communicate; in this case, special function blocks, defined for communication purposes, need to be used. In the case shown in Figure 7.15(c), the two FBs exchange data values through the use of *unsolicited* data send and receive (USEND and URCV blocks), over an application association specified as a communication block parameter. The case in Figure 7.15(d), shows the use of *confirmed* service used to obtain the value of a remote variable, by using the READ block executing the MMS service with the same name.

Besides the communication blocks shown in Figures 7.15(c) and (d), Table 7.3 lists all the standard blocks defined.

7.5.4 New services introduced

The major new type of operation introduced by the companion standard for process control is the possibility of performing event man-

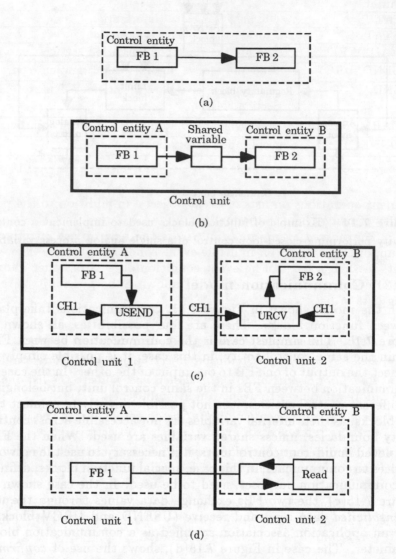

Figure 7.15   Communication between function blocks: (a) communication within the same control entity, (b) across control entity boundaries, but within the same control unit, (c) across control unit boundaries using non-confirmed services, (d) across control unit boundaries, using confirmed services.

Table 7.3 List of standard communication blocks.

Function block	Usage
STATUS	Obtain VMD status information
USTATUS	Provide VMD status information
READ, WRITE	Execute the corresponding MMS services
USEND, URCV	Send and receive unsolicited information report
SEND, RCV	Send and receive data in interlocked mode (see Section 7.4)
ALARM, NOTIFY	Management and notification of alarm occurrence
CONNECT	Application association management

agement operations on lists of event objects, in addition to the possibility of using them individually.

The *named event condition list* is the new object introduced to support operations on multiple event condition objects. The elements in such a list can be event condition objects or other named lists of event condition objects; thus allowing the possibility of creating lists of lists.

The new services defined are as follows:

- *DefineNamedEventConditionList*: defines a new object;
- *DeleteNamedEventConditionObject*: drops a list (if deletable);
- *AddNameEventConditionListReference*: adds to the list one or more references to event condition objects;
- *RemoveNameEventConditionObject*: remove from the list one or more references to event condition objects;
- *GetNamedEventConditionListAttributes*: obtains the list of components currently included in a named event condition list;
- *AlterNamedEventConditionListMonitoring*: alters the values of the enable and group priority attributes of all the event condition objects included in the list.

The *group priority override*, mentioned in the last service listed above, is an additional attribute of the event condition objects, introduced by the process control companion standard along with the *list of referencing named event condition list reference*. The latter attribute just gives references to all the named event condition lists including the current event condition object. The group priority is an attribute that, if not undefined, holds a priority value to be used by the VMD in servicing the different events, instead of the priority attribute (see Section 6.9). The possible values for the group override attribute are: *undefined* (in this case the priority attribute gives the event priority) or an integer value from 0 to 127 (0 being the highest priority). This attribute is a group attribute because it can only be modified by using the AlterNamedEventCondition-ListMonitoring service, hence the same value is assigned to all the condition objects in a list, creating a whole group of event conditions at the same priority level.

Additional extensions are also introduced in other services dealing with event condition objects, in order to take account of the new attributes and the new type of objects introduced.

7.6   Conclusions

The protocols in the application layer of the ISO–OSI model are intended to lessen the implementation effort of distributed applications, by providing a set of objects and related services that are as close as possible to the entities manipulated by the application itself.

In the manufacturing messaging and operation environment, this role is played by MMS, as discussed in Chapter 6. However, the model provided by MMS is deemed to be too generic for providing efficient support in some application fields; on the other hand, pushing the details of MMS specification further would lead to an overly specialized standard, which would no longer cover the whole manufacturing spectrum.

Companion standards are the solution to this problem. One such standard has been defined for each of the relevant application fields within the manufacturing environment. In each companion standard, it is possible to define: new objects and service, and how the core MMS elements should be defined. A companion standard can take account of the peculiar characteristics of the specific field of application it is intended to address, thus providing a higher degree of standardization.

It should be noted, however, that companion standards represent a step forward in providing *interoperability*, defined as the possibility of interconnecting devices from different manufacturers with minimum effort to allow communication at the maximum level. But they do not allow for the substitution of a manufacturing device by another performing the same operations, without modifying the application program. This additional feature, often referred to as *interchangeability*, is the subject of further work, and it is aimed at pushing the standardization process even further, entering into the application sitting on top of the ISO–OSI protocol stack. Only a little work has been done on this subject, and in any case it is outside of the scope of this book.

References

[RoboCS89] ISO TC 184/SC 1/WG 3, *Robot Companion Standard to MMS*, Working Draft N. 6, February 10, 1989.

[ProcCS89] ISO TC 184/SC 5/WG 2 N. 181, *Companion Standard for Process Control*, June 1989.

[NCCS89] ISO TC 184/SC 1/WG 3, *Companion Standard for Numerical Control*, working draft, Feb. 1989.

[PLCCS89] IEC SC 65A/WG 6/TF 7, *Companion Standard for Programmable Logic Controller*, working draft, Jan. 1989.

[ProdCS88] ISO TC 184/SC 5/WG 2 N. 141, *Production Management Companion Standard*, Aug. 1988.

Chapter 8

File Transfer Access and Management

8.1 Introduction

One of the major objectives of protocols in the application layer of the OSI model is to provide a network-wide model for application objects, which are actually implemented in different ways in the different network stations.

The file transfer access and management (FTAM) protocol, defined by the standard ISO 8571 [ISO8571], deals with the definition of a uniform model for file operations in an open system, including file structure, services and protocol definitions.

It is worth noting that the model provided by FTAM only covers the aspect of a filestore related to file transfer, while file storage is not dealt with. The typical situation of an application program accessing a remote filestore, by using FTAM, is shown in Figure 8.1. The FTAM presents to its user, with the aid of the underlying protocols, a virtual filestore that can be manipulated by the remote user, according to the FTAM model.

As the *virtual* attribute indicates, the filestore model seen by the user does not exactly correspond to the real filestore. The mapping between the virtual and real objects is implemented by an FTAM user standing on the same station as the real filestore.

344

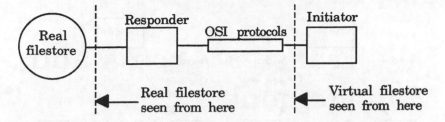

Figure 8.1   Architecture for file transfer.

No storage operation is encompassed by FTAM, which only provides mechanisms for transferring files between two parties. Hence the FTAM cannot be regarded as a specification for distributed file systems or distributed data bases, because important aspects (such as file replication, copy management and atomic execution of transactions) are out of the scope of FTAM.

8.2   Control of the operations

The model provided by FTAM for the operations on a file involves three participating entities:

- *controller*: this entity starts the operation and takes control until completion;
- *destination virtual file*: this entity, instructed by the controller, initiates the operation;
- *responder*: this entity acts as a passive element, as it just performs actions requested by the initiator.

The whole scheme for the execution of an FTAM operation is shown in Figure 8.2. With this scheme it is possible to start a file access that involves two entities which are different from the controller which starts the operation. However, in the commonest situation, the roles of both the controller and the initiator are played by the same entity.

The responder implements the virtual filestore, where the virtual file to be accessed is located. The model of operation in Figure 8.2 is also valid for transfers between two filestores, as the protocol does not need to use any information on the filestore at the initiator side.

It can be seen that two types of information are transferred during file operations: data values (shown by the solid lines in Figure 8.2) and a description of the file structure (shown by dashed lines). It is important to note that the latter is also transferred during FTAM operations, because in the following it will be seen that it is possible to open a file just to manipulate its structure.

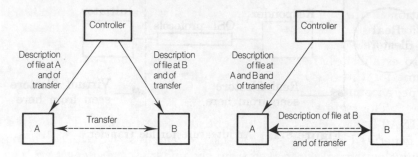

Figure 8.2   Scheme of the file transfer operations.

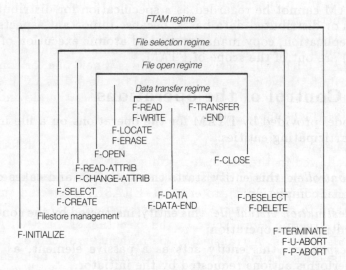

Figure 8.3   FTAM regimes and associated services.

8.3   File transfer regimes

File operations, as defined in FTAM, are only possible if a suitable environment, called a regime, has already been set up. Different nested regimes are defined, as shown in Figure 8.3; the figure also indicates the operations allowed in each regime.

Within the scope of one regime, only one instance of an inner regime is allowed; it turns out that if an initiator has opened a file in a filestore (responder), by establishing FTAM, file selection and file open regimes, it cannot open another file in the same filestore. Therefore only one file can be transferred at a time between the same pair of partners. However, different initiators may transfer files with the same filestore, and the same FTAM user can open several files on different virtual filestores.

The FTAM regime establishment is used to ensure the application environment (that is the availability of the application association), and to negotiate the functional units and service classes (see Section 8.6.1) to be used; furthermore, the execution of F-INITIATE also establishes the initiator and responder roles, as they are the same for this service, and some other parameters, such as access type, accounts and passwords, which will be used later on.

The regime may terminate in an orderly way , if an F-TERMINATE is executed, or it may be aborted, if either a F-U-ABORT is generated by either FTAM user, or an F-P-ABORT or a local equivalent signal is received from the underlying presentation layer.

The filestore operations allowed in the FTAM regime are not defined by the standard.

The file management regime allows the initiator to perform some general file operations, without accessing its contents; in particular, it is possible to manipulate the file attributes (F-READ-ATTR and F-CHANGE-ATTR). This regime is initiated by either using the F-CREATE service (if the file is a new one, or some special attributes have to be manipulated) or the F-SELECT one. It is closed with either an F-DELETE, which erases the file and all its attributes (filename included), or with an F-OPEN that keeps the file status.

The access to the file contents and structuring information is only allowed in the file open regime. The initiator is allowed to select a suitable subset of the file on which subsequent operations are applied (F-SELECT), to erase (F-ERASE) a selected subset of the file and to read or write the selected subset.

This regime is bracketed by the execution of the F-OPEN and F-CLOSE services. A transient or permanent error can be reported on the file open regime closure; this information may be used to decide whether or not it is possible to start a recovery action (provided that standard recovery mechanisms are implemented), as explained in Section 8.6.4.

The read and write operations open the data transfer regime, where the data units are actually exchanged, as will explained more clearly in Section 8.6.3.

8.4   Virtual file model

The information associated with a virtual file may be divided into two broad classes: contents and attributes. While the former are optional (as the file may be empty), the latter are mandatory, because the file name attribute must exist, at least. In this section, we look first at the attributes and then at the structure of the file contents.

8.4.1 Attributes

Two types of attributes are defined for the virtual file and related operations:

- *file attributes*: describe some of the general characteristics of the file; the set of these attributes is in one-to-one correspondence with the file, and their values are seen by all the initiators manipulating the same file;

- *activity attributes*: a set of attributes of this class is associated with each FTAM regime, and they can be divided into:

  - *active attributes*: describe the active value of file attributes as perceived by the initiator; they are in one-to-one correspondence with some of the file attributes, and their value may not be the same for all the initiators accessing the same file, as they perform different types of access;

  - *current attributes*: describe the facts established about the initiator and the current value of the state information concerning the file transfer; these values are derived by those exchanged in the protocol data units.

The list of attributes defined in FTAM are given in Table 8.1, divided into three classes listed above. Most of them are self-explanatory, because they may be found in most popular file systems. However, some of them deserve some explanation.

Contents type

This attribute describes the type of file and is set when the file is created and cannot be modified. Two types of information are required to maintain the file structure and semantics during transfers:

- a file structure description, given by a constraint set name (see section 8.4.2)

- the name of the abstract syntax to be used in transfer operations

This information may be specified either by giving the pair of names or by referencing a document type name (possibly with parameters) among those defined by FTAM (see Section 8.4.4). Any access to the file contents must not be in conflict with the value of this attribute in order to be executed.

Active contents type

This attribute specifies the name of the document type or the pair of structure and abstract syntax names used for accessing the file by

Table 8.1   List of virtual file attributes.

Attribute Name	Attribute type	Group
Filename	File attr.	Kernel
Permitted actions	File attr.	Kernel
Contents type	File attr.	Kernel
Active contents type	Activity attr.	Kernel
Current access request	Activity attr.	Kernel
Current initiator identity	Activity attr.	Kernel
Current location	Activity attr.	Kernel
Current processing mode	Activity attr.	Kernel
Current calling application title	Activity attr.	Kernel
Current responding application title	Activity attr.	Kernel
Storage account	File attr.	Storage
Date and time of creation	File attr.	Storage
Date and time of last modification	File attr.	Storage
Date and time of last read access	File attr.	Storage
Date and time of last attribute modification	File attr.	Storage
Identity of creator	File attr.	Storage
Identity of last modifier	File attr.	Storage
Identity of last reader	File attr.	Storage
Identity of last attribute modifier	File attr.	Storage
File availability	File attr.	Storage
Filesize	File attr.	Storage
Future filesize	File attr.	Storage
Current account	Activity attr.	Storage
Current concurrency control	Activity attr.	Storage
Current locking style	Activity attr.	Storage
Access control	File attr.	Security
Legal qualification	File attr.	Security
Current access passwords	Activity attr.	Security
Active legal qualification	Activity attr.	Security
Private use	File attr.	Private

the initiator; it is possible to have different values for each initiator, because a file with a complex structure also supports access according to simpler document definitions. Hence they can be accessed by different users according to different structure models. The value of this attribute must not be in conflict with the value of the *Contents Type* attribute.

Current access request

This attribute specifies which operations are allowed in the particular selection regime in effect; the selected operations may only be a subset of those allowed by the access control file parameter.

Current location

This attribute stores information about the current element accessed within the file.

Current processing mode

This attribute specifies the operations allowed in the open regime currently in effect; the scope of this attribute is the current open regime. Therefore, it is a subset of the current access request parameter, and it may be changed by closing and re-opening the file, without changing the current access request parameter.

File availability

Indicates whether or not some delay should be expected in opening the file. The real meaning of the delay is known only to the responder; a possible cause of delay may be the need to mount the device where the file is stored. An initiator operation changing the value from *deferred* to *immediate* availability may indicate that the responder should eliminate the cause of the delay (for example, the file should be copied to a permanently mounted device).

Filesize

Gives the nominal size in octets of the whole file.

Future filesize

Indicates the nominal file size that can be reached when the file is updated. When this size is reached, the responder has three options: increase the value of this parameter, increase the value and give a warning, or indicate an error.

Current concurrency control

This attribute contains, for each of the operations mentioned for the access control parameter, the type of lock to be used (locks are discussed in Section 8.5).

Current locking style

This attribute indicates whether or not the locking of portions of the file is currently selected, or whether the file must be locked as a whole.

Access control

This attribute maintains all the information regarding the access rights to the file. It contains two types of information:

(1) *statement of access* containing an indication of which operations are allowed from the following: *read, insert, replace, erase* and *extend.* Moreover, it shows the locks required for these operations (see also Section 8.5);

(2) *test terms* that may contain a name for the only (or group of) initiator(s) entitled to manipulate the file, a vector of passwords, one for each operation manipulating the file contents or attributes and for deleting the file, and a (or group of) location(s) for the application entity entitled to manipulate the file.

Legal qualifications

The meaning of this attribute is related to data protection legislation, but it is not defined by FTAM.

Current access passwords

This attribute consists of a vector of passwords, each one associated with an operation accessing the file contents or attributes. The values are derived from the parameters used in the Select and Create services, and they are checked against the corresponding values of the access control attributes, in order to decide whether or not each operation is permitted.

Active legal qualification

The meaning of this parameter and its relationship to the legal qualification attribute are not defined by FTAM.

Private use

This attribute is intended to be for use of the specific system, and its semantics is not defined by FTAM.

The attributes of all the three types are subdivided into groups, as shown in Table 8.1; the groups are introduced in FTAM in order to allow different standard implementations with different degrees of complexity.

The *kernel group* is always defined, as it is mandatory for all the FTAM implementations. The *storage group* is defined if it is possible to read the parameter values set by previous activities on the same file; in other words, the virtual filestore must be able to store all the attributes fully supported (not all the attributes are mandatory). The *security group* deals with security and access control, hence it can be implemented only if the virtual filestore is able to enforce the access and security rules specified by FTAM (not all the attributes are mandatory). The *private group* only includes the private use attribute.

8.4.2   Virtual file structure

The virtual file defined by FTAM has a hierarchical data structure based on the following properties:

- the file access structure is an ordered tree;
- each node may or may not have a data unit associated with it;
- each node in the tree gives access to the underlying sub-tree; each sub-tree is referred to as a File Access Data Unit (FADU); the access to the whole file is given by the root node;
- a node may or may not have a name assigned to it;
- the height of the tree and the number of children for each node is unconstrained.

Figure 8.4 shows an example of the structure of a virtual file, where a different name has been assigned to each node. It is worth noting that the file contents consist of two types of information: data units and structure information. The importance of this distinction lies in the fact that the file contents may be accessed in order to transfer either or both types of data elements.

The ordering of nodes in the tree is in accordance with the so-called pre-order traversal; this ordering implies that each FADU precedes in the file structure all its descendants in the tree structure. In Figure 8.4 for example, the names have been assigned so that FADU ordering in the file corresponds to the alphabetical ordering of the associated names.

The FADUs of a file are in a one-to-one correspondence with the sub-trees, and they are identified by giving either the name of the root node, or the path to reach the root of the sub-tree from the file root. In a similar way, data units are identified by the node they are associated with. A FADU may also be identified by the number indicating its position in the file, according to the pre-order traversal of the tree; the root node has the position 0.

An alternative method of determining a FADU identity is to use its relative position with respect to the last FADU accessed or to the whole file, according to the following mechanisms:

- *first*: identifies the first node, in the pre-order traversal, with an associated data unit;

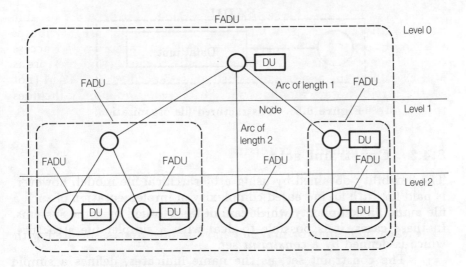

Figure 8.4 General structure of a virtual file.

- *last*: identifies the last node, in pre-order traversal, with an associated data unit;
- *current*: identifies the *current* location in the file;
- *previous*: identifies the FADU preceding the *current* one, in pre-order traversal;
- *next*: identifies the FADU following the *current* one, in pre-order traversal;
- *begin*: is used to go back to the beginning of a file; the *next* FADU corrsponds to the first one in pre-order traversal;
- *end*: there is no longer a current location, however the *previous* FADU corresponds to the *last* one.

As with any other data structure, the virtual file can be described by using a suitable ASN.1 definition. In particular, a file description is divided into two parts, as already seen in the definition of the access control attribute: a description of the file structure with an associated standard ASN.1 object identifier, and the abstract syntax for the data units.

FADUs are the access elements of a file; in other words, it is possible to transfer a complete sub-tree or lock it, without transferring or locking the whole file. This property gives more flexibility to the operations on files; for example, it is possible to transfer a whole sub-tree with a single F-READ or F-WRITE, or it is possible to lock it, allowing other users to access the rest of the file.

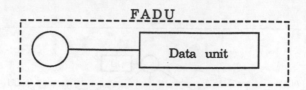

Figure 8.5   Unstructured file organization.

8.4.3   Constraint sets

The flexibility obtained by using a hierarchical file model, however, is paid for with an increased complexity of implementation of such a file model, a complexity which cannot be afforded by some systems. In these cases, it is possible to deal with a simpler file structure, which is defined by a *constraint set*.

The constraint set, as the name indicates, defines a simple file structure by constraining the hierarchical model so that its constrained version assumes the desired structure. Two types of restriction are imposed by a constraint set: restrictions on the file structure and restrictions on the operations permitted in the open regime.

Each user can define their own constraint sets, however, the standard already provides some definition of constraint sets that define some of the commonest file structures and which are simpler than the hierarchical one assumed as a general model.

Unstructured constraint set

This type of file is such that it can only be read or written to as a whole, hence it is not really structured. The file tree can only assume the structure shown in Figure 8.5, where all the data in the file are associated with the root node, as no other node is allowed in this structure. The operations permitted on this type of file in the open regime are: read, replace, extend and erase.

Sequential flat constraint set

This constraint set defines a typical sequential file, structured as a stream of records (possibly of different sizes). The structure of a sequential flat file is depicted in Figure 8.6; the tree is composed of a root without a data unit and a set of leaves, each one with an associated data unit. FADUs can be accessed by using either a sequence number or the relative position (first, last, previous, current, next, begin and end). The operations permitted in the open regime are: locate, read, insert and erase.

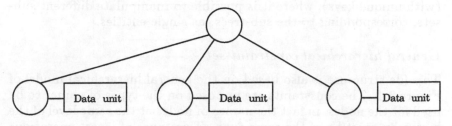

Figure 8.6   Structure of a sequential flat file

Ordered flat constraint set

The file structure defined by this constraint set is similar to that of a sequential flat file, hence the general structure of Figure 8.6 is still valid. The only difference is that, in this case, the root node is not allowed to have an associated name, while the name is mandatory for the leaves; moreover, the names are ordered according to some rule not specified in the standard.

The operations permitted are: locate, read, insert, replace, extend and erase. However, the ordering of names imposes some constraint on the execution of some of these actions. An insert operation with a FADU identity of *begin* inserts a new leaf node in a position which keeps the nodes ordered by name. It is possible to specify for the erase and replace operations the name of the node to be erased or replaced; if the FADU entity is *begin*, then the node(s) matching the name are changed, if the identity is *current*, *previous* or *next*, the FADU is changed only if its name matches the one given.

Ordered flat constraint set with unique names

This constraint set defines a file structure identical to the ordered flat file, except that the names associated with the nodes must be unique. Note that in this case, as in the previous one, the names may be used as access keys for the data records, thus providing a simple structure for keyed files.

Ordered hierarchical constraint set

There is no structuring constraint on this type of file, hence it may be described by the tree in Figure 8.4. The constraints apply to the node names, as each node must have a unique name associated with it, and they are ordered according to the values of node names. The type for the node names must be the same for all the nodes. The only constraint on operation is related to insertion; in this case, the new node to be inserted must have a name not already present in the structure, and it is inserted so that the name ordering is preserved.

This file structure allows the implementation of keyed files (with unique keys), where it is possible to manipulate different subsets, corresponding to the sub-trees, as single entities.

General hierarchical constraint set

This file structure is also based on the general hierarchical model of Figure 8.4. The constraints are imposed on the types of names to be used for the nodes, in fact the names of nodes at the same level of the hierarchy must be of the same type. Two types of insert operations are possible: insert a new FADU as a sister of the current one, and insert a new FADU as a child of the current one. The former type of insertion is not permitted if the current FADU specifies the root.

General hierarchical constraint set with unique names

This file structure is very similar to that defined by the general hierarchical constraint set, as the only difference is that, in this case, the node names of the children of any particular node must be unique.

8.4.4   Documents

The constraint sets mentioned above may be used to define *documents* (see also Section 8.4.1). A document is a more complete definition of a type of file; in fact, it specifies the format and meaning of the data units and/or node names that may be stored in the file, along with a constraint set selecting a particular file structure. A description of the standard documents defined by FTAM is given below.

Unstructured text file

This text file uses the unstructured constraint set, and its contents are composed of one or more character strings, whose semantics are not specified in the standard. Three optional parameters are allowed with this document, which identify:

- the ASN.1 (see Chapter 4) universal class number (i.e. the alphabet) of the characters in the file
- the maximum string length
- the significance of the maximum string length; three options are possible: the strings in the file are shorter or equal to the maximum, their length is exactly equal to the maximum, or the string length is not significant, as they may vary when the file is stored elsewhere.

Structured text file

This document uses the sequential flat constraint set to define the file structure. Each data unit present in the file is composed by zero or more character strings, whose semantics are not specified in the standard. The parameters of this type of document are the same as for the unstructured text.

Unstructured binary file

The constraint set defining this type of document is the unstructured one. The only data units of the file are composed of a set of binary information, organized as a string of octets. The parameters of this type of document are identical to the two last parameters of the unstructured text file, the first being unnecessary, because it is not necessary to select an alphabet, as the data are raw binary items.

Structured binary file

The constraint set used for this document is the structured one. Each data unit in the file is composed of zero or more binary strings organized in octets. The parameters for this document are the same as for the unstructured binary file.

Simple hierarchical file

This type of document does not specify any constraint set. The only additional specification for the general file model is that the node names must be unique strings. This type of document is intended to be referenced by other document definitions, which will specify the syntax for the data elements and the parameters. Hence this definition has to be regarded only as a platform upon which it is possible to build structured document types.

8.5 Concurrency control

When several initiators access the same virtual filestore, it is possible for them to perform actions on the same files. In this case, it is necessary to have some mechanisms to control concurrent access to these files.

Concurrency control is used to ensure the time and space consistency of the file contents. Data held in a file are time consistent if they represent the state of a data set at some point in time; that is, it is never possible for both updated and old values of the data set to be accessible at the same time (except for the updating entity). Space consistency ensures that the same data values are available for all the possible clients of the filestore (except for an updating entity).

Not all the files need concurrency control mechanisms, because either they are not shared, or consistency enforcement is not required. At the other end of the spectrum, some files must not be accessed at all.

All the other files need to be *locked* before accessing their contents. As far as read-only operations are performed, the only concurrency control action to be taken is to avoid write operations, while reading is still in progress, because this would lead to a violation of time consistency. The shared lock, when it succeeds, gives a user the ability to block write operations, while allowing other users, performing other shared-lock operations, to read the file contents.

Write operations should be performed after performing a successful exclusive lock operation; when this lock is in effect, no other user is allowed to access the file, for either reading or writing.

When the FTAM regime is set up, the initiator can specify the type of lock to be used during the file transfer operations. The type of access may be selected from the following: no control required, shared lock, exclusive lock and no access. The enforcement of the concurrency control rules is left to the real filestore.

In addition to locks on whole files, it is possible to lock only the FADU that is manipulated. In this way, concurrency is increased, as different users accessing different FADUs can operate on the file at the same time, regardless of the locks used.

8.6   Services

The services provided by FTAM are divided into two hierarchical classes: internal and external services. This classification is needed because all the recovery operations are completely hidden to the FTAM user. The whole situation may be represented as in Figure 8.7. For each entity, there is a basic file protocol machine (FPM) implementing the internal services, and a file error recovery protocol machine (FERPM) implementing the external services, by using the internal services and the recovery protocol.

Note that the external services are a subset of the internal ones, as the recovery primitives are not exposed to the FTAM user. The difference in the execution of the same service at the external and internal level is that the former are, in general, more reliable, as their execution may include error recovery actions.

8.6.1   Functional units and service classes

The set of services defined by FTAM is grouped into functional units and service classes, in order to allow standard implementations with different levels of functionality, according to the cost and technical limitations that each implementor has to comply with. The grouping is also useful to negotiate a common subset of functionalities

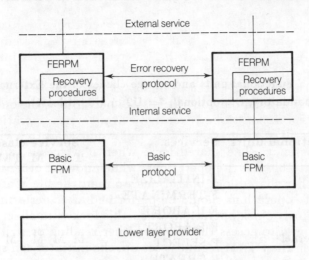

Figure 8.7   Internal organization of an FTAM entity.

Table 8.2   Functional units and service classes of the Internal File Service (M= mandatory, O= optional, *= U2 or U3, at least).

Functional units	Services	Service classes				
		T	A	M	TM	U
U9 Recovery	F-CHECK F-RECOVER F-CANCEL	O	O		O	O
U10 Restart Data Transfer	F-CHECK F-CANCEL F-RESTART	O	O		O	O

supported by a pair of FTAM entities.

Tables 8.2 and 8.3 show the classification of the FTAM services into ten functional units, eight for external services and two for internal ones. For each functional unit, the applicability to each service class is also shown. The service classes are: transfer (T), access (A), management (M), transfer and management (TM) and unconstrained (U). Not all the combinations of these classes are allowed, as there is a clear dependence between some of them. The permitted combinations are: T, M, A, T-A, T-M-TM and A-T-M-TM. Each combination may be used in conjunction with the unconstrained class (U).

Table 8.3   Functional units and service classes of the External File Service (M= mandatory, O= optional, *= U2 or U3, at least).

Functional units	Services	Service classes				
		T	A	M	TM	U
U1 Kernel	F-INITIALIZE F-TERMINATE F-U-ABORT F-P-ABORT F-SELECT F-CREATE F-SELECT F-DELETE	M	M	M	M	M
U2 Read	F-READ F-DATA F-DATA-END F-TRANSFER-END F-CANCEL F-OPEN F-CLOSE	*	M		*	O
U3 Write	F-WRITE F-DATA F-DATA-END F-TRANSFER-END F-CANCEL F-OPEN F-CLOSE	*	M		*	O
U4 File Access	F-LOCATE F-ERASE (requires U2 or U3)		M			O
U5 Limited File Management	F-CREATE F-DELETE F-READ-ATTRIB	O	O	M	M	O

Table 8.3   (*cont.*)

U6 Enhanced File Management	F-CHANGE-ATTRIB (requires U5)	O O O O O
U7 Grouping	F-BEGIN-GROUP F-END-GROUP	M O M M O
FADU Locking	use locking service parameters (requires U2 or U3, and U4)	O O

8.6.2   Grouping

File services may be executed individually, determining the success or failure of each of them by examining the value of the response parameters. In this case, a request cannot be issued if the response for the previous request has not yet been received.

Another mode of issuing a sequence of services is grouped execution. In this case, the sequence should be considered as a single group, whose overall success depends on the success of a sufficient number of group members.

Requests for services in the same group are issued even though one or more previous requests are still outstanding, as shown in the time diagram of Figure 8.8. However, the responses must be received in the same order as the corresponding requests, as a list of expected responses is kept by the FTAM entities. This list is like a FIFO buffer, where an element is inserted at the tail when a new request is issued, and an element is extracted from the head when a response matching the head contents is received.

A threshold sent as a parameter in the F-BEGIN-GROUP request set is the minimum number of successes of individual services in the group, which is required to take even part of the operations in the group. In other words, sending all the service requests in a group allows the responder to check whether a number of operations greater or equal to the threshold can be executed; if so, all the operations in the group are really executed, otherwise none succeeds.

Some grouped sequences are defined in the standard and are reported in Table 8.4, along with the names of the service classes permitting them. The notation used is as follows:

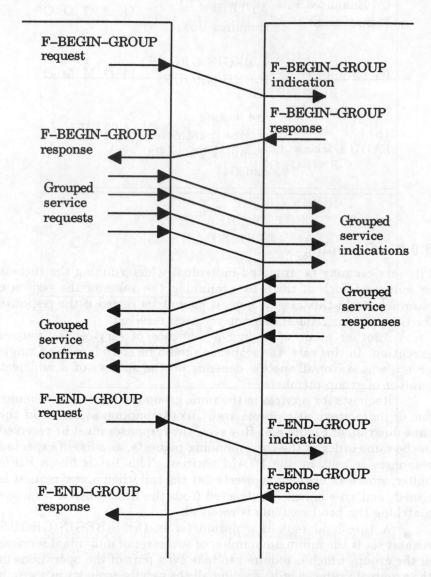

Figure 8.8   Time diagram of the execution of grouped services.

Table 8.4   Standard service groups.

(a)	F-BEGIN-GROUP (F-SELECT | F-CREATE) [F-READ-ATTRIB] [F-CHANGE-ATTRIB] F-OPEN F-END-GROUP
(b)	F-BEGIN-GROUP F-CLOSE [F-READ-ATTRIB] [F-CHANGE-ATTRIB] (F-DESELECT | F-DELETE) F-END-GROUP
(c)	F-BEGIN-GROUP (F-SELECT | F-CREATE) [F-READ-ATTRIB] [F-CHANGE-ATTRIB] (F-DESELECT | F-DELETE) F-END-GROUP
(d)	F-BEGIN-GROUP (F-SELECT | F-CREATE) [F-READ-ATTRIB] [F-CHANGE-ATTRIB] F END-GROUP
(e)	F-BEGIN-GROUP [F-READ-ATTRIB] [F-CHANGE-ATTRIB] (F-DESELECT | F-DELETE) F-END-GROUP

- items included between brackets '[' and ']' are optional
- the vertical bar '|' is used to separate alternative actions
- parentheses '(' and ')' have the normal algebraic meaning.

For all the sequences in Table 8.4, the threshold parameter is set equal to the number of services in the group (except F-BEGIN-GROUP and F-END-GROUP); that is, all the services must be successful in order to consider the whole group, or part of the group as successful.

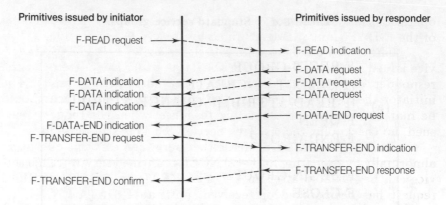

Figure 8.9 Bulk data transfer operations for a read.

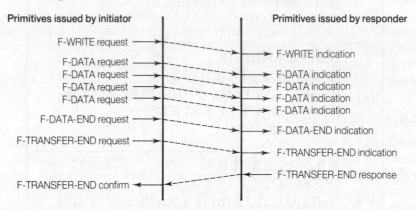

Figure 8.10 Bulk data transfer operations for a write.

8.6.3 Bulk data transfer

File data transfer is performed by reading or writing a whole FADU. As seen in Section 8.4.2, a FADU may be a quite complex data structure, or even the whole file. Therefore, although a fragmentation service is provided by intermediate protocol layers, data transfer should take place by transmitting the whole FADU in several application-level data units.

The F-READ and F-WRITE non-confirmed services are used to start the transfer to or from the initiating entity, respectively. Each of these service primitives carries a parameter with the identification of the FADU. A typical sequence for a read data transfer is shown in Figure 8.9, while Figure 8.10 shows a typical write data transfer.

After an F-READ or F-WRITE is issued or received, data units are sent with the non-confirmed service F-DATA. Each data unit, as well as other bulk transfer service primitives, is numbered, because this number can be used as a checkpoint identifier for all the operations related to error recovery (see Section 8.6.4). The direction of the F-DATA units is determined by the type of operation.

The sequence of data units is closed by an F-DATA-END service issued by the entity sending the data (either the initiator or the responder, according to whether the operation is write or read). The initiator then sends an F-TRANSFER-END request, which should be matched by the corresponding response; when the request is issued, no checkpoint request (see Section 8.6.4) is still outstanding.

During bulk data transfer, either party can exit this operation abnormally by executing an F-CANCEL confirmed service. This service can be initiated after an F-DATA-READ or F-DATA-WRITE request has been issued or received, until an F-DATA-END is issued by the data sender or the entity has issued either a request or response for an F-TRANSFER-END.

The execution of an F-CANCEL terminates the bulk data transfer, deleting also all responses and indications that are pending, and canceling any restart activity. The file remains open, but the two parties can have different views of the state of the activity, as the result of the interrupted operation is not defined by the standard.

8.6.4 Error recovery

Error recovery operations are performed by the FERPM entity shown in Figure 8.7, which is implemented in the upper part of the whole FTAM entity. Thus the operations described in this section are not visible to the external user, as they involve only internal entities. In fact, normal service primitives, not related to recovery, are just passed up and down by the FERMP, after adding or deleting some parameter related to recovery only. Vice versa, the primitives of the services illustrated in this section are generated by and addressed to either of the two FERPMs; hence they are totally hidden from the FTAM user.

Checkpoint insertion

The error recovery procedure is performed by re-executing some of the operations of the sequence that failed. A key point for implementing this type of strategy is to keep track of the operations performed, so that they can be repeated during the error recovery operations. In FTAM, each of the two parties maintains a *docket*, where all the information relevant to a possible recovery procedure is recorded.

The docket management operations follow the rules listed below:

(1) a docket is created whenever an F-OPEN request is issued (initiator) or received (responder), and it is initialized with some general information on the two participating entities;

the state is set to *starting*;

(2) if the response to the F-OPEN that caused the docket creation reports a failure, then the docket is deleted;

(3) whenever a request for an F-READ or F-WRITE is issued or received, the state *in progress* is recorded on the docket;

(4) the entity sending data adds the checkpoint identifier of an F-CHECK request to the docket, before issuing it; the same operation is performed by the receiver upon receipt of the corresponding indication;

(5) after securing all data units received before the F-CHECK indication, the data receiver acknowledges the checkpoint with an F-CHECK response; upon the issue or receipt of this primitive, all the earlier checkpoints are deleted from the list in the docket;

(6) upon the execution of the F-DATA-TRANSFER service, the *data transfer finished* is recorded on the docket;

(7) the initiator records *terminating* on its docket when it issues an F-CLOSE request;

(8) the receipt of an F-CLOSE response reporting either success or permanent failure causes the deletion of the docket, while a response reporting any other type of result causes the activation of the recovery procedure, while keeping the docket.

As a checkpoint is acknowledged only after securing all the data received, the real meaning of this operation is to record the point where all the data transmitted so far need not be re-transmitted, in any case. This allows the recovery procedure to be shortened, as it should only deal with those data units with no information on their correct reception and storage.

Recovery

Three levels of recovery actions are possible, according to the level of damage caused by an error:

I – damage of the data transfer regime only

II – damage of the select or open regimes

III – loss of association.

A recovery operation for level I is shown in Figure 8.11. During a data transfer, the receiver can issue an F-RESTART request with the number of the most recent checkpoint in its docket (if any). This primitive requests the data sender to restart the data units transmission from the checkpoint indicated (if any), or from the beginning, if an immediate restart is not possible. The restart can also be requested by the data sender, but it cannot specify the checkpoint, which is provided in the response from the receiver.

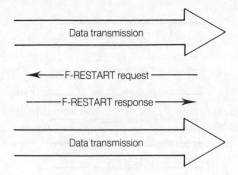

Figure 8.11   Recovery procedure for level I errors.

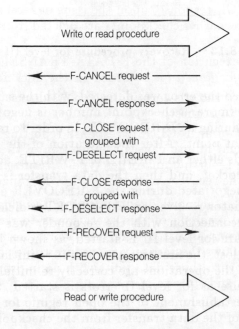

Figure 8.12   Recovery procedure for level II errors.

If the restart functional unit is not implemented, errors of level I may be processed as errors of level II.

The recovery operations for level II are shown in Figure 8.12. In this case, the F-CANCEL service is executed upon the detection of a level II error, causing the abrupt termination of the bulk data transfer regime; the F-CANCEL parameter should indicate a transient (recoverable) error. Then the initiator closes and de-selects the file with a grouped request. In this case, both parties retain the docket on file closure, as a transient error has been indicated.

Once the file has been closed and de-selected, the true recovery action is started by executing the F-RECOVER service. This operation re-establishes (if possible) the open regime on the same file

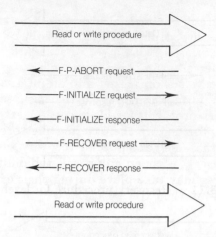

Figure 8.13   Recovery procedure for level III errors.

manipulated when the error was detected, with the same parameters as before; furthermore, a checkpoint number is negotiated between the two parties, during an F-RECOVER, in order to resume the data transfer from that point. After the execution of the F-RECOVER, the initiator sends either an F-READ or F-WRITE, according to the contents of its docket, and then the data transfer is resumed from the checkpoint negotiated during the F-RECOVER execution.

If the initiator receives an F-P-ABORT indication or a local signal that the connection with the responder was lost, then the recovery procedure for level III is started, as shown in Figure 8.13. As any regime is lost, the first thing to do is to re-initialize the FTAM regime. Then, if the operations are correctly re-initialized, the same recovery procedure as for level II errors is started; this procedure leads to the re-establishment of the open regime for the same file, and to a restart of the data transfer from the checkpoint negotiated.

8.7   Conclusions

FTAM provides a uniform model for file transfer in an open system. Only those aspects related to communication are included in this model, as the storage operations are left to the real filestore implemented in one of the two party stations.

The operations are performed by a sequence of nested environment set ups, each one allowing the initiator to perform a new set of operations. However, each environment can encapsulate only one instance of an inner environment. This constraint leads to some limitations in accessing the files; for example, it is not possible for the same user to manipulate more than one file at a time, even when the user is on a diskless station and its files are in the same remote filestore.

The structure of the virtual files should be general enough to incorporate all the file structures used by today's real filestore. A tree-like structure is used, with a set of standard restrictions available, in order to describe simple, popular file structures.

An FTAM entity is organized into an internal filestore and an external one. The former provides all the basic services, while the latter adds recovery protocols for file access operations. It turns out that the services provided by the external filestore are the same as those for the internal one (except that recovery services are hidden to the external user), with an improved reliability level, because recovery procedures may take place during their execution, without any intervention from the external user.

Reference

[ISO8571] ISO 8571, *File Transfer Access and Management, Parts 1 to 4*, first edition, 1988.

Chapter 9

Office Application Protocols

9.1   Introduction

Office automation has introduced many requirements which have soon led to the development of *electronic mail systems* so that inter-personal message exchanges can be facilitated, and *virtual terminal* supports in order to handle data representation on heterogeneous devices.

The electronic mail system's main purpose is to support information transfer both from an originator to a single recipient and from an originator to multiple recipients. An ideal solution requires an environment able to accept messages from a number of information sources and to deliver to a different variety of information sinks. In this case information transferred is not restricted to simple text but may contain various information types such as voice, graphics and facsimile. Furthermore, specific services make it possible to submit and deliver messages either interactively or in a spooled approach, depending on the characteristics of the devices involved in the system.

Many solution have been proposed up to now, however most of such implementations are characterized by some limitations, since in most cases they are closed corporate systems, or vendor specific implementations. It should be considered that the advantages of electronic mail system can be pointed out by enhanced systems not

370

limited to the reduced environment of a single organization or a single implementation.

Standardization organizations are currently making a considerable effort to define office document architectures and office document interchange formats, and particular attention has been devoted by CCITT and ISO to the specification of services and protocols for message handling. In this chapter the message handling services and protocols according to the *X.400 recommendations for Message Handling Systems* (MHS), which have gained broad acceptance among user communities and computer manufacturers, are introduced and discussed [X400]. It is worth noting that CCITT X.400 is used as the basis for ISO's *Message Oriented Text Interchange System* (MOTIS).

Application writers have often faced problems related to the lack of *terminal standards*. Applications written for a specific terminal cannot be correctly executed using devices coming from other vendors, or even for a different type of terminal coming from the same manufacturer. This fact is mainly due to different implementation approaches for the control character sequences, generally named as *escape sequences*, which are used to position the cursor, change the background and/or foreground colour, set the blinking mode for characters, and visualize special characters not included in the printable set. Even though the ANSI organization, together with many other international organisations, has introduced specific standards for output and input data, device implementors seem not to be interested in that. In fact, in many cases, they continue to propose proprietary solutions which are incompatible with those of every other manufacturer. This makes writing display-oriented applications difficult. As an example, problems arise when anyone tries to use a screen editor that works with an arbitrary keyboard and display. Even if a given terminal has a key labeled *insert character*, it is very unlikely that an existing editor will be able to use that key for the function for which it was intended. Another example is given by an application devoted to hotel reservations, where a list of the free-hotels can be scanned by the user: it would be nice if the operator could move the cursor to the desired item by means of the arrow keys on the keyboard, or the mouse, and then use the carriage return key or click a mouse button to select the hotel. This problem can be solved by buying the main computer, the terminal and the software from a single manufacturer, so everything works together. However, as the system grows and more and more terminals and personal computers gain access to the network, the incompatibility problem has to be faced in some way. A solution, which is adopted in some cases, provides for a *configuration* object which is based on a sort of data base allowing immediate conversion of an escape sequence into that required by the selected device. In this way it is possible to define the characteristics of the terminal currently used. Typical elements considered in the data base are the screen size, the operating modes supported by the device, such as the escape sequences activated by function and arrow keys and so on. This approach was introduced first by the Berkeley Unix, and now is widely used in many other software tools.

The OSI solution is rather similar to the concept discussed above, since it introduces the idea of a *virtual terminal* implemented as an abstract data structure, which can describe the abstract state of the real terminal, and can be accessed and updated by both the computer and the keyboard.

The ISO Virtual Terminal specifications are also described in this chapter, in order to give a complete overview of those protocols which play a basic role in the efficient operation of an office environment.

The TOP specifications [TOP3.0] address the requirement for message handling systems and virtual terminals by defining a TOP MHS Application Profile, which specifies the message handling services needed to allow users to exchange messages on a store and forward basis, and a TOP VT Application Profile, which provides an object-based, remote, interactive terminal service between heterogeneous end systems. It is worth noting that MAP specifications do not include both the application modules, being typical functions oriented to the office environment.

9.2   MHS overview

Figure 9.1 describes the X.400 architectural model. A layered solution has been used as a basic structuring technique for representing the communication functionalities of the message handling system. This comes from the fact that this approach is applied in all modern network architectures to control their complexity and to achieve independency of logically disjointed functions.

Layering is based on the concepts of service, protocol and interface, already introduced for the description of the lower communication layers in Chapter 2.

It should be noted that no ACSE module is provided for managing associations which are, in fact, handled within the MHS. At the present time, however, there are harmonization activities going on between ISO and CCITT to bring the two MHS standards activities together.

As shown in Figure 9.1, the system is based on two layers; the lower layer, called the *message transfer layer*, is composed of *message transfer agent entities* (MTAE) and *submission and delivery entities* (SDE). The protocol which governs the communication between a couple of MTAEs is indicated as the *message transfer protocol* (P1) and is concerned with the store and forward mechanism for the transfer of messages. This means that messages are sent from one end or intermediate MTAE to another end or intermediate sys-

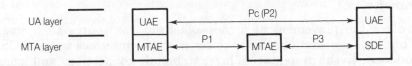

Figure 9.1 The Message Handling System model based on a layered architecture.

tem. Besides the routing operations, the MTAE provides storage for messages and supports specific control actions, which are carried on by referring to the control information provided by the protocol itself. The MTAEs may also transfer the message to a sequence of further MTAEs in order to implement a multi-recipient delivery mechanism. The communication between an SDE and an MTAE is based on the protocol P3 which provides reliable message exchange facilities without supporting particular end-to-end electronic mail functions. Its main purpose is to provide a distant application process with access to the message transfer functions. Both P1 and P3 protocols are based on the OSI presentation service and cooperate in a coordinated manner to manage the message transfer service, which is then available to the entities in the upper layer composed of *user agents entities* (UAE). At this level different protocols may be defined, each one corresponding to a specific syntax and semantics of data. For message transfer, only the P2 protocol is available, which may be compared to paper-based mail exchange between users.

9.2.1 Message transfer functions

X.440 or MOTIS is related to all aspects of electronic mail systems, starting from when the originator decides to write a message and ending when the recipient finally throws it in the garbage can. Those aspects include the following activities:

Composition

This concerns the task of creating a message or an answer to a message; the system itself may provide assistance with addressing and the various header fields related to a single message; in fact, even if the body may be prepared by means of a normal text editor, when a message is received and an answer must be provided, the mail system can get the originator's address from the incoming mail and automatically insert it into the proper place in the answer message.

Transfer

Involves the movement of a message from the source to a single or multiple destination; this requires a proper interface to the ACSE module or to the presentation layer to handle connections and transfer mechanisms, these aspects should be managed by the mail system without the user being involved.

Reporting

This mechanism informs the originator about sent messages, in particular, the user is informed if the message was delivered, rejected or lost during transfer.

Conversion

Since heterogeneous terminals may be used by the mail system, this feature plays a basic role for allowing incompatible sending and receiving devices to be integrated in the system; a typical example is given when a message has to be sent from a computer terminal to a facsimile device; in this case, the message has to be prepared for a scanning process in order to build up a facsimile image for the receiver.

Formatting

Concerns the form of the displayed message on the recipient's terminal, which means that each message has to be suitably processed before being sent to the terminal.

Disposition

Concerns actions to be performed by the recipient on the message after it has been received and processed; they include the possibility of throwing it away immediately before reading or after reading it, saving it and so on; these actions may involve operations to reread the message after saving in order to process it in other ways.

When a UAE has prepared a message to be sent, message transfer services are used to transfer data to one or more recipients and if the message cannot be delivered the UAE will be informed in some way about this problem. No connection is established for carrying on the transfer, this means that a message is passed to the MTAE without any previous contact with the destination entity being required.

The message transfer protocol supports the service introducing, among others, the following functionalities:

- notification of successful delivery of a message or prevention of notification in case of non-delivery

- conversion of the encoded information type for a message as specified by the UAE or prevention of any conversion
- definition of the submission and/or delivery time and date for the message
- deferring delivery of a message until a specified time and date
- selection of a priority for the delivery of a message: a message can be *urgent, non-urgent* or *normal*
- availability of multi-recipient delivery mechanism
- disclosure of the identification of all other recipients to each destination upon delivery of the message
- returning of the message contents when a non-delivery notification is produced
- alternate recipient delivery mechanism, which allows a message to be delivered to a second recipient indicated in the submission request
- testing mechanism for verifying the capability to deliver a message
- holding mechanisms in order to allow a UAE to request that the MTAE holds its message until a later time.

The message transfer service is based on the primitives listed in Table 9.1, which has been organized according to functionality requirements so that the different functions have been grouped according to their effects. A further classification would suggest dividing those functions into *local* and *remote* primitives. In the former case, no action is required from entities outside the originating user site since the user interacts with the local communication environment, while in the latter case at least one user in another system interacts with the originating one in a coordinated manner. Such interactions are supported by the services provided by the underlying distributed communication subsystem. All primitives classified as *remote* are considered as global activities and include all transfer operations which represent the basic service primitives for the message handling system. However, such classification has to be considered in more depth. In fact the locality concept involves other entities being able to interact through services and protocols, too. Local and remote activities described in Table 9.1 refer to a specific model for the interaction between a UAE and an MTAE. In particular it is expected that the user agent and its message transfer agent be located on two different physical sites managed by two different management and implementation authorities, however the X.400 recommendations also define different operating models.

Table 9.1   Message transfer service primitives.

Class	Primitive	Type	Description
Transfer	SUBMIT	Req, conf	Submission of a message
	DELIVER	Ind	Delivery of a message
	PROBE	Req, conf	Submission of probe
	NOTIFY	Ind	Delivery/probe notification
Logon/logoff	(UAL) LOGON	Req, conf	User logon
	(MTL) LOGON	Ind, resp	System logon
Access	(UAL) CHANGE PASSWORD	Req, conf	Change of user's password
management	(MTL) CHANGE PASSWORD	Ind, resp	Change of system's password
Transfer	REGISTER	Req, conf	Registration of user's receipt
restrictions	(UAL) CONTROL	Req, conf	Change of user's receipt restrictions
	(MTL) CONTROL	Ind, resp	Change of system's password
Transfer cancel	CANCEL	Req, conf	Cancel request for a message

The model and its applications

The user agent is a program used to interface the user to the mail system; it provides functions to compile, send and receive mail from user agents and to start it on its way. In practice, the message transfer agent works as an electronic post office and, just as in the postal system, a message may visit several electronic post offices before being delivered. It is possible for the user agent and the message transfer agent to reside on the same host computer; however, it is normal for the user agent to be run on a personal computer in one site and the message transfer agent to be run on a mainframe managed by the telephone company, PTT, or some other public or private service.

Functions carried out locally by the UAE are those functions which do not require cooperation with other UAEs. A typical example is given by text editing functions or alerting of the user in the case of reception of newly arrived messages. Local functions are not standardized by the specifications even if they are communication related. The user agent entity, in fact, embodies those aspects of UA which have to do with the representation of the message's contents and other functionalities [X401]. Users access a UAE for creating, presenting or storing messages. Some UAE implementations provide storage in which a user can manage outgoing and incoming messages. An example is represented by a workstation having suitable mass storage devices, although the user can manage its messages using a simple intelligent terminal. In the former case the UAE, other than providing local functions for message processing, also provides mechanisms and an adequate amount of storage so that messages can be stored locally instead of in the MTAE system. Interactions between the UAE and the MTAE use standardized protocols specified for message handling. On the other hand, if a UAE is implemented in the same system with an MTAE, the UAE accesses the message transfer service interacting directly with the MTAE, without any protocols being involved. Figures 9.2, 9.3 and 9.4 show different physical configurations, where the different elements may be connected by means of dedicated lines or switched network connections.

In Figure 9.2 the UA is represented by a set of processes interacting directly with the MTA since they are located in the same physical system. The user interacts with the UA by means of a serial line which connect the I/O device to the system.

If the user agent and the message transfer agent run on separate machines, the interaction between them is a subject for standardization and OSI has specified the P3 protocol for this purpose. Figure 9.3 represents a UA located on a workstation, interactions with the MTA are carried out by the P3 protocol. Figure 9.4 proposes a different solution from those exemplified previously since, in this case, one or more UAs are located in an independent system provided by as many I/O devices as are required by the number of UAs. Even in this case I/O devices may communicate with the corresponding UAs with a dedicated line, while standardized protocols and services are used for interactions between UAs and MTAs.

Since an electronic mail system involves wide geographical areas, organizational mapping rules are also defined in the specifications. The main concept is that mail services are always provided by specific private or public organizations, each one controlling its specific *management domain* (MD). A management domain is composed

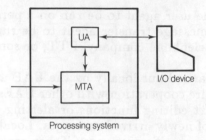

Figure 9.2   UAs and MTAs reside on the same processing system, users interact with the UA by means of simple terminals.

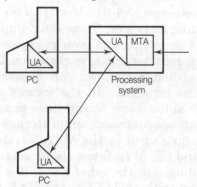

Figure 9.3   The UA is located in a workstation and communicates with a remote MTA by a standard communication protocol.

of at least one MTA and zero or more UAs owned by a specific organization and is indicated as a *private management domain* (PRMD) if the controlling organization is private, while, if the organization is public, it is called an *administration management domain* (ADMD). The role of a management domain is to provide message transfer and interpersonal message exchange services, which can be granted at different levels. An administration, in fact, may provide access for a user to an administration supplied UA, or for a private UA to an administration MTA or for a private MTA to an administration MTA.

In the case of an administration supplied UA two solutions may be implemented. In the former, the user has only an input/output device, such as a telephone or teletypewriter, and interacts with the UAs made available by the administration. In the latter, intelligent terminals provided with UAs may be proposed to the user. However, in both cases the UAs are under the control of the administration.

In case of private UAs, the user may use its private stand-alone UA process, which can be installed on a workstation or a personal computer. The UA interacts with the MTA supplied by the admin-

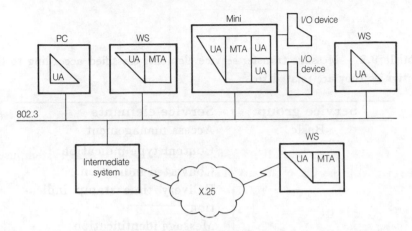

Figure 9.4   Multiple UAs located in a single system (mini) and communicating with a remote MTA system.

istration using standardized procedures based on the submission and delivery primitives to obtain the MT service. In this case the UA is defined as associated with the MD, which makes the transfer service available.

A user may have the availability of an MTA other than a number of UAs. This environment represents a private management domain, which may interact with the administration management domain at the level of the MTA. A private domain is considered to exist entirely within one country and within that country the private domain may have access to more administrative domains as shown in Figure 9.5. However, it should be noted that, even if the private domain may interact with many other administrative organizations, it cannot operate as a relay between two administrations. Moreover, when interactions are active, the responsibility for the operations is with the PRMD and, because of this, the ADMD performs any control to verify that the operations of accounting, logging, quality of service and other functions are correctly executed by the PRMD.

9.2.2   The message transfer service

The message transfer service allows messages to be exchanged between UA and the activation of the probing mechanism to verify the reachability of a given destination. Other than the basic services, the UA may select optional service elements at each message submission so that specific requirements may be satisfied as already introduced in Section 9.2.1. In Table 9.2 service elements are grouped in five different classes regarding submission and delivery, conversion, query and status and inform [X411].

To transfer a message the UA submits the message to the

Table 9.2   Message transfer service elements classified according to the activities they are related to.

Service group	Service elements
Basic	Access management
	Content type indication
	Converted indication
	Delivery time stamp indication
	Message identification
	Non-delivery notification
	Original encoded information types indication
	Registered encoded information types
	Submission time stamp indication
Submission and delivery	Alternate recipient allowed
	Deferred delivery
	Deferred delivery cancellation
	Delivery notification
	Disclosure of other recipients
	Grade of delivery selection
	Multi-destination delivery
	Prevention of non-delivery notification
	Return of contents
Conversion	Conversion prohibition
	Explicit conversion
	Implicit conversion
Query	Probe
Status and inform	Alternate recipient assignment
	hold for delivery

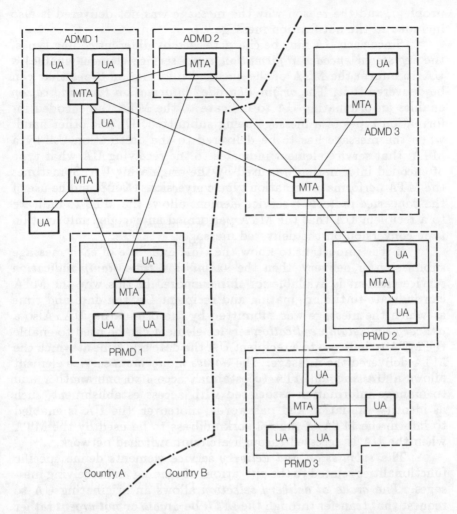

Figure 9.5 Interconnections of private and administration domains.

MTA, specifying also the name and the address of the recipient; at this point the MTA completes the transfer operation delivering the message to the destination UA together with the originator's name and address. When the *message identification* service element is indicated by the requestor, the MTA is enabled to provide a UA with a unique identifier for each message submitted or delivered by the MTS. This approach is useful for subsequent references to the received or sent messages, when notification information is also required. Notification functions are activated when the *non-delivery notification* service element is introduced in the request by the originating UA. In this case, in fact, if a message cannot be delivered to the specified recipient, the originating UA is informed about the problem, and the reason why the message was not delivered is also included in the notification message.

Since each UA may be characterized by different coding types, the *registered encoded information types* service element enables a UA to inform the MTA of the encoded information types that can be delivered to it. The *original encoded information types indication* enables an originating UA to indicate to the MTA the encoded information types of a message being submitted. On the other hand, when the message has to be delivered to the destination UA by a MTA, that service element indicates to the receiving UA what type of encoded information was used by the originating UA. Sometimes the MTA performs information type conversions [X408], so the use of the *converted indication* service element allows the MTS to indicate to a recipient UA that the MTA performed an encoded information type conversion on the delivered message.

If it is important to know the time and date of each message submission or delivery, then the *submission time stamp indication* service element is available for this purpose. In this way the MTA can indicate to the originating and recipient UA the date and time at which the message was submitted by the originating UA. Also a *delivery time stamp indication* service element can be used to enable the MTA to indicate to a recipient UA the date and time at which the MTA delivered the message. The *access mangement* service element allows a UA and an MTA to establish access to one another and to manage information associated with access establishment, such as identity validation and passwords, moreover, the UA is enabled to inform the MTA of the network address to be used by the MTA when the UA is accessed through a circuit switched network.

The *submission and delivery* service elements define specific functionalities related to the operations of sending and receiving messages. The *grade of delivery selection* allows an originating UA to request that transfer through the MTA be *urgent* or *not urgent* rather than normal, in this way different priorities are available for transferring documents. *Multi-destination delivery* enables an originating UA to specify that a message being submitted is to be delivered to more than one recipient UA, while the *disclosure of other recipients* service element enables the MTS to disclose the recipient names to each destination UA upon delivery of the message. Since a primary recipient is always indicated in the request, the UA may also indicate alternative recipients using the *alternate recipient allowed* service element, so that, if the main recipient is unreachable, other destinations can be selected.

A message can be delivered to its destination by the MTA after a specific time and date indicated by the UA when the submit request is passed to the MTA, the service element to be used is called *deferred delivery*. A deferred delivery message, if not yet delivered, can be cancelled by using the *deferred delivery cancellation* service element.

If an explicit notification is needed, then the *delivery notification* service element enables the originating UA to request that an explicit reply be returned when the submitted message has been successfully delivered to a recipient UA. A specific message identifier is used to put into relation the message previously sent with the response message containing also the date and time of delivery. The reply is generated without any specific actions being required from the UA or the user.

If the originating UA does not want to receive any notifications about delivery failures, the *prevention of non-delivery notifications* must be used by the originating UA.

If the originating UA needs a copy of the message sent to one or more destination, the *return of contents* service element allows an originating UA to request that the content of a submitted message be returned with any non-delivery notification; such action cannot be successful if a conversion has been done by the MTA.

The *conversion* service elements manage operations related to encoded information type conversion. In particular a user may also request that conversions are not performed for a particular submitted message using the *conversion prohibition* service element. On the other hand *implicit conversion* enables the MTA to perform any necessary conversion for a period of time, the recipient UA is informed of the original encoded information types as well as the current encoded information types in the message. *Explicit conversion* also enables a UA to request the MTA to perform a specified conversion, such as that required when interworking between different telematic services. The UA is also informed of the original information type other than the current encoded information type.

The *query* and *probe* service elements allow a user to examine and test the correct operation of the system; in particular the former permits a UA to request information related to the control and operation of the MTA, while the latter enables a UA to establish, before submission, whether a particular message can reach a specific destination. In this case the MTA acts as if it had to transfer a real message, so it generates delivery or non-delivery notifications indicating whether a message characterized by the same submission information could be delivered to the specified recipient UAs. This service can also check whether the message size, content type, and encoded information types would render it undeliverable. The result of the probe service depends upon the attributes with which the recipient is registered with the MTA, such as encoded information type, maximum message size and content type.

The *status and information* service elements include the *alternate recipient assignment* which enables a UA to receive certain messages: the selection of messages is based on the definition of a set of attributes, a typical example is represented by an organization which states that a certain UA has to receive all those messages

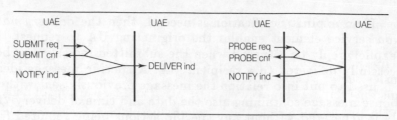

Figure 9.6   Time sequence diagrams for message submission and probing of a message transfer.

which have a specific country name, administration management domain name and organization name without the personal name of the receiver being defined. In this way even if the real destination is not known to the message handling system, the message can be delivered to the UA for which a subset of the attribute set assigned to the message matches those selected for it.

Another service element of this class is represented by the *hold for delivery* parameter, which enables a recipient UA to request that the MTA holds its message for delivery and returning notification until a later time. This happens when the UA informs the MTA that it is unavailable for receiving messages or notifications, and, in the same way, it can inform the MTA when the delivery procedure can be resumed.

When a message has to be transferred, first, the UA submits the message to the message transfer service using a *SUBMIT* request, which will be locally confirmed by a *SUBMIT* confirmation. Service elements can be indicated in the request by setting appropriate parameters. It should be noted that some of these parameters are optional, while others must be inserted. If the submit confirmation indicates that the submission operation has been completed successfully, the destination entity will be informed of the availability of the document by the use of a *DELIVER* indication primitive. If at the time when the message was submitted the originating user specified an appropriate parameter, then the destination entity will reply with a *NOTIFY* primitive to the originator so that the requestor is informed about successful or unsuccessful deliveries.

A mechanism to test whether a message could be delivered to one or more recipient, is represented by the *PROBE* request, which is locally confirmed as the submit primitive. The success or failure of the operation is reported back to the originating user agent by a *NOTIFY* indication primitive.

Figure 9.6 reports two schemes where submission, delivery notification and probing are described in terms of time sequences.

The message transfer protocol

Three entities represent an MTAE executing the transfer protocol: the message dispatcher, the association manager and the reliable transfer server (RTS) [X410] [X411]. The message dispatcher performs the relaying of messages, generation and forwarding of delivery reports and information type conversion, while the association manager supports the establishment of associations between MTAEs. The reliable transfer service provides and maintains the association requested by the association manager and also provides for releasing them if requested by the association manager. Table 9.3 describes the services used by the three modules cited above. It should be noted that the association manager uses only the *OPEN* and *CLOSE* primitives for establishing or releasing an association and employs information locally available. Two different message protocol data units (MPDUs) are used by the message dispatcher, so that data referring to user information can be distinguished from control information contained in status reports. In particular the *user MPDU* carries a message submitted by a user agent for delivery, while the *service MPDU* carries either a probe or a delivery report. The message protocol data unit is mapped onto the user data parameter of a data transfer primitive made available by the RTS module.

The reliable transfer server, other than creating and maintaining associations between an application entity and the corresponding remote end, supports the reliable transfer of application protocol data units. In particular an association created by the RTS may handle both one-way and two-way alternate transfers of MPDUs. If the two-way alternate functionality is active, then the right to transfer is controlled by the turn, which can be transferred from one end to the other.

The following service primitives are made available by the RTS:

- **open**: this function is related to the establishment of an association between remote entities; when a user issues an *OPEN* request primitive, a new association with another RTS user is opened. This is a confirmed service.

- **close**: this function supports the release of an association; when the initiating RTS user has its turn, it can issue a *CLOSE* request primitive, which terminates the association previously opened; this also is a confirmed service.

- **turn-please**: this function handles the exchange of the turn. To request the turn, the user issues a *TURN-PLEASE* request primitive, the other entity currently owning the token can compare the priority of the request with its own state, if the request has a higher priority the token is sent back to the requester. The request is unconfirmed.

Table 9.3 Service primitives used by the association manager, message dispatcher and reliable transfer server.

Association manager	Message dispatcher	RTS
SUBMIT	OPEN	CONNECT
DELIVER	CLOSE	RELEASE
PROBE	TRANSFER	DATA
NOTIFY	TURN-PLEASE	TOKEN-PLEASE
	TURN-GIVE	TOKEN-GIVE
	EXCEPTION	ACTIVITY-START
		ACTIVITY-INTERRUPT
		ACTIVITY-RESUME
		ACTIVITY-END
		ACTIVITY-DISCARD
		SYNCHRONIZE-MINOR
		U-EXCEPTION-REPORT
		P-EXCEPTION-REPORT
		U-ABORT
		P-ABORT

- **turn-give**: this function provides the exchange of the turn; when an RTS user issues a *TURN-GIVE* primitive the turn is assigned to the requestor. This is an unconfirmed service.

- **transfer**: this operation performs a reliable transfer of a protocol data unit.

- **exception**: indicates a transfer failure and is generated by the RTS if it cannot complete the transfer of an application protocol data unit.

The reliable transfer server is supported by the OSI presentation and session services. It can be interfaced to the presentation layer with minimal requirements and uses extensively the session services made available through the presentation layer. The presentation layer is, in practice, totally transparent to RTS operations. As an example, when a connection has to be established and the RTS is interfaced to the presentation layer, a *P_CONNECT* primitive will be used, which implies that an *S_CONNECT.request* primitive will be invoked by the session layer. This primitive will transfer a *Presentation Connect* data element in its *UserData* parameter. At the other side of the connection, the *S_CONNECT.response* primitive will contain a *Presentation Accept* data element or a *Presentation Refuse* data element depending upon the result provided by the presentation layer.

If the association established by the association manager is two way alternate the message dispatcher manages the turn for sending MPDU by using the *TURN-PLEASE* and *TURN-GIVE* primitives, and, if the transfer of the MPDU cannot be completed for some reason in the *transfer time* indicated by a suitable parameter, it will receive an *EXCEPTION* indication primitive containing the protocol data unit, which has been previously submitted. After an exception indication has been received, a rerouting procedure may be attempted, if this new attempt fails then a *service MPDU* containing a negative delivery report is generated.

As has been said before a MPDU is mapped onto the user data parameter of the transfer request, this parameter is known as the *application protocol data unit*. It must be pointed out that an APDU transfer constitutes a single *session activity* and after an activity has started the APDU can be transferred in one or more presentation data units, each one submitted by using a *DATA* request primitive. Hence, multiple data requests may be used to transfer an APDU, and this can be done if *checkpointing* was agreed in the phase of the connection establishment. In this case an APDU is divided in several parts and a checkpoint is inserted to separate each part from the following. All checkpoints must be confirmed by the remote RTS, taking into account that it is possible at the session establishment phase to define a maximum number of outstanding unacknowledged checkpoints for a session activity. This number is indicated through the definition of the so-called *window size* which is negotiated during the connection establishment phase. Figure 9.7 describes an APDU transfer by the use of a time sequence diagram. When transfer problems arise, the sending RTS entity will receive presentation exception report or presentation abort primitives; in this case the sending RTS will attempt to recover the transfer in some way starting from the last confirmed checkpoint. However, if the transfer cannot be completed successfully, the activity is discarded and an exception indication is generated by the sending RTS to the message dispatcher.

The message transfer interface

Figure 9.8 describes a solution for the message transfer interface. It should be noted that the configuration defined in the specifications is based on the interaction of two protocols, the message transfer protocol P1 and the submission and delivery protocol P3, which are concatenated to one another. The protocol P3 supports the communication between an SDE and an MTAE and not between two SDEs. In other words the SDE functionality is hidden in the operations of the MTAE. In this case, in fact, while SDE provides

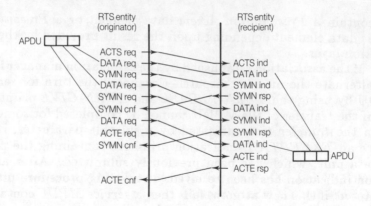

Figure 9.7   An APDU transfer performed using the session service.

an interface for activating remote actions, (SDE) acts as a server for those requests and passes the requests to the MTAE so that they can be correctly executed.

The definition of the submission and delivery protocol is obtained with the help of a general framework for interactive protocol definition, referred to as *remote operations* [X410]. Since the submission and delivery protocol is inherently interactive, the remote operations provides the way to manage such interactivity. In fact, in P3 either the submission and delivery entity or the message transfer agent entity may request that a particular operation be performed, the corresponding remote entity attempts to perform the operation and then reports the outcome of the attempt. The remote operations framework defines four basic protocol data unit types called *operation protocol data units*:

- *invoke*: this PDU specifies an operation and is sent by an entity which invokes a specific operation to be performed by a remote entity

- *return result*: this PDU is returned by the remote entity which has to perform the requested operation; the PDU contains the result of the operation when it is successful

- *return error*: this PDU is returned by the remote entity and reports on the error which occurred during the execution of the operation

- *reject*: this PDU may be sent by both the entities on receipt of any invoke, return result or return error when the PDU is malformed and cannot be processed for this reason.

For any protocol which makes use of the remote operation definition, actions must be defined which map correctly on the operations of that protocol. The submission and delivery protocol defines, for all the primitives introduced previously, the associated operations. Only

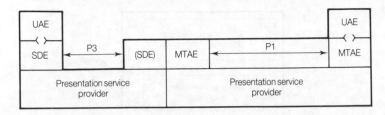

Figure 9.8 Submission and delivery interface.

the *LOGON* and *LOGOFF* primitives are directly mapped onto the RTS *OPEN* and *CLOSE* primitives.

Interpersonal messaging user agent layer

This layer makes available to the user the *interpersonal messaging* (IPM) service [X411]. This service is composed of the services provided by the message transfer layer plus those provided by the cooperation of UA entities, which interact by means of the P2 protocol. The P2 protocol consists of:

- the definition of a set of protocol elements, each having a standardized syntax and semantics which are used to build up *user agent protocol data units* UAPDU, also containing the contents of the message to be exchanged between user agent entities.

- the operations related to the exchange of these protocol elements that each user agent must perform.

- the rules to be applied in using the message transfer layer service when providing the interpersonal messaging service.

Two UAPDUs are defined: the former is an interpersonal message UAPDU (IM-UAPDU), the latter is a *status report* UAPDU (SR-UAPDU). In the first case the protocol data unit carries a message generated by an originator UA and transferred to a destination UA, composed of two parts, a *heading*, which represents the control information such as subject, destination and so on, and a body, which is the information the user wishes to communicate, consisting, for example, of paragraphs of text, voice comments, facsimile diagrams and so on. In the other case, a status report represents information generated for use by the destination UA or may be conveyed directly to the user. It works as an acknowledgment of the receipt or non-receipt of an intermessaging of a UAPDU. The definition of a UAPDU is based on the following data types:

- *IP message identifier*: which identifies a particular IP-message being unique and unambiguous; it may also include the originator name for the identifier;

- *time*: defines a calendar date and time to be conveyed in the protocol.

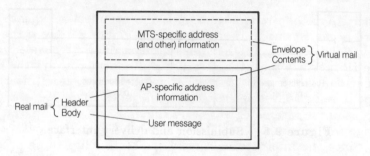

Figure 9.9   Structure of the document to be transferred.

As pointed out previously, an interpersonal messaging UAPDU is composed of *heading* and a *body*. Figure 9.9 shows the document structure related to the UAPDU contents. The heading includes the *originator name*, which is the name of the user who submits an IP-message and the name of the *authorizing users*, representing the users which authorized the sending of an IP-message. The recipients of the message are specified in terms of *primary recipients*, *copy recipients* and *blind copy recipients*, which represent the users specified by the originator to receive the IP-message in those particular roles. A *reply to* field is also provided, so that a previous IP-message is identified to which this IP-message is a replay. It is also possible to indicate previous messages, which are obsoleted or cross referenced by this IP-message, this is obtained by two fields indicated as *obsoletes* and *cross references*. A *subject* component conveys information about the message contents as specified by the user, while an *expiry date* element indicates the date and time by which the originator considers the message to be no longer valid. The time by which the originator would like to have a reply sent, is specified by the *reply by time* field, while the *reply to users* indicates to which users replies have to be sent after reception of the current IP-message. A parameter is also used to indicate the IP-message importance, which can be *low*, *normal* or *high*. Another parameter, called *sensitivity* is used to indicate if the message is *personal*, *private* or *company confidential*.

The *body* parts of the message represent the information the user wishes to transfer to the destination. Each part of the message carries with it an indication of its type. In particular the text, telex, voice, fax, videotex and other types are provided for representing different kinds of information for various office devices.

The status report UAPDU is used to return notification of receipt or non-receipt of an IP-message to its originator, and each report may be composed of one of the elements described in the following. *Non-receipt*: this is included if, and only if, notification of non-receipt is being conveyed. This field includes a *reason*, which indicates either whether the UAE has discarded the message for local reasons or whether the UAE has autoforwarded the message to another UA. A *non-receipt qualifier* is also included to indicate if the discard occurred due to the arrival of the expiry date or if the message was obsoleted by another one. If the originator requested return of the IP-message sent, the *returned* component conveys the entire interpersonal message UAPDU that was delivered. If notification of receipt is being conveyed the *receipt information* field is included. It also contains a parameter to specify the date and time by which the message was received.

Since the interpersonal messaging service has to be provided by the user agent, then it must support specific operations for each service element, including those related to management functions. Hence two types of interactions can be identified for the UA: cooperation with a remote UA and information exchange with the underlying message transfer layer (MTL).

To send a message a UAE uses the message transfer service as a means to perform the transfer. The primitives already shown in Table 9.1 represents the operations related to access management.

The sending and receipt of a message requires actions by both the originator's and recipient's UAE. In particular, the originator UAE has to construct an IM-UAPDU containing the interpersonal message identifier and the body parts of the document to be sent according to the P2 syntax. After this it issues a *SUBMIT* request primitive to the MTL, whose parameters include the constructed IM-UAPDU. If the *SUBMIT* confirmation primitive returned by the message transfer layer indicates that the submission of the protocol data unit failed, then the UAE must pass this information to the user; if the *SUBMIT* primitive indicates that the submission was successful, the primitive also provides the submission time and an identifier for the submit operation which can be used to correlate further notifications with the message being submitted.

After a successful submission, the UAE may receive a *NOTIFY* indication primitive to indicate that the IM-UAPDU was not delivered, in this way the UAE may inform the user of the failure.

At the recipient's UAE, when the protocol data unit is delivered, a *DELIVER* indication primitive with the parameters of the basic MT service is received from the MTL. The main parameter of this primitive is represented by the IM-UAPDU, which contains the message identifier and the body element.

As pointed out in the previous paragraphs a number of IPM service elements exist which can be selected when the protocol data unit is submitted to the MTL. These elements activate other actions in addition to those related to the basic service of sending and receiving.

Submission, delivery and conversion service elements are provided as an option of the basic service of sending and receiving IP-messages. In particular, the *grade of delivery, multi-destination delivery, disclosure of other recipients* and *explicit conversion* are made available to IPM service users by an interaction between originator and recipient UAEs, in more detail, the originator's UA specifies the corresponding parameter of the *SUBMIT* request primitive, when the IM-UAPDU is sent, while the recipient's UAE makes the corresponding parameters of the *DELIVER* indication primitive accessible to the recipient when the protocol data unit (IM-UAPDU) is received.

In the case of the *alternate recipient allowed* service element, the originating UAE sets the corresponding parameters in the *SUBMIT* request primitive when the IM-UAPDU is sent; when an IM-UAPDU is delivered to an alternate recipient's UAE, the *DELIVER* indication primitive indicates the name of the originally intended recipient. If the attempt to deliver the message to an alternate recipient fails for some reason, an appropriate *NOTIFY* indication primitive indicating the delivery failure is issued to the originator's UAE, which will pass this information to the originating user. On the other hand, if the IP-message is successfully delivered then a *NOTIFY* indication primitive signaling the success of the operation may be issued to the originator's UAE.

For the *delivery notification* service element, the UAE requests the notification by specifying the appropriate parameter in the *SUBMIT* request primitive when the protocol data unit is passed to the MT layer. If the delivery of the protocol data unit occurs and is suitably signaled by a *NOTIFY* indication primitive, then the UAE must make the originator aware that the notification has occurred. The notification information contained in the notify primitive must be made available to the user.

The *return of content* service element actions are based on the fact that if the delivery of an IM-UAPDU fails, the returned content parameter of the *NOTIFY* indication primitive will convey the returned IM-UAPDU available to the originator.

The *blind copy recipient indication* requires that the originator's UAE constructs two or more IM-UAPDUs in the P2 syntax. These protocol data units are identical except for the inclusion of the *blind copy recipients* parameter. One protocol data unit without the blind copy recipient component is sent by using a *SUBMIT* request to only those recipients specified as primary or copy recipients of the IP-message, while the blind copy recipients are sent a different IM-UAPDU. At the receiver side the IM-UAPDUs are received through the deliver indication primitive, and, if they do not contain the blind copy recipients element, the recipients are not aware of the blind copy destinations.

The *non-receipt notification* is required by the originator for a particular recipient of an IP-message specifying a suitable parameter in the report request component for that recipient in the IM-UAPDU which is sent to the recipient by means of a submit request primitive. This may include a request to return the IP-message with the non-receipt notification. The protocol data units are then delivered to all the recipients' UAEs by means of a deliver indication primitive. Each destination for which a non-receipt notification is required, receives from its UAE the appropriate notification generated by two possible events:

(1) the protocol data unit is not received by the destination specified by the originator, but is auto forwarded by the recipient's UAE to another UAE

(2) the UA finds that no messages can be delivered to the destination indicated by the originator.

In both cases the UAE builds up an IPM status report (SR-UAPDU), whose main components are the message identifier, which is identical to that of the IM-UAPDU currently under processing, and information related to the reasons for non-receipt. If the originator requested that messages were to be returned, then the IM-UAPDU is returned as a component of the SR-UAPDU. When the originating UA receives the status report, it must pass the information obtained to the user, so that it is made aware that the non-receipt notification has occurred.

For the *receipt notification* service element, the originator's UAE specifies the appropriate parameter in the *report request* component for a specific recipient in the IM-UAPDU, which is sent to the recipients by means of a submit request primitive. The IM-UAPDU is then delivered by a deliver indication primitive to the UAEs to which recipients belong. When the IM-UAPDU is received, the UAE will automatically generate an SR-UAPDU to convey the receipt notification and send it back to the originator. A second solution provides for the UAE to inform the recipient that a receipt notification is required, then it waits for a confirm from the user so that an SR-UAPDU can be prepared and sent back to the originator. For both solutions the UAE constructs an SR-UAPDU including among other things the message identifier of the IP-message, to which the notification applies, and the receipt time. The notification is sent by the UAE issuing a submit request primitive to the MTL. At the originator's side, a deliver indication from the MTL conveys the SR-UAPDU and the UAE must make the originator aware that the receipt notification has occurred.

The *multipart body* service element allows an IP-message to consist of several different parts which may be of different body types. To activate this service the UAE must include in the IM-UAPDU the various body parts along with their type indication in the *body* component. When this protocol data unit is received by a UAE without any conversion having been performed by the MTL, then the encoded information types parameter will be the same as that supplied by the originating UAE. If some conversion has taken place, the encoded information types parameter will indicate the new body part types resulting from the conversion and the original encoded information types parameter will indicate what type of body parts were originally sent.

The *probe* service element is activated by the UAE when a probe request primitive is issued to the MTL supplying the appropriate parameters. If the probe confirmation primitive returned by the MTL indicates that the request for a probe was not accepted, then the UAE must make the probe originator aware of the failure, providing also the failure reasons parameter. On the other hand, if the probe confirmation primitive indicates that the probe request was accepted, the confirm primitive also provides a probe time and an event identifier which can be used to correlate further notifications with this probe. For an accepted probe, the UAE which requested it receives a notify indication primitive containing a delivery or non-delivery notification, in the case of a 'delivery' notification, the UAE should inform the probe originator that an IP-message submitted with the same set of parameters as the probe could have been successfully delivered, if a 'non-delivery' notification is received, the UAE should inform the user that a corresponding message could not be delivered to the specified destination.

Other than the provision of interpersonal messaging service elements, the UAE must perform certain functions necessary for the proper operation of the service. These functions require cooperation between remote UAs and between a UA and the underlying MTL. One of the most important functions deals with flow control, which is used by the MTL as a means to handle its resources. To this purpose the MTL uses the *CONTROL* indication primitive, which conveys information which defines the maximum length, priority, and type of messages the UAE is going to accept. Using this information, the UAE should tune its operations so that the new constraints imposed by the MTL are observed and should issue a *CONTROL* response primitive signaling by means of a suitable parameter that, as a result of the new restrictions, it has messages or probes to submit.

The OSI approach

The message handling system in the OSI architecture, composed of the message transfer service and the associated protocols, represents another service element based on the presentation service, and all of the modules previously described can easily be interfaced to the communication subsystem.

It should be noted that the OSI Transport layer service provides a reliable and cost-effective data transport capability. Two remote transport entities may negotiate a suitable protocol class depending on the required quality of service and on the characteristics of the underlying communication system. To this purpose it can also be noted that the reliability introduced by the transport protocol is enforced by the recovery mechanisms of the RTS module, which enable survival of protocol malfunctioning and connection losses. The RTS service also duplicates some transport functions since it is supposed that only class 0 and class 1 can be negotiated by the transport protocol.

It should also be noted that the RTS makes minimal use of the presentation layer service. To this purpose there was a considerable effort by ISO to transfer the data representation facilities into the presentation layer, taking into account the fact that X.409, which is the notation used for the definition of the protocol data units in the X.400 specifications, slightly diverges from the abstract syntax notation used by ISO. Since a universal representation of data can be available at the presentation layer, the information type conversion function of the message transfer protocol should be considered as an information processing task pertinent to the presentation layer and not to the message transfer layer.

9.3   Virtual terminal concept

When complex display-oriented applications are to be used in a distributed environment where different screen devices are used, the most effective approach requires the use of a shared data structure maintained by a virtual terminal application module. This structure has to be accessed for reading and writing operations by both the terminal user and the application program running in a station connected to the network. The responsibility to update the screen image, whenever its abstract representation is modified, is left to the virtual terminal software. Two different models can be used for this.

The first model is based on a solution where the virtual terminal software supports two copies of a single shared data structure representing all the information to describe the screen image. A copy is handled by the virtual terminal software running on the terminal and the other supported by the virtual terminal software running on a distant host computer where the application program resides. The use of a shared data structure plays a basic role for the efficient handling of the operations, since each change in its structure can be immediately replicated on the screen image. Figure 9.10 shows a block scheme for an application and a user interacting by means of a replicated shared data structure. The operator at the terminal can modify the terminal copy of the abstract data structure by typing on the keyboard as shown in Figure 9.10 by arc 1. These changes are visible on the screen, since the display reflects the state of the local data structure. The terminal then sends virtual terminal commands to the distant host over the network using the virtual terminal protocol. This action is represented by arc 2 in the figure. The PDU causes the remote copy of the data structure to be brought up to date with the local one. The modified data structure can be read by the application program by means of appropriate commands, as shown in Figure 9.10 by label 3. In the same way, the application program can modify its copy of the data structure, which causes a PDU to be sent to the terminal, to update the local data structure and the related image on the display: these actions are represented by the arcs labeled 4, 5 and 6. Hence, the terminal user can act on the shared data structure through *virtual terminal* commands, which update both the local image and the remote one. This last is modified through the use of a specific protocol which allows the transfer of the protocol data units containing the virtual terminal commands. In this way, both data structures are consistent and both the terminal users and the application have the correct view of their respective images. During virtual terminal operations, it may happen that simultaneous updates are performed by the users. In order to avoid inconsistencies, a mechanism is used to control access to the data structure, based on the availability of a token which assigns the right to perform updates to a single user. The token may be requested and passed between the users in a similar way to the method used in the session layer. This model, indicated as *synchronous*, suffers from a problem due to the fact that characters cannot be echoed immediately, since the availability of the token is required. To overcome this problem an *asynchronous* model has been defined. It is based on the existence of two data structures for each end of the connection, one is used for input and the other for output. Thus, two single-way channels are available as compared with a two-alternate-way channel made available by the *synchronous* model. Figure 9.11 shows that the input data structure for the first virtual terminal user corresponds to an output data structure for the other user and vice versa. This means that, when the first user modifies its input data structure, the remote output data structure is changed, while the output data structure of the originating user and the input area of the remote application are not directly affected. This approach states that each copy of the data structure can be accessed for reading or writing purposes by a single user. Such a solution avoids the problems pointed out by the synchronous model, but involves more storage and a more difficult mechanism to handle the communication.

The abstract data structure is based on a screen area whose purpose is to replicate exactly the screen contents. Actually, in most cases this area is structured as a two-dimension or three-dimension array, where each element is represented by a screen character in a specific screen position. The two-dimensional structure represents a single page, whilst a three-dimensional array handles multiple pages or windows. It should be noted that each character is also accompanied by other control information, which describes completely the way it has to be represented on the screen. In particular other information involves the indication of the font the character belongs

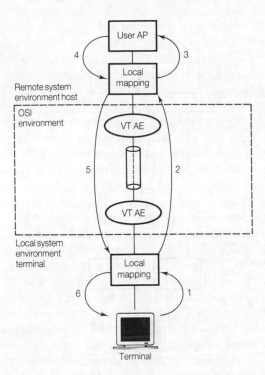

Figure 9.10 Virtual terminal model: the synchronous approach.

to, the foreground and background colours, the emphasis and so on. These attributes can be negotiated when a connection between remote terminal users is established. The operations which can be supported by a virtual terminal function applied to the character array are the basic operations generally provided by an intelligent terminal controller. Table 9.4 lists these basic operations.

Such operations can be roughly classified into *addressing*, *text*, *attribute* and *erasing* commands. The addressing commands are used to point to a specific character in the array, the attribute commands set specific representation modes, text commands are generally based on a single function handling character insertion, and the erasing commands include different functions to erase a single character, a group of characters, a line, a set of lines, a page or a group of pages. It should be noted that if only the cited commands are available, operations like scrolling of the image become quite difficult and time consuming, in fact it is necessary to copy and update the whole of the pages involved in the array. The way to overcome this point is to operate with an update window which can be moved along the y dimension which is supposed as being infinite. In this way only the characters contained in the window need to be screened and

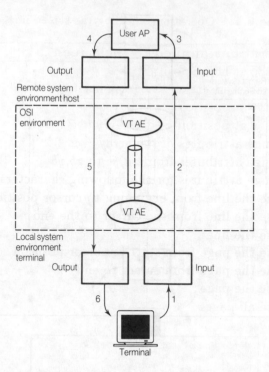

Figure 9.11   Virtual terminal model: the asynchronous approach.

modified. An evolution of this approach is represented by a form
which can be defined and downloaded into the terminal. It consists
of different fields and the basic commands are also provided, adding
those functions which allow relative motion of the cursor between
the fields defined in the form. Attributes associated with the fields
can also be managed: for example, erase field commands are supported. A typical example of a form is given in Figure 9.12, which
is composed of read-only and readable and writable fields. Taking
into account the requirements to support form updates, it is obvious
that virtual terminals cannot specify when characters or control information can be moved to the remote part of the connection. If a
protocol data transfer occurs after each character insertion, a consistent performance fall would occur, hence the better solution is based
on the capability of gathering a certain number of commands and
data before performing a transfer. This is quite obvious when the actions of an operator filling a form are considered. This activity may
involve repeated insertion and corrections involving cursor moving
commands, also, from one field to another. In order to obtain the
best result in terms of performance, the net effect of the whole of the
operations on the form should be transferred, and not just the single

Table 9.4   Operations affecting the screen image.

Operations applied to the screen
Cursor at home position
Character insertion at cursor position
Cursor at position x,y
Cursor at position $x+dx$, $y+dy$
Change attributes of the array
Change attributes from xa,ya to xb,yb
Change attributes for the following characters
Erase the line from beginning to cursor position
Erase the line from the cursor to the end
Erase the line
Erase the page from start to cursor position
Erase the page from cursor to end
Erase the page
Erase all pages

```
Membership application – Pigeon Fancier's Society

Name:                    Telephone:
Address:                 # of Pigeons:
```

Figure 9.12   A form example.

actions performed on a field. It should be noted that this approach is widely used for database update transactions. The way the virtual terminal implements the update mechanism is indicated as *delivery control*. The simplest solution provides for a buffering mechanism which terminates when buffer limits are exceeded. In this case the delivery control is represented by space unavailability. In other cases a specific character, such as form feed is used to identify the time at which the sending operation has to be performed. Other solutions use a time limit to decide when the transfer has to occur. Certain solutions are based on the availability of a suitable primitive which forces the transfer to be performed, in this way the user has complete control over the deliver operation.

A further function made available by the virtual terminal tool is a sort of *attention* command which allows a previous command to be interrupted, sometimes it is obtained by a *break* or *del* key, which may generate the transfer of expedited data to stop the previous command.

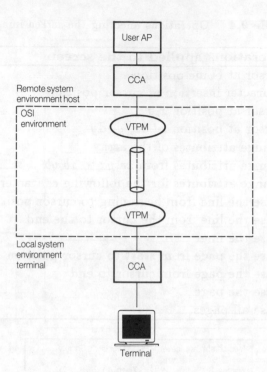

Figure 9.13   Communication interactions between a terminal user and an application.

9.3.1   The OSI virtual terminal

The basic concept of the OSI VT is a *shared conceptual communication area* (CCA) [ISOVT9040] [ISOVT9040A], which maps very well onto the model described above.

Both the *synchronous* and *asynchronous* modes are supported; however, the TOP VT Application Profile suggests that the asynchronous mode only has to be provided. From the point of view of the protocol aspects, Figure 9.13 gives a scheme of the communication interactions between a user and an application. It should be noted that two *virtual terminal protocol machines* are defined, one for each end of the connection. Each protocol machine includes its own CCA shared area, which is accessed by VT users via service primitives in which information is transferred to or from the VT user or application program.

The CCA contains a number of abstract objects and object type definitions. All information transfers imply the update of the shared area, which is then made available to the remote VT user. One of the principal elements is represented by the *conceptual data store* (CDS), which contains one or two display objects, directly re-

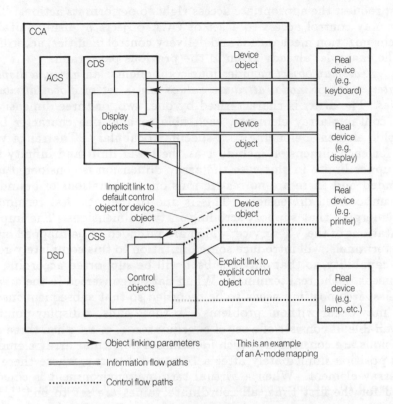

Figure 9.14   VT objects interrelationship.

lated to the management of visual data.

A *control and status store* (CSS) contains control objects which are used for signalling purposes and reporting information. An *access control store* (ACS) maintains all the access right assignments. *Device objects* are also defined. Each of them represents a mapping between a display object and a real device; moreover it provides specific parameters which exercise suitable control over such mapping functions. In particular, a device object is linked to one display object and to one or more control objects. A *data structure definition* is also available. It contains the object type definitions for the display objects, device objects, control objects and other parameters which are part of the *virtual terminal environment*.

All these elements are shown in Figure 9.14, which also points out the interrelationship between the various object elements.

The data structure definition element is initialized at the association establishment phase, and subsequent changes may only occur by negotiation. Other area components may be changed when the association is in existence and negotiation is not in progress. Hence, if the CDS or CSS objects have to be modified by the VT user, this must request the appropriate access right to perform its actions. The user may control access to a set of CCA objects by using suitable synchronization mechanisms and delivery control facilities, according to the examples already given in the previous paragraph.

A *display object* includes four components: an *array*, a *display pointer*, a set of *modal attribute values* and a set of *global attribute values*. The array is characterized by one, two, or three dimensions and contains array elements, each able to hold one character box graphic element belonging to a specific vocabulary. The range values for each dimension include 1 as the lower limit and infinity for the upper limit. In this case the array dimension is considered unbounded and there are no restrictions on combinations of bounded and unbounded dimensions. This is due to the fact that terminals are emerging that support scrolling in two dimensions. The implementations of the VT service, which are intended to be mapped onto real terminals, will introduce some limitation to this completely general capability, so that only a subset will be supported according to the needs of the real terminals. When data are inserted in the array, the first free position needs to be recorded so that subsequent insertion may occur without problems. To these ends, a display pointer is available; it consists of a set of coordinates, x, y, x, when three dimensions are considered, which identifies a particular array element or a position immediately after a bounded X-array, where there is no array element. When a virtual terminal environment is constituted for the first time, all coordinate values are set to one. Any array element may be empty or may select a character box graphic element belonging to a specific repertoire. This selection is also indicated as the *primary attribute value*. Each array element is also characterized by a set of *secondary attributes*, such as the indication of the *character repertoire*, the *emphasis* (blinking, reverse, boldface and so on), foreground colour, background colour and font. The last four are also indicated as *rendition* attributes, each independent from the others. Hence, an array element composed of its primary and secondary attributes is completely defined and independent of all other array elements. *Modal attributes* consist of a value for each of the secondary attributes, while *global attributes* consist of a value for each of the secondary attributes except character repertoire.

The *control object* allows the VT user to handle control information associated with virtual terminal functions and real devices. These functions are not related to the functions for displaying text, such as ringing bells, turning lights on and off, modeling function keys and mouse buttons. The semantics for the control object are not given in the specification, however, a detailed discussion is given for echo control. In particular, the standard points out that in the asynchronous mode of operation, updates input by the terminal user may be echoed locally on the displaying device or at the opposite end of the virtual terminal association. Control of when and where echo control has to be performed usually resides in the remote VT user. In fact it must be pointed out that both local and remote echo are of no concern to the VT service, since echoing may be handled outside the VT environment by the remote VT user. However, the VT service provides the appropriate mechanism to inform the VT user process at the local end of the association when the echo function is set and when it is disabled. The mechanism is based on a simple switch; it should be noted that this does not imply that the VT service is involved in the process, but just provides a switch so that the VT user process can be informed as to whether or not it should echo input updates. In this way the echo function becomes a local concern without involving any VT service. The switch represents an echo control object which can be turned on or off by the remote VT user using an appropriate VT service. This control object contains a boolean value which tells the local VT user whether input updates have to be echoed or not; furthermore, a second boolean value informs the VT user if the input updates may be printed immediately on the output device or whether they should be queued, so that they can be echoed later. This fact is due to the need to coordinate output coming from the remote end user with the output to be echoed. To perform this control, the user is expected to maintain another boolean, called the *locking boolean*. When this boolean is true, then updates to be echoed are queued until its value changes to false. On the contrary, when its value is false updates to be echoed are sent to the viewing device.

Each real device can be described in the abstract data structure using a *device object*. In this way a keybord, a printer, a display and other devices can be fully described so that mapping between the display object and the device can be performed correctly.

Table 9.5 lists services which are available to the VT user. The first four primitives are devoted to association management. For the association establishment, in addition to the various parameters related to the identification of the application entities and the definition of the functional unit to be selected, the *VT-mode* parameter allows the synchronous or asynchronous mode to be negotiated. The subsequent primitive allows a standard profile to be negotiated. If no standard profile is available then all parameters can be negotiated one by one using the NEG primitives. The *VT-DATA* primitive updates display or control objects. A *VT-object-update* parameter contains the object identifier and the value to be used for the update. Updates of control and display objects can be performed in different ways according to the delivery control used. The service provider can be thought of as a queue, which stores a sequence of update requests to those objects. Each request is the result of a *VT-DATA* request primitive. Every time a user issues a *VT-DATA* primitive an item of update data is added to the queue tail. When an update is delivered to the remote VT user an item is taken from the head

Table 9.5   Virtual terminal services; C = confirmed service, U = unconfirmed service.

VT service primitive	Description	C/U
VT-ASSOCIATE	Establish an association	C
VT-RELEASE	Release an association	C
VT-U-ABORT	User requested abort	U
VT-P-ABORT	Provider requested abort	U
VT-SWITCH-PROFILE	Negotiate a standard profile	C
VT-START-NEG	Start the parameter negotiation process	C
VT-END-NEG	End the parameter negotiation process	C
VT-NEG-ACCEPT	Accept a proposed value for the parameter	U
VT-NEG-INVITE	Invite the other user to propose a parameter value	U
VT-NEG-OFFER	Propose a parameter value	U
VT-NEG-REJECT	Reject a proposed parameter value	U
VT-DATA	Data transfer	U
VT-DELIVER	Transfer all buffer data	U
VT-ACK-RECEIPT	Acknowledge VT-DELIVER	U
VT-GIVE-TOKEN	Send the token (synchronous mode)	U
VT-REQUEST-TOKEN	Request the token (synchronous mode)	U
VT-BREAK	Overtake data in transit	U

of the queue and inserted in the *VT-DATA* indication primitive.

Objects which are assigned an update priority other than normal are characterized by update queues not subject to delivery control. If no delivery control is used, it is the virtual terminal software which determines when to send the protocol data units related to the update sequence [ISOVT9041].

Three kinds of delivery control are supported: none, simple and quarantine. When no control is provided for, the role of determining when PDUs are to be sent is for the virtual terminal software. If simple delivery control is used, the same rule applies, but the sending operations are managed by the VT-DELIVER primitive, which flushes the buffer. When quarantine delivery control is defined, PDUs are only sent if the VT-DELIVER is invoked. The VT-ACK-RECEIPT is used to acknowledge the VT-DELIVER primitive.

The last two primitives are used for token management.

9.4   Conclusions

Message interchange functions and virtual terminal support play an important role for the efficient progress of activities in the office environment.

Various countries have developed computer-based store and forward message services by means of suitable organizations associated with public data networks. This fact has made apparent the need for standardizing international message exchange between subscribers to such services. TOP architecture is fully based upon CCITT Recommendations except for some aspects related to the lower layers of the architecture. An example is given by the fact that, while CCITT X.400 specifications require a Transport Class 0, the TOP MHS specifications require a Transport Class 4.

It should also be noted that differences from ISO standard implementations do exist, such as the lack of the presentation layer, since conversion mechanisms are an integral part of the message transfer layer located in the application layer.

Future work will be related to the *distributed user agent* and *mailbox service*, which defines a distributed model for the UA. It is based on the concept of distributed interface: one part located near the MTA to support message submission and delivery of messages from the MTA other than message storage and login services, and the other located near the UA to support fetching and dispatching of messages between the mailbox of the message transfer agent and that of the user. Since the distribution of UAs requires a specific mailbox access protocol to support interactions between the remote mailboxes involved in the communication, a standard protocol, named P7, is going to be defined for this interface. This will be included in the TOP specifications when available.

In the TOP environment VT users may reside on different

heterogeneous end systems and each user has a set of objects representing the VT. The current TOP VT protocol operates only in the full duplex asynchronous mode.

References

[X400]   CCITT:*Message Handling Systems*, Recommendation X.400, Red Book, Vol. 8, Fascicle 8.7, 1984.

[X401]   CCITT: *Message Handling Systems: Basic Service Elements and Optional User Facilities*, Recommendation X.401, Red Book, Vol. 8, Fascicle 8.7, 1984.

[X408]   CCITT: *Message Handling Systems: Encoded Information Type Conversion Rules*, Recommendation X.408, Red Book, Vol. 8, Fascicle 8.7, 1984.

[X409]   CCITT: *Message Handling Systems: Presentation Transfer Syntax and Notation*, Recommendation X.409, Red Book, Vol. 8, Fascicle 8.7, 1984.

[X410]   CCITT: *Message Handling Systems: Remote Operations and Reliable Transfer Server*, Recommendation X.410, Red Book, Vol. 8, Fascicle 8.7, 1984.

[X411]   CCITT: *Message Handling Systems: Message Transfer Layer*, Recommendation X.411, Red Book, Vol. 8, Fascicle 8.7, 1984.

[X420]   CCITT: *Message Handling Systems: Interpersonal Messaging User Agent Layer*, Recommendation X.420, Red Book, Vol. 8, Fascicle 8.7, 1984.

[ISOVT9040]   ISO 9040 *Information Processing Systems – Open Systems Interconnection – Virtual Terminal Service – Basic Class*, Dec. 1987.

[ISOVT9040A] ISO 9040 *Information Processing Systems – Open Systems Interconnection – Virtual Terminal Service – Basic Class – Addendum 1*, Dec. 1987.

[ISOVT9041]   ISO 9041 *Information Processing Systems – Open Systems Interconnection – Virtual Terminal Protocol – Basic Class*, Dec. 1987.

[TOP3.0]   *Technical and Office Protocol Specification – Ver. 3.0*, MAP/TOP Users Group, 1987.

Chapter 10

Office Document Architecture and Interchange Format

10.1 Introduction

One of the most important features of an integrated office environment is the capability of interchanging documents composed of various content types, such as characters for text, geometric and raster graphics, between dissimilar application systems. A basis for this is given by the ISO work for the office document architecture (ODA) and interchange format, known as ISO 8613 [ISO8613/1]. Before it, no comprehensive international standard was available to address the interchange of compound documents. However, it should be noted that this standard also, like others [ECMA101] [CCITT-T73], is very accessible and flexible in its approach to the subject in order to address the broadest number of requirements. As a result, implementors of this standard are not guaranteed interoperability because of the number of options allowed in the specifications. Since equivalent implementations on dissimilar systems are required to achieve electronic compound document interchange, TOP specifications [TOP3.0] have introduced the so-called *TOP office document architecture application profile*, which focuses implementors on ODA features commonly found in electronic compound documents and enables them to build products that will interoperate. In particular, the TOP ODA AP specifies an implementation of the ISO specifications that supports interchange of formatted or revisable compound documents composed of characters, computer graphics, or raster graphics objects.

10.2   ODA overview

The document architecture introduces a structured approach to document description and construction so that transfer operations can occur between different systems. The basic concept states that different types of contents, including text, graphics, image and sound, can coexist in a document. Further support is given for editing, formatting and presenting a document in such a way that those operations may be performed with the same effect on the various devices connected to the network. Hence, the aim of the specification of the document architecture is to support specific activities in an integrated and distributed environment, as listed in the following points:

- **document interchanging**, which is a process able to provide a document or a part of it to a remote user or device; this can be done using the communication subsystem available or by means of an exchange of storage media;

- **document editing**, which includes all those operations associated with the creation and changing of the structure and contents of a document;

- **document formatting**, which refers to the operations required to define the layout of a document including the appearance of its contents on a presentation medium;

- **document presentation**, which is the operation carried out to make the document contents available in a form perceptible to a human operator on paper or screen media.

Three different forms are provided for by the specification for the representation of a document. A *formatted form* allows a document to be represented according to the intention of the originator, which means with the correct number of chapters and paragraphs suitably organized in relation to the physical support features. A *processable form* is used for editing purposes and to be formatted during a subsequent phase. A *formatted processable form* allows a document to be presented as well as edited according to the user requirements.

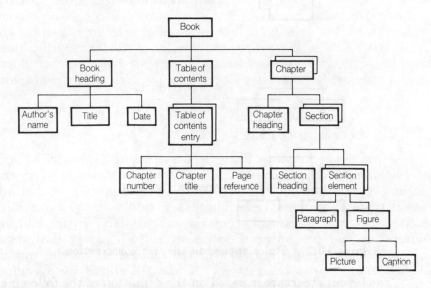

Figure 10.1   A logical structure describing a book representation.

10.3   Logical and layout structure

A basic concept in the document architecture is that of *structure*, which refers to the repeated subdivision of the document contents into increasingly smaller parts generally referred to as *objects*. Hence, it can easily be demonstrated that the document structure may be correctly described by using a tree form.

Two approaches are adopted for a document description: one refers to its *logical structure*, while the other indicates the *layout structure* of the document. The former describes the document in terms of subdivisions performed according to the meaning of the document contents, such as chapters, sections, figures and paragraphs; the latter provides for a subdivision obtained referring to layout objects such as pages and blocks. Figure 10.1 describes the logical structure of a book, while Figure 10.2 shows some aspects of the description rules used in the tree form. It should be noted that the logical structure and the layout structure provide alternative but complementary views of the same document. Hence, if we refer to the book description shown in Figure 10.1, it can be considered as consisting of chapters containing figures and paragraphs, or alternatively, as consisting of pages that contain text and graphics elements. Those elements which cannot by further subdivided into smaller objects, are called *basic objects*, while all other elements are indicated as *composite objects*.

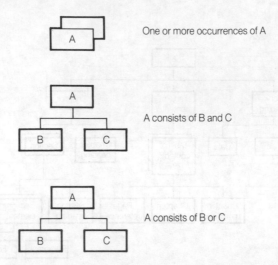

One or more occurrences of A

A consists of B and C

A consists of B or C

Figure 10.2   Rules applied in the tree construction.

The layout structure is based on the definition of the following objects:

- **Block**, which is a basic layout object and corresponds to a rectangular area that is contained entirely within the area of the object to which it is immediately subordinate. It is positioned such that its sides are parallel to the sides of the enclosing page. In other words a block is an area for the positioning and imaging of portions of the document content. It can be immediately subordinate to a page or a frame.

- **Frame**, which represents a composite layout element corresponding to a rectangular area on the presentation medium and containing one or more frames or one or more blocks.

- **Page**, which can be a basic or composite layout object referring to a rectangular element of the representation medium; it can be composed of one or more frames or one or more blocks.

- **Page set**, is a set of one or more pages or page sets.

For the logical structure only two elements are defined, referred to as *basic logical objects* and *composite logical objects*. These elements are then classified according to their application features in *chapters*, *sections* and so on.

Another important aspect of document architecture is represented by the document content which is composed of *content elements*. A content may consist of *character text* so that the content elements are characters, while if images or graphics are considered, the content elements are *picture elements* or *graphics elements*, such as lines, arcs, polygons and so on. When both a logical structure and a layout structure are given for a document, then each content

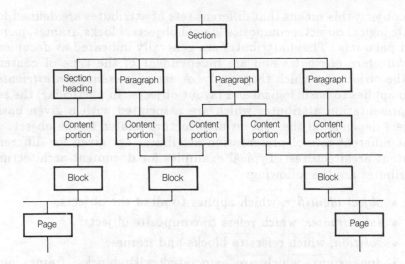

Figure 10.3 Logical and layout representation of a book.

element belongs exactly to one basic logical object and one basic layout object. Moreover, a set of related content elements that belong to one basic logical object and one basic layout object is called a *content portion*. It is then possible for a basic logical object and a basic layout object to have more than one content portion, however only an integral number of content portions is allowed. It should also be noted that, in general, there is no one-to-one correspondence between logical and layout objects. Figure 10.3 shows both possible views of the book layout already introduced. The ODA specifications also give a more detailed internal structure for a basic logical object or layout object and the rules related to such an internal structure depend on the type of content. This structure is indicated as *content architecture*. The ODA specifications describe in detail the content architecture for characters, raster graphics and geometric graphics [ISO8613/6] [ISO8613/7] [ISO8613/8].

10.4 Attributes

The ODA specification provides for the association of specific *attributes* to each document component, such as a logical or layout object, a logical or layout object class or a content portion [ISO8613/2]. In this way specific characteristics are indicated for each document component. In particular, attributes may be associated with the document as a whole, in this case they give rise to a *document profile*, which represents reference information about the document and may repeat information belonging to the document content, such as the title, the organization and the name of the author. The set of attributes used for a logical or layout object depends on the type of the object; this means that different sets of attributes are defined for basic logical objects, composite logical objects, blocks, frames, pages and page sets. These attributes are generally indicated as *document architecture attributes* and are independent of the type of content of the objects to which they apply. A set of *presentation attributes* also applies to basic logical and layout objects. In particular, the set of presentation attributes which are associated with a given basic object depends on the content architecture related to the object, so that different sets of presentation attributes are given for different content architectures. Typical examples for document architecture attributes are the following:

- *object identifier*, which applies to all of the objects;
- *subordinates*, which refers to composite objects;
- *position*, which refers to blocks and frames;
- *dimensions*, which are associated with blocks, frames and pages.

Examples for the presentation attributes are listed below:

- *line spacing*, which refers to character content architectures;
- *clipping*, which is related to raster graphics content architectures;
- *line rendition*, which refers to geometric graphics content architectures.

It should be noted that presentation attributes may be collected and organized in the form of *presentation styles*, to which references may be made from both logical and layout objects. Moreover, the attributes that apply to a content portion identify it through the content identifier, which is then followed by a set of coding attributes which depend on the coding used for the content portion. A typical example is given by a facsimile-coded raster graphics image where the *number of picture elements (pels)* attribute can be used. The logical structure of a document is, in general, independent of the corresponding layout structure, since the logical structure is directly indicated by the author during the *editing phase*, while the layout structure is determined by the *formatting process*, which is controlled by specific attributes called *layout directives* associated with the logical structure. An example can be represented by the requirement that a chapter start on a new page or that the title of a section and the first two lines of its first paragraph be represented on the same page, or, again, that a certain amount of indentation for a list of items be used and so on. Layout directives are then collected into *layout styles* which may be referred to by one or more than one logical object.

10.5   The document profile

The *document profile* [ISO8613/4], as stated previously, consists of a set of attributes associated with a document as a whole. The document profile contains a summary of the document architecture features that are used in the document in order that a recipient can easily determine what approach is needed to process or visualize the document. Besides that, the title, organization, author's name and date are also included so that the storage and retrieval processes are considerably facilitated. For the architecture features, attributes, such as a form specification, the content architecture, the character set, fonts and styles, other than the type of emphasis, are given to compose the *document characteristics* set of attributes.

The various logical and layout objects can be classified into groups according to similarities related to the objects features. The similarity may be related to logical features such as *chapter, paragraph* or to layout features such as *style, size,* or to content, such as *page headers* and *footers*. A class can be described by specifying the set of properties that are common to its members. This is obtained by defining a set of rules to indicate the value of the attributes related to the common properties.

The set of logical and layout classes and their relationship associated with a document are indicated as a *generic logical structure* and *generic layout structure,* while the structures that are referred to a particular document are indicated as *specific logical structure* and *specific layout structure*.

It should be noted that a *document class* is described by a *generic logical structure* together with a *generic layout structure* and the *generic logical structure* represents the set of all potential *specific logical structures,* while the *general layout structure* is composed of the set of all potential *specific layout structures* that can be used for the document class concerned. It is worth noting that the generic logical structure can be used as a set of rules from which specific logical objects and structures are derived during the editing process; the same approach can be stated for the generic layout structure from which specific layout structures can be derived during the formatting process. For this purpose Figure 10.1 represents a generic logical structure, while Figure 10.4 shows a generic layout for a page composed of a frame for the header, the footer and the body text.

As an example, Table 10.1 reports a list of attributes, which constitute an effective document profile. The *presence of constituents* set of attributes indicates the presence of document constituents associated with the document body when interchanged. In this way can be pointed out what elements take part in the document description: in this case a *generic layout structure,* a *specific layout structure,* and a *specific logical structure* are provided along with the *resource document* description. The *document characteristics* set also

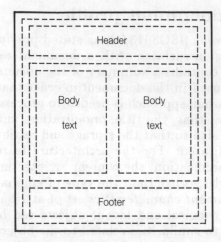

Figure 10.4   A page layout composed of a header, footer and text body.

specifies the *ODA version date* along with the *interchange format class* [ISO8613/5] and *document architecture class*. The *document constituent attributes* refer to the page dimensions, expressed in *basic measurement units*, and the level of protection. Other attributes refer to the *date and times* and to management properties such as the *title*, the *subject* and the *document type*. The *originators* attributes indicate the producer and the author of the document, while the *external reference* attributes allow other documents to be referenced as an explanation of the contents of the current one. *Security attributes* are also introduced to manage access control functions.

10.6   The document processing model

Figure 10.5 shows the basic model for document processing. Three main processing phases have been identified. The *editing process* is concerned with creating a new document or modifying a previous one. It is for the document architecture to provide data structures for representing the document emerging from this phase and to describe that control information which affects this activity. This phase produces a new document independently of the fact that a modification phase has been carried on instead of a creation operation. Hence, the result is a new document arranged in a *processible form*, which means that a new editing phase may be repeated or can be passed to the *layout process*. This new process is devoted to the organization of the document content according to a page-oriented form. Two different approaches are provided. In one case, the layout process generates a *formatted* document, which is not intended to be modified and can only be used as input for the imaging process.

In the other case the layout process may also generate a *formatted processible* form document, which can be processed further by any one of the three phases: editing, layout or imaging. The document architecture provides the data structure for representing both forms of formatted documents and control information to be used by the layout process. The *imaging process* is concerned with presenting an image of the document in a form a human being may easily perceive on a screen or on paper.

10.7 A document representation

In order to obtain an efficient instrument for illustrating document structures, a notation has been defined, for which a structure diagram is provided, being based on components represented by rectangular boxes. The document root is placed at the top of the diagram and subsequent hierarchical levels are added to the tree starting from the top and going towards the bottom. Arcs, which go from one object to the immediately subordinate objects, represent the subdi-

Table 10.1   A document profile.

Attribute	Value
Presence of constituents	
Generic layout structure	Partial
Specific layout structure	Complete
Specific logical structure	Complete
Resource document	Communication course
Document characteristics	
Document application profile	TOP AP
Document architecture class	Formatted processible
Content architecture class	Formatted processible
Interchange format class	A
ODA version date	ISO 8613 1987-12-15
Document costituent attributes	
Page dimensions	10200, 13200
Protection	protected
Additional document characteristics	
Unit scaling	12, 10
Document management attributes	
Title	ODA features
Subject	Standards
Document type	Report
Abstract	ODA overview

Table 10.1   *(cont.)*

Attribute	Value
Date and times	
Document date and time	1989-12-12
Creation date and time	1898-12-31
Expiry date and time	1992
Release date and time	1989-12-31
Originators	
Organization	Polytechnic
Preparers	A.Smith, B.Bush
Owners	Polytechnic of Turin - Italy
Authors	Robson, John, Steven
External reference	
Reference to other documents	ISO 8613
Filing and retrieval	
Keywords	Document, layout, format
Local file reference	odadoc
Content attributes	
Document size	50.000
Number of pages	20
Languages	English
Security attributes	
Authorization	Informatic Dept.
Encryption indicator	not encrypted
Password	myname

vision of the superior object into its components. When diagrams representing generic structures are considered, mnemonic symbols are used to specify how the subordinate objects are to be generated starting from a specific box. These symbols support a simple and complete description of the structure:

- **SEQ**, which indicates a sequence construction, in other terms the subordinate objects have to be considered according to the order in which they are written from left to right;

- **AGG**, this indicates that the immediately subordinated objects are to be generated in any order;

- **CHO**, this indicates that a choice has to be made between the immediately subordinated objects, since only one has to be generated.

Other mnemonics can be placed at a branch to indicate how many times the object can be generated.

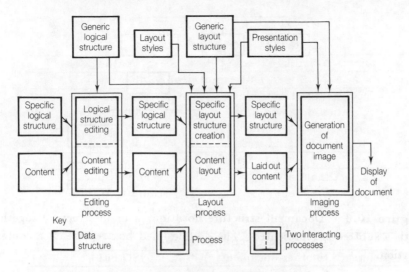

Figure 10.5   The document processing model.

- **OPT**, this indicates that the object or group of objects is optional and thus it must not occur or must occur once only;
- **REP**, this indicates that the object may occur one or more times;
- **OPT REP**, these symbols indicate that the object is not to occur at all, or to occur one or more times.

The absence of the symbols OPT and REP means that the object must occur once only. These symbols are not used when specific structures are considered, since the diagrams explicity report the occurrence of each object involved in the structure. When a content portion has to be specified in the diagram, the box shown in Figure 10.6 is used. Each box in the diagram contains a name to identify the object and may be used in a user's application to process a document.

10.8   Specific logical and layout structure

The example reported in the following presents an application of the document architecture. In this case a simple report has been considered and the document structure, as well as the document layout process are discussed. First, a specific layout structure and a specific logical structure are given in order to demonstrate that an originator may have two distinct views of the same document. This is obtained by showing how the same document can be represented in both formatted and processible form.

The subsequent aspect includes a generic logical structure and

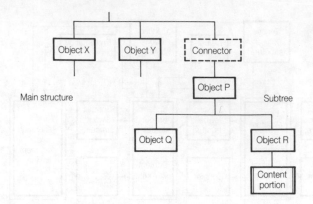

Figure 10.6   Document structure notation: a main structure together with a subtree is represented. The double lined box represents a content portion.

a generic layout structure in addition to the processible form. In this case the generic structures are examples of document classes. In particular the generic logical structure can be viewed as the document class from which the specific logical structure, described previously, has been generated. In addition, the generic layout structure may be used to control the layout of the document obtained from the layout process.

The attributes associated with each document element are also specified, together with the corresponding attribute names according to an appropriate table form. The name is indicated in the right column of the table, while the value is reported in the left one.

Figures 10.7, 10.8 and 10.9 show a document class named *report*. It consists of three pages. The first one contains a logo, an organization name, a title, the name of the author and an abstract, while the second page contains two paragraphs, a part of a third paragraph and a figure. The last page contains the other part of the third paragraph, acknowledgments and the bibliography. Since the document must define a general architecture for reports, contents are expressed in symbolic terms. Figure 10.10, 10.11 and 10.12 describe the layout structure of the document, pointing out the various blocks belonging to the different pages.

The specific layout structure diagram reported in Figure 10.13 shows the blocks and pages presented in Figure 10.10, 10.11 and 10.12 organized into a hierarchical form. It can be noted that the contents are divided into a number of content portions, each one assigned to a block. Hence, there is a block for the logo, one for the organization name, one for the title, one for the author name and so on. It should also be noted that the content portions of the document are represented, according to the notation, by using double

Politecnico di Torino
Corso Duca degli Abruzzi 24
1-10129 Turin Italy

Office Document Architecture and Interchange Format

John Smith

Abstract

One of the most important features of an integrated office environment, is the capability of interchanging documents composed of various content types, such as characters for text, geometric and raster graphics, between dissimilar application systems. A basis for this is given by the ISO work for the Office Document Architecture (ODA) and interchange format, known as ISO 8613 [ISO8613/1]. Before it, no comprehensive international standard to address interchange of compound documents was available. However, it should be noted that, this standard also, like others [ECMA101][CCITT-T73], is very reach and flexible in its approach to the subject in order to address the broader number of requirements. As a result, im

Figure 10.7   Document example: the first page of a report.

lined blocks. The third paragraph is assigned to two blocks belonging to two different pages. Each layout object is also characterized by a set of attributes as reported in Table 10.2, which refers only to a part of the specific layout structure.

The *object type* and *object identifier* are used to uniquely identify the component to which attributes apply. For layout objects,

Paragraph A   imilar application systems. A basis for this is given by the ISO work for the Office Document Architecture (ODA) and interchange format, known as ISO 8613 [ISO8613/1]. Before it, no comprehensive international standard to address interchange of compound documents was available. However, it should be noted that, this standard also, like others [ECMA101][CCITT-T73], is very reach and flexible in its approach to the subject in order to address the broader number of requirements. As a result, im

Paragraph B   his standard are not guaranteed interoperability because of the number of options allowed in the specifications. Since equivalent implementations on dissimilar systems are required to achieve electronic compound document interchange, TOP specifications [TOP3.0] has introduced the so called *TOP Office Document Architecture Application Profile*, which focus implementators on ODA features commonly found in electronic compound documents and enable them to build products that will interoperate. In particular the TOP ODA AP specifies an implementation of the ISO specifications that supports interchange of formatted or revisable compound documents composed of characters, computer graphics, or raster graphics objects.

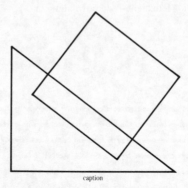

caption

Paragraph C1   *nt Architecture Application Profile*, which focus implementators on ODA features commonly found in electronic compound documents and enable them to build products that will interoperate. In particular the TOP ODA AP specifies an implementation of the ISO specifications that supports interchange of formatted or revisable compound documents composed of characters, computer graphics, or

Figure 10.8　　Document example: intermediate page of a report.

Paragraph C2 to the subject in order to address the broader number of requirements. As a result, implementors of this standard are not guaranteed interoperability because of the number of options allowed in the specifications. Since equivalent implementations on dissimilar systems are required to achieve electronic compound document interchange, TOP specifications [TOP3.0] has introduced the so called *TOP*

Paragraph D important features of an integrated office environment, is the capability of interchanging documents composed of various content types, such as characters for text, geometric and raster graphics, between dissimilar application systems. A basis for this is given by the ISO work for the Office Document Architecture (ODA) and interchange format, known as ISO 8613 [ISO8613/1]. Before it, no comprehensive international standard to address interchange of compound documents was available. However, it should be noted that, this standard also, like others (ECMA101)[CCITT-T73], is very reach and flexible

Acknowledgment – Acknowledgment

Bibliography

[ISO8613/1] ISO DIS 8613 "Office Document Architecture (ODA) and Interchange Format – Part 1 – Introduction and General Principles" July 1987.

[ISO8613/2] ISO DIS 8613 "Office Document Architecture (ODA) and Interchange Format – Part 2 – Document Structures" July 1987.

[ISO8613/4] ISO DIS 8613 "Office Document Architecture (ODA) and Interchange Format – Part 4 – Document Profile" July 1987.

Figure 10.9   Document example: ending page.

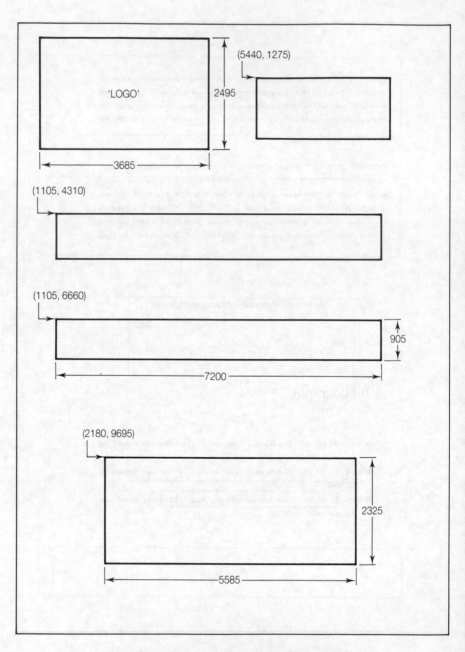

Figure 10.10   Document example: first page layout.

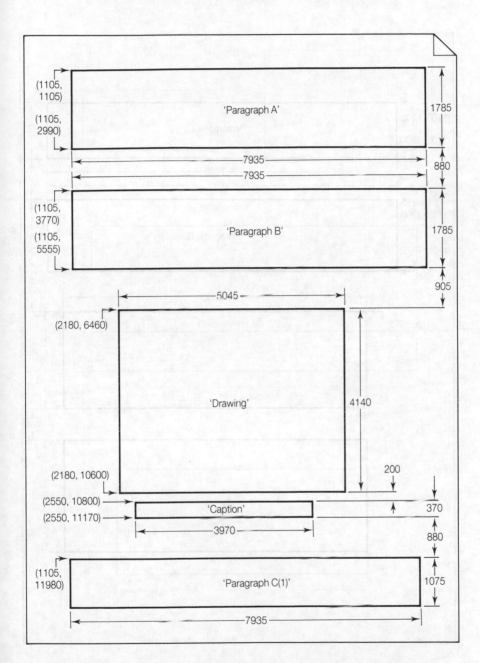

Figure 10.11 Report document example: intermediate page layout.

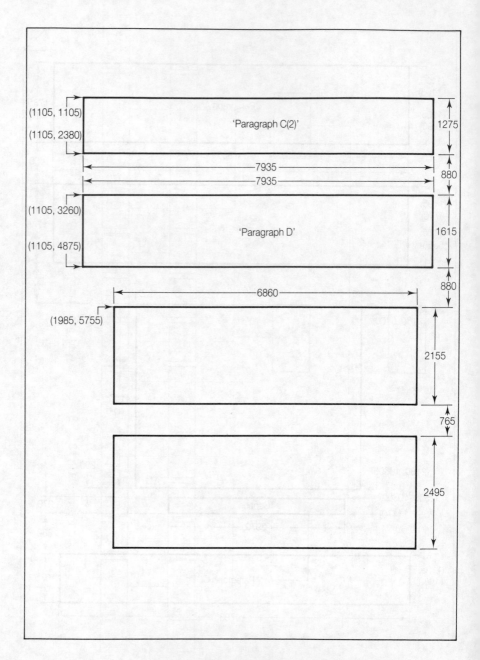

Figure 10.12   Report document example: last page layout.

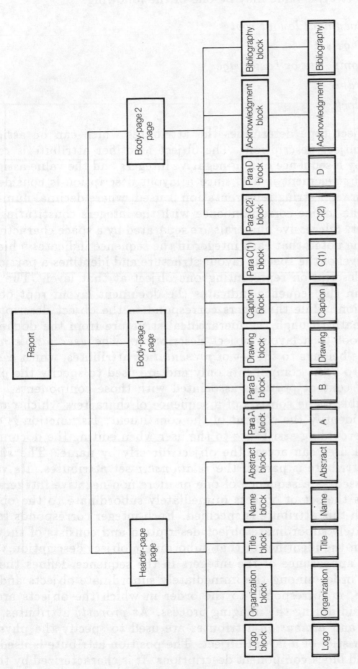

Figure 10.13   Specific layout structure of the *report* document.

the object type value may be one of the following:

- *document layout root*
- *page set*
- *composite or basic page*
- *frame*
- *block.*

The object type determines the attributes which can be assigned to the object description. The object identifier attribute is represented by a sequence of non-negative integers and the value assigned to the first element is a 1, since a layout description is considered. The character string representation is used, where decimal numerals are in one-to-one correspondence with the integers constituting the identifier. Successive numerals are separated by a space character. It should be noted that each integer in the sequence indicates a hierarchical level of the specific layout structure and identifies a particular object description representing one object at that level. The first integer in the sequence indicates the document layout root object description, while the others correspond to the object descriptions on the path through the hierarchical structure from the document layout root to a layout object description. The *user visible name* attribute belongs to the set of *presentation* attributes, which can be applied to basic components only and are used to specify the properties of content portions associated with those components. The user visible name consists of a sequence of characters which can be used to identify the content of the constituent. Its function is only that of providing assistance to the user when editing the document: in fact a user can access the object directly by name. The *subordinate* attribute is part of the *relationship* set attributes. Its value is expressed as a sequence of one or more non-negative integers. It indicates the set of objects immediately subordinate to the object for which this attribute is specified. Each integer corresponds to an immediately subordinate object description and consists of the last integer in the identifier of that subordinate object description. The order of appearance of the integers in the sequence defines the sequential order among the immediately subordinate objects and, in this case, it corresponds to the order in which the objects are to be overlaid during the imaging process. As *property* attributes, the *position* and *dimension* attributes are used to specify the physical characteristics of a layout object. The position attribute is used for frame and block component descriptions. It is characterized by three parameters, even if only two are used in the example:

- *horizontal position*, which is represented by a non-negative integer
- *vertical position*, which is a non-negative integer

- *positioning rule*, which is characterized by three subparameters: *distance, centering* and *order*.

This attribute specifies the position of the object referred to the object at the next higher level in the hierarchical structure, which can be represented by the immediately superior page or frame. The vertical and horizontal position corresponds to the vertical and horizontal distances from the reference point provided by the immediately superior object to the reference point of the object to which this attribute applies. The parameter *positioning rule* may be specified by itself or together with either or both the other parameters. It specifies the rule to be used for positioning the object.

The *dimensions* attribute is characterized by two parameters to specify both the vertical and horizontal dimensions of the object to which the attribute applies.

The *content identifier* attribute, belonging to the set of *identification* attributes for content portions, identifies a content portion description uniquely within the context of the document, while the *content information* attribute specifies the part of the content portion description which is composed of content elements, such as graphics characters, pixels, and so on.

The specific logical structure is also described according to a hierarchical approach as depicted in Figure 10.14. Here it is shown that the document consists of two directly subordinate composite logical objects representing the *header* and the *body* of the document. The header consists of basic logical objects representing the *organization*, the *title*, the *author* and so on. Content portions are assigned to the basic logical objects. There is no basic logical object for the logo because it is an integral part of the layout structure. Each logical object is characterized by its attributes in the same way as for the layout objects. Table 10.3 reports the attributes associated with the various objects belonging to a part of the logical structure, while Table 10.4 defines the presentation styles. In the case of the logical structure the *object type* may assume the following values:

- *document logical root*
- *composite logical object*
- *basic logical object*.

The *object identifier* has the first integer in the sequence set to 3 to specify that the logical object structure is considered. When needed, each basic logical object refers to an appropriate *presentation style*. Presentation attributes define how the contents are to be imaged on the presentation support. In the case of character contents, as an example, the presentation attributes indicate the line and character spacing intervals, whether or not the content has to be justified, how many lines have to be skipped at the beginning of the page, and so on. In Table 10.3 the *presentation style* attribute is used

Table 10.2   Part of the specific layout structure description.

Specific layout structure	
Object type	Document layout root
Object identifier	1
User visible name	Report
Subordinates	0, 1, 2
Object type	Page
Object identifier	1 0
User visible name	Header Page
Subordinates	0, 1, 2, 3, 4
Object type	Block
Object identifier	1 0 0
User visible name	Logo
Position	X=550, Y=530
Dimensions	W=3600, H=2500
Content architecture class	Formatted raster graphics
Content portions	0
Content identifier - layout	1 0 0 0
Content information	Array of raster graphics content elements

to establish a relationship between a basic component description and a presentation style. Looking at Table 10.4 it can be seen that each style is defined by an appropriate *presentation style identifier* attribute, which is constituted by a sequence of two integers, the first of which is always five. The representation of such an identifier is obtained by using a string of two decimal coded numerals with a space character as a separator between them.

In order to complete the information needed to layout the document contents, additional information may be used concerning the document layout structure, which involves a detailed description of the internal organization of pages. It should be noted that this information can be supplied by the recipient, which provides the description of the layout according to the characteristics of the pages it is going to use. The next example also gives a guide line for the use

Table **10.2**   *(cont.)*

Specific layout structure	
Object type	Block
Object identifier	1 0 1
User visible name	Date
Position	X=5450 , Y=1250
Dimensions	W=3000, H=500
Content architecture class	Formatted raster graphics
Content portions	0
Content identifier - layout	1 0 1 0
Content information	Turin, 12 December 1989
Object type	Block
Object identifier	1 0 2
User visible name	Addressee
Position	X−1100 , Y=4300
Dimensions	W=4500, H=550
Content architecture class	Formatted raster graphics
Content portions	0
Content identifier - layout	1 0 2 0
Content information	To members of UNIPREA
Object type	Block
Object identifier	1 0 3
User visible name	Subject
Position	X=1120 , Y=6600
Dimensions	W=7200, H=900
Line spacing	300
Content portions	0

of the generic layout structure, which contains sufficient information to represent the layout required for the document. In the next example the same document is represented through the corresponding logical form, along with a generic layout structure to describe the layout required.

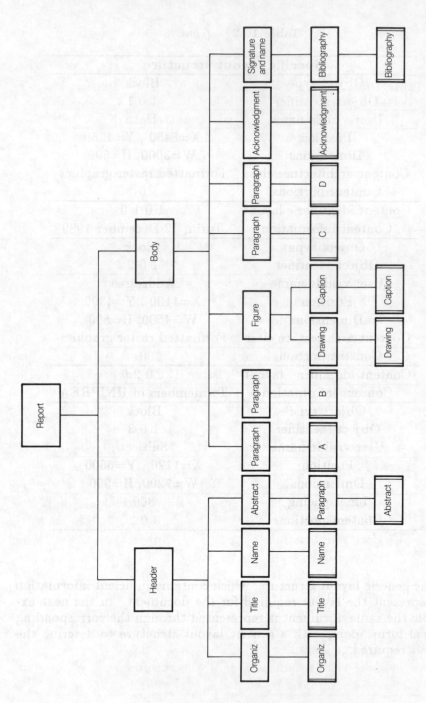

Figure 10.14   Specific logical structure of the *report* document.

Table 10.3 Part of the specific logical structure description.

Specific logical structure	
Object type	Document logical root
Object identifier	3
User visible name	Report
Subordinates	0, 1
Object type	Composite logical
Object identifier	3 0
User visible name	Header
Subordinates	0, 1, 2, 3
Object type	Basic logical
Object identifier	3 0 0
User visible name	Date
Content portions	0
Content identifier - logical	3 0 0 0
Content information	Turin, 12 December 1989
Object type	Basic logical
Object identifier	3 0 1
User visible name	Addressee
Content portions	0
Content identifier - logical	3 0 1 0
Content information	To members of UNINFO
Object type	Basic logical
Object identifier	3 0 2
User visible name	Subject
Presentation style	5 0
Content portions	0
Content identifier - layout	3 0 2 0
Content information	Subject: ODA overview
Object type	Composite logical
Object identifier	3 0 3
User visible name	Summary
Subordinates	0

Table 10.4   Presentation styles.

Presentation styles	
Presentation style identifier	5 0
Line spacing	3 0 0
Presentation style identifier	5 1
First line format	First line offset=1200
Line spacing	300
Presentation style identifier	5 2
First line format	First line offset 1200
Alignment	Justified
Line spacing	300
Presentation style identifier	5 3
First line format	First line offset 1000
Alignment	Justified
Line spacing	300

10.9   Generic logical and layout structure

The aim of this example is to show how a document can be interchanged in a processible form by the use of a generic logical structure and a generic layout structure associated with the specific logical structure.

The generic logical structure is used to facilitate the subsequent editing of the document performed by a recipient. In particular, the generic logical structure presented in Figure 10.15 is one which may have been used to generate the specific logical structure of the document shown in Figure 10.14.

The generic layout structure introduced here is used to control the layout of the logically structured document, when it is applied to the document layout and imaging processes. It specifies what types of layout object can be created during these processes and in what order they have to be made available. In particular, the generic layout object will create an image of the document which corresponds to that which could be produced by the specific layout structure reported in the first example and shown in Fig. 10.13. A logically structured document can be laid out if each logical object description in the document may be related to a layout object description created by the document layout process using the generic layout structure. Such a relationship is obtained by means of layout styles, each of which is composed of a set of attributes called *layout directives*. Each object description in the specific logical structure

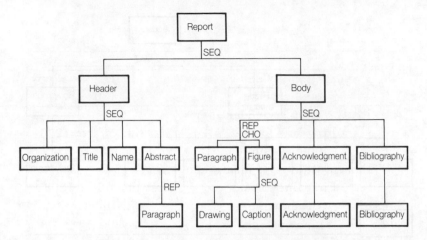

Figure 10.15 Generic logical structure of the *report* document.

contains an attribute which refers to a particular layout style with that object description. The attributes in the layout style then relate the logical object description to the appropriate layout object description and guide the correct layout of the logical object during the document layout process.

The document also contains *presentation styles*, each of which contains a set of attributes called *presentation attributes*, which are used to affect the layout and imaging of the content of the basic logical object descriptions within the document. As for layout styles, a basic logical object description may contain a reference to a certain presentation style and this has the effect of associating a particular set of presentation attributes with that object description.

In this example, the reference to layout and presentation styles are not contained within the attributes of the specific logical object descriptions, but are contained within the attributes of the object class description corresponding to the specific logical object description. This approach can be used to reduce the number of coded bits required to interchange a document or facilitate subsequent editing.

Figure 10.15 reports the generic logical structure of the document, which specifies the logical object descriptions that may occur in a corresponding specific logical structure and their permitted sequential orders. The order in which the object descriptions are specified is important since it indicates the order in which the objects are to be processed by the document layout and imaging processes. The document is described by a tree whose root node is the *logical root description*, called the *report*, which generates two subordinate composite logical object descriptions, called the *header* and the *body*. These logical object descriptions must occur once only in any corresponding specific logical structure. The use of the

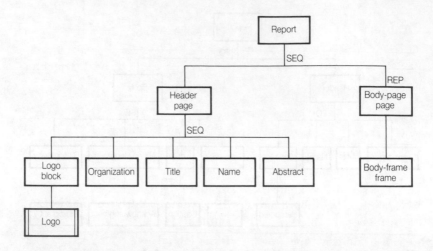

Figure 10.16   Generic layout structure of the *report* document.

mnemonic symbol *SEQ* should be noted, placed below the document
level, which indicates that the sequential order of these composite
object descriptions, in any corresponding specific logical structure,
implies that the *header* is in first position followed by the *body*. The
header consists of four subordinate elements: the *organization*, *title*,
author and *abstract*. They occur once in any corresponding specific
logical structure and must occur in the order shown in the diagram.
The *abstract* is a composite logical object description composed of
one or more basic logical object descriptions, called *paragraphs*. The
body is also a composite logical object consisting of any number and
combination of the logical objects *paragraph* and *figure* as indicated
by the mnemonics REP, CHO followed by the object descriptions
acknowledgment and *bibliography*, which may occur only once. The
object class description *acknowledgment* contains a generic content
portion description. Any specific logical object generated from this
generic logical structure would contain a logical object description
corresponding to *acknowledgment* but no content portion description
would be associated with this object description.

For the generic layout structure, Figure 10.16 describes the
document named *report* as composed of a *header* page followed by at
least one *body page* page. The first type of page contains one generic
content portion description for a *logo* and four layout object class
descriptions for frames: *organization*, *title*, *author* and *abstract*.

Each *body page* page contains a subordinate frame. It should
be noted that the diagram also specifies that the order in which the
pages are generated, along with their subordinate layout objects, has
to be taken into account.

Table 10.5 reports the object class description pertaining to

Table 10.5   Part of the generic logical structure description.

Generic logical structure	
Object type	Document logical root
Object class identifier	2 (report)
User visible name	Report
Generator for subordinates	SEQ (header, body)
Object type	Composite logical
Object identifier	2 0 (header)
User visible name	Header
Generator for subordinates	SEQ (date, addressee, subject, summary)
Object type	Basic logical
Object identifier	2 0 0 (date)
User visible name	Date
Layout style	4 0
Content architecture class	Processible characters
Object type	Basic logical
Object identifier	2 0 1 (addressee)
User visible name	Addressee
Layout style	4 1
Content architecture class	Processible characters
Object type	Basic logical
Object identifier	2 0 2 (subject)
User visible name	Subject
Layout style	4 2
Presentation style	5 0
Content architecture class	Processible characters
Object type	Composite logical
Object identifier	2 0 3 (summary)
User visible name	Summary
Layout style	4 3
Generator for subordinates	REP summary-paragraph

the general logical structure, while Table 10.6 describes the presentation styles associated with the document. Table 10.7 lists the object descriptions for the objects in the specific logical structure. The object descriptions in this table must be interpreted together with the object class descriptions given in Table 10.5. Table 10.8 presents the object class descriptions pertaining to the generic layout structure.

Figure 10.17 describes the specific layout structure generated

Table 10.6   Styles associated with the generic logical structure.

Styles for the generic logical structure	
Presentation style identifier	5 0
Line spacing	3 0 0
Presentation style identifier	5 1
First line format	First line offset 1200
Alignment	Justified
Line spacing	300
Presentation style identifier	5 3
First line format	First line offset 1200
Alignment	Justified
Line spacing	300
Presentation style identifier	5 4
First line format	First line offset 1000
Alignment	Justified
Line spacing	300
Layout style identifier	4 0
Layout object class	0 0 1 (date)
Offset	Trailing=700, right-hand=400
Layout style identifier	4 1
Layout object class	0 0 2 (addressee)
Layout style identifier	4 2
Layout object class	0 0 3 (subject)
Layout style identifier	4 3
Layout object class	0 0 4 (summary)
Layout style identifier	4 4
Offset	Left-hand=705
Layout style identifier	4 5
Layout object class	0 1 (body-page)
Layout style identifier	4 6
Indivisibility	0 1 0 (body-frame)

Table 10.7   Part of the constituents for the specific logical structure.

Specific logical structure	
Object type	Document logical root
Object identifier	3
Object class 2 (report)	
User visible name	Report
Subordinates	0, 1
Object type	Composite logical
Object identifier	3 0
Object class	2 0
User visible name	Header
Subordinates	0, 1, 2, 3
Object type	Basic logical
Object identifier	3 0 0
Object class	2 0 0 (date)
User visible name	Date
Content portions	0
Object type	Basic logical
Object identifier	3 0 1
Object class	2 0 1 (addressee)
User visible name	Addressee
Content portions	0
Object type	Basic logical
Object identifier	3 0 2
Object class	2 0 2
User visible name	Subject
Content portions	0
Object type	Composite logical
Object identifier	3 0 3
Object class	2 0 3
User visible name	Summary
Subordinates	0
Object type	Basic logical
Object identifier	3 0 3 0
Object class	2 0 3 1 (summary-paragrph)
User visible name	Summary-paragraph
Content portions	0

by the document layout process from the specific logical structure, the generic logical structure and the generic layout structure described above. If a document is generated in formatted processible form, then this structure would be generated by the originator and interchanged together with the other document structures.

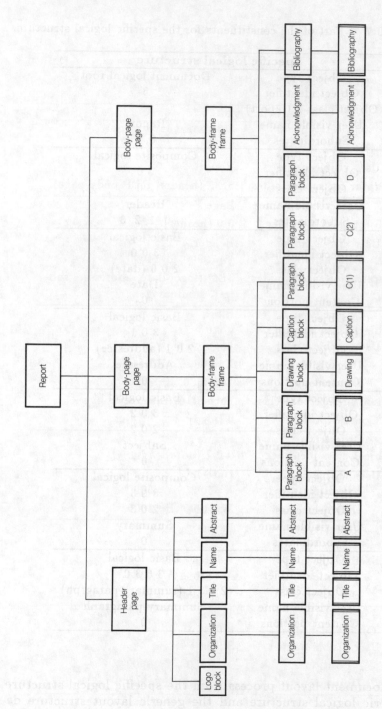

Figure 10.17 Specific layer structure generated by the document layout process from the specific logical structure of the *report* document.

the generic logical structure and the specific layout structure described above. If a document is generated in formatted processable form, then this structure should be generated by the originator and interchanged together with the other document structures.

Table 10.8   Part of the generic layout structure description.

Generic layout structure	
Object type	Document layout root
Object class identifier	0 (report)
User visible name	Report
Generator for subordinates	SEQ (header, REP body-page)
Object type	Page
Object class identifier	0 0 (header)
User visible name	Header
Dimensions	W=9900, H 14000
Generator for subordinates	SEQ (logo, date, addressee, subject, summary)
Object type	Block
Object class identifier	0 0 0
User visible name	Logo
Position	X=700, Y=720
Dimensions	W=3600, H=2500
Content architecture class	Formatted raster graphics
Content portions	0 (logo)
Object type	Frame
Object class identifier	0 0 1 (date)
User visible name	Date
Position	X=5000 , Y=500
Dimensions	W=4000, H=1600
Object type	Frame
Object class identifier	0 0 2
User visible name	Addressee
Position	X=1100 , Y=4300
Dimensions	W=5300, H=1400
Object type	Frame
Object identifier	0 0 3
User visible name	Subject
Position	X=1120 , Y=6600
Dimensions	W=7200, H=1800

Table 10.9   Part of the specific layout structure description.

Specific layout structure	
Object type	Document layout root
Object identifier	1
Object class	0 (report)
User visible name	Report
Subordinates	0, 1, 2
Object type	Page
Object identifier	1 0
Object class	0 0 (header)
User visible name	Header
Subordinates	0, 1, 2, 3, 4
Object type	Block
Object identifier	1 0 0
Object class	0 0 0
User visible name	Logo
Content architecture class	Formatted raster graphics
Object type	Frame
Object identifier	1 0 1
Object class	0 0 1 (date)
User visible name	Date
Subordinates	0

This specific layout structure differs from that proposed in Figure 10.13 in the fact that this one contains frames, while the other does not. Another aspect is related to the fact that the previous specific layout structure contains a content portion description for the object description named *logo*, while here the content portion description is omitted because it is specified as part of the generic layout structure. The object descriptions contained in Figure 10.17 are listed in Table 10.9, which are to be interpreted in conjunction with the layout object class descriptions listed in Table 10.8. It should be noted that in Table 10.9 the presentation attributes associated with the content corresponding to various blocks are specified by means of presentation styles, which are described in Table 10.4.

10.10   Interchange format

The *office document interchange format* (ODIF) specifies the format of the data stream used to interchange documents structured

Table 10.9 *(cont.)*

Specific layout structure	
Object type	Block
Object identifier	1 0 1 0
Position	X=400 , Y=700
Dimensions	W=3000, H=500
Content portions	0
Content architecture class	Formatted processible characters
Object type	Frame
Object identifier	1 0 2
Object class	0 0 2 (addressee)
User visible name	Addressee
Subordinates	0
Object type	Block
Object identifier	1 0 2 0
Dimensions	W=4500, H=550
Content portions	0
Content architecture class	Formatted processible characters

according to the standard definitions.

A document arranged according to the ODA approach is represented by a data stream consisting of one or more data structures listed below:

- document profile descriptor
- layout object descriptor
- layout object class descriptor

- logical object descriptor
- logical object class descriptor
- presentation style descriptor
- layout style descriptor
- text unit.

These data structures are named *interchange data elements*, which are inserted in a data stream according to certain rules. The first interchange data element in a data stream is always a document profile descriptor. The other elements may be chosen between the interchange data elements mentioned previously. The order in which the elements have to be organized in the data stream is based on the sequence specified below:

- document profile descriptors
- layout object class descriptors
- logical object class descriptors
- text units representing generic content portions
- presentation style descriptors
- layout style descriptors
- logical object descriptors
- text units representing specific content portions.

Each element consists of subordinate data structures and data items representing the attribute of the constituent concerned. Each document profile, each object class, each style and each object is represented by one descriptor. In particular a text unit consists of two main parts:

- *an attribute field*, which may be represented by a data structure consisting of subordinate data structures and data items representing the attributes of the content portions concerned
- *an information field*, which may be represented by a data structure that is either a data item or a set of data items representing the content elements making up the content portion concerned.

Each content portion is represented by one text unit.

It should be noted that data formats of the data stream and its subordinate data structures are reported in the specifications using the abstract syntax notation ASN.1 [ISO8824], so that a formal description is available. For the coding process the basic encoding rules defined by those specifications for a concrete syntax [ISO8825] are also used.

10.11 Conclusions

ODA is an ISO standard for interchanging integrated text and graphics documents between dissimilar systems in an Open Systems Interconnection environment. The ODA Standard provides for the interchange by defining an independent model of the content, logical and layout sub-structures found in office documents. ODA's abstract model caters for technical papers and reports, manuals and other representations where contents may include mixtures of character text, facsimile and drawings. Hence, ODA supports processible document interchange where the paragraphs and page layout information can be transferred between previously incompatible systems, edited and reformatted by these systems. The TOP environment also includes the ODA architecture in the so-called TOP ODA Application Profile. In this case the specification wants to suggest an implementation approach able to guarantee interoperability between different physical environments.

References

[ISO8613/1]   ISO DIS 8613 *Office Document Architecture (ODA) and Interchange Format – Part 1 – Introduction and General Principles* July 1987.

[ISO8613/2]   ISO DIS 8613 *Office Document Architecture (ODA) and Interchange Format – Part 2 – Document Structures* July 1987.

[ISO8613/4]   ISO DIS 8613 *Office Document Architecture (ODA) and Interchange Format – Part 4 – Document Profile* July 1987.

[ISO8613/5]   ISO DIS 8613 *Office Document Architecture (ODA) and Interchange Format – Part 5 – Office Document Interchange Format (ODIF)* July 1987.

[ISO8613/6]   ISO DIS 8613 *Office Document Architecture (ODA) and Interchange Format – Part 6 – Character Content Architectures* July 1987.

[ISO8613/7]   ISO DIS 8613 *Office Document Architecture (ODA) and Interchange Format – Part 7 – Raster Graphics Content Architectures* July 1987.

[ISO8613/8]   ISO DIS 8613 *Office Document Architecture (ODA) and Interchange Format – Part 8 – Geometric Graphics Content Architectures* July 1987.

[CCITT-T73]   CCITT Recommendation T.73 *Document Interchange Protocol for the Telematic Services*, 1984.

[ECMA101]   *Office Document Architecture.*

[TOP3.0]   *Technical and Office Protocol Specification* – Ver. 3.0, MAP/TOP Users Group, 1987.

[ISO8824]   ISO DIS 8824 *Specification of Abstract Syntax Notation One (ASN.1)*, 1986.

[ISO8825]   ISO DIS 8825 *Specification of Basic Encoding Rules for Abstract Syntax Notation One (ASN.1)*, 1986.

Chapter 11

The Application Program Interface

11.1 Introduction	12.6 Private communication
11.2 General issues	application interface
11.3 The interface model	12.7 Conclusions
architecture	References
11.4 Event management	
11.5 Connection management	
interface specification	

11.1 Introduction

A basic requirement for a user oriented to distributed application development in a MAP/TOP environment is to know how programs can talk to the application layer. It is a fact that OSI standards do not specify this high-level interface in much detail and the mechanisms made available, based on the *indication* principle, cannot be implemented easily. In order for the user to be able to choose among competing communication MAP/TOP boards on the basis of performance and price, it is necessary for all the boards to support the same interface to the user program as shown in Figure 11.1. In other words, there is a need for a standard application service interface so that moving application programs from one board to another does not require changing user programs. MAP and TOP specifications define this interface and this chapter introduces the methodology for describing application program interfaces, which include a set of utilities, a model of interaction for the application program and the underlying protocol services and a general call format specification. The aim of this approach is to establish a framework within which

445

the external behavior of an interface can be described in a general way. As a consequence, implementations do not need to be perfectly consistent with the model described here, but it is necessary for the external behavior of the interface to correspond to that introduced by this model. In particular, the use of a general call format will ensure that all the application program interfaces described using this methodology have a single style.

11.2   General issues

The MAP Application Interface Specification [MAPTOPAPI] describes an application program interface for a multi-tasking environment supporting inter-process communication and coordination.

Operating system aspects are not taken into account: the specification describes asynchronous and synchronous mechanisms only, which can be implemented easily by means of different operating system functions. For asynchronous functionality a multi-tasking environment is assumed, supporting the basic inter-process communication and coordination facilities. To this purpose an event-based mechanism is introduced to allow an application program to interact asynchronously with network services. In particular, the issuing of an asynchronous function call will cause a message to be sent to the corresponding interface service provider. As soon as a message has been sent by the function, the user task regains control and continues execution. The service provider must be implemented by means of a separate task which is, then, independent from the user program issuing the request as described in Figure 11.1. This task is constantly waiting for incoming messages to process and can perform its operation executing in parallel with the user task which originated the call. To perform its work the service provider has its own data space, can share the user's data space when needed and can access network connections set up by the user. All function calls having asynchronous capabilities are also provided with a specific parameter called *return_event_name*. This name refers to the event which occurs when the service to be performed has come to a full completion, which means either a correct termination of the function has been achieved or an unrecoverable error has arisen.

On the other hand, when a synchronous function is used, the behavior of the process can be compared to that obtained by means of an asynchronous function call plus a wait for the event associated with the asynchronous function call itself. Figure 11.2 reports the program behavior for both the asynchronous and synchronous cases.

The interface model for the communication between the user program and the service provider is based on the exchange of data of various lengths. These data are passed by means of an area or buffer under the control of the user. Different conditions may arise, since, in some cases, the size and amount of data passed across the

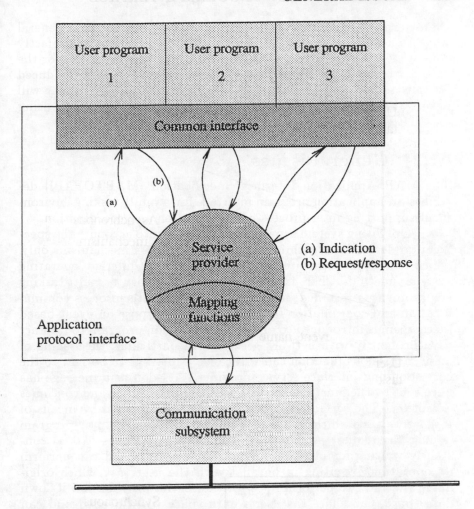

Figure 11.1   Interaction between an application program and the service provider.

interface may vary according to the different times when the function is called by the user. Furthermore, when information returned by functions is considered, the user may have no idea in advance of how much data will be returned. To solve these problems, two different strategies for buffer management have been specified:

- the user program may directly allocate space for buffers to pass data to the service provider;
- specific parameters may be used in the function call to trigger automatic buffer allocation by the interface; in this case, if the user does not provide the buffer, the interface performs the allocation of a buffer obtained from the users' buffer pool.

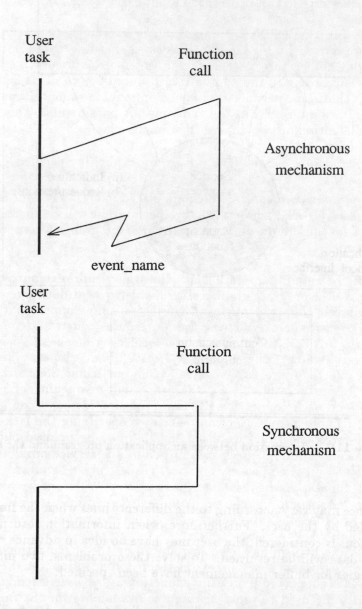

Figure 11.2   Asynchronous and synchronous behavior of a function call.

It should be noted that the user of the interface is made responsible for freeing the buffers allocated for data exchange, while the interface is responsible for informing the user if an overflow condition arises, due to the fact that the current amount of data cannot be stored in the allocated buffer.

A function call is structured in such a way that some parameters are passed by means of an argument list associated with the call, while others are gathered and stored in a preallocated area handled according to the approach introduced before. This is due to the fact that some parameters may be optional in some calls and not all users are interested in the same output parameters. This leads to the definition of two different parameter classes:

- *mandatory parameters*, which are explicitly specified on the call;
- *optional parameters*, which are placed in an input *data control block* (DCB), whose structure declaration will be included in a specific file to be used by the user program at compilation time.

It should be noted that, since DCB allocation requires resource availability, a user program can become unable to send data due to the user's system resource constraint. In fact, it may happen that, on a network service invoked by the user, a resource constraint condition arises: in this case the user will be informed by means of a suitable error code. On the other hand, the service provider operations may also be affected by resource contraints: in particular there is a limit on the resources available for the processing or queuing of service requests on each connection. If this condition arises, a connection service request from a user can be refused specifying the lack of resources for connection establishment. It must be pointed out that when a connection has been established by the service provider, the resource required to process an abort request must be always guaranteed. Similarly, when the interface service provider presents to the user an *a_associate indication*, it must also guarantee the ability to queue or process a subsequent user request to respond to such an indication.

A mechanism has been introduced by the specification to inform a user when a resource constrained connection can be used again: it is supported by a utility function called *note when cleared*, which is only used to monitor resource availability for the function call which has just produced an error for lack of resources. In this way the lack of resource for connection is considered a transient problem, which can easily be solved by the user cleaning up some resource usage.

Application interface functions are divided into a set of classes according to their characteristics:

- *high level*: the high-level service makes a user environment available where high-level functionality plays a basic role; in particular a high-level function may require the execution of a set of low-level service functions;

- *low level*: low-level services make an environment available where all aspects of the underlying protocol machine are accessible to the user; this fact makes this module useful for protocol testing, since at this level there is a direct correspondence between application service primitives and function calls;

- *requester and responder mode*: the requester mode functions give the user the capability to request network services, while the responder mode functions are associated with the other end of a request; these services set up mechanisms to accept and automatically respond to requests received from a remote application entity.

11.3   The interface model architecture

The model includes two different components: the former, composed of the set of interface services, can be considered as an integral part of the user program, while the latter represents the interface service provider, which works as an independent process. Figure 11.3 indicates the functional blocks belonging to both the model components.

11.3.1   The user region

As shown in Figure 11.3, the *user program region* of the model is composed of library calls, which can be viewed as a part of the *application process* (AP) which makes use of such calls. These have the responsibility of generating service requests according to specific formats and of queuing them for processing to the interface service provider.

The *high-level service* (HLS) gathers a set of *grouped* elementary services available to the AP, while the *low-level service* (LLS) includes those elementary service primitives which can also be reached directly by the AP. In particular, the low-level service block includes three service categories:

- *paired services*, for which requests and corresponding confirm services are paired;

- *non-confirmed services*, which handle response and request service primitives;

- *indication service*, which receives *indication* service primitives.

The *responder service* (RS) supports the set of services which automatically process incoming unsolicited service indications. These functions, which are connection specific, can be active to respond to

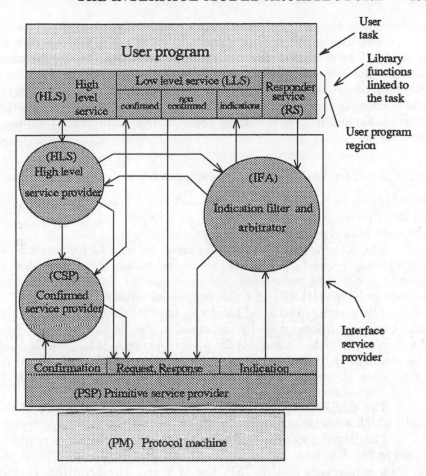

Figure 11.3   The application program interface model.

any number of requests before ending; in particular, some responder functions may be active for the whole life of the connection to which they belong. It should be noted in Figure 11.3 that the functional mechanism describing the responder activity is based on interaction with the interface service provider. In fact, the intelligence of a responder function is based on the facilities provided by the *indication filter and arbitrator* (IFA), which is usually a dormant task. The IFA may be activated by means of a responder service call immediately after a connection has been established. In this way each specific responder function call forces a responder service to process a particular type of service indication. Once activated, the function will filter incoming unsolicited indications in order to respond to the ones to which it has been activated to respond. When an indication has been detected, a confirm primitive may be generated as a response to the indication request. This answer will be positive or negative according to the acceptance criteria provided by the user.

The *user program region* contains all necessary processing required before a request can be formatted and sent to the interface service provider. All functions included in this block can be generally described as library functions. In particular, they provide for the queuing of service requests verifying whether the service provider is available and if local resources are sufficient to perform the queue operation.

11.3.2   The interface service provider

Interface services are provided by a task not belonging to the Application Process, since it is viewed as an independent entity to which the user may repeatedly submit service requests.

The interface service provider must be able to process all the outstanding requests in the correct order, taking into account that specific processing orders may be specified for both the *high-level service provider* (HLSP) and the *confirmed service provider* (CSP).

The various functional blocks in the interface service provider may exchange information by means of messages and note services. As an example, when a request for a service is sent, it is done through the availability of an interface to the service provider, which, in its turn, when the requested service has been completed, sends a note to the requester.

The HLSP supports high-level services and makes use of the CSP, which associates requests with the corresponding responses.

The HLSP determines if one or more connections are required to serve the function call and the sequence of requests to be made on each connection of the CSP, the IFA and the *primitive service provider* PSP so that the requested service may be satisfied. In particular, for each request in the sequence, the HLSP provides for the matching of parameters specified in the call to those required by the service primitive as defined in the specific *application service element* (ASE) (i.e. MMS, FTAM and others). After the request has been passed to the appropriate destination, the HLSP waits for its completion to be noted by the CSP, IFA or the PSP.

When the sequence of requests has been completed, the HLSP puts the result in an output data area and notes the completion of the requested service.

The CSP has to pass primitive requests to the PSP and then waits for a response from it indicating if the request is accepted or rejected. If the request is accepted, the CSP solicits confirmation from the PSP and waits for the completion of such solicitation. When the completion is signaled, the CSP reports the positive or negative result, noting the completion of the submitted request.

The IFA is responsible for screening incoming unsolicited or solicited indications to be processed by the *responder function* (RS) or by the HLSP. This activity can be made available at the moment when an association is activated.

When a request is received from the RS, the responder mode filter is adapted to the indication type to be processed. In particular, the acceptance criteria and the responder actions are defined only for that specific type. Termination criteria for the responder mode function are also specified.

Whether a solicitation sent by the LLS or by the HLSP is received by the IFA, the filtered indication buffer area is scanned to see if any indication exists. If no indication is available, then the IFA will wait for a primitive indication; in the other case, the indication is identified and related data returned to the requestor.

When an indication coming from the PSP is received, the IFA checks to see if the indication type is one of those to be filtered or to be received by the HSLP; if not, the indication is stored in the IFA filtered buffer area or, in response to an outstanding LLS solicitation, it is passed to the LLS module. If the indication belongs to the set of those to be filtered, the indication is checked against the acceptance criteria defined for it; in the case of a positive check a confirmation is sent to the PSP and actions associated with a successful indication are triggered, in the other case, a negative confirmation is sent to the PSP. At the end of these operations, as long as the termination criteria are satisfied, the indication type may be removed from the filter list.

The PSP sends request and response primitives to the *protocol machine* (PM) and receives confirmation and indication primitives from it. It also provides error reporting on behalf of the PM and informs all its users when an unsolicited indication arrives.

The PSP processes confirmations and receives requests on a FIFO basis; all confirmations will be delivered to the CSP and all indications will be delivered to the IFA. In particular, when a send request is processed, whether it is a response or a request primitive, and providing that the association is active, it is immediately passed to the PM; after that, the completion of the request is noted to the requestor. When an indication or confirmation primitive is received from the PM, the PSP verifies whether outstanding valid solicitations are available, if so the solicitation is satisfied by passing any information contained in the confirmation or indication primitive to the solicitation source. Finally, a note for the completion of the solicitation is issued. When no solicitation is available then the request is saved for later processing.

The Protocol Machine (PM) is the functional block which contains the state table and the set of rules related to the application protocol (i.e. it could be the MMS protocol machine).

11.4   Event management

Event management (EM) support functions allow the user to define an event when a function is called and to specify which event or combination of events is to be awaited. A further facility provides for the implicit deletion of an event at the time that the user is notified of an event's occurrence. To implement this function the host operating system has only to support process activation and deactivation either by a direct request to the dispatcher or by means of other solutions.

The basic functions required by an event management system are listed in the following:

- the capability of writing event-based programs and of handling multiple connections within a single process; a user must be able to wait on one or more multiple events, where an event is defined as the completion of an operation started via an asynchronous function call;

- the capability of minimizing assumptions concerning operating systems support and of not precluding the use of the same mechanism for non-MAP events.

The EM introduced in MAP specifications can be considered as a generalization of the semaphore definition introduced by Dijkstra [DIJKSTRA]. The semaphore, in fact, does not specify what events are, but rather allows the user of the facility to define events. A further aspect deals with the fact that a process is not forced to wait on an event prior to the occurrence of the event itself. The event management system has the usual semaphore features plus a facility related to the fact that a process may wait on a disjunction of multiple events.

The EM mechanisms can be used by programs or routines which either wait on events or note the occurrence of events. To do this, unambiguous names must be associated with the various events. EM does not specify how to generate or agree on event names, but when they are defined, it needs to be informed which names are to be used. This is accomplished by having each asynchronous application interface function specify an event name representing its completion. In this way the program which implements the function can use the event name to note the occurrence of that event.

Since a process may send more than one function call before it decides to wait, each event name is saved by the interface and this set of event names represents the waiting event expression for the process. In other words the process waits for the occurrence of one event included in the expression issuing the wait function. Until an event occurs, the process is deactivated; it resumes when any event in the expression occurs and is noted: the note service activates the process and returns to it the name of the event. The latter is also

PWI

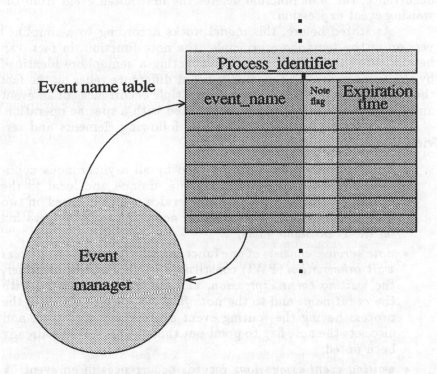

Event name table

Process_identifier		
event_name	Note flag	Expiration time

Event manager

Figure 11.4   The event management model.

removed from the waiting event expression. If during the process execution other asynchronous operations are started before issuing another Wait, the associated event names are added to the waiting event expression.

The EM facility is composed of a basic service called *wait*, which allows a process to wait until an event occurs. As shown in Figure 11.4 the wait service is based on a function which affects the *process wait information* (PWI), represented by a time-ordered list of entries. Each entry contains an event name and a switch to indicate whether the event has been noted. An expiration time is also associated with the event so that if the declared time limit is exceeded, the process is restarted anyway. In particular, when the expiration time is set to FOREVER the wait function causes the issuing process to wait until the waiting event expression is true, while, if the expiration time is set to a specific value, the waiting process waits until either the waiting expression is true or the specified expiration time has elapsed. If the expiration time is zero, the wait function does not cause the process to wait for the event expression to become true, but it returns immediately.

When the wait function returns as a consequence of an event occurrence, the wait function deletes the first noted event from the waiting event expression.

As stated before, this model works according to a simplified version of the semaphore principle: the note function, in fact, can be compared to a *signal* primitive affecting a semaphore identified by the event name. The most significant difference relies on the fact that the EM model cannot support multiple occurrences of an event and only a single event may be associated with a specific operation.

The model for EM includes the following elements and services:

- *name service*: this service is used by all asynchronous application interface functions; a name, unique and local to the calling process, is passed to this service, which is based on two different functions, *name add* and *name delete*, both operating on the *event name table*;

- *note service*: consists of one function, which acts on the *process wait information* (PWI) constituted by the process identifier, the *waiting event expression*, and the *queue* associated with the *event name* and to the *note flag*; this service activates the process having the waiting event expression set to true, and also sets the note flag to point out that the process has already been noted;

- *waiting event expression*: records occurrences of an event by specifying an entry for each specific event, only a single occurrence for an event is supported by the model, which enforces only one event name for each operation;

- *note function*: is used to note the occurrence of a single event; it checks for the noted event in the waiting event expression; if found, the event expression is set to true and the process waiting on that expression is activated;

- *expression service*: this service is used to build and maintain waiting event expressions; a waiting event expression is associated with each local environment and is implicitly referenced by the wait and other application interface functions called within the local environment; whenever an asynchronous application interface function specifying a local event name is called, the event is added to the local environment's waiting event expression by means of an *expression event add* function; whenever the wait function returns successfully, the single event returned by the wait is removed from the local environment's waiting event expression by means of an *expression event subtract* function used before returning from the wait.

Figure 11.5 shows the objects involved in the event management environment:

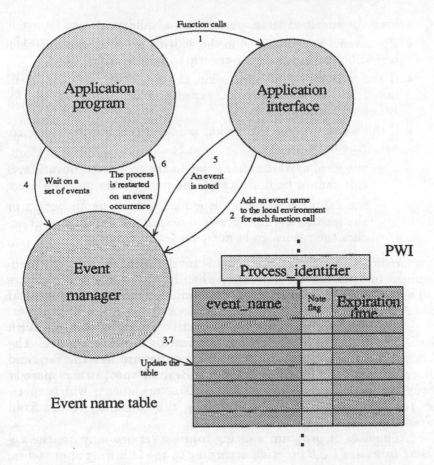

Figure 11.5   Objects involved in the event management environment.

- an application process, whose activity is affected by events;
- the application interface accessed by the application program;
- the event manager, which provides services to handle the event name table.

The only EM service to be developed and exposed to the user is the *wait* function, together with support functions needed to implement the mechanisms previously described. The call format used for the service expressed in the C_language is the following:

```
Return_code em_wait(time, local_event_name, result)
Em_t time;
Local_event_name *local_event_name;
Api_rc *result;
```

In particular, this function performs the following steps:

- load the specified time, performing a validity check;
- if no events are contained in the waiting event expression, then a specific warning code is generated for the user;
- if the waiting event expression is true, then the first event noted in the waiting event expression identified by the *local_event_name*, is returned;
- if the waiting event expression is false the following steps are performed:
  - the local system timer is set to the requested duration; if this cannot be done a suitable return code must be used;
  - the calling process is suspended until timeout occurs or the waiting event expression becomes true; if timeout occurs the return code must be set to describe it.

Support functions are used to provide mechanisms for memory management and parameter handling, when interface function calls are to be invoked. Other general-purpose functions also used in the EM model are described in MAP specifications.

The *dynamic initialize DCB* function allocates and initializes the DCB which will be used by an application interface service. The *dcb_type* parameter used in this function determines the required allocation area for fixed parameters. Beyond that, other space is requested by means of the *additional_size* argument, which specifies the total size of the area excluding that assigned to the fixed parameters.

The user or program wanting to use a service may use the *dynamic initialize DCB* function according to the following approaches:

- the user may call it before invoking the service call and then passing it the returned DCB pointer;
- the user may pass a null value for the DCB pointer of the called function, which will provide for the allocation and the initialization of the DCB, using the dynamic initialize DCB function.

Each ASE will have specific *dcb_type* parameter values due to the different syntax and semantics of data.

When called, the initialization function will provide for the examination of the *dcb_type* and the output parameters generating error messages when incorrect formats are detected. Subsequently, memory is allocated and the DCB initialized according to three different solutions:

- *default*: in this case the allocation function assigns a default value for the object;
- *default indication*: this parameter requests that the service call supplies the default value;

- *no-value indication*: this is used to signal that a parameter does not require any value, if it is not supplied.

The function call structure is the following:

> *Return_code xx_didcb (dcb_type, additional_size, dcb_pointer, result)*
> *Xx_dcb_type dcb_type;*
> *Uint32 additional_size;*
> *Octet **dcb_pointer;*
> *Api_rc *result;*

In this case, the function name is preceded by the *xx_* prefix, since these kind of functions are bounded to a specific application service element (ASE); for example if the MMS ASE is considered, function names become *mm_gperror* or *mm_didcd*, while for the FTAM ASE the name is *ft_gperror* or *ft_didcb* and so on.

To deallocate the DCB used for a specific service, the following function is used:

> *Return_code xx_dfdcb (dcb_pointer, result)*
> *Octet **dcb_pointer;*
> *Api_rc *result;*

This function provides for the freeing of the area addressed by the *dcb_pointer* and allocated by the *dynamic initialize DCB* function.

The *get_printable_error* routine translates return codes to printable strings for a particular service. The function call structure is the following:

> *Return_code xx_gperror (input_result, return_string, vendor_string, result)*
> *Api_rc *input_result;*
> *Octet **return_string;*
> *Octet **vendor_string;*
> *Api_rc *result;*

This function can be used to translate any return code from any application interface function to a printable string which is the abstract description of the return code as defined in the function call specification. The return code and the vendor code are part of the *input_result* parameter. It is suggested that the vendor also implements this function to translate its codes into printable strings. For the wait function call as specified for the C language, when an incorrect value is specified for the timer, it is expected that the code EME004_TIME_INV is returned to indicate that kind of error. When the *get printable error* function is called with a *return code* set to EME004_TIME_INV, it will return a pointer to the string: *invalid timer value*.

Another support function is the *note when cleared* primitive, which is issued when a previous no connection resource error has cleared. In particular, it is used after a return code of no connection resource on a previous function specifying the same connection identifier has been detected: it is expected that a note is made on the *return_event_name*, once the unavailable resource becomes available. The note indicates that, at the time of its generation, the previously unavailable resource is newly available. This fact cannot guarantee that the resource will remain available until the previously called function is called again. In order to obtain the funtionality of the call that was previously unsuccessful because of resource constraints, the same call must be issued again.

It should be noted that the function *note when cleared* applies only to the more recent function call, specifying the same *connection_id*, which means that multiple requests cannot be simultaneously outstanding on the same connection.

11.5   Connection management interface specification

This specification gives a definition for the interface towards the *Association Control Service Element* (ACSE) and deals with all aspects of the application association establishment.

In order for an application process, generally called an *Application Entity*, at the application layer of the OSI reference model, to be able to use the services of the application interface, a *presentation address* must be assigned to it. Furthermore, each AE should be registered with the network directory, or, where the AE has to be unknown to the network community, it should be registered only on a local basis. Another parameter to be considered is the number of associations per AE invocation: any network invocation of the same AE will be checked against this bound. The same approach will be followed for the parameter related to the number of AE invocations per presentation address.

When a *p_connect indication* service primitive is received at a specific presentation address, the AE management function passes the indication to any corresponding AE invocation which has requested receipt of the *a_associate* indication. If multiple invocations are available for that indication, only the first is satisfied, adopting the first-come-first-served approach. If no active AE invocation is available, the *a_associate* indication will be queued.

When an AE activation has to be performed, supposing that the AE has already been registered, it must be declared each time the activation is requested to the interface service provider. This must be done at run time and before using any network service. The result of the activation procedure is a *label* assigned to the activated AE, which must be used for subsequent association requests. The AE label is generated to identify uniquely the application entity within the local environment. When the AE is deactivated, then the label will be invalidated. Before deactivation is performed, the user of an AE invocation must terminate all pending or active connections and declare that other *a_associate* indications will not be accepted in order to initiate the deactivation procedure. Though multiple AE activations could be implemented, the MAP specification considers only single associations, in other words, each AE can only have one AE invocation.

In the association procedure, an AE label will be used as the calling AE invocation identifier value related to the user attempt to initiate an association. In the same way it is also used as the responding AE invocation identifier value, when the user attempts to respond to an *a_associate* indication.

To receive incoming *a_associate* indications, an AE must obtain explicit permission. This is granted by the issue of a *listen* function call from the user of any invocation of the same AE. If *a_associate* indications are received before, they will be rejected by refusing the presentation connection. When users want to declare that they are no longer interested in receiving any association indication, they can issue a *stop listen* function.

An association request is always related to a specific *application context*, which can be suitably selected. The MAP *application context*, in fact, can only have a single *application service element* (ASE) activated at a time (a typical example could be the FTAM ASE). The ACSE service interacts with the selected ASE to establish a connection. An ASE association request, after a check on the ASE specific information provided by the user, generates an ASE specific *initiate APDU* together with the *a_associate* service parameters required by ACSE; an ACSE association request, after checks for ACSE information provided by the ASE returns an approval to it and generates the *a_associate* service request to the ACSE protocol machine.

The connection established between remote AEs will be defined by means of a unique identifier within a local open system. This identifier refers to a pending association being negotiated, an active association or a terminated association which still contains user information. A connection identifier is assigned as soon as an association indication is received by means of the *listen* function or an association request is issued via a *connect* function.

If a connection identifier has been defined by means of the *listen* function, only *abort* and *answer* services can make use of that identifier; other service calls making use of that identifier will receive a code indicating a protocol error.

If a connection has been aborted by means of an *abort* indication and there exist unsolicited indications on the connection that have not been matched with a user *indication receive* call and have not caused the corresponding event to be noted, only the abort and indication receive functions can make use of the same identifier used by the aborted connection. Subsequent function calls making use of the same identifier should receive an error code related to the invalid use.

If a connection is released by the user, which has yet to receive all the unsolicited indications on the connection, only the abort and indication receive functions can make use of the connection identifier of this released connection.

Since each application association can control a certain amount of resources within a local open system, which has a limited resource pool, it is possible for a condition to arise where no new connections can be supported and no old connection is released for a long time period. To overcome this problem, the *connect* function provides a timer indicating how long a user is willing to wait for the availability of a connection resource, so that the user is allowed to avoid entering a potential deadlock.

An application entity is identified through the use of specific identifiers, in particular the parameters *my_dir_name* or *called_dir_name* define a distinguishing name which can be used for access to the network directory. Parameters such as *my_ae_title*, *called_ae_title*, or *responding_ae_title* define AE titles to be used on ACSE PDUs.

11.5.1   Connection management services

The *application entity activation* function is responsible for generating an AE invocation to the local interface service provider. This must be done before any other network service is issued, so that a specific identifier, called the *ae_label* is returned to be used by the connection establishment functions. In particular, subsequent *connect, listen, stop, answer, application entity deactivation* function calls can be used referring to that specific AE. The function structure is as follows:

> Return_code xx_aeactivation (my_dir_name, input_dcb,
> return_event_name, inout_dcb, ae_label)
> Ae_dir_name my_dir_name;
> Local_event_name return_event_name;
> struct Xx_aeactivate_in_dcb *input_dcb;
> struct Xx_output **inout_dcb;
> Ae_label *ae_label

The user can indicate a specific value in the *my_ae_title* parameter (contained in the *Xx_aeactivate_in_dcb* data structure) to be provided for the ACSE *calling_ae_title* and *responding_ae_title*.

According to the ISO–OSI model an AE invocation may have a set of application associations each using a different application layer service. However, when this interface is used, each AE invocation generated by an AE *activation* function can only make use of one application layer service element (ASE) in addition to ACSE. This fact is an obvious consequence of having a specific language binding of the AE activation function for each ASE interface (xx must be chosen according to the ASE).

The service provider actions associated with the execution of the function call are listed below:

- a test is performed to see if the current AE invocation will exceed the number of AE invocations per presentation address limit; if the limit is exceeded a suitable error code is returned, otherwise the number of AE invocations is incremented;

- an AE invocation label is returned to be used for subsequent network requests;

- identifiers to be used in the ACSE *a_associate* request PDU are suitably processed.

The *application entity deactivation* function can be issued after all connections within an AE invocation have been terminated. At the completion of this function, the *ae_label* corresponding to a specific AE invocation will no longer be valid and the network will also be informed that subsequent services will be rejected. An AE invocation cannot be deactivated when there are active connections maintained for it and when the user of that invocation has unresolved listen functions outstanding for this AE invocation. The structure of the function call is described below:

> *Return_code xx_aedeactivation (ae_label, return_event_name, inout_dcb)*
> *Ae_label ae_label;*
> *Local_event_name return_event_name;*
> *struct Xx_output **inout_dcb;*

The server provider deletes the *ae_label* associated with the AE invocation and updates the local open system management information base. In addition, the number of AE invocations per presentation address is decremented by one unit. After an AE invocation has been established, connection management functions can be successfully used.

The *connection* function, which is a requester mode high-level function call, has the basic aim of creating a connection with a remote AE returning a connection identifier related to the established connection. This operation is performed by using the *ae_label* returned by the AE activation function.

The connection function has also a retry option, so that transient problems can be overcome such as resource limitations: the user can specify a number of retries and a delay between consecutive retries. Another parameter is used to set the waiting time limit related to connection resource availability for a single connection request.

The structure of the function call is as follows:

Return_code xx_connect(ae_label, return_event_name,
input_dcb, called_dir_name, inout_dcb, connection_identifier)
Ae_label ae_label;
Local_event_name return_event_name;
Ae_dir_name called_dir_name;
*struct Xx_connec_in_dcb *input_dcb;*
*struct Xx_connec_out_dcb **inout_dcb;*
*connection_id *connection_id;*

This function involves several actions to be performed by the HSLP and CSP modules. In particular, the HSLP module performs the following steps:

- an *a_associate* request service primitive is received from the ASE and a corresponding *a_associate* request is passed to the CSP;
- if the return information indicates a successful completion, the connection identifier is initialized and the appropriate event is noted;
- if the return event was not signaled from the CSP, then the retry counter must be set and the action repeated until a return event is noted.

When the CSP return event is signaled, the user of the CSP module is informed that the CSP completed its task. The operations performed by the CSP module include a check to see if the current request exceeds the number of associations per AE invocation, after that resource allocation is performed. An *a_associate* request is then passed to the PSP module waiting for the corresponding response, which will subsequently be solicited. Successful or unsuccessful completion will be suitably notified.

The *listen* function declares the intention of the AE to accept an *a_associate* indication from another AE invocation. The successful completion of this function will provide the connection identifier, which can be used for subsequent operations. When the *a_associate* indication has been processed by the listen function, it has already been approved by both the ACSE and the corresponding ASE. The structure of the function call and of the related *stop listen* call is reported in the following:

> *Return_code xx_listen(ae_label, return_event_name, inout_dcb, connection_id)*
> *Ae_label ae_label*
> *Local_event_name return_event_name;*
> *struct Xx_listen_out_dcb **inout_dcb;*
> *connection_id *connection_id;*

> *Return_code xx_slisten(ae_label, return_event_name, inout_dcb)*
> *Ae_label ae_label*
> *Local_event_name return_event_name;*
> *struct Xx_output **inout_dcb;*

An outstanding asynchronous *listen* function can be terminated by a *stop listen* function.

When a *listen* function is issued, the AE invocation is recorded as being interested in receiving indications. An indication solicitation is passed to the PSP and a response is waited for from it, which will be reported when the return event is noted.

If a *stop listen* function is issued, the interface service provider is informed about the fact that a particular AE invocation is no longer interested in receiving *a_associate* indications. In this case, if outstanding unresolved *listen* function calls are not yet resolved, these functions will be served, and, after that, subsequent association indications will be rejected until a new listen call is performed by the same AE. The service provider actions include generation of information for the ACSE management information base, which must be updated according to the fact that the user of the AE invocation no longer wants to receive associate indications. Outstanding requests for associate indication solicitations, which came from the same AE invocation but have not been honored, are removed from the solicitation queue established for the PSP and, subsequently, the appropriate code is returned noting the event.

The *answer* function generates an *a_associate* response, and is used to accept or reject a connect request from a remote AE invocation. The function call uses the connection identifier obtained through a listen function call. When a connection is established as a result of the use of this function call, then all ASE context-sensitive function calls such as *abort, release request, release response and indication receive* can be used. The structure of the function call is the following:

> *Return_code xx_answer(connection_id, return_event_name, input_dcb, inout_dcb)*
> *Connection_id connection_id*
> *Local_event_name return_event_name;*
> *struct Xx_answer_in_dcb *input_dcb;*

> struct Xx_answer_out_dcb **inout_dcb;

When the answer function is called the HLSP receives the association response service primitive from the ASE, and, if correct, sends a synchronous request to the PSP so that it provides to send out an *a_associate* response primitive. At the end of this operation, the corresponding return event is noted.

The *release* request is a requester mode low-level function call, which pairs request and confirmation primitives. A connection established by a *connect* or *answer* function call is terminated via the release request. This function can be issued as soon as the intended connection is established by means of a *connect* or *answer* function call. The function call format is shown below:

> Return_code xx_rrequest(connection_id, return_event_name,
> input_dcb, inout_dcb)
> connection_id connection_id;
> Local_event_name return_event_name;
> struct Xx_relreq_in_dcb *input_dcb;
> struct Xx_relreq_out_dcb **inout_dcb;

When this function call is used, the CSP gets the release request primitive from the ASE and passes the *a_release* to the PSP waiting for the response from the PSP indicating the acceptance or rejection of the request. If no response is received, a solicitation is generated to the PSP waiting for the confirmation. If a confirmation or an error is notified, then a suitable return event is generated. If the function completes successfully, the number of associations per AE invocation for the AE invocation associated with the connection identifier is decremented.

When a *release* indication is received and processed by the protocol machine associated with a connection established by the *connect* or *answer* functions, an *a_release* response will be issued:

> Return_code xx_rrsp (connection_id, return_event_name,
> input_dcb, inout_dcb)
> connection_id connection_id;
> Local_event_name return_event_name;
> struct Xx_relresp_in_dcb *input_dcb;
> struct Xx_relreq_out_dcb **inout_dcb;

In this case the HSLP receives the release response primitive from the ASE and then sends it to the PSP waiting for the result, noting the related event.

The *abort* function is used to terminate an association. When used, all application interface service provider resources associated with the connection identifier are freed and the request is processed by the protocol machine associated with the connection identifier. In this case, the HLSP receives the abort request from the ASE and generates an abort request to the PSP. The number of associations per AE invocation for the AE invocation associated with the connection identifier is decremented. The structure of the function call is as follows:

> *Return_code xx_abort (connection_id, return_event_name,*
> *input_dcb, inout_dcb)*
> *connection_id connection_id;*
> *Local_event_name return_event_name;*
> *struct Xx_abort_in_dcb *input_dcb;*
> *struct Xx_output_dcb **inout_dcb;*

When applications are developed in an asynchronous environment, programs should always have an outstanding *indication receive* call to accept incoming indications such as abort or release ones, taking into account that all applications should be prepared to deal with an indication whenever it arrives.

The use of this function involves the IFA module, which performs the following actions:

- if an indication is not available, it waits until either it is received or the connection is aborted or released;
- received information is placed in the input/output area, and the event is noted.

The function call is structured according to the following syntax:

> *Return_code xx_Indication Receive (connection_id, input_dcb,*
> *return_event_name, inout_dcb)*
> *connection_id connection_id;*
> *Local_event_name return_event_name;*
> *struct Xx_indication_out_dcb **inout_dcb;*
> *Uint32 *indication_name*

11.6 Private communication application interface

The private communication application interface has been designed to support communications between two application entities which have agreed to exchange data via a specific MAP context called *private*. It provides users with direct access to the ACSE and presentation layer services. In order to do that, an application entity must be activated using the application entity activation service introduced in the previous section. When an AE has been activated, it can attempt to establish an association with a remote AE by means of a connection service specifying that the *private* application context has to be used. The remote AE may use a *listen* service to wait for incoming association indications, and, when an indication is received which specifies the private application context, the *listen* service informs the user about that. The user, in his turn, can respond by means of an *answer* service.

When an association has been established between the two AEs involved in the communication, data may be transferred using the *private data transfer service*. When the transfer is complete and no more data exchanges are needed, the association can be terminated by means of a *release* request service or the corresponding *release* response service, or the *abort* service request. At the remote end of the connection, data are retrieved by means of the *indication receive service*.

The basic aim of the *private communications application interface* is supporting the exchange of user data between remote users; hence, a key role of this interface is to pass user information to the network service provider. In this framework the *UserData* type becomes an important reference point to describe information to be transferred. In particular the type *UserData* refers to a sequence of one or more pairs of *presentation context identifier and data element*. The presentation context identifier indicates the abstract syntaxes used to describe the corresponding data to be transferred. It is assumed that the *UserData* parameter, provided as input by the user, will be used by the network service provider to perform the encoding of the exposed values into the transfer representation negotiated by the presentation service provider.

It should be noted that, even if the *private communication application interface* provides direct access to presentation layer services, this is not the only interface to these services. Even if, as described in Chapter 4, the presentation layer includes the encoding of a user representation of an abstract syntax into the negotiated transfer syntax and the decoding of a negotiated transfer syntax into the user representation of the corresponding abstract syntax, the private communication interface may specify that the encoding and decoding functions be handled in the private communication interface or, even, in the application itself.

The reasons for this choice depend on the fact that the user is allowed to tune a specific configuration with the aim of getting better performance. As an example, the user may not be satisfied with the possibly slow encoding/decoding process provided by the presentation layer. In this case, it can obtain a faster operation outside the communication facilities, using, for example, external hardware support.

A specific service for the private communication application interface is the *private data transfer service* which prepares and sends a user-generated buffer to be transferred by the network service provider. This request is considered complete when the service provider has copied the user data out of the user provided buffer or when an error has been found. When an asynchronous call is used, the private data transfer service only initiates an event asking the service provider to transfer the data available in the user buffer. To do this, the service provider makes its own copy of the data and notes a return event when this operation has been completed. In this case, the user may still reuse the posted buffer. It should be noted that while the service is in progress, which means that the return event has not yet been noted, the user must not change the buffer contents.

If the data transfer service is issued synchronously, the function will return after the service provider has finished copying the data from the source buffer and has completed any other required operation. In this case, the source buffer can be reused without problems.

The *private data transfer* function call definition is as follows:

Sint32 pc_pdtransfer (connection_id, return_event_name,
inout_dcb, user_data, eom)
Uint32 connection_id;
Local_event_name return_event_name;
*struct Pc_output_dcb **inout_dcb;*
*struct UserData *user_data;*
bool eom;

To exemplify the connection procedure, Figure 11.6 describes the model for connection establishment.

11.7   Conclusions

Since users must be able to to choose between competing communication MAP/TOP boards on the basis of performance and price, it is necessary for all the boards to support the same interface to the user program. For this reason, MAP and TOP specifications define a common and generalized application program interface. In particular, it has been specified that when a process has to establish an association the *activate* function call has to be used, whose format has also been defined in detail. This call provides for the authentication of the process and the registering of it as a legal network user. The activate call returns a 32 bit integer to the caller which will use it as its own identifier in subsequent calls. After this, the process acting as a server has to perform a *listen* function call, which prepares the process to accept connection requests coming from remote client processes. Two options are available for the call: in the former the function is blocked waiting for an indication reception, in the lat-

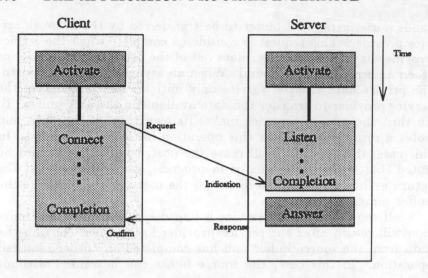

Figure 11.6   Connection establishment in the Private Communication Interface.

ter the function does not block the process, which may continue its computations. In this case a *wait* function call can be used to stop the process activity, specifying the event related to the reception of an indication.

When a client performs a *connection* request (corresponding to an *a_associate* request), the server is awakened and parameters associated with the incoming parameters are transferred to it by means of the *a_associate* indication. The server examines the parameters and can reject or accept the association by means of an *answer* call which generates an *a_associate* response. The PDU transferred to the originator (the client) contains an *a_associate* confirm, which completes the transaction establishing or denying the connection.

References

[DIJKSTRA]   Dijkstra, E.W., *Cooperating Sequential Processes in Programming Languages*, ed. F.Genuys, Academic Press, New York, 1968.

[MAPTOPAPI]   *Manufacturing Automation Protocol Specification*, Version 3.0, Vol. III, 1988.

Chapter 12

Pilot Applications

12.1 Introduction

The MAP and TOP specification [MAPTOP] represents the most publicized work in the area of standardization for factory automation in the United States of America. European industries also saw the organization of a complementary project on manufacturing networks as vital. This led to the foundation in January 1986 of a project addressing a Communication Network for Manufacturing Applications (CNMA), supported by the European Communities under the ESPRIT initiative. This project gathers together a set of European industries coordinated by British Aerospace. It should be noted that the aim of CNMA is the definition of the same final profile for manufacturing applications as the MAP program. MAP strongly represents North American needs, while CNMA follows European users' requirements for multivendor internetworking down to the level of device controllers. Within a manufacturing cell, in most cases, American industries use primarily a single vendor's controllers and related proprietary communication systems, since their main need is linking together a variety of different manufacturing cells. In Europe, many companies do not have the same financial capability, and so ask for multi-vendor equipment down to the level of robots, machine tools

471

and so on.

The main purpose of CNMA is to focus its activity upon higher layers (application and presentation) and this is also a major topic of the MAP project which has been addressed in MAP 3.0. CNMA has contributed greatly to the MAP evolution through its research and implementation work in this area, in order to aid the definition of a single international profile of communications for use in the manufacturing environment. In particular, CNMA is making strenuous efforts to maintain compatibility with MAP. One of the main activities in meeting the user requirements is the selection of a suitable unambiguous profile of communication protocols incorporating both existing and emerging standards. This work can be considered as an integration of the activities which led to version 3.0 of the MAP and TOP specifications.

This chapter also emphasizes reduced protocol profiles oriented to real-time requirements often present at cell-level operations. A case study developed by the research group to which the authors belong is described in the following, and attention is drawn to implementation details.

12.2   The CNMA project

The profile is documented in an implementation guide [CNMA40] which represents the specification for all CNMA implementations. The structure of the guide includes the following elements:

- *transport profile*, whose purpose is to address the issues of network connections, addressing and reliable data transfer;
- *application profile*, which contains mechanisms for the control and exchange of messages between application-specific protocols and services such as MMS, FTAM, and Directory Service;
- *application interfaces*, which standardizes the interface to the communication software, so that the portability of user applications is greatly improved; MMS and FTAM are specified in that document.

Each document assigns a chapter to each layer or service. In particular, for layers 1 and 2 CNMA acknowledges the benefit to users of providing a choice of LAN type. In this way, a user may choose a type according to cost, performance, mantainability and installed base.

Initially, MAP opted only for the broadband technology and then extended it to cover carrierband with token bus access, but studies in Europe showed that 98% of LAN installations have opted for baseband technology. As a consequence, CNMA chose also to include baseband in its profile, which is the same as that supported by the TOP specification.

Layers 3 to 5 are designed to conform to MAP; these layers are more stable than layers 6 and 7 and are thus defined as *background* layers of the architecture. For layer 6 CNMA specifies the use of a kernel subset, while layer 7 protocols are defined in a set of chapters, the first of which defines the ACSE, referring to the latest ISO draft international standard protocol. Other chapters present FTAM, Network Management and Directory Service.

In particular, CNMA's MMS is based on the International Standard (IS) specification, while MAP MMS is based on a Draft International Standard (DIS). Moreover, in the absence of companion standards, which are currently under final approval by ISO, the current CNMA implementation guide specifies subsets of services for PLCs (programmable logic controllers), NCs (numeric controllers), and other devices. CNMA has also proposed certain extensions to the MAP specifications, probably the most notable being MAP over Ethernet, and will continue to work in this direction based on the input of the CNMA users.

However, it should be noted that CNMA is not an alternative to MAP, since both have a common goal, which is the use of international standards to implement a communications network for manufacturing applications.

MAP needs to ensure that future specifications are unambiguous and implementable and can therefore take advantage of CNMA's experience. Moreover, it must be pointed out that MAP and TOP specifications are the building blocks around which CNMA develops. Figure 12.1 points out the structure of the CNMA architecture.

By applying CNMA implementations to real production environments, CNMA partners have gained considerable experience which is now used to provide OSI products such as MAP 3.0 by CNMA vendors and to apply such products by CNMA users. It should also be noted that CNMA products, in terms of software developed for the application layer, represent an improvement with respect to the MAP 3.0 specifications, since they include more recent ISO/OSI features. Hence those products are marketed both as MAP V3.0 products and MAP V3.0 compatible with OSI enhancements.

12.3 The ISW pilot project

The *Institut fur Steuerungstechnik der Werkzeugmaschinen und Fertigungseinsichuungen* of the University of Stuttgart (ISW) has provided an experimental pilot facility where the benefits of open systems communications are demonstrated. The pilot comprises all the features which are typical of a CIM environment and provides applications for each of the CNMA's vendors. Computer equipment (including minicomputers, PCs and controllers) from each participant vendor is used and, in this way, the pilot represents a real heterogeneous environment. It is divided into two independent parts:

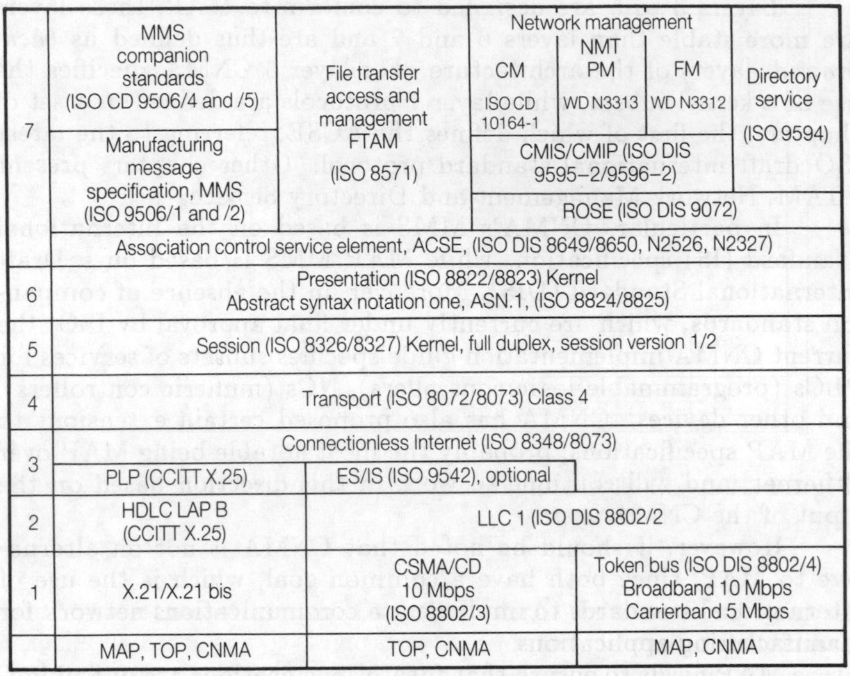

	MMS companion standards (ISO CD 9506/4 and /5)	File transfer access and management FTAM (ISO 8571)	Network management			Directory service (ISO 9594)
				NMT		
			CM	PM	FM	
7			ISO CD 10164-1	WD N3313	WD N3312	
	Manufacturing message specification, MMS (ISO 9506/1 and /2)		CMIS/CMIP (ISO DIS 9595–2/9596–2)			
			ROSE (ISO DIS 9072)			
	Association control service element, ACSE, (ISO DIS 8649/8650, N2526, N2327)					
6	Presentation (ISO 8822/8823) Kernel — Abstract syntax notation one, ASN.1, (ISO 8824/8825)					
5	Session (ISO 8326/8327) Kernel, full duplex, session version 1/2					
4	Transport (ISO 8072/8073) Class 4					
3	Connectionless Internet (ISO 8348/8073)					
	PLP (CCITT X.25)	ES/IS (ISO 9542), optional				
2	HDLC LAP B (CCITT X.25)	LLC 1 (ISO DIS 8802/2)				
1	X.21/X.21 bis	CSMA/CD 10 Mbps (ISO 8802/3)	Token bus (ISO DIS 8802/4) Broadband 10 Mbps Carrierband 5 Mbps			
	MAP, TOP, CNMA	TOP, CNMA	MAP, CNMA			

Figure 12.1   CNMA communication profile.

the first, which is a fully automated manufacturing cell, is used to show time-critical data exchange between controllers, while the second part consists of a single five-axis milling machine and is used to demonstrate the information flow between computer aided design (CAD), computer aided programming and the numerical controller (NC).

The manufacturing cell consists of the following elements:

- a turning center (INDEX GU 600)
- a machining center (EX-CELL-O- XS 800)
- a local pallet store
- a linear portal robot.

Both centers are standard numerical controlled machine tools equipped with automatic clamps to fix the workpieces for the machining process. The turning center is based on three numerical control axes: two linear and one rotary axis, while the machining center has three numerical controlled linear axes and a switched rotating table.

It can be seen in Figure 12.2 that a pallet store is also available. It includes four conveyors belts arranged in a rectangle where a maximum number of sixteen pallets with one workpiece per pal-

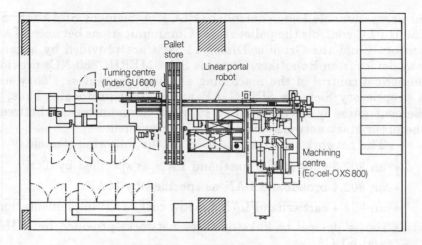

Figure 12.2 Fully automated manufacturing cell at ISW: mechanical layout.

let may be circulated. An output and input position is also made available for manual exchange of workpieces to and from an external store. At a second point exchanges of workpieces to and from the machine tools can take place.

Between the pallet store and the machine tools within the cell, there is a linear portal robot, which provides for workpiece handling. It is provided with two linear and one rotary axis which allow the gripper to move into any position within the portal's area.

The five-axis milling machine (Deckel FP2H) has three linear and two rotary axes. It is used to produce single parts of complex workpieces, such as models for casting tools. There is no automatic workpiece handling in this part of the pilot. This task, as well as the starting of the machining process, has to be done manually by an operator. Part-programs for the machining process are downloaded from a file server onto the machine controller.

12.3.1 Computer and devices

Seven European vendors provided fourteen computers and controller devices to be connected to the network. In particular, the configuration of the system is based on the availability of a Nixdorf Targon 35 which supports Computer Aided Design (CAD) operations and order entry functions, while an Olivetti LSX 3020 minicomputer provides computer aided programming (CAP) and fileserver functions for management of partprograms. A BULL DPX 2000 minicomputer supports a shopfloor control system, while the cell control software runs on a Bull IBM 600 personal computer (PC).

The linear portal robot is controlled by means of a GEC GEM

80 programmable logic controller (PLC). A Siemens SIMATIK S5 150 U PLC controls the pallet store. Communications between MAP protocols and the Grundig Dialog 11 NCs are provided by a gateway device from Robotiker. Siemens SINUMERIK 880 NCs provide numerical control of the machining and turning centers. They use a proprietary Siemens SINEC AP automation protocol. Thus, a Siemens gateway is employed to support communications between the proprietary network and the OSI environment.

The network structure is based on the following elements:

- an 802.3 CSMA/CD baseband LAN as specified by TOP;
- an 802.4 broadband LAN as specified by MAP;
- an 802.4 carrierband LAN for low cost MAP implementation;
- router devices to link the three networks provided by BULL and GEC.

To integrate the different applications, MMS and FTAM are used, and, since MAP products do not implement a complete set of network services directly, fault and configuration management are supported by BULL and the Fraunhofer Institute, while performance management is provided by Siemens.

12.3.2   The software structure

Five important areas for CIM are covered:

- production management
- computer aided design
- shopfloor control
- cell control
- machine control.

Figure 12.3 gives a mapping scheme for application software on the various parts of the system architecture. The shopfloor and cell control software are used within the manufacturing cell, while the CAP and CAD software are used within the five-axis milling part of the pilot.

Production management is a simple order entry application and performs those functions necessary for generation, modification and deletion of manufacturing orders to be processed by the shopfloor control system. A standard software package has been adopted for shopfloor control. It is called AGIS and has been developed for Bull and adapted to CNMA's OSI communication requirements by Alcatel-TITN.

Data exchange between the shopfloor control system and the relevant machine controllers occurs through a cell controller whose software has also been developed by Alcatel TITN. The cell architecture is based on the following elements:

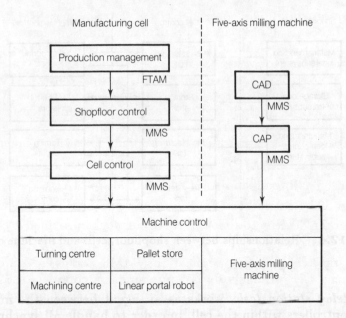

Figure 12.3 Application software configuration.

- *Manufacturing task*: this acts as an agent between the manufacturing local control system of AGIS and the NCs of the turning and machining centers. When a machine tool is ready for the next machining process, enabling requests are generated to the shopfloor controller. If a positive response is received from the controller, then part-programs and command sequences are downloaded to the corresponding NCs and the machining process is started. When the machining process has been completed, AGIS is informed in order to take appropriate actions.

- *Storage task*: operates as an interface between the storage local control subsystem of AGIS and the PLC of the pallet store. It manages action sequences of the PLCs for internal or external input or output of workpieces. In the case of internal activity, pieces are exchanged between the machine tools and the local pallet store, while for external activity workpieces are exchanged between the local and an external store.

- *Material handling task*: works as an interface between the material local control subsystem of AGIS and the PLC of the linear portal robot. It handles action sequences for the PLC for the transport of workpieces from the pallet store to one of the machine tools and vice versa.

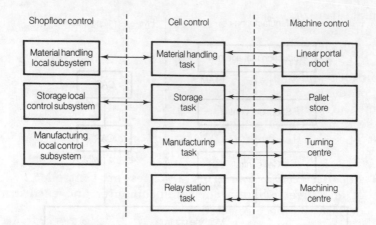

Figure 12.4   Relationships between shopfloor, cell, and machine control.

- *Relay station task*: works as an agent between the machine controllers within the cell, in order to handle all synchronization requirements between the controllers. This has been provided since no wired I/O signals are used for those functions.

Figure 12.4 shows the interrelationships between the different elements.

Specific software has been developed for implementing the various functionalities of each machine within the manufacturing cell. The pilot's network administration application covers three of the five functional areas of network management, in particular:

- *Performance management*: provides monitoring of network behavior and detection of bottlenecks within the network;
- *Configuration management*: which provides the administration of communication parameters;
- *Fault management*: which provides the detection and diagnosis of faults.

Security and accounting management functions have not been implemented according to the suggestions provided by MAP 3.0 specifications.

12.4   Magneti Marelli

This pilot implementation within the CNMA project is currently under development in the San Salvo area, which is about 700 km south of Milan. This plant belongs to the Electromechanical Group of Magneti Marelli and represents a highly productive and flexible manufacturing organization devoted to the production of starter motors, alternators, rotators for wipers and batteries for cars and other motor vehicles.

The production line for alternators has been chosen for developing the pilot project, which includes three different sections: shaft production, rotor production and final assembling. Stators are manufactured independently and then assembled to the rotors in the final section of the pilot line.

The pilot line includes 24 stations organized into two different sections. The basic elements of the line are the following:

- *Robotized cell 1*: four arms (1–3 axes) are controlled by means of an Olivetti Sigma 8600 minicomputer and each arm can declare the piece rejected;
- *Robotized cell 2*: three arms are controlled by an Olivetti minicomputer; after any operation the piece can be declared rejected and in this case subsequent operations are inhibited;
- *Automatic test station*: in this station the handling system is controlled by a Siemens PC and dedicated CPUs monitor testing procedures; the operator can specify or examine the following parameters:
  - list of workpiece types
  - parameters associated with each type
  - accepted average values
  - statistics.

Pieces not conforming to the specified parameters and performance are transferred to the repair station.

12.4.1   Application software

Application software implements general monitoring functions, production tracking control and diagnostic signals management.

Production monitoring collects data about the system efficiency and performance to be used as a feed-back for production planning and control. Tracking represents a different approach for data collection at the shop floor level, since traces for work in progress are made available. While monitoring functions detect information about automated equipment, tracking allows direct control on production characteristics. Diagnostic signals management carries out acquisition of data related to the machines involved in the manufacturing process, in order to point out the technical causes of faults and the device's physical state.

Referring to the CIM architecture as defined in the literature and depicted in Figure 12.5, the pilot project includes the two lower layers, while only few functions have been developed for the plant controller layer.

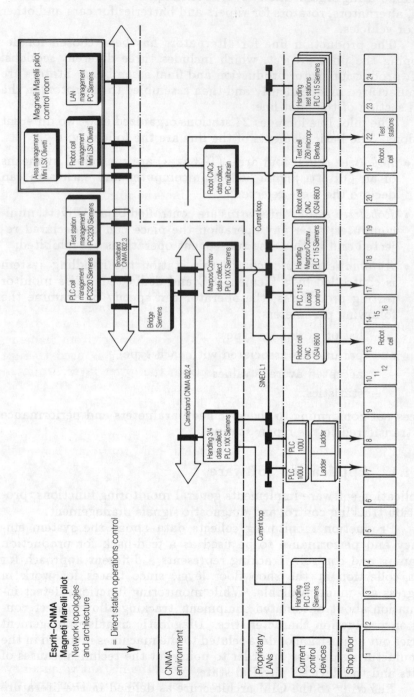

Figure 12.5 CIM architecture.

12.4.2 Hardware and communication issues

At the lower layer of the CIM architecture PLCs and NCs are allocated represented by Siemens PLCs for the *handling systems*, microprocessors-based units (Bertola processing units) for the *test stations* and Olivetti OSAI 8600 CNC for the *robot assembly stations*. The second layer involves Siemens PCs to implement PLCs Cell Control and an Olivetti minicomputer LSX used as a *robot cell controller*. At the third layer an Olivetti minicomputer LSX is devoted to *area control* functions.

The network architecture is based on the use of two different technologies chosen according to performance requirements. For the lower layers an IEEE 802.4 carrierband-based solution has been chosen to connect the Siemens PLC controlling the simpler devices. The two robotized assembly stations and the test stations are currently not connected directly to the network.

A 802.3 baseband technology has been introduced to support communication involving the higher layer of the architecture, which means data exchanges occurring between the Siemens PCs, the Olivetti minicomputer devoted to station subgroups management and the area controller. A station devoted to backup functions is also connected to this segment of the LAN. It can be noted that the two segments are connected by means of a bridge from Siemens. Proprietary solutions are also used: a *SINEC L1* is used to support data exchange involving PLCs from the lower layer, while an *OLINET LAN* is used to handle data exchange between OSAI NCs and the baseband network through an Olivetti PC-250.

The complete stack of CNMA 4.0 (MAP 3.0) has been implemented on the area and cell controllers. All communications performed between the CNMA environment and proprietary networks take place by means of gateways.

12.4.3 Cell controllers and shop-floor devices

Device status is examined periodically by the cell controllers, which can reach PLCs through the concentrators responsible for data collection. Other information to be collected concerns operation cycle times associated with the different devices. In fact each device on the shop floor carries out a specific operation within a time interval which is typical for the device itself. This interval includes the following elements:

- *loading time*: this is the time between the instant when a new part is loaded on the device for the next operation and the start of the operation itself;
- *device time*: this is the time needed to complete the operation specified by the program related to the device;

- *unloading time*: this is the time between the operation terminating and the instant when the piece is transferred from the device to the line.

The time interval obtained by the sum of those three time parts is the time elapsed between the beginning of a loading phase for a workpiece to the next one and constitutes the *cycle time* for the device. This information plays a basic role for the evaluation of the efficiency of the device, hence, it must be made available to the cell controller by means of a reliable mechanism. For this purpose an unsolicited confirmed service has been used and each line device controller sends to the cell supervisor information related to loading, work, and unload time at the end of the operation on the part currently involved in the process.

To collect status information on devices and controllers, a simple polling mechanism is used, which is based on a time period of 5 seconds. Tracking information is also collected by means of the same approach and using a time period of one minute.

Diagnostic data are generated by the device itself, which sends them, when available, using an unsolicited service.

12.4.4   Area manager and cell controllers

The minicomputer Olivetti LSX is devoted to area management (AM) functions and interacts with the three cell controllers by means of application associations. In this context, cell controllers transfer information related to the controlled devices by means of unsolicited services. The AM processes that information to develop statistical evaluation for the production process.

It should be noted that two cell controllers implement gateway functions too. In particular the Robot Cell Controller interacts with the multibrain unit (Olivetti PC 250) by means of the OLINET protocols on a baseband physical channel. This was possible since the first four layers of both CNMA and OLINET protocol profiles are the same. The application software includes an interface to convert MMS-like data typical of the CNMA environment into the syntax and semantics needed by the OLINET approach.

The test cell controller and the test banks communicate by means of dedicated point-to-point links and specific non-standard protocols. At the application level, MMS-like services have been translated into data and commands typical of the proprietary environment.

12.5   The FAIS project

The FAIS (Factory Automation Interconnection System) is a project pursued by the International Robotics and Factory Automation Center (IROFA) under a commission from the Ministry of International

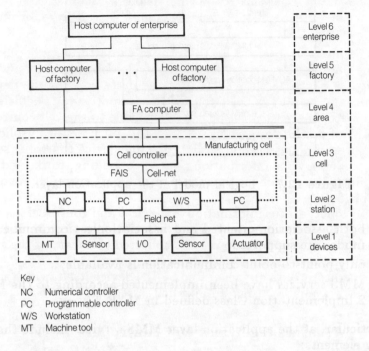

Figure 12.6   Aim of the FAIS network: interconnectivity.

Trade and Industry. The aim of the project concerns the development of a common and generalized solution for the interconnection of automatic equipment used in manufacturing.

Activities have been concentrated on the development of a technology oriented to solving interconnection problems at the cell level, with the final purpose of providing easy interconnectivity between equipment from different vendors.

Since MAP commercialization started with 'FullMAP' systems, generally unsuited to cell-level real-time requirements, the MiniMAP approach has been chosen for the project [MiniMAP]. For data transmission, optical fiber cables have been chosen in addition to the coaxial cable.

12.5.1   The communication architecture

A three-layer architecture has been adopted, in accordance with the MiniMAP specifications, so that MAP compatibility is ensured. Figure 12.6 shows the protocol architecture defined for the FAIS project. The functions specified for MiniMAP and MMS have been chosen according to the following points:

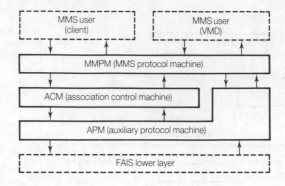

Figure 12.7   Logical model of the application layer.

- both association-oriented and associationless communication modes are supported;
- only point-to-point communication is available;
- MMS services have been implemented according to the MAP 2 Implementation Class defined in MAP 3.0.

In particular, at the application layer MMS services include the following elements:

- Initiate
- Cancel
- GetNameList
- Write
- Conclude

- Reject
- Identify
- GetVariableAccessAttributes
- Abort
- Status.

Figure 12.7 describes the model for the upper layer of the protocol profile. Dotted lines are used to indicate elements not included in MiniMAP specifications, hence not considered in FAIS specifications. The application layer is composed of three different modules:

- *MMPM*: the *manufacturing message protocol machine* implements the MMS protocol mechanisms;
- *ACM*: the *association control machine* is responsible for associations management;
- *APM*: the *auxiliary protocol machine* handles interface mechanisms to the lower layer.

Connections to the lower layer are carried out by means of LSAPs oriented to the type of communication modes. In fact, three types of LSAPs have been introduced: association oriented, associationless and association unspecified. Six types of PDUS have also been defined:

- ASOC_ORIENTED_PDU
- INITIATE_PDU
- ABORT_PDU
- ASSOCIATION_LESS_PDU
- CONCLUDE_PDU
- REJECT_PDU

At the application layer, each protocol data unit contains auxiliary protocols as a prefix of the MMS PPDU in order to specify PDU types. The basic specifications for the application layer may be stated as follows:

- both association-oriented and associationless communication modes are required;
- both association-oriented and associationless LSAP orientations are required;
- the maximum length of upper layer PDUs is 1024 octects.

12.5.2 Lower layers

For the logical link control (LLC), the FAIS implementation specifications assume the standard ISO 8802-2 LLC Class III specification, while the MAC sublayer and the physical layer specification refer to the ISO 8802-4 token passing bus mechanism. In particular, the following guidelines have been taken into account:

- priorities for service and access classes are required;
- Request_with_Response functions are required;
- data transfer with confirmation functions for LLC Type 3 must be supported.

Parameter values for the MAC sublayer depend on the size of the whole system. However, specifications report sample settings for an assumed system of 500–1000 meters with about 32 nodes.

In case of fiber optics, two different aspects are considered. Table 12.1 shows parameters for a moderate and a high sensitivity approach: values specified conform to IEEE 802.4 specifications.

12.5.3 Testing procedures

Thirteen companies were involved in the project, as shown in Table 12.2, and twelve systems have been developed, using carrier band and optical transmission lines. Specific tests have been developed to experience interoperability at the level of the service for both the application and data-link layer. However, communication between

Table 12.1   Fiber optic implementation specification.

Implementation specification		
Items	Moderate sensitivity	High sensitivity
Topology	Passive star	Passive star
Number of nodes	8	32
Maximum distance between nodes and starcoupler	500 mt	500 mt
Maximum number of splices between nodes and starcoupler	2	2

Table 12.2   Companies involved in the FAIS project.

Companies involved in FAIS
Fanuc Ltd
Fuji Electric Co., Ltd
Fujitsu Ltd
Matshushita Electric Industrial Co., Ltd
Mitsubishi Electric. Corp.
NEC Corp.
Omron Corp.
Sumitomo Electric Industries Ltd
Yamatake-Honiwell Co., Ltd
Yokogawa Electric Corp.

application programs simulating real life have also been developed to create imaginary situations and check interconnectivity at the application level. Application programs were planned on the base of the following situations:

- *Robot equipment control*: the cell controller handles a robot which mounts and removes parts and an NC (numerically controlled) unit to process them;

- *Handler and electric furnace control*: the cell supervisor controls an electric furnace which is fed and voided by a handler;

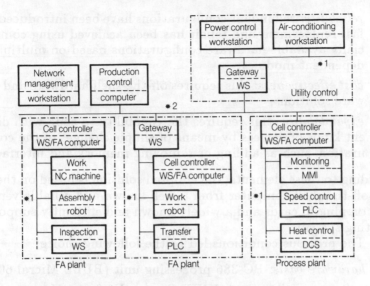

Figure 12.8 Plan for the FAIS project demonstration.

- *PCB mounting system*: the cell controller controls two different component mounting units based on either ICs or discrete components on printed circuits boards;
- *Water management system*: the cell controller handles motors and values to supply or remove water to the system.

Currently, work is going on to implement an entire plant, Figure 12.8 reports the whole scheme. Interconnection between MiniMAP and FullMAP networks is also planned.

12.6 Migration strategies

New standards-based approaches may be introduced in the factory in a non-traumatic way only if previous investments can be saved and proprietary solutions integrated in the system to be developed. The problem may be partially solved by using gateways to OSI LANs.

In particular, all the projects examined before always include proprietary subnetworks connected to the standard environment by means of gateways. As an example, within the framework of CNMA, ROBOTIKER developed an example of a cost effective tool oriented to the integration into a production environment of a great number of existing industrial devices. This solution is based on a *programmable network interface unit* (PNIU), which is generally known as *gateway*. The following requirements have been taken as a reference point for the development of this equipment:

- *protection*: electrical and mechanical aspects have been taken into account;

- *reliability*: redundant configurations have been introduced and fast replacement and repair has been achieved using commercially available hardware configurations based on multiple independent modules;

- *cost effectiveness*: this requires off-the-shelf hardware and software solutions;

- *expandability*: this requires the capability to cope with different kinds of devices by means of simple changes of the configuration, such as adding or removing memory and interfaces.

According to these elements, the adopted solution is based on the use of an off-the-shelf computer from a well known and reliable vendor, based on plug-in cards and a widely known and efficiently supported operating system.

The previous conditions led to the following choice:

- *hardware basis*: PC-386 processing unit (BULL Micral 600)
- *software environment*: UNIX System V3.2 from Interactive
- *communication interface boards*:

    - CONCORD's MAPware series 1200 for PC Bus System with LLC interface PROM for the CNMA network and carrier modems;
    - RS 232 and RS 485 interface boards for proprietary devices.

Figure 12.9 reports a schema of the gateway architecture, which includes the following elements:

- *CNMA stack*, that implements the OSI side of the gateway and performs the functions of server in the CNMA network; it should be noted that layers one and two are supported by a CONCORD MAP board, while layers three to seven are installed on the PC386; the higher layers have been ported from BULL, which participates in the CNMA project as a vendor;

- *proprietary stack*: this implements the proprietary side of the gateway and can work as either a client or a server for the proprietary connections, depending on the user-defined configuration; each stack is also responsible for translating MMS elements into the corresponding items of the proprietary protocols;

- *gateway application*: the basic function provided by this module is routing management between the CNMA stack and the proprietary ones.

Figure 12.10 shows a more detailed representation of the proprietary stack architecture, pointing out the following modules:

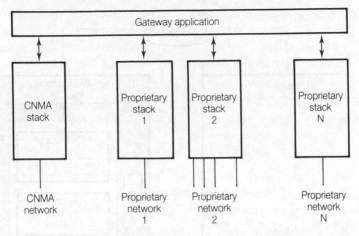

Figure 12.9 Gateway architecture.

- *MMS interface*: this module provides a partial MMS interface to applications, the same as that provided by the CNMA stack; this allows a cell controller application running on the gateway to perform a direct use of the proprietary stack; in this case, gateway and cell control use the same hardware support;
- *VMDs manager*: each device directly connected to the gateway has a VMD associated with it containing a software image related to the behavior of the device itself;
- *MMS/proprietary application protocol translator*: this performs protocol translation between MMS and the Proprietary Application Services;
- *Proprietary protocol libraries*: this module implements the proprietary protocol;
- *Device driver*: this gives access to the proprietary network interface;
- *Proprietary network interface*: this module supports part of the proprietary protocol;
- *Timer process*: this is used to implement MMS timeouts;
- *Receptor process*: this is used to collect incoming messages from the serial board or network interface when this board is not able to interrupt processes running in the gateway CPU.

Two different pilot systems in the CNMA project are based on the use of the ROBOTIKER gateway and are described in the following section.

Stuttgart pilot installation

In this implementation a numerical controller from GRUNDIG (Dialog 11), can exchange information with other devices through the

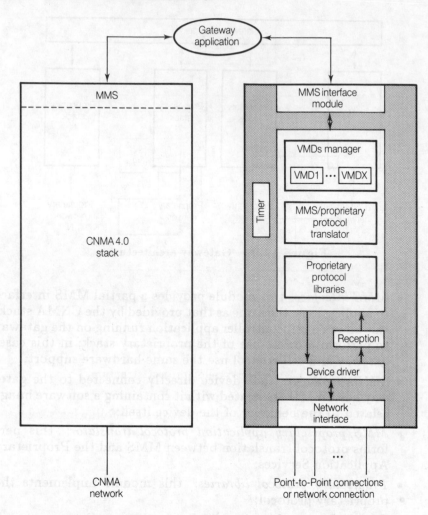

Figure 12.10   Gateway detailed organization.

CNMA networks. The gateway is used to allow CAD/NC links as shown in Figure 12.11. The geometrical desciption of a designed workpiece is transferred from a Nixdorf Targon processing unit into an Olivetti LSX3020, which provides for the generation of the NC part-programs using that geometrical description. NC programs are then downloaded to the NC unit by means of MMS services provided by the gateway. The Grundig NC controls a five-axis milling machine, where part-programs are executed under the direct control of an operator. Since no automatic material flow is available and reduced data exchange functions are provided by the proprietary protocol of the NC, communication to it is reduced to download and upload operations, which are started by the operator of the NC.

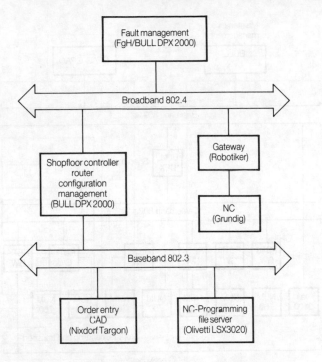

Figure 12.11 ISW pilot project structure.

In this case the gateway only provides the following services:

- *Context management*
    - Initiate
    - Conclude
    - Abort
    - Reject.
- *Domain management*
    - InitiateDownloadSequence
    - DownloadSegment
    - TerminateDownloadSequence
    - InitiateUploadSequence
    - UploadSegment
    - TerminateUploadSequence
    - RequestDomainDownload
    - RequestDomainUpload.

No hardware is used to communicate with the NC: the Grundig Dialog 11 protocol is supported completely by the gateway CPU and messages are interchanged by means of a standard RS 232 board. At the OSI side, the gateway is connected to an 802.4 broadband segment.

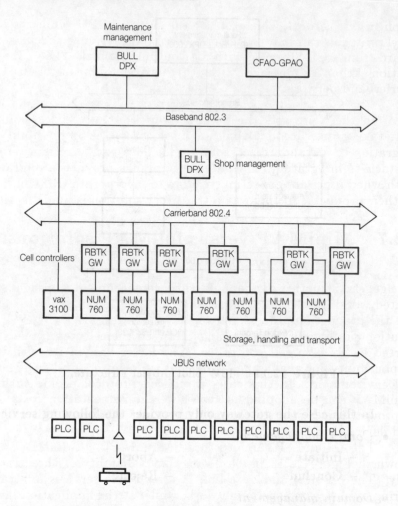

Figure 12.12   AEROSPATIAL pilot installation.

Aerospatial pilot installation

This implementation provides translation between MMS and UNI-TEL WAY messages, so that seven NUM 760 numerical controllers can exchange information with other devices through the CNMA networks, as shown in Figure 12.12.

The NC equipment controls four machining centres and three lathes and, by MMS links provided by the gateways, exchanges data with two applications. One application runs in the same processing unit as the gateway and performs a cell control task, the other is an application, installed on a BULL DPX 2000, devoted to the maintenance of data gathered accessing all field equipment. In this application the complete list of MMS services is provided by the gateway. The gateway implementation includes the UNITEL WAY application protocol, which runs on the gateway CPU, while the low-level protocols run in a processor located on a separate special serial board from ACL-Stargate with four output channels. The gateway station exchanges messages with other devices by means of an 802.4 carrierband network.

In these projects the gateways functions have been pointed out, taking into account that, in most cases, the impossibility of migration to a standardized solution for data exchange is a serious obstacle to integration. The gateway approach provides a migration path when users are expecting vendors to incorporate OSI solutions to their products. In this way a transitory solution is made feasible.

12.7   MiniMAP versus fullMAP solutions: a case study

The general structure of a manufacturing environment envisages separated working cells able to exchange information in order to carry out the production process. At this level, the full MAP [MAPTOP] solution can handle data exchange between the cells, each one supported by its own cell controller. The latter has, in its turn, the responsibility for managing operations at a lower level inside the cell environment. In this case, a reduced protocol profile such as MiniMAP can be adopted so that lower implementation costs and improved time responses for message transfer between cell control and devices can be guaranteed.

The MiniMAP architecture [MiniMAP], [EMiniMAP] as shown in Figure 12.13, is based on the availability of three layers only. The physical and data-link layers provide services for transferring byte streams on the network, while, at the application layer, more complex functions are made available, such as MMS (see Chapter 6) and DS (see Chapter 5). Moving from the full MAP protocol stack to the MiniMAP reduced solution means that some important functions provided by the intermediate protocol layers are lost, so that a different approach is required. Logical connections must be handled by MMS directly, since the application common service element (ACSE) is not available. Parameter negotiation is not required since predefined values are used: a typical example is given by the message maximum size, which is assumed to be 1Kb. Message coding and decoding to and from an abstract notation is also provided by MMS, the presentation layer not being available. The flow control is obtained by defining a suitable parameter for the maximum number of pending requests for each application association, while routing aspects are not considered since applications operate inside a bounded area. The lack of the transport and network layers implies that communication reliability is guaranteed by the data-link

application protocol which runs on the network side, while the low-
level protocols run in a microcomputer board integrated to special serial
board from G.D. Serarc, which offers 6 digital channels. The gateway
system exchanges messages with the field devices by means of an 80324
card and a network.

Also, *thinness* project developments have been pursued
culminating into account that, in all cases, the impracticability of
conversion to a standard-based solution for data exchange is a serious
obstacle to integration. The practical implementation provides a somewhat
cumbersome decision something always to incorporate Osi solution
to their conductor architecture, but this implementation made feasible,
and uses a *thinness* exchange by this implementation made feasible.

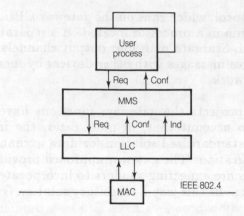

Figure 12.13   MiniMAP system architecture.

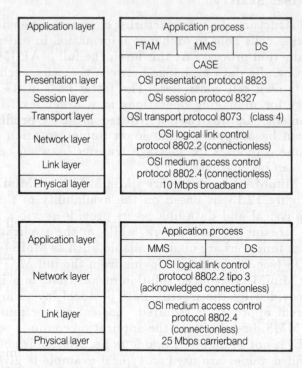

Figure 12.14   MiniMAP and full MAP protocol profiles organization.

layer, where an 'acknowledged-connection' logical link control (LLC)
provides acknowledge messages for frames received from the network
and also guarantees the correct correspondences between messages
sent and their respective acknowledgments.

Figure 12.14 compares the MiniMAP reduced protocol profile
to the full MAP solution.

Since a department Ethernet network was available and previous studies performed on the subject [IEEE1] showed that in most cases the CSMA/CD solution guarantees good performances in spite of its non-deterministic nature, the prototype architecture was developed for CSMA/CD technology. In any case, in accordance with the CNMA protocol profile specification, the development approach allows an easy migration of the implementation to the token bus technology without software changes being required. The logical link control has been developed according to the ISO IEEE 8802.2 [ISO88022] and its addendum for the unacknowledged-connectionless and acknowledged-connectionless services.

At the application layer, MMS services have been developed and user application processes have also been implemented. MMS implementation has been carried out referring to the standard ISO 9506 [ISO9506], while the coding and decoding procedures from/to ASN.1 (see Chapter 4) data format descriptions have been implemented according to the standard ISO8825 [ISO8825]. Since MMS introduces 80 different types of services, not all useful for the purpose of this application, only more general functions have been developed for the prototype network. In any case, work is currently in progress for the development of other functions not available at this time.

12.7.1 MMS – manufacturing message specifications

This protocol has been introduced to support message exchange between equipment used in the factory environment.

In general terms, a factory communication architecture is based on the interaction of manufacturing cells, each one composed of numerical controllers (NC) and programmable logical computers (PLC). These devices exchange information with their cell controller which is reachable through a local network, which provides physical support for information transfer. Figure 12.15 gives an example of such a communication architecture. Typically, automatic equipment, such as numerical controls or programmable logical units, are connected to the physical device to be controlled (robot actuators, conveyors, machine tools, etc.) at one side, while at the other side the connection to the network is provided. In this framework, MMS makes available a set of services to manage the communication between applications executed by the various devices connected to the network.

The basic element of the MMS protocol is represented by the Virtual Manufacturing Device (VMD), which can be used to represent each programmable device. In particular, the VMD describes the device interface towards the external world as depicted in Figure 12.16. Each VMD may contain one or more (if the real device is based on a multiprocessor unit) Application Processes (APs), which may be users of MMS services. In fact, MMS can be thought of as a

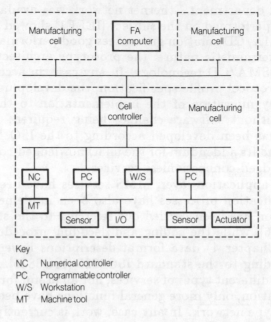

Figure 12.15   A local area network together with the equipment involved in the information exchange process.

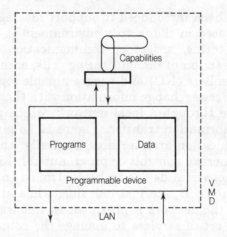

Figure 12.16   The VMD configuration and functionalities.

service library, providing communication and management facilities to the application processes. In this way, functions to read and write remote variables are available, remote programs may be started or stopped and asynchronous events may also be handled.

The MMS standard specification describes such services in abstract terms. These are classified into *confirmed services*, which in-

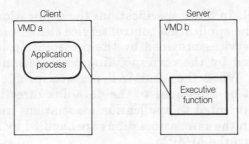

Figure 12.17   Communication between two remote processes by means of an application association.

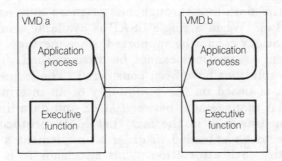

Figure 12.18   A bidirectional channel on an application association.

clude a response from the remote entity about the status of the corresponding request, and *unconfirmed services*, which do not require any response from the destination of the request. The MMS specification involves two basic elements: the *protocol machine* (MMPM – manufacturing message protocol machine) describing the mechanisms to be supported to provide a specific service, and the *executive function* (EF), which is responsible for responding to the requests received from the remote entities. For a better understanding of the MMS functionality, the application entities involved in the communication must be considered as a client interacting with a server. The client, which may be one of the VMD application processes, generates the request and the server, represented by the executive function of the addressed remote entity, provides the requested service. Information exchange between remote entities is accomplished through a virtual channel called an application association (AA), as shown in Figure 12.17. This channel is bidirectional and can be used by two couples of application processes at the same time as described in Figure 12.18.

According to the ISO standard communication architecture, the MMS is a specific application service element (SASE), hence it must be assigned to the application layer (layer 7) in the ISO reference model. In MAP specifications the application association is supported by the application control service element (ACSE), which, in turn, uses services provided by the presentation layer so that it can be identified by the corresponding presentation service access point (PSAP). When the MiniMAP protocol profile is considered, the VMD must be interfaced to the data-link directly, since ACSE functionalities oriented to application associations management are not available. In the case, associations are handled by an appropriate module added to the MMPM.

The standard specifications for MMS state that a VMD may be connected to the lower layer (i.e. presentation) through one or multiple PSAPs: this is possible since application associations are handled by the ACSE module. In case of MiniMAP, a VMD is interfaced to the data-link through one or more link service access points (LSAPs). When a single LSAP is available, multiple application associations cannot be supported, since messages corresponding to different associations cannot be distinguished. To solve this problem two solutions have been considered. The former, proposed in [ISO/TC], is based on the availability of an intermediate layer supporting AA management between MMS and data-link. This approach has a drawback in the fact that MMS protocol data unit formats have to be extended in order to implement a mechanism able to identify each association. This also leads to a violation of the MMS PDU format defined in MMS specifications.

The other solution involves the use of more LSAPs so that each association can be identified by three elements: a local LSAP, the destination node physical address, and a remote LSAP. According to this approach, each VMD in the network is identified by a single LSAP, which can be used by other application processes for their AAs if those associations are not already active. In this case, a new local LSAP must be created in order to support the new association giving it a unique identifier. Figure 12.19 introduces such a mechanism.

Virtual manufacturing device

The virtual manufacturing device (VMD) is a piece of general virtual programmable equipment which includes a manufacturing message protocol machine, to handle protocol and interface mechanisms, and an executive function (EF) able to handle service requests submitted by application processes belonging to other remote VMDs. Inside a VMD there is also a set of application processes, which control the operations to be performed by the real machine represented by the VMD. The application processes and the executive function share a set of variables, which are owned by the real device. These variables must be reachable both by the local and by the remote application processes, which may access them by means of the executive function. As a consequence, a mechanism must also be provided capable of

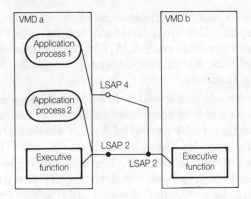

Figure 12.19 An example to address the use of multiple LSAPs to manage several application associations.

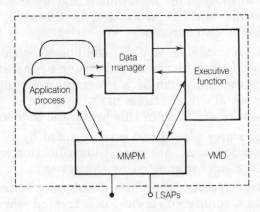

Figure 12.20 The virtual manufacturing device components.

supporting sharable accesses to variables.

The VMD has been implemented using three processes:

- A *manufacturing message protocol machine* (MMPM), to handle protocol mechanisms;

- An *executive function*, to process service requests;

- A *data manager*, to ensure mutual exclusion for shared access.

Application processes are also part of the VMD, as shown in Figure 12.20. Information exchange between processes has been implemented using the mailbox mechanism.

The basic elements needed to create a VMD are:

- *Capability*: represents a local resource of the real device; services available to the user allow one or more capabilities to be managed. MMS standard specifications do not indicate how a capability may be implemented, they only state that different capabilities must be identified by unique names in the VMD environment; each VMD is characterized by a fixed set of capabilities, which are assigned to specific domains by the executive function.

- *Domain*: represents a well defined set of resources belonging to the real device; it is composed of an information field containing a program to be executed by the real machine, or general data to be used by the real device to handle the resource set associated with the domain. For this implementation, the information field has been used to specify the name of the file containing the program to be executed; a domain may be static or dynamic: if static, its structure is defined when the VMD is configured so that resource are permanently assigned to the domain, when dynamic the domain may be created or deleted using specific MMS services and, in this case, the resource association is also dynamic;

- *Program invocation*: is a VMD component with which one or more domains may be associated. Using a program invocation, the MMS user may handle a program executing on the real device; program invocations may be static or dynamic and both cases are available in this prototype implementation;

- *VMD and status identifiers*: is represented by a table containing the vendor name, the model identification and the list of abstract syntaxes supported by the system;

- *Transaction object*: represents an object created by the EF to execute a confirmed service, it is created whenever the EF receives an indication and deleted when the service has been executed and the corresponding answer has been sent to the originator of the request.

The VMD configuration is carried out when the executive function is activated. The aim of the configuration phase is to define all resources of the real device represented by the VMD itself. This is accomplished by the EF reading a memory area or a file where configuration data are stored. In this prototype implementation, the EF reads information from a file where, using a specific notation, all device resources are specified. In particular, the configuration file specifies:

- *Capabilities*, representing real machine resources defined as a character sequence;

- *Static domains*, which are specified by a name, an initial state, and the names of the associated capabilities;

- *Physical variables*, also called *unnamed variables*, to distinguish them from the *named variables* defined in the MMS specifications; these variables must be shared by the EF and application processes; MMS users, by means of using MMS variable handling services, may associate a *named variable* with one or more *physical variables*.

MMS services

MMS services are classified into nine categories [ISO9506] according to the kind of objects processed when services are executed. Each class is composed of a set of specific services. However, in order to meet various application needs, the MMS specification defines nine *conformance building blocks* (CBB) [ISO9506] according to which only a part of the whole set of services of a class must be implemented and, for each service, not all functions have to be developed. Hence, the set of functions to be implemented for each service depends on the CBB choice performed by the implementors.

For this prototype implementation, only a subset of the services provided for by MMS specifications has been developed. Work is currently going on to introduce those functions not yet supported. The pilot implementation includes, today, the following service classes, which have also been tested for performance evaluation:

- Environment and general management services
- VMD support services
- Program invocation management services
- Variable access services.

Static domains only are considered and they are defined at VMD configuration. The following CBBs have also been taken into account:

- STR1: states the validity of array variables;
- STR2: states the validity of structured variables;
- VNAM: enables or disables access to MMS objects by name;
- NEST: indicates the maximum number of levels in the description, in this case NEST=1;
- TPY: enables communication towards a third party, as an example, a user may ask the EF to read a file allocated to a specific filestore.

For the sake of simplicity, each program invocation has been associated with a single domain and, since the TPY conformance block has been chosen, a file store has been made available. In the following, services developed for the prototype architecture are examined in more detail.

The *environment and general management services* include the following functions:

- *initiate*: opens the communication session with a remote user activating an application association and negotiating suitable parameters;
- *conclude*: negotiated termination of the association;
- *abort*: unilateral termination of the association;
- *cancel*: is used to cancel a service pending request;
- *reject*: is used by the remote VMD to send back information about protocol violations.

These services have been developed according to the standard specifications, since they do not depend on any CBB. For the abort service a particular approach has been followed. In fact, when the ACSE module service is available, the abort service is mapped directly onto that provided by ACSE, while in this case a specific PDU has been introduced to transfer the abort request to the other entity involved in the communication. The PDU is handled by the MMPM, which can send it on the AA that has to be cancelled: the receiving remote VMD will consider it as an abort command and will proceed to the deletion of the AA descriptor sending an abort indication to the AA users.

The *VMD support services* allow users to get general information from a remote VMD and to modify object names. In particular, a user is enabled to read the VMD state and to get the list of objects and capabilities defined in the VMD environment. The following functions are available:

- *Get status*: by this service the user can get the logical and physical status of the VMD.
- *Get name list*: the list of objects belonging to a specific class is obtained; the available object classes are defined in the standard specifications. In this case study, the named variables, domain and program invocation classes have been implemented. Another parameter to be used for this service is which set of objects belonging to the chosen class are to be listed, i.e. objects related to a specific domain, to a specific association or to the whole VMD.
- *Identify*: is used to identify the VMD in terms of vendor name, model name, revision and the available abstract syntax notations list.
- *Rename*: this service allows an object name to be changed by the user.
- *Get capability list*: the VMD sends back the list of available capabilities.

The *program invocation management services* are based on the *program invocation* (PI) object, which is a VMD object by which program execution can be controlled. The PI contains a status information about execution, which includes the following conditions:

- IDLE: PI does exist, but the corresponding program is not yet in execution, or has been completed and can be reactivated;
- STARTING: a command to put the program in execution has been used, but the program has not yet started;
- RUNNING: the program entered the execution phase;
- STOPPING: a command to stop the program has been used, but the command has not yet been completed;
- STOPPED: program execution is suspended, but it can resume at the point where it was interrupted;
- RESUMING: a command, not yet completed, has been given to resume the program;
- RESETTING: a command is being completed so that the PI state may pass from the STOPPED to the IDLE (or UNRUNNABLE) state;
- UNRUNNABLE: no way exists to resume the program activity, the only transition allowed is due to the PI deletion.

The PI model introduced in the standard specification supports three flags named: REUSABLE, DELETABLE and MONITOR. When REUSABLE is set, the program can be reactivated after completion, while the DELETABLE flag enables the PI deletion. The MONITOR flag specifies whether the events monitoring service can be used. According to the standard specification, a domain list describing the program environment is associated with each PI. A domain at least has to specify the program entry point along with a field called *execution argument* used to pass parameters to the program when activated.

Figure 12.21 shows a state transitions diagram for the program invocation object.

The *variable access services* operate on MMS variables, which are dynamic objects, in the sense that they can be created and deleted by the user. They are identified by a name and by a definition context, which indicates whether the variable is global to the VMD environment, local to a domain or to an application association.

An MMS variable is an abstract element with which VMD real variables may be associated. Real variables, also called 'unnamed', are defined permanently at the VMD configuration phase. When an MMS variable is read or written, the corresponding real variables are affected, while, when an MMS variable is deleted, only the mapping table between the MMS variable and the real ones is deleted.

Variable access is performed in different ways according to the CBB chosen for the implementation. In this case study each variable can be accessed by name. Since a nesting level of one has been

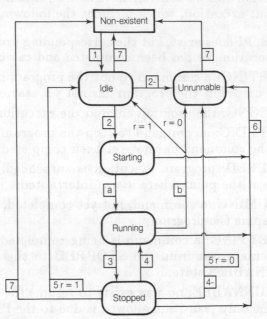

1 create, 2 start, 2- start error, 3 stop, 4 resume, 4- resume error, 5 reset,
6 kill, 7 delete, a begin signal, b end signal, r = 1 reusable true, r = 0 reusable false

Figure 12.21   A program invocation state diagram.

adopted, structured variables definition is allowed so that variable subelements may also be composed of structured variables containing simpler ones. This holds for arrays also, which can be constituted of structured variables composed of simpler ones.

Five kinds of services have been developed to manage variables:

- *Define variable names*: a new MMS variable may be defined; this is accomplished by specifying the name, the context (VMD, domain, association), the type and the real variable associated with it; the variable type has to be chosen so that adjacent real variables can be associated with the abstract one specified in the parameter of the service; the EF will provide the mechanism for the mapping, verifying whether real variables are already assigned to other MMS variables; this is accomplished by testing a specific flag, called *in_use*, associated with each real variable of the device. When an association table cannot be set by the EF, an *INCONSISTENT TYPE* error is sent back to the user.

- *Delete variable access*: this service supports MMS variable erasing; in particular, EF removes from the VMD database the structure definition related to the MMS variable, freeing the real variables associated with it. To control the erasing operation, an MMS variable has a flag associated with it, called *MMS_deletable*, which can be set to zero so that the variable cannot be deleted; when a read function is active on a variable, the associated flag is always set to zero and remains so until the end of the operation.

- *Write*: this service allows new data to be inserted in a real variable associated with the MMS variable specified in the request; data must be provided in the ASN.1 format; the EF first verifies the existence of the specified variable and then tests whether data are compatible with the variable type. If both tests are positive then a write request is addressed to the *data manager* for each real variable. When confirms are received for all write operations, the EF will inform the user about the operation completion.

- *Read*: the user sends a read request to the EF specifying one or more variable identifiers; the EF interacts with the DM and the data got from it are passed to the user in the ASN.1 format.

- *Get variable access attributes*: by this service a user can get information about an MMS variable type expressed according to the ASN.1 standard notation.

12.7.2 Manufacturing message protocol machine

The MMPM handles protocol mechanisms and supports interactions between VMD and the underlying data-link layer. MMPM also exchanges information with the executive function (EF) and application processes as pointed out in Figure 12.22. Furthermore, in the MiniMAP protocol profile where only three layers are provided for, the MMPM has to support mechanisms to handle application associations (AA).

The communication protocol

The communication protocol is based on the exchange of MMS protocol data units (PDUs), defined according to the MMS standard specification, between system components as stated in the following:

- application processes send service requests to the MMPM through the use of 'request' PDUs, while they receive the corresponding confirms by means of 'response' or 'error' PDUs.

- the executive function receives service requests from the MMPM by means of 'indication' primitives and sends back to the MMPM 'response' or 'error' PDUs, when confirmed services are to be processed.

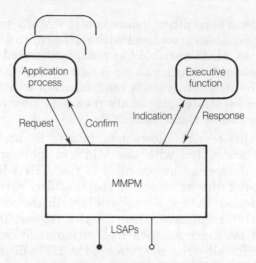

Figure 12.22   The manufacturing message protocol machine.

An extended MMS PDU, as described in the following, has been used to support communication between the MMPM and the users of the EF:

```
typedef struct extended_mms_pdu{
AA_ID aa_id;
PRIORITY priority;
MMS_PDU mms_pdu;
};
```

Besides the MMS PDU, it is composed of the application association identifier, AA_ID, and the priority level of the request, *PRIORITY*. For the priority aspects, even if the fact that CSMA/CD technology supports priorities at the MAC layer has been taken into account, a priority mechanism has also been introduced at the MMPM level for future extensions. At present, the MMPM supports two different priority levels (0, 1), which are implemented by means of separate queues: the queue at priority 0 is always served first.

MMS protocol defines the rules which enable the client (AP) to access services made available by the server (EF).

The procedure is based, first, on the establishment of a virtual connection (AA) between the client and the server. To manage this channel, five primitives are available as introduced in the previous section: initiate, conclude, cancel, abort and reject. When the user asks the MMPM to open an AA with a remote EF, a suitable data structure for handling data transfers is made available so that confirmed services can be stored awaiting service completion. In that data structure, a field is also available to store the status word related to the association. In fact, when the open process is in progress, the state variable is set to the *establishing MMS environment* state, and an *initiate* request is sent to the remote MMPM. This, on receiving the request, creates its own data structure, sets the status variable to *establishing MMS environment* and passes the request to the local EF. In the case of a positive response from the EF, a new AA may be opened, the *MMS environment* state is entered and a confirm primitive is sent back to the calling MMPM. If a negative answer is obtained from the EF, the data structure associated with the AA is deleted and a negative answer is sent back to the calling MMPM.

When the calling MMPM receives a confirm from the remote one, it enters the *MMS environment* state and passes a confirm to the user. In the other case, the data structure associated with the AA is deleted and a negative answer is passed to the user. The *initiate* primitive includes negotiation of some parameters used in the communication phase. The user suggests specific values for those parameters, which can be reduced, in turn, by the local MMPM, the remote MMPM or by the EF. The resulting value is returned to the user again, by means of an *initiate* confirm.

An AA may be terminated by using a *conclude* or an *abort* request. When a *conclude* request is used, the MMPM enters the *relinquishing MMS environment* state and sends a request to the remote MMPM, which, in turn, enters the *relinquishing MMS environment* state, passing the conclude request to the EF. If a positive answer is received from the EF, then the MMPM deletes the AA data structure and enters the *non-existent* state, in the other case, the *MMS environment* state is entered again. When an *abort* primitive is used, the AA is deleted immediately without any confirm being sent to the user. Figure 12.23 shows the state diagram for an AA on a calling MMPM, while Figure 12.24 reports the state diagram for the called MMPM. The MMPM processes user requests not related to AA management only if the *MMS environment* state is active, in other cases a *reject* primitive is used to inform the user about the protocol violation.

When non-confirmed service requests are received from the user, the MMPM will only pass them to the EF, while confirmed services need a more complex processing mechanism for the following reasons:

- One of the parameters negotiated with the *initiate* service is the maximum number of services waiting for completion (in a *pending* state). Hence, the MMPM must always know how many confirmed services are waiting for completion in order to reject new requests when that limit has been reached.

- A name is associated with each confirmed service, so that the service is uniquely identified inside each association. This identifier is provided by the user when a service request is activated, and passed back to the user whenever a confirm

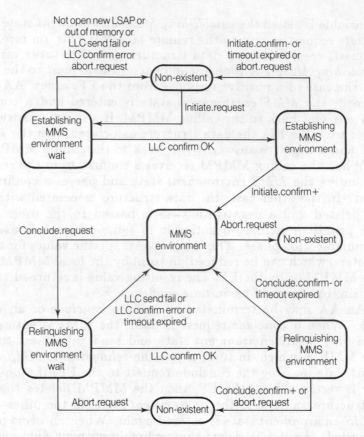

Figure 12.23   State diagram of an AA related to the calling MMPM.

is received, so that the answer can be correctly associated with the corresponding answer. The MMPM has to verify the unicity of such an identifier in the bounds of each association. This is accomplished by scanning the service requests list corresponding to each association, looking for a *pending* request having the same identifier. If a request is found, then a *reject* primitive is generated for the user to point out the protocol violation.

- A *cancel* service is a general function to ask the EF to delete a confirmed service currently in the *pending* state. The request identifier must be used in the service. When this request is received, the service descriptor is forced into the *cancelling* state and the request is passed to the remote MMPM, which will send it to the EF. If the EF accepts the request, the service will be deleted from the list, otherwise it will be set into the *pending* state again.

Figure 12.25 shows the state diagram for confirmed service requests.

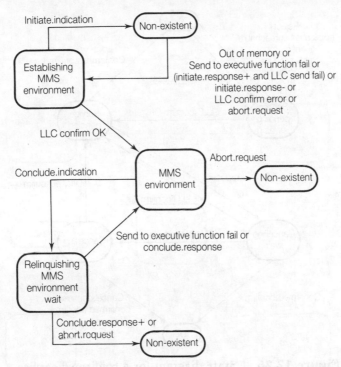

Figure 12.24   State diagram for an AA related to the called MMPM.

Application associations management

Application associations are the virtual communication channels available between an application process (client) and an EF on a remote VMD (server). Since the ACSE module is not available in the reduced protocol profile, AAs have to be managed by the MMPM directly. Each AA is identified by three elements: a local LSAP, a remote LSAP and the remote node physical address. In this way, for each message received by the LLC, the corresponding AA can be selected.

Since the MMPM is interfaced to the LLC directly, it can call for LSAP creation or deletion. The first LSAP is created when the MMPM is started up, so that messages addressed to the EF can be received and processed. The MMPM holds an active LSAPs list. Each active LSAP has a list whose elements are couples of addresses: one is a remote LSAP identifier, the other the remote node physical address. When an MMPM has to activate a new association, the active LSAPs list is scanned looking for whether, for one of them, the couple of remote LSAP identifier and physical address of the new AA does exist in the corresponding sublist. If it is not found in one of the scanned LSAPs, then it can be used to define the new association, otherwise a new LSAP will be created.

This approach allows a minimum number of active LSAPs

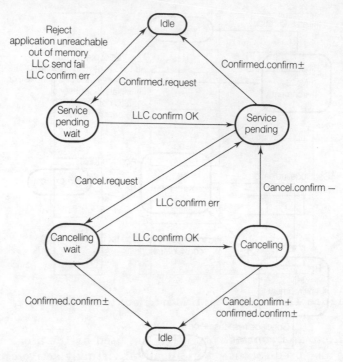

Figure 12.25   State diagram for a confirmed service.

to be involved to identify all associations requested by application processes.

MMPM software structure

The MMPM has been developed using a single process, known to the system as *MMPM_SERVER*, and a set of routines activated by asynchronous events, such as timer expiration or frame receipt from the network, from a user or from the EF. Each routine implements a specific function as shown in Figure 12.22. The MMPM structure includes the following elements:

- *MMPM module*: the core of the protocol machine based on interface primitives to get and put messages from/into the queues related to the network, the user, the timer and the EF; when all the queues are empty, the process is put into hibernation until a new message is inserted in one of the queues by the asynchronous routines which handle data received from the external environment; the operating system calls have been gathered into a *sysdef.h* file so that by updating this file the module can be easily transferred onto other systems.

- *MMS_timer module*: this module contains functions used to implement a system timer to handle the communication protocol; timers are activated to shorten waiting times, when the

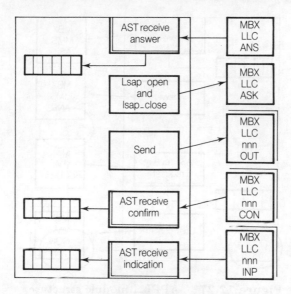

Figure 12.26   The MMPM interface to the LLC layer.

initiale and *conclude* primitives are used by the user. Timers are also used to verify periodically if virtually active users are still alive.

- *LLC_I module*: this module includes all LLC interface functions; to support the information exchange between protocol layers, mailboxes are used. In particular, two predefined mailboxes, named *MBX_LLC_ASK* and *MBX_LLC_ANS* in Figure 12.26, are used, respectively, to pass SAPs activation and deactivation requests to the lower layer and to receive answers from the logical link control; in the former the MMPM may write *open_sap* and *close_sap* primitives defined in the LLC_I module; an asynchronous routine gets messages from the *MBX_LLC_ANS* and puts them in the corresponding queue, where they can subsequently be read from the MMPM main process. Each active LSAP handles four mailboxes to send messages on the network (*MBX_LLC_nnn_OUT*), to get confirm messages from the network (*MBX_LLC_nnn_CON*) and to get data frames from the network (*MBX_LLC_nnn_INP*). The MMPM sends data frames on the network by means of the *send* primitive, which writes messages into the (*MBX_LLC_nnn_OUT*) mailbox associated with the SAP; confirm mailboxes are associated with an asynchronous routine, which receives messages and puts them in the corresponding queue; analogously a different asynchronous routine gets messages from the *indication* mailbox putting them in the corresponding queue. Figure 12.26 gives a complete scheme of the MMPM interface to the LLC layer.

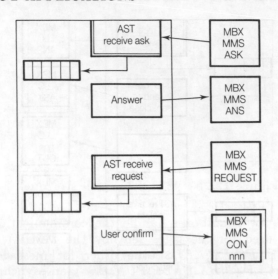

Figure 12.27   APPL_I module structure.

- *APPL_I module*: this module contains interface mechanisms supporting message exchange between the MMPM and application processes (APs). Mailboxes are used to exchange messages; four predefined mailboxes are available, two of them are used for connection management, while the third and fourth are used to receive service requests from the various application processes and to process related responses. Connection management mailboxes are used by application processes to ask for associations before service requests are sent; in the *MBX_MMS_ASK* mailbox an AP writes a message to ask for opening or closing of a connection with the MMPM; the *MBX_MMS_ANS* mailbox is used by the AP to receive confirm messages; in the AP_I module, an asynchronous routine is used to read messages available in the *MBX_MMS_ASK* and to put them in the corresponding queue so that they can be processed by the MMPM; an *answer* primitive is also available so that the MMPM can reply to the AP request. The *MBX_MMS_REQUEST* mailbox is used by the APs to pass MMS service requests to the MMPM; a specific asynchronous routine reads those requests and puts them in the right queue. Reply messages are sent back to the application processes through the *MBX_MMS_CON_nnn* mailbox; every time an AP asks for a connection to the MMPM, a confirm mailbox is dynamically created so that a reply for the request can be received. Figure 12.27 shows the *APPL_I* module structure.
- *EXFN_I module*: this module supports interface procedures handling data exchange between the MMPM and

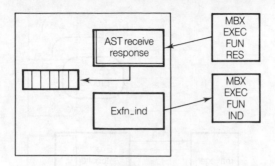

Figure 12.28   EXFN_I module structure.

the EF; two mailboxes handle the communication, the former is used for messages sent by the MMPM to the EF (*MBX_EXEC_FUN_IND*), the other for messages received from the EF (*MBX_EXEC_FUN_RES*); an asynchronous procedure is associated with the last mailbox, so that messages received from the EF can be put into the right queue to be processed by the MMPM; this module is described in Figure 12.28.

- *ASN.1 encode/decode modules*: messages passed to the MMPM are in ASN.1 format, hence, a decoding mechanism is required; this is accomplished by using functions defined in the *from_asn.c* file and contained in the *from_asn* file. In some cases, the MMPM, by itself, must generate information items, which have to be passed to the user in the ASN.1 format. To perform such a conversion, suitable functions have been made available in the file *to_asn.h*.

Executive function

The executive function (EF) is associated with a VMD and provides MMS variable access services to application processes. The EF is connected to the MMPM so that communication with application processes located on remote nodes is possible. Since the EF must process local messages for application processes located in its VMD, a channel for the EF is also available to all local processes. Figure 12.29 shows a scheme representing all possible connections between the EF and the other parts of the VMD.

The MMS standard [ISO9506] does not specify the EF organization, but gives general guidelines for processing a confirmed service. The approach is based on the *transaction object* (TROB), which is generated whenever an indication primitive for a confirmed service request is received. The TROB is cancelled at service completion. The basic components of a TROB are the following:

- *Invoke_ID*: identifies the request and is unique within the application association; it is provided by the user as a parameter

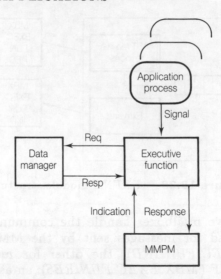

Figure 12.29   Connections between the EF and other VMD elements.

contained in the service request, and it will be returned to the user as a parameter in the reply message so that the user may associate the response with the corresponding request.

- *AA_ID*: identifies an association; in this implementation it is represented by three elements: a local LSAP, a remote LSAP and a remote physical address.

- *Pre_execution modifiers list*: this is the list of the objects to be used by the confirmed service, including semaphores and events to synchronize execution of services.

- *Service identifier and associated parameters*: no indication is given in the standard specification about the identification of TROBs; in this implementation a two-field identifier has been used, one field refers to the service, while the other is a structured field composed of all parameters associated with the request.

- *Post_execution modifiers list*: this is a semaphore list to be released at service completion.

- *Cancelable flag*: this may enable service deletion performed via a *cancel* primitive.

Other parameters are also included in the prototype implementation:

- *computable flag*: set to false when the service, represented by the TROB, is waiting for a reply to be provided by the variable handler in the VMD or by a local application process; it assumes a true value when the TROB is created or when the expected reply is received;

- *label*: this is a counter used to implement services requiring

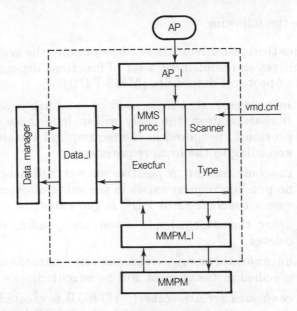

Figure 12.30   Exec function structure.

more than one request addressed to the variable handler in
the VMD; when the TROB is created it is set to zero;

- *priority*: this is the priority level assigned to the request and
  the corresponding reply;
- *data*: this field contains the reply provided by the variable
  handler;
- *result_list, last_result*: these are pointers referring to the result
  list related to *read* and *write* services.

The EF is composed of a single process, known to the system as
EXEC_FUNC, including a set of asynchronous routines activated on
message reception from the MMPM, from an application process or
from the *variable manager* in the VMD. Figure 12.30 demonstrates
the EF basic modules.

The *EXEC_FUN* is the core of the EF and contains most
of the procedures and data structures implementing services and
global variables. Other modules implement interface and configuration mechanisms, MMS variable handlers and program invocation
objects. Figure 12.31 shows a flow chart related to the EF process. It
can be seen that, at the startup phase, the EF initializes communication channels and configures the VMD, reading data and parameters
from an appropriate file accessed by means of the *scanner* module.
The main activity of the process is reading messages from the various queues related to the interface modules. If all queues are empty,
the process is placed in a *hibernation* state and can be awakened by
a message appended to a queue. The message types handled by the

process are the following:

- **Indication** primitives: these correspond to the *service_request* primitives and implement a set of functions depending on the kind of protocol data units (MMS-PDU):
  - *initiate_request*: this is used to establish a new application association; the reply will include those parameters previously proposed in the request and suitably updated according to the local requirements;
  - *conclude_request*: a positive answer will be generated if no pending request exists in the association, in the other case a *conclude error* PDU is generated;
  - *abort*: the association is closed, and pending requests are deleted;
  - *unconfirmed service requests*: the unconfirmed service specified in the request will be executed;
  - *confirmed service request*: a TROB is created to handle the request and is inserted in the TROB list available in the EF.

- **Data manager** frame: contains the identifier of the physical variable related to the request and data associated with it; the identifier of the TROB related to the request is also available so that data received can be stored in the corresponding field and the *computable* flag set to true.

- **Signal from AP**: this is used for *program invocation* services, two different kinds of signals are provided for:
  - *BEGIN_AP*: this signal is generated by an AP activated by the *start* MMS service; according to the process identifier (PID) associated with the signal, a *program invocation* is identified, which indicates the TROB corresponding to the *start* service so that the *computable* flag can be set to true;
  - *END_AP*: this signal is sent at completion by an AP associated with a *program invocation*; when this signal is received, the program invocation is put into the *idle* or *unrunnable* state, according to the state of the *reusable* flag.

Whenever a message is extracted from the queue, the *executive_function()* procedure is executed: it scans the TROB list and executes services for TROBS having the *computable* flag set to true. At service completion, an answer is passed to the user and the TROB is deleted from the list.

Operating system calls are made through macros defined and gathered in a specific file, named *sysdef.h*, so that, when the whole

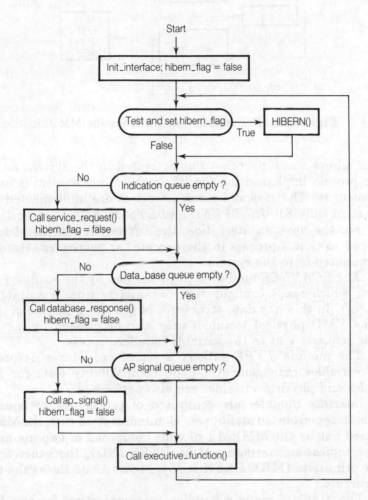

Figure 12.31 State diagram describing the executive function.

software has to be ported on other machines, the updating process can easily be performed.

The *MMS_PROC* module contains the *start*, *stop*, and *resume* services related to the *program invocation* management. The *start*

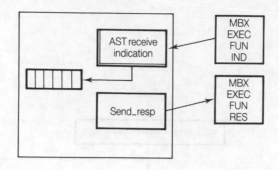

Figure 12.32   Interface modules for the MMPM.

service allows a new process to be activated in the system as a *son* of the process implementing the EF: a *fork()* mechanism is used to implement it. The *stop* and *resume* services are implemented using the system calls *SYS$SUSPEND and SYS$RESUME*, respectively.

For the *program invocation*, the *kill* service has also been introduced so that a process in the *execute* or *suspended* state may be eliminated from the system.

The *SCANNER* module is implemented by the *scanner()* procedure, which reads configuration parameters from a suitable file (*vmd.cnf*). In this way data structures of the EF are made available and the VMD physical variables may also be created by means of specific requests sent to the variable handler process.

The module *TYPE* gathers a set of procedures devoted to MMS variables management. Type compatibility tests for MMS variables and physical variables are also performed.

Interface modules are composed of procedures to read and write messages from/to mailboxes. Communication with the MMPM is carried out by the MMPM_I module composed of two mailboxes: one for *indication* messages (MEX_EXFN_IND), the other for *response* primitives (MBX_EXFN_RES). Figure 12.32 shows the module structure.

The *DATA_I* module handles communication for the VMD physical variables handler. Two mailboxes are also available as pointed out in Figure 12.33.

The module *AP_I* handles signals generated by application processes and received through the MBX_AP_COM as shown by Figure 12.34.

Other modules are also provided for conversion to/from the ASN.1 format.

A specific process, called the *data manager* has been developed to handle VMD physical variables. The aim is providing shared access to variables, so that local application processes as well as remote users may access data without conflicts. Two modules are included in the process, as shown in Figure 12.35: the module *DATA_MNG*

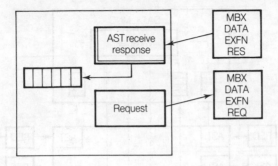

Figure 12.33   Interface module for the VMD physical variables handler.

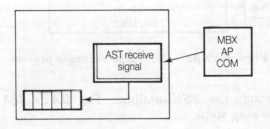

Figure 12.34   Interface module for the application process.

handles variable access, while the module *DATA_MBX* provides communication functions with the other modules in the VMD.

When the system starts, the data manager executes the initialization function so that mailboxes may be created for message exchange with the EF (DATA_MBX_REQ and DATA_MBX_RES). Two more mailboxes are also created for handling connections with application processes (ASK and ANS); two other mailboxes are used to handle service requests related to the data manager operations on variables (REQ, RES).

When initialization is complete, the process hibernates. It will be awakened only when a message is appended to one of the queues.

One of the most common operations the data manager has to provide is variable creation. These operations occur when the executive function performs its initialization procedure submitting a *create* request to the *DATA_MANAGER*, providing also an identification number and the ASN.1 type of the variable. In this way the *DATA_MANAGER* may allocate a specific memory area to contain the variable, which is also added to the internal data structure. Figure 12.36 describes the time diagram for the operations to be performed at system startup.

When an application process wants to access the local VMD variables, a connection request to the DATA_MANAGER has to be

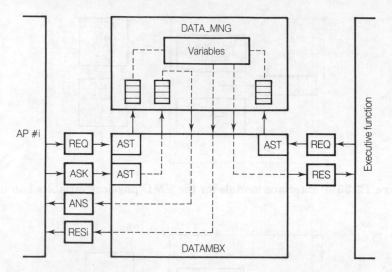

Figure 12.35   The data manager process.

sent first, through the *ASK* mailbox. The *DATA_MANAGER* executes the following steps:

- the new user is added to an internal list;
- an identification number is given to the user;
- a maibox is created (*MBX_DATA_RES_nnn*) to handle replies related to read/write requests for a variable;
- a reply is sent back to the user as a response for the connection request through the *ANS* mailbox.

When these steps have been executed, the AP may ask for read/write services on local VMD variables. The connection to the *DATA_MANAGER* may be closed by the AP, by sending a disconnection request to the ASK mailbox. As a consequence of the request, the *DATA_MANAGER* will proceed to delete the user identifier from the internal list and the DATA_MBX_RES_nnn mailbox related to the AP.

A suitable data structure is used to transfer data during the read/write operation:

```
struct DT_Mbx_Data {
char service; /* Command: CREATE, WRITE, READ */
              /* Response: CREATED, WROTE, READ */
              /* or < 0 if error */
void *id; /* request service identifier */
unsigned long var_name;
unsigned short data_length;
unsigned char data[data_length];
} DT_DATA;
```

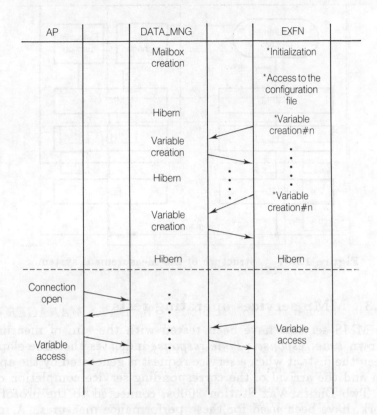

AP	DATA_MNG	EXFN

Figure 12.36 Time diagram for the operations performed at system startup.

The *id* field can be used to express an identification parameter for the request, while the *var_name* field contains the variable identifier; in the case of a write operation, the field *data* contains the new value for the variable to be written. In the case of a response, the field *service* contains a description for the operation just completed, while the *id* field contains the identifier of the operation previously specified in the request. For a read operation, the *data* field contains the value got from the variable.

When variable access is requested by a local application process, the request is appended to the *MBX_DATA_REQUEST* mailbox and variables are considered as simple byte sequences. Transfers are performed by means of a copy operation between memory areas.

When remote requests are to be satisfied the EF is involved, which passes the request to the *DATA_MANAGER* through the *MBX_DATA_EXFN_REQ* mailbox. Since the communication now involves systems which may be different in their structure, conversions to and from ASN.1 format must be performed.

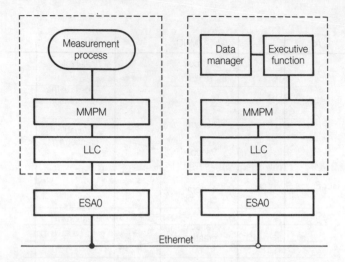

Figure 12.37   Structure of the measurement system.

12.7.3   MMS services operating tests

Some MMS services have been tested with the aim of measuring their own *time response*. *Time response* indicates the time elapsed between the instant when a service request is generated by the application and the arrival of the corresponding service completion confirm. Two Digital Vax Station 2000s, connected to the prototype network, have been used for these performance measures. A measurement program has also been developed, representing an MMS user which generates MMS service requests addressed to a remote VMD. Figure 12.37 gives the structure of the measurement system.

Time response is computed by reading the timer immediately before the request is performed and again when the corresponding reply is received. The time difference gives the time response for that service request.

These measurements are performed for a statistically significant number of repeated tries for each service, so that a minimum, medium and maximum value for time response may be given for each kind of MMS service.

First, the *initiate* and *conclude* services for AA management have been considered. Since a sequence of initiate services cannot be used, because of system limitations on the maximum number of AAs available at the same time, a sequence of initiate and conclude services has been used. According to such an approach, the same AA is opened and then closed repeatedly. The time response measure for the initiate service is performed by reading the local system clock immediately before any initiate request and again after the corresponding response has been received. The difference between the two values is then computed. This procedure has been repeated

Table 12.3   Time response for the initiate and conclude services.

Time response (msec)			
Service type	Minimum	Average	Maximum
Initiate	80	90.4	260
Conclude	60	74.6	140

Table 12.4   Time response for the define named variable and delete variable access services.

Time response (msec)			
Service type	Minimum	Average	Maximum
Define	70	82.6	400
Delete	70	84.2	470

1000 times; in this way, a minimum, medium and maximum value for time response could be evaluated. Results are shown in Table 12.3.

In the *variable handling* set of services, the following functions have been examined:

- *Define named variable and delete variable access*: even in this case, since a limitation does exist for the maximum number of allowed new variable creations, the mechanism chosen for measuring time responses is based on a sequence of requests where both services, define and delete, are used. Analogously to the procedure described before, the internal clock is read before requesting the service and at answer reception so that the effective time involved for each service can easily be computed. In this case 1000 requests were also measured and results are shown in Table 12.4.

- *read and write*: these requests can be replicated without any limitations. Individual measures have been performed in order to evaluate the minimum and maximum values for the service time response. For the computation of the average value, the error due to the clock read operation has been taken into account. Since the system call involves 0.25 ms of wasted time, the time elapsed includes 0.5 msec due to the delay related to clock read operation. Table 12.5 gives results for the MMS variable write service, while Table 12.6 gives time response values for the read function. In both cases the average value has been computed on a sequence of 1000 service requests.

Table 12.5   Time response for the MMS variable write service.

Write service	
Response time (msec)	
Minimum	80
Average	93.1
Maximum	200

Table 12.6   Time response for the MMS variable read service.

Read service	
Response time (msec)	
Minimum	78
Average	91.5
Maximum	187

For the *program invocation management* services, other than activation and deactivation services (*start, stop*) for the associated process, the creation and deletion services have also been chosen. This measure has been performed by repeating the following steps 1000 times:

- create a program invocation;
- start a process;
- delete a program invocation.

For each of the listed services a measure of the response time has been performed by reading the clock before the request and after the related confirm has been received. All measures have been saved in a table, which was subsequently used to compute the minimum, average and maximum value for time responses. Table 12.7 reports the results of the test.

12.8   Conclusions

This chapter has introduced some issues related to the development of MAP/TOP applications. It has been pointed out that the CNMA project, supported by the European Communities under the ESPRIT initiative, plays a basic role in the experimentation of MAP/TOP based solutions for factory communications. In particular, specific pilot projects have been examined and a case study related to the development of a time-critical prototype network has also been presented and discussed.

Table 12.7   Time response for create program invocation, delete program invocation and start services.

Service type	Time response (msec)		
	Minimum	Average	Maximum
Create program invocation	70	119.8	380
Start	60	115	320
Delete program invocation	70	122.7	350

MAP and TOP products are currently supported by many companies from the USA, Japan and Europe, and several development projects are being carried on in the USA (General Motors, Xrox, Dupont) and Japan (Isuzu Motors, Omron).

The current MAP Version 3.0 installations are supported by the following leading suppliers: Concord Communications, AEG Computrol, Motorola, Sisco, Hewlett-Packard, Digital Equipment, Allen Bradley and GE Fanuc, which represent, for the moment, a reference point for the development of MAP/TOP installations.

References

[MAPTOP]   *Manufacturing Automation Protocol Specification*, Version 3.0, Vol. III, 1988.

[MiniMAP]   *Manufacturing Automation Protocol Specification*, Version 3.0, Vol. III, 1988.

[IEEE1]   L.Ciminiera, C.Demartini, A.Valenzano, *A Priority Mechanism for Industrial Networks*, IEEE Transactions on Industrial Electronics, June 1988.

[ISO88022]   *Logical Link Control*, 1985.

[ISO9506]   *Manufacturing Message Specification*, Parts 1 & 2, 22 December 1988.

[ISO8825]   ISO/DIS 8825 *Specification of Basic Encoding Rules for Astract Syntax Notation One (ASN.1)*, 1986.

[ISO/TC]   ISO/TC 184/SC 5/WG 2 N. 196, *Factory Automation Interconnection System (FAIS) – Cell Implementation – 2nd Draft (1989.6)* by International Robotics and Factory Automation Center (IROFA).

[CNMA40]   *CNMA Implementation Guide*, Version 4.0, 1989.

[EMiniMAP]   EMUG, *Manufacturing Automation Protocol Specification*, Version 3.0, Vol. I, 1989.

Index